MIME INTO PHYSICAL THEATRE: A UK CULTURAL HISTORY 1970–2000

This is the first book to investigate the social, political, cultural, artistic and economic forces which created conditions for the rise, success and decline of mime and physical theatre in the United Kingdom, from the 1970s to 2000.

Unpicking the various routes through which mime and physical theatre emerged into wider prominence, this book outlines key thematic strands within this history of practice. The book blends historical description and reflective analysis. It aims to juxtapose the various histories at play within this field, giving critical attention to the voices of the artists, funders and venue managers who were there at the time, particularly recognising the diversity of practitioners and the network of relationships that supported their work. Drawing upon over 40 original interviews, including, amongst others: Joseph Seelig, Helen Lannaghan, Steven Berkoff, Julian Chagrin, Annabel Arden, Nola Rae, Denise Wong, David Glass, Justin Case and Toby Sedgwick, the book offers unique testimonies and memories from key figures active during these three decades. This wide-ranging account of the history, social context, key moments and practical methods gives an unparalleled chronicle of one of the UK's most vital and pioneering forms of theatre.

From undergraduate students to established scholars, this is a comprehensive account for anyone studying contemporary theatre, theatre history, mime, physical theatre and the structures that support the performing arts in the United Kingdom.

Mark Evans is Professor of Theatre Training at Coventry University. He has written widely on movement, actor training and physical theatre. His recent publications include *Frantic Assembly* (with Mark Smith); *Performance, Movement and the Body*; *The Routledge Companion to Jacques Lecoq* (with Rick Kemp); and a critical introduction to *The Moving Body* by Jacques Lecoq.

Simon Murray teaches contemporary performance and theatre studies at the University of Glasgow. Previously Director of Theatre at Dartington College of Arts, he was co-founder/co-editor (with Jonathan Pitches) of the *Theatre, Dance and Performance Training* journal and has been a professional theatre practitioner. His disparate writings include publications on Jacques Lecoq, physical theatres, lightness, WG Sebald and performances in ruins.

MIME INTO PHYSICAL THEATRE: A UK CULTURAL HISTORY 1970–2000

Mark Evans and Simon Murray

LONDON AND NEW YORK

Designed cover image: 'Dancing with an angel' Lindsay Kemp and David Houghton in *Flowers*. c. 1979–81. By kind permission of David and Richard Houghton. Photo by Richard Houghton.

First published 2023
by Routledge
4 Park Square, Milton Park, Abingdon, Oxon OX14 4RN

and by Routledge
605 Third Avenue, New York, NY 10158

Routledge is an imprint of the Taylor & Francis Group, an informa business

© 2023 Mark Evans and Simon Murray

The right of Mark Evans and Simon Murray to be identified as authors of this work has been asserted in accordance with sections 77 and 78 of the Copyright, Designs and Patents Act 1988.

All rights reserved. No part of this book may be reprinted or reproduced or utilised in any form or by any electronic, mechanical, or other means, now known or hereafter invented, including photocopying and recording, or in any information storage or retrieval system, without permission in writing from the publishers.

Trademark notice: Product or corporate names may be trademarks or registered trademarks, and are used only for identification and explanation without intent to infringe.

British Library Cataloguing-in-Publication Data
A catalogue record for this book is available from the British Library

ISBN: 978-0-367-35248-6 (hbk)
ISBN: 978-0-367-35249-3 (pbk)
ISBN: 978-0-429-33020-9 (ebk)

DOI: 10.4324/9780429330209

Typeset in Bembo
by Apex CoVantage, LLC

This book is dedicated to Isla Henderson, Wendy Kirkup and Vanessa Oakes.

CONTENTS

List of Figures	*x*
Foreword	*xiii*
Authors' preface	*xiv*
Acknowledgements	*xvi*

1	Introduction – piecing mime together	1

Defining mime and physical theatre 2
Understanding mime 4
Why mime matters 5

2	The moment of mime	7

Revealing mime history 7
Mime and the 1960s 16
Venues: putting mime in its place 25
The next generation: mime in the 1970s 27
International influences 33
Conclusion 39

3	Cultural economies of mime and physical theatre: ecologies of support	40

Political and economic landscapes 41
Structures of support and funding 43
A home for mime 52
Mime Action Group: for and of its times 56

viii Contents

*Festivals as vehicles for community, conviviality, collaboration
and cultural production 67*
After-words 80

4   Mime and physical theatre beyond the centre   81

Mime and physical theatre in the English regions 81
The Northern Region – a profile in time 88
Scotland 96
From Scotland into Wales 108
Northern Ireland 117
A note on traffic across the seas 120

5   Making mime and physical theatre   124

The economics of devising 126
Improvisation – the body and soul of devising 128
Play, creativity and 'le jeu' 132
The etude and physical scoring 138
Objects and masks 142
Dance, choreography and choreographic building blocks 147
The influence of visual and live art on devising 153
Popular performance 158
From collaborator to director and back 161
Conclusion 166

6   From scarcity to abundance: training, education,
    dissemination and debate in mime and physical theatre   169

Landscape, provision and discourse 169
A time of workshops 174
*Learning mime in the community: a challenge to the conventions
of drama teaching 193*
*Teaching mime and physical theatre in higher education: drama
schools and universities in an ambivalent relationship 202*
Concluding and continuing training 213

7   All mimes are equal?   214

The wider picture 215
Working class mime 217
Women in mime and physical performance 219
Gender, sexuality and physical performance 228
Race and mime 231

Contents **ix**

Mime, physical theatre and interculturalism 242
Disability, mime and physical theatre 246
Conclusion 252

8   Conclusion – the rise and fall of mime as a
cultural phenomenon   254

Making content – mime and physical theatre
  about something 257
Critical reception 260
Mime and physical theatre into the new millennium 261

Bibliography   *264*
Index   *273*

FIGURES

2.1 *L'Enfant Prodigue*, with Irene Mawer as Pierrot and Ruby Ginner
as Pierrot Père. 14

2.2 'Dancing with an angel' Lindsay Kemp and David Houghton in
Flowers, c. 1979–1981. 18

2.3 Jacques Lecoq and Julian Chagrin at Ecole Jacques Lecoq,
Paris, c. 1960. 21

2.4 Julian Chagrin in performance. Date unknown. 22

2.5 Nola Rae in *Upper Cuts*, c. 1980. 28

2.6 Justin Case performing his restaurant sketch in Budapest,
Hungary, 1984. 30

2.7 Moving Picture Mime Show (David Gaines, Toby Sedgwick
and Paul Filipiak) in *The Examination*, 1978. 32

2.8 Dartington Dance School interior with Dance Mime Group, c. 1935. 36

3.1 *Total Theatre* (Front cover), Vol 9, Issue 3, Autumn 1997. 60

3.2 *Twin Houses*, Compagnie Mossoux-Bonté, London International
Mime Festival 1996. 72

3.3 *Sur La Route de Sienne*, Theatre le Ranelagh, featuring Stanislav
Varkki, London International Mime Festival, 1997. 73

3.4 Festival of Mime, Dance, and Visual Theatre, Brewery Arts
Centre, Kendal. Brochures for 1986 and 1989. 77

4.1 *Contes Mauriciens, Théâtre Sans Frontières, 1999*. Featuring
Rebecca Jameson and Helen Iskander. 95

4.2 Lindsay Kemp, St Nicholas Graveyard, Aberdeen, 1971. 99

4.3 Mark Saunders: *The Clown and the Jockey*, Traverse Theatre,
Edinburgh, 1984. 101

4.4 Mark Saunders, *The Chaplin Obsession*, 1988. 102

4.5 Cardiff Theatre Laboratory First Statement, Mike Pearson, October 1973. 110

4.6	*Origin of Table Manners* (Director: Richard Gough), Cardiff Laboratory Theatre, 1985.	111
4.7	Odin in Wales: Barter Evening (publicity leaflet), Cardiff Laboratory Theatre, 1980.	112
4.8	Grotowski's Teatr Laboratorium Workshops (publicity leaflet), Cardiff Laboratory Theatre, 1982.	114
5.1	Trickster Theatre (Mary Stuart, Rachel Ashton, Michele Hine, Roger Ennals, Mark Hopkins and Robert Thirtle) in *Mantu*, 1983.	143
5.2	Trestle Theatre Company (Toby Wilsher and Thomasina Carlyle) in *Top Storey*, 1987.	144
5.3	The Kosh (Mark Hopkins and Siân Williams) in *Endangered Species*, 1990.	152
5.4	Hesitate and Demonstrate (Janet Goddard and Geraldine Pilgrim) in *Points of Departure* at Oval House Theatre Upstairs, London, 1977.	155
5.5	Mummer&Dada (Ana Vasquez, Gregoire Carel, Kevin Brooking and Bim Mason, with Lee Beagley on percussion) street performance in Covent Garden, London, 1986.	159
5.6	Trickster Theatre (Roger Ennals, Robert Thirtle, Mark Hopkins, Maria Stengard, Mary Stuart and Rachel Ashton) in *Charivari*, 1984.	160
5.7	David Glass in *The White Woman*, directed by Rex Doyle, 1982.	163
5.8	David Glass Ensemble (Hayley Carmichael, Richard Atlee, Peter Bailee, Paul Hamilton, Neil Caplin, Di Sherlock, Sally O'Donnell) in *Gormenghast*, 1992.	165
6.1	*Since 1988, 189 teachers*: International Workshop Festival, (centenary publication, 1998).	182
6.2	Workshop/training opportunities, *Total Theatre*, Volume 4, Number 2/3, Summer/Autumn 1992.	188
6.3	*Moving into Performance* programme (1), MAG, Manchester 1994.	194
6.4	*Moving into Performance* programme (2), MAG, Manchester, 1994.	195
6.5	Mark Saunders, mime workshop for children, Edinburgh 1983.	202
6.6	Mark Saunders, mime workshop for students, Royal Scottish Academy of Music and Drama, Glasgow, 1991.	207
6.7	CPR *Past Masters Etienne Decroux*, workshops and symposium.	209
6.8	*On the Braille in the Body.* Touchdown Dance integrated workshops with the visually impaired and the sighted at Dartington College of Arts, 1993. Featuring Gerry Overington and Dartington performer, Sharon Higginson.	211
6.9	Devised theatre class led by writer, Deborah Levy in Tilt Yard, Dartington College of Arts in the 1990s.	212
7.1	Peta Lily preparing to perform in Three Women Mime's show *High Heels*, 1981.	224

xii Figures

7.2 Peta Lily in *Wendy Darling*, 1988.   227

7.3 Mbongeni Ngema and Percy Mtwa in *Woza Albert!*, 1981.   233

7.4 Black Mime Theatre (Tracey Anderson, Cassi Pool and Arosemaya Diedrick) in *Drowning*, 1991.   234

7.5 Trickster Theatre Company (Robert Thirtle and Roger Ennals) in *Time of Lies*, 1982.   245

FOREWORD

The late 1960s and 1970s saw a growth of interest in many new forms of physical and visual performance in the UK, including mime, circus-theatre, puppetry and live art. This occurred despite almost no infrastructure or full-time training for would-be performers, many of whom studied their craft and found most of their work abroad. The burgeoning scene was recorded by a few, mostly short-lived alternative performance journals. Thanks to the efforts of many people mentioned in the following pages, and with some initiatives from the Arts Council of Great Britain from the end of the 1970s, that situation gradually changed. In the intervening half century, British artists in these disciplines have ranked amongst the very best in the world.

We live in the country of Shakespeare, and our tradition of spoken drama is universally admired, almost to the exclusion of other forms of theatre. Physical and visual theatres have been deemed marginal, fringe, or something for children; often defined by what they aren't – not really dance or 'proper' theatre. Otherwise glowing reviews often start with the words 'I hate Mime, but . . .'. It is a tremendous testament to many people's talents and determination that not only have physical and visual theatre flourished, but become an integral part of mainstream theatre in Britain. Artists who started their careers in street theatre, mime, circus and puppetry have in recent years been involved in creating some of the biggest hits at the National Theatre, English National Opera, and the West End.

A serious study of this important chapter in British theatre history is long overdue. Simon Murray and Mark Evans' carefully researched survey fulfils an important mission in shining a light on pioneering work which could otherwise remain unrecognised, and on names little known beyond a coterie of enthusiasts. Mime, physical and visual theatre are an inspiring and rich resource for today's flourishing UK theatre culture. This book is the first to record their contribution.

Joseph Seelig and Helen Lannaghan
London International Mime Festival

AUTHORS' PREFACE

Unknowingly, this feels like a book which we have been preparing for all our working lives as performers, theatre makers, researchers and teachers. It has been a rich and rewarding project for many reasons, but two in particular stand out. Firstly, it has folded – or catapulted might be a more appropriate verb – us back in time to our younger selves, when we (without knowing each other) were an active part of the mime and physical theatre landscape which this volume describes and reflects upon. Writing, therefore, born out of lived and embodied knowledge as much as from books and computer screens. Secondly, the process has enabled us to have rich and hugely generative conversations with practitioners of myriad hues and experiences. Few good things came from COVID-19 and lockdown, but for us what had been planned as no more than 10 face-to-face interviews metamorphosed into over 40 Zoomed encounters, the products of which you will see before you across the following eight chapters. Most of our research publications (see bibliography) have circled around the themes, practices and people that inform this book. It has been these writings, and the preoccupations which have informed them, that have brought us together, forged our friendship, and have led us to this joint project. The book has been propelled by a strong and shared sense that the period under examination (1970–2000) was special in nourishing the complex social, cultural, artistic and political conditions which gave rise to the multitude of deeply embodied performance practices we account for in this volume. Periodisation, of course, is an artificial construct, and easily demolished, but nonetheless through a combination of evidence, intuition and the telling of stories we hope that our book does offer robust testimony that these three decades were indeed 'special' for mime and physical theatre. Finally, our writing might be seen as a brave but foolhardy attempt to rescue mime from silence: to cannibalise the words of the renowned social historian, E.P. Thompson, we have sought to rescue the poor mime artist (and physical theatre practitioner) 'from the enormous condescension of posterity'[1].

Mark Evans and Simon Murray

---

1 In the 1963 preface (p. 9) to his seminal work, *The Making of the English Working Class*, (2013) EP Thompson wrote 'I am seeking to rescue the poor stockinger, the Luddite cropper, the "obsolete" hand-loom weaver, the "utopian" artisan, and even the deluded follower of Joanna Southcott, from the enormous condescension of posterity'.

ACKNOWLEDGEMENTS

It was always our aim in writing this book to include the voices of many of those who were there at the time and whose practice or work is the central spine of this book. We are very grateful to the many people who we interviewed or corresponded with for this book. We have also had considerable help from our interviewees and others in acquiring images and seeking appropriate copyright permissions. In many cases, this has been a complex task since we have been searching for the provenance of photographs taken 30–40 years ago. Our sincere thanks go out to: Paul Allain, Annabel Arden, Deborah Barnard, Michael Bennett, Steven Berkoff, Patrick Boillaud, Clare Brennan, Ben Buckley, Geoff Buckley, Susanne Burns, Ian Cameron, Justin Case, Joff Chafer, Franc Chamberlain, Julian Chagrin, John Cobb, Ruphin Coudyzer, Janet Curtis, Gemma Dalby, Dartington Trust and the Elmgrant Trust, Judith Dimant, Manon Dumonceaux, Jack Eastman, Stewart Ennis, Sean Foley, David Gaines, Helen Gethin, David Glass, Janet Goddard, Lynette Goddard, Richard Gough, David Grant, Graham Green, David Houghton, Richard Houghton, Sue Hoyle, Nigel Jamieson, Coneyl Jay, Sarah Kemp, Helen Lannaghan, Peta Lily, Robert Lister, London International Mime Festival, Dick McCaw, Tom Maguire, Bim Mason, Dorothy Max Prior, Roberta Mock, Geoff Moore, Kevin Mount, Kate Mount, John Mowat, Peter Mumford, Tessa Musgrave, Lloyd Newson, Glenn Noble, Geraldine Pilgrim, Jonathan Pitches, Nola Rae, Benji Reid, Simon Richardson, Matthew Ridout, Douglas Robertson, Mhora Samuel, Mark Saunders, Toby Sedgwick, Joseph Seelig, Fern Smith, Liam Steel, Eileen Stewart, Ian Stewart, Jamie Taylor, Robert Thirtle, Trestle Theatre Company, Mikha Wajnrych, Ris Widdicombe, David Williams, Siân Williams, Alan Caig Wilson, Frank Wilson, Thomas Wilson, Denise Wong, Richard Woodcock and John Wright.

The staff at Routledge have been consistently helpful, supportive and understanding, particularly as the COVID-19 pandemic intervened so drastically in our plans for the research underpinning this project. Our special thanks go to Ben

Piggott, Laura Soppelsa, Zoe Forbes and Steph Hines. Additional thanks to Laura Guthrie at Graeae for her invaluable feedback on the disability section in Chapter 7.

We gratefully acknowledge the support of the Society for Theatre Research for this project, with an award for theatre research made in 2020. We also acknowledge the support of our respective institutions, through the Centre for Dance Research at Coventry University and Theatre Studies and the School of Culture and Creative Arts at the University of Glasgow. We also wish to thank David Richmond (University of York St. John) for his support and hospitality during a key phase in the writing of this book.

With great sadness we conclude by noting that a number of leading figures associated in various ways with the fields of mime, physical theatre and theatre scholarship have died since we began this project. We wish to take this opportunity to acknowledge their significant contributions and the generosity they have shown to other artists and scholars over the years: Geoff Buckley, Mike Pearson, Philip Zarrilli, Noel Witts, Hans-Thies Lehmann, Marcello Magni and Peter Brook.

1

INTRODUCTION – PIECING MIME TOGETHER

Our history of UK modern mime and physical theatre is made of fragments, pieces of unfinished history. The ephemerality of UK mime and physical theatre means that the experiences that we have sought to examine are dispersed within the memories of those involved, dislocated in time and space. There are so many stories that could be told, that it is impossible to imagine a definitive version. Bringing together those that we have gathered thus offers a coherence and significance that is not necessarily intrinsic to the material. Writing history can operate as a source of power, shaping the way we understand practice; our interpretation of the field, therefore, needs to recognise the diversity of practices and practitioners which have otherwise been hidden from historical scrutiny. We have aimed to fill the empty spaces within the existing documentation of this field with the words and images of those who created its landscapes. Instead of linearity we have examined spheres of connection and association. As Marie-Louise Crawley (2020) points out, fragmentation is exactly what is interesting in these histories and is what marks the effects of time upon our subject. In some important senses, it is this fragmentation that has enabled us to make sense of the multiple perspectives we have encountered, including features that are seldom referenced in contemporary histories of devised theatre practice. It is our experience that the history of mime and physical theatre during this period resists being fixed – it is a history in transition, in motion and in play. We have been constantly aware of the multiple and diverse changes and evolutions at work within the field, and thus within this, *our* history of that field. Our process has encouraged us to value the anecdotal – a form of narrative which allows access to the personality and passion of the speaker and gives the individuality of the voice force and meaning. Our relationship with the history of mime and physical theatre has had to be personal, discursive and critical, even and especially as we have sought to gather and reveal evidence. We have tried to be alert to subtle interconnections and wary of our own positions within this history. The interviewees

DOI: 10.4324/9780429330209-1

2 Introduction – piecing mime together

and case studies for this book were chosen in response to the diversity of the field, the current scholarship around historic mime practice and our focus on interconnectedness over linearity. We have sought to ensure that a wide range of voices are included, from across the UK, from funders, administrators and venue managers as well as practitioners, and recognising the importance of both established practitioners and previously marginalised artists. Crawley writes about the choreographer in the museum ' "doing" history' (2020: 93) – we have felt like the academics in the midst of practice, reversing this dynamic and 'undoing' history. Our chapters refer to the lived experiences of those making and presenting mime and physical theatre, acknowledging that the past can offer up important experiences for those of us revisiting this domain.

Defining mime and physical theatre

What do we mean by 'mime'? Mira Felner observes that such a question requires a historical perspective, as, 'what is denoted by the term is different for each generation' (1985: 15). Mime has fulfilled a different function within each historical and cultural context, and each mime artist effectively represents an embodied network of different practices and movement heritages. Throughout this book, therefore, we have tried to trace how understandings of what mime and physical theatre are and how they might be practised have flexed in response to local/regional needs, personal interest and wider social, political, economic and historical shifts. Despite the fact that a number of mime practitioners (Desmond Jones, Pat Keysell and Nola Rae, for example) strongly advocated for the retention of the word, many of the practitioners that we have spoken to bemoaned the limitations they felt that the word 'mime' put upon their work. In John Mowat's opinion, 'mime's a strange word now, isn't it? I don't quite know what the definition of mime is' (2020). Toby Sedgwick (2020) lamented that '[i]f someone says, "Oh, you're a mime", I get shivers up my spine'. Joff Chafer (2021) recalled that '[w]hen we started, mime was very much a problematic word, in that theatre programmers didn't book it because mime was seen as part of dance . . . losing the name "mime" was definitely good'. Some leading teachers disparaged the term – Simon Murray recalls that one of Philippe Gaulier's most withering critiques was to the effect that the student was performing 'like a tubercular little mime artist'. Nigel Jamieson (2020) seems to sum up the feelings of many mimes when he states, 'I think we all felt that title around our necks'. Uninformed media representation often presented mime in very limited ways – people trapped behind glass walls or walking in the wind. These clichés have haunted mime throughout the period in question – and continue to do so.

This love/hate relationship with mime as a title in some ways defines UK practice and the transformation of mime into a broader field – physical theatre. For some, mime was about silence and a lack of objects: 'The only reason we called it mime was because there is nothing there' (Sedgwick, 2020). For others, these elements were only symptoms of a form of theatre that was attempting to ask itself some big questions: 'What do you need for theatre? You need people watching

Introduction – piecing mime together **3**

and people doing, to an extent. And you don't need sets, or lighting even; you just need that relationship. I think that's fundamental' (Glass, 2020). Silence operated as a threshold, the edge of language and text, such that even when that threshold was eventually crossed physical theatre still held within its various configurations the sense of a physical homeland that was pre-/non-verbal. The difficulty in defining mime and physical theatre is however part of the flexibility that allowed it to stay at the forefront of theatre practice over the 1980s and 1990s. Mime and physical theatre in this sense represented a serious and profound response to Peter Brook's provocation in his book *The Empty Space*:

> I can take any empty space and call it a bare stage. A man [*sic*] walks across this empty space whilst someone else is watching him, and this is all that is needed for an act of theatre to be engaged.
>
> *(Brook, 1968: 11)*

If the artists were undecided about what mime was, audiences were clearly not going to find any simple answers. Respondents to a 1992 survey of mime audiences[1] identified 'modern mime', 'visual theatre', 'theatre', 'comedy' and 'physical theatre' as the most popular descriptions of this kind of work (McCann Matthews Millman, 1992). An earlier 1989 McCann Matthews Millman [MMM] report on audience perspectives suggests that labels such as 'physical theatre' or 'visual theatre' are 'not only unhelpful, but also create further barriers' (1989: 22), suggesting that these terms are strange, pretentious and too avant-garde (1989: 67). The report identifies audiences' negative perceptions of mime as being derived from television and films – in particular the work of Marcel Marceau et al. (1989: 8). Practitioners reported feeling too easily pigeonholed by the terminology, and promoters saw the word 'mime' as a barrier to marketing work (McCann Matthews Millman, 1991: 4–5). The MMM 1991 report suggests that promoters viewed mime as 'thin on the ground in Great Britain' (1991: 6), despite the fact that the 1994 UK Mime and Physical Theatre directory, which was by no means exhaustive, listed over 65 companies and artists.

For our purposes then, mime can be defined as a form of performance that is predominantly silent (with minimal/limited use of words and sounds, such that movement dominates dramaturgically) and that makes minimal use of set and props (the illusion of objects is created through movement, or set and props are present to facilitate the movement). The limitations imposed by such a definition are what eventually led to the use of the more encompassing phrase, 'physical theatre', by the end of the 1980s[2]. Within physical theatre, the emphasis on movement over text remained but text, voice and sounds became more prominent and/or were not

---

1 The survey respondents had seen performances by Black Mime Theatre, Dorothy Talk, Mime Theatre Project, Right Size, Théâtre de Complicité and Trestle Theatre.

2 For a more detailed consideration of the term physical theatre, its meanings and etymology, and the contexts within which it might be used, see Murray and Keefe (2016: 16–82; and 2007: 9–114, 151–155).

4 Introduction – piecing mime together

set in opposition to movement and gesture. Set designs that enabled movement in imaginative ways were also an increasing feature of this work, in particular in the 1990s as funding for mime and physical theatre grew. We have understood physical theatre in its broadest context – as encompassing some forms of visual theatre, performance art and popular performance. Despite the porosity and elasticity of these definitions, we have avoided positioning mime as a subset of physical theatre, since we consider that it has a historical significance of its own. In Chapters 2 and 5 we trace how different European influences have shaped this field over the three decades in question. Eventually, by 2000, definitions became general enough to be near meaningless, such that although we might all generally claim to know what we mean or recognise by the term physical theatre, we would be hard-pushed to explain it in specific terms. In addition, its overuse has contributed to its demise as a critical tool.

Understanding mime

A number of theoretical positions, several of which emerged into prominence during the last quarter of the twentieth century, are useful to bear in mind in relation to how we understand mime and physical theatre. Murray and Keefe provide a comprehensive discussion of these theories and their relation to physical theatres – kinesic semiotics, phenomenology, cultural materialism, feminism and reception theory (2016: 28–39). Theory did not, however, drive most of the practitioners we examined. Their work was a response to the world around them and the environments in which they found themselves working. We are not, therefore, seeking to over-theorise mime and physical theatre performance during this period. Rather we intend to reveal some of the significant interactions between the relevant social, cultural, economic and ideological contexts within which mime and physical rose to prominence and then faded.

We contend that focusing on this period between 1970 and 2000 reveals much of interest in the relationships between theatre and performance practice and wider social, aesthetic, economic and political forces. Our chapters, therefore, focus on the relationship between these various factors and explore their impact on who created what, where, how and for whom. Chapter 2 examines the recent cultural history of mime and physical theatre, seeking to identify the trajectory that brought mime into prominence in the last quarter of the twentieth century and to recognise the contribution of a number of key figures in that journey. Chapter 3 addresses the systems of funding during this period (e.g. Arts Council, Regional Arts Boards, Local Authorities, the National Lottery and private sponsorship) and the national and regional arts policies that shaped the development of mime and physical theatre (e.g. the Arts Council decision to move responsibility for mime from the Dance Department to the Theatre Department, and the inauguration of the advocacy organisation Mime Action Group). In addition, this chapter reviews the influence of festivals such as the London International Mime Festival and regional equivalents. In Chapter 4 we look at the organisational and venue structures 'beyond the centre' which enabled mime to flourish, and specifically the ways in which the Regional Arts Boards offered support for the development of mime across the UK. We look in particular at the Northern region of England and at Scotland, Wales and Northern Ireland. Case studies and short profiles refer to the individual artists, companies, administrators and venue managers who shaped mime and physical theatre for these regions during this period. Chapter 5 focuses on identifying general approaches to the making of mime and physical theatre, exploring their defining features and the principles that underpin them, positioning them within a wider context and then examining one or more practitioners as case studies for each approach. These case studies are not chosen as definitive examples but selected in an attempt to provide a varied profile of the field that represents its breadth as well as its depth. Chapter 6 explores the opportunities for training, education and debate in mime and physical theatre in the UK. Whilst recognising the importance of the mime schools that emerged during this period, the chapter also interrogates the significance of the development of workshops, residencies and festivals as part of the UK mime and physical theatre training ecology. Chapter 7 reviews the extent to which the field of mime and physical theatre offered equality of opportunity for female, disabled and global majority practitioners. Case studies include the ground-breaking work of companies such as Three Women Mime, Black Mime Theatre and British Theatre of the Deaf, as well as others.

Why mime matters

Jacques Lecoq declared that '[a]t the end of the nineteenth century, the human body was rediscovered' (in Lust, 2000: 105) – however, this was not a moment but the beginning of a century-long journey. Throughout the twentieth century, the body and its physical expression increasingly became something that was public and not just intimate. In undertaking this journey, the body has (re)emerged as a central space for performance practice. Mime and physical theatre matter because they represent the coming together of social, cultural and aesthetic changes over the last century. What is represented in this coalescence is a series of snapshots of the ways in which physical performance embodied the conditions within which it was made and to which it was responding. It presages a period of change within the UK theatre industry, a period that saw the body and the various identities that bodies represent, the playful and transformative power of the physical imagination, and the creative energy of movement, be unleashed in ways that they had never been in UK theatre. It may be hard to believe now, but there was a time when what mime was, what physical theatre was and how both were important as forms of theatre mattered intensely to those practising these forms.

Our case studies are not exhaustive – we have sought to ensure a fair representation whilst keeping the number of interviews manageable. White, straight, nondisabled male voices have tended to dominate within this field (and we are aware of our own position in this context), so we have wanted where possible to forefront other perspectives. In addition, where extensive documentation and/or analysis

6 Introduction – piecing mime together

of an artist or company already exists, we have chosen sometimes to focus on less well-known examples and to value breadth as much as depth. We have sought to ensure that each chapter intersects judiciously with the other chapters, building a picture of the ways in which physical devising across a wide range of practices and contexts enabled the articulation of individual 'voices'. We contend, for example, that it is valuable to understand the 'how' of making mime and physical theatre not just through a critical examination of process, but also through an interrogation of what companies wanted to say, why, where and to whom, as well as acknowledging the socio-economic and political pressures that shaped their work.

2
THE MOMENT OF MIME

This chapter investigates the rise of modern mime and physical theatre leading into and across the 1960s and 1970s. We begin by identifying the antecedents to modern mime and physical theatre and examining the pioneer figures in the field during this period. Our aim is to place the professional lives of individual artists within the context of the mime and physical theatre ecology and UK society at that time. In doing so, we will point to the ways in which mime and physical theatre can be understood as the confluence of themes and histories that inform the structure of this book. Class, culture, location, gender and funding all played their part in relation to the opportunities UK mime and physical theatre practitioners have experienced and the routes that they were able, encouraged or motivated to take. The mime genealogies that we will examine were all shaped by the availability of training, public and artistic taste, and government arts policy. Chapters 3 and 4 will examine the ways in which government arts funding policy and wider socio-economic and political forces impacted mime and physical theatre practice, but first, this chapter lays out the broader trajectory of UK mime practice over the twentieth century that brings us to the period in question.

Revealing mime history

Our understanding of 'mime' is of course shaped by its history. At the Desmond Jones School in Shepherd's Bush, London, in the early 1980s, the small school noticeboard would often feature a card with a quote chosen from the various literatures on mime. For many of his students, this represented their first introduction to the history of the form they were learning. Few, if any, of the schools in London or Paris devoted time to explaining the history of the techniques that were being

DOI: 10.4324/9780429330209-2

8 The moment of mime

taught. A trip to Samuel French's Theatre Bookshop[1] in the 1980s would reveal a small selection of books on mime, mostly dedicated to practical instruction – for instance, Claude Kipnis' *The Mime Book* (1974), which includes flick-through photographs depicting mime sequences. With a little detective work, the interested reader might unearth Jean Dorcy's *The Mime* (1961) – a brief history of the work of Jacques Copeau (1879–1949), Etienne Decroux (1898–1991), Jean-Louis Barrault (1910–1994) and Marcel Marceau (1923–2007). They might also come across Bari Rolfe's comprehensive compilation, *Mimes on Miming* (1979) and Mira Felner's *The Apostles of Silence* (1985). The 'French connection' was further strengthened by mentions of the teaching and practice of Copeau's nephew, Michel Saint-Denis (1897–1971), in books such as Irving Wardle's biography of George Devine (Wardle, 1978: 44–118), as well as Keith Johnstone's *Impro* (1981: 144) and William Gaskill's *A Sense of Direction* (1988: 42–43). The first English translation of Jacques Lecoq's book *Le Corps Poétique* (*The Moving Body*) was not published until 2000.

Copeau and after – Bing, Saint-Denis, Decroux, Barrault, Marceau and Lecoq

The French mime tradition, which for many Western Europeans represents the dominant tradition of mime practice, started with the physical performance skills developed by Jacques Copeau and his assistant Suzanne Bing (1885–1967) at the Ecole du Vieux-Colombier, founded in 1919, and with the young company, Les Copiaus, that Copeau set up in Burgundy in 1924. Etienne Decroux studied at Copeau and Bing's school and acknowledged the work with Bing in particular as vitally important in his development of corporeal mime. After Les Copiaus was dissolved, a new troupe emerged, La Compagnie des Quinze, led by Copeau's nephew Michel Saint-Denis[2]. This troupe first toured to London in 1931 with their productions of *Noé* and *La Viol de Lucrèce*, and returned each year until 1935, when Saint-Denis dissolved the company and moved to England. Jane Baldwin reports how London critics 'singled out the actors' movement for its spontaneous and natural appearance' (2003: 50). In 1936 he started the London Theatre Studio, which lasted until the outbreak of the Second World War in 1939. After the war, in 1947, he opened the Old Vic School (Baldwin, 2003). Both schools became influential in the development of UK actor training and promoted Copeau and Bing's techniques including silent improvisation, mime, mask work, choral work and the importance of movement. Saint-Denis helped change the disposition of British theatre towards mime, movement and mask work, and encouraged interest

---

1 Samuel French's Theatre Bookshop on Fitzroy Street in London was the leading specialist theatre bookshop in the country. It closed in 2017. Before the internet, such shops were the main source of information on what books were available.
2 For more information on Copeau and Bing, see Evans (2017), Evans and Fleming (2019) and Donahue (2007). For more information on Saint-Denis, see Baldwin (2003) and Saint-Denis (1960 and 1982).

in the French tradition; nonetheless, during this period the drama conservatoires generally saw mime and mask work as no more than additional skills that might enhance an actor's employability.

Decroux assembled a small mime company after the Second World War, which toured Europe, including England (Leabhart, 2019: 23), but his profile remained obscure amongst all but those 'in the know' and his notorious perfectionism made the experience challenging for English audiences. Barrault, who had worked along-side Decroux to develop mime as a technique, abandoned his teacher to develop his own form of theatre that included mime, masks and movement. Amongst his most influential productions were *Autour d'une Mère* (1935, based on William Faulkner's novel *As I Lay Dying*), *Christophe Colombe* (1953) and *Rabelais* (1968). The company that Barrault formed with his wife, the actress Madeleine Renaud, toured several times to the UK between 1951 and 1971, ensuring that his vision of a total theatre that was richly physical was at least recognised in the UK. Along with Saint-Denis, Decroux and Barrault's international reputation and their ability to profile mime as a serious art form prepared the way for the success of the British mimes who emerged from the 1950s to 1970s.

The other important reference point was, of course, Marcel Marceau, who had studied in Paris with Decroux in 1944–1945. Marceau first performed his own *mimodrames* in 1947. He started touring to the UK in 1952, during which time he made his debut on BBC television and performed at the Arts Theatre, London, for four weeks. He subsequently toured to the UK almost every five years. By his UK/London performances at the Old Vic Theatre in 1984, Marceau's total repertoire included 44 'style mimes' (sketches built around a specific theme, for example: 'The Maskmaker', in which the mask becomes tragically inseparable from the wearer's face) and 37 mime sketches built around the character of Bip, his mime alter-ego. His success meant that for many he was the face of mime, and his influence was extensive. The English mime Julian Chagrin recalls how he encountered Marceau one day in a theatre, 'he opened the door – and he said, "*Ah! Chagrin. Tu es venu boire a la source*". Isn't that magnificent! The ego! How would you translate that – "You have come to drink at the source"? Isn't that wonderful!' (Chagrin, 2020). Marceau opened his own school in Paris in 1969, which a number of UK students attended (including Nola Rae, who studied shortly after the school opened). Marceau's version of the completely silent white-faced mime in black tights, whose actions give the illusion of a world of invisible objects, dominated popular conceptions of the mime artist – as evidenced in the mime parodies later performed by popular entertainers such as Kenny Everett[3] and Rowan Atkinson[4]. This has been a cross that mime has had to bear and that partly explains the artistic/aesthetic snobbery which UK mime has lived with ever since.

---

3 See, for example: www.youtube.com/watch?v=msO2v5G5P2A.
4 Atkinson performed a sketch in the BBC comedy series *Not the Nine O'Clock News*, in which he played a mime artist, Alternative Carpark, who announced, 'I am a mime, my body is my tool'.

10 The moment of mime

Jacques Lecoq, though less well-known than Marceau, was arguably the closest to achieving Copeau's vision. Having trained originally as a physiotherapist, Lecoq became involved with theatre groups during the German occupation of France. After the War, he joined Jean Dasté's company, Les Comédiens de Saint-Etienne, as an actor and choreographer. Subsequently, he travelled to Italy, where he taught at the Piccolo drama school in Milan, researched the performance traditions of Commedia dell'Arte and Greek Tragedy, and directed and performed with Dario Fo. He returned to Paris in 1956 to establish his school, which he ran with his wife Fay until his death in 1999. In 1959, Lecoq directed a production of *Peter and the Wolf* for BBC television. He also visited the UK a number of times during the 1980s to present his lecture demonstration *Tout Bouge* (*Everything Moves*), occasionally to teach a LEM workshop, and to lead one of the British Summer School of Mime international summer school events.

The history of French mime is covered in detail by a number of authors (Evans (2017), Felner (1985), Leabhart (1989, 2019), Lust (2000), and Murray (2018)); however, mime has a much longer history than this. Various authors (e.g. Mawer (1925 and 1936) and Lust (2000)) have outlined a common ancestry for modern mime that stretches back as far as Ancient Greek and Roman culture. This lineage is traced through the troubadours of the Dark Ages and Medieval Britain, the clowns and fools of Tudor England, the Commedia-inspired clowning of Joseph Grimaldi, the tumbling and acrobatics of the Hanlon-Lees troupe, the advent of the Pierrot character (see Evans, 2015) and the comedy routines of Stan Laurel and Charlie Chaplin[5]. Chaplin and Laurel were accomplished silent comedy performers. They both developed their physical performance skills within the live popular entertainment industry and found their abilities ideally suited to the medium of early film comedy. Laurel's bashful, shy film persona together with his slightly surreal approach to comedy seem to owe something to Commedia characters such as Tartaglia[6] and the ways in which mime allows the transformation of objects[7]. Chaplin's comic routines were clearly an inspiration for many subsequent mime artists – acrobatic, making use of whatever comes to hand. Marceau freely admitted that his Bip character was in part inspired by Chaplin's Little Tramp. British pantomime, a traditional seasonal entertainment form, is based in large part on the slapstick routines of Commedia, mingled with other elements such as fairy tales and fantasy, cross-dressing and music-hall routines. 'Panto' performance may contain occasional elements of mime, but should not be confused with pantomime as a form of silent mime relying upon gestures for the telling of stories. These forms are lineages that, within UK theatre history, firmly link mime and physical theatre to popular entertainment (comedy,

---

5 'In England we've got great clowns, we've got Grimaldi, we've got a theatre tradition of fine comedians – Chaplin and Stan Laurel being a couple of them . . . We have a tradition here which really hasn't been recognised' (Rae, 2020).

6 A timid, stuttering character.

7 See, for instance, the pipe smoking routine in Block-Heads (1938) (available at: https://youtu.be/rqL7WN9T7-s).

acrobatics, clowning and silent movies) and with notions of skill rather than art. This historical association with the popular perhaps explains why the French mime traditions, which sought specifically to elevate mime to the level of an art form, gradually gained ground in the UK in the latter half of the twentieth century, as tastes and aspirations changed. The recognition of mime as a post-Second World War art form interestingly also coincides with the emergence of Samuel Beckett as a significant figure in French and British post-war theatre – connecting with his fascination with silence and physical routines (e.g. *Act Without Words 1*, which premiered at the Royal Court Theatre, London, in 1957).

Mime, dance and ballet

Several other approaches to mime and physical performance also can be identified in the early part of the century. The number of publications that emerged between 1920 and 1960 indicates that mime enjoyed significant popularity at this time (Perugini, 1925; Chisman and Wiles, 1934; Welsford, 1935; Mawer, 1936; Pickersgill, 1947; Lawson, 1957; Bruford, 1958). Perugini[8] saw mime as derived from Greek and Roman dance/drama and Commedia dell'Arte, but essentially as an important element of ballet. Welsford[9] offered a historical view of the fool/jester from Ancient Greece through to Commedia dell'Arte and the Elizabethan court. Chisman and Wiles make no mention of any particular mime history, but encourage the aspiring mime artist to focus on the 'foundations of movement, position, balance, relaxation, walk, etc., with the study of some subjects requiring rapid co-operation between mind and body' (1934: 8), perhaps informed by contemporary developments in physical education. Pickersgill, who was for a time Principal of the London School of Dramatic Art, follows in the footsteps of Perugini and places mime in the context of Greek and Roman culture and the Italian Commedia dell'Arte. Like Chisman and Wiles, she places great emphasis on blending mind and body, and developing poise and rhythm. Her focus on the use of gestures to communicate ideas and emotions indicates the possible influence of François Delsarte[10] or perhaps the *pantomime blanche* techniques of the Pierrot tradition.

Two interesting examples of this dance and Commedia lineage are Harold Cheshire and Clifford Williams. Cheshire trained in mime and ballet in New York[11], as well as training as an actor, and performed and toured extensively and

---

8 Mark Perugini (1876–1948) was a ballet critic. He was married to the mime artist Irene Mawer.

9 A fellow of Newman College, Cambridge, Enid Welsford (1892–1981) was a neighbour of Simon McBurney's family when he was growing up (Giannachi and Luckhurst, 1999: 75).

10 François Delsarte (1811–1871) was an influential French teacher who devised a codified system for the analysis of movement. At the start of the twentieth century his method was very popular in France, the UK and particularly in America.

11 Cheshire trained with Elizabetta Menzeli. Menzeli's advert in the January 1919 issue of *The Two Step*, a monthly New York dance magazine, indicates that her training included ballet, Delsarte, Physical Aesthetics and Grace Culture.

12 The moment of mime

internationally both before and after the Second World War. His most successful mime piece was 'The Hands', in which the whole performance focused solely on the expressive use of his hands[12]. The rest of his repertoire drew on Commedia dell'Arte (in particular Pierrot), Eastern dance traditions and liturgical drama. Cheshire died in 1970 at the age of 82. Few records remain of his work, one brochure for his tour giving tantalising glimpses of the flavour of his performances.

Williams also trained as a dancer. He founded the Mime Theatre Company in 1950 and for the next three years wrote and directed 20 mime plays, before moving into theatre directing. He eventually joined the Royal Shakespeare Company (RSC), where he directed a Commedia-inspired production of *The Comedy of Errors* in 1963 that was a huge international success for the company and revived interest in a previously neglected play. In addition, he directed a ground-breaking, modern-dress, all-male production of *As You Like It* for the National Theatre in 1967, and Kenneth Tynan's controversial erotic review *Oh! Calcutta!* in 1969.

Irene Mawer

Perhaps one of the most intriguing figures from this period is Irene Mawer (1893–1962). It seems that she had little or no formal training in mime, although she was trained as an actress; however, she became a very successful mime teacher and performer and established a successful school with her colleague, the dancer Ruby Ginner. Mawer's practice brings together the influences of dance, classical Greek theatre and Commedia dell'Arte, yet her achievements and legacy have been largely forgotten since her death in 1962. Mawer taught mime at both Central School of Speech and Drama and Rose Bruford College. Rose Bruford (1904–1983) was herself a former student and she acknowledged Mawer's influence on her own teaching (Bruford, 1958: 7). Robert Lister, an actor who trained with Rose Bruford in the 1960s, recalls details of some of the mime exercises:

> I remember that the first half of every mime class was given over to exercises designed to improve posture and suppleness in each part of the body. Precision and economy of movement and gesture were foremost considerations. As far as I recollect, much of her work focussed on the five senses; exploring them through the imagination. . . . There was also a fairly intense study of Commedia as a source of mime. We studied the various characters and learned the gestures of the stylised mime vocabulary: *man, woman, love, money*, etc.
>
> *(Lister, 2021)*

Mawer's own book on mime (1936) begins with a historical survey ('The History of Mime and of Symbolic, Expressive, and Dramatic Movement') that supports

---

12 Andrew Dawson and Jos Houben's production *Quatre Mains* (1997) is an echo of this piece, with its focus on the expressive use of their hands.

the description Lister gives earlier – covering mime from Ancient Egypt and Greece through to Harlequinades in the nineteenth century. Tracing such a lineage is clearly also about asserting a cultural value to mime and locating it alongside the established European theatrical traditions and the perceived civilising power of European culture[13]. Late nineteenth- and early twentieth-century anthropology, inspired by James George Frazer's *The Golden Bough* (1890), had asserted the cultural importance of myth and ritual. Frazer's text and the work of the Cambridge Ritualists[14], together with Friedrich Nietzsche's celebration of the Dionysian energy of the dancing Chorus in *The Birth of Tragedy* (1872), no doubt informed Mawer and Ginner's passionate revival of Ancient Greek dance and physical expression. Ancient Greek culture was seen as offering a wholeness of being that had been lost through the prudery of Victorian social mores and the brutal savagery of the First World War (Mawer and Ginner first met in December 1915). Ginner is clear that from the start of the Ginner Mawer School in 1918 'the Greek ideal' was 'the basis of it all' (Ginner, 1963: 100). Both Ginner and Mawer enjoyed reasonable success up until the outbreak of the Second World War in 1939 – an Institute of Mime was established and there are numerous examples of Mawer giving demonstrations and lectures about mime across the UK – although Macintosh (2011) notes that interest started to wane from the end of the 1920s. The pinnacle of Mawer's success came in 1928 when she starred as Pierrot in a production of *L'Enfant Prodigue*, a role she reprised several times over the next decade (see Fig. 2.1). During the war, the School was evacuated to Boscastle in Cornwall. The war depleted the School's financial resources and many of those associated with the School, the Institute and Ginner's Revived Greek Dance Association were lost to active service. The momentum was lost, and aesthetic taste after the war started to turn away from the techniques offered by Ginner and Mawer. Dance and free movement in the early part of the century had felt like 'forbidden territory' to many young women, encouraging freedom of movement and relaxed dress. Ginner and Mawer's work was part of this social change in the perception of women's bodies and must have seemed liberatingly innovative to many young women at this time. Their school, with its distinctive blending of dance, movement and mime, and as an institution founded and run by women, was indeed an important and trail-blazing enterprise. After the Second World War, their work seemed like 'the end of a long tradition that began with Duncan' (Macintosh, 2011: 55), and was perceived as less in tune with post-war aesthetics. Financial pressures forced Ginner's Association to undergo incorporation into the Imperial Society of Teachers of Dance in 1951. Ultimately, Mawer's mime practice fell out of favour – it did not speak so convincingly to the post-war generation of the 1960s who were looking for something to

---

13 Macintosh (2011: 55) sounds a note of caution in relation to Ginner's emphasis on physical perfection and her possible connections with the eugenicists (2011: 55), and points out the cultural nostalgia evident in the call for a return to the 'idyllic classic days, for inspiration . . . beauty, joy and – sanity' (Perugini, 1928: 9) by Mark Perugini, Mawer's second husband.

14 A group of scholars, including Jane Harrison, Gilbert Murray, Francis Cornford and Arthur Cook, who had a shared interest in ritual and sacrifice as a driving force in Ancient Greek drama.

14 The moment of mime

FIGURE 2.1 *L'Enfant Prodigue*, with Irene Mawer as Pierrot and Ruby Ginner as Pierrot Père. By kind permission of Eileen Stewart.

Source: Date and photographer unknown.

The moment of mime **15**

shake up the theatre establishment of the time. However, one of her former students, Eileen Stewart, recalls that towards the end of her career, Mawer,

> continued to broaden her researches into the use of masks, mime and body language in the theatrical performances of other cultures as well as exploring mime as a way of developing children's imaginative play to become a meaningful form of *shared visual* conversation between 'performer' and 'audience'. . . . She was a person with a strong intellectual curiosity, an acute awareness of the importance of the human imagination and a warm concern for people even though she remained a very 'private' person and published little. . . . She was a pioneer in many respects and a woman who wanted us to see movement as important in all aspects of human expression and communication.
>
> *(Stewart, 2022)*

By the 1960s, the impact of Michel Saint-Denis and the French mime teachers (Decroux, Marceau and Lecoq) meant that the balance had swung firmly away from Ginner and Mawer. The post-war revival of Paris as a centre for artistic and cultural innovation (in particular with respect to fashion, film, philosophy, theatre, photography and literature) gave the arrival of French mime a certain novelty and allure. Marceau's Bip seemed to fit effortlessly into this image of a stylish, sophisticated French cultural scene that was informed by the tragedy of the war but also by the grace and humanity that emerged in its aftermath. The silence of mime represented an eloquent response to the horror and trauma of two world wars. Copeau, Bing, Decroux, Barrault, Marceau and Lecoq had all lived through an appalling period in European history. Marceau, born Marcel Mangel, helped fellow Jews to escape the Holocaust; Lecoq was part of the French Resistance and his sister was for a period interned in one of the concentration camps. Communication through mime in the decades after the Second World War enabled the constitution of an arena in which a common humanity might possibly be re-established[15].

The association of mime with Greek and Roman dance/drama and Commedia dell'Arte, and specifically with ballet, explains some of the cultural assumptions that placed mime originally alongside Dance in the Arts Council's departmental structures. Mime was taught in ballet schools, as the use of a silent language of gestures was required for several dances in the classical ballet repertoire. A number of post-war mime teachers trained initially as dancers: for example, Barry Grantham[16],

---

15 Lecoq recalls how he worked as a drama animateur in German teacher-training colleges after the war: 'I like to think I helped a little in the "denazification" of Germany: I tried out a relaxation exercise which consisted of lifting the arm and letting it drop. I found that their way of doing the gesture was stiffer and different from ours, so I taught them to loosen up!' (2020: 5).

16 Grantham worked as a dancer and a mime before specialising in the teaching of Commedia dell'Arte. See: Grantham (2000) and www.chalemie.co.uk/Grantham.htm.

16 The moment of mime

Adam Darius[17] (1930–2017) and Lindsay Kemp. Joan Lawson (1907–2002), who wrote the 1957 book *Mime*, was an influential teacher of dance and ballet and taught mime at the Royal Ballet School from 1963 to 1971.

Mime and the 1960s

Sandy Craig (1980) writes about how the counter-culture of the 1960s embodied a willingness to enjoy: the rough, physically adventurous and simple; a delight in the strange, bizarre and imaginative; an appetite for sensation and change. Events such as the Edinburgh Festival Fringe and venues such as the Arts Lab in London became hubs for many experimental theatre companies at this time (Pip Simmons, Freehold and the People Show) and acted as a model for alternative venues around the country such as York Arts Centre and St George's Project in Liverpool (Craig, 1980: 16). The cultural impact of the *Summer of Love* in San Francisco in 1967 and '*les événements*' in Paris in 1968[18] was substantial and assisted in the setting up of new informal and experimental art venues (Ansorge, 1975: 56). Paris once again became an exciting and iconic intellectual environment – Barrault allowed the student protestors to use the Théâtre de l'Odéon as a centre for debate, and invited Peter Brook to develop an experimental production of *The Tempest* that became the seed for his relocation to Paris in the 1970s[19]. The political energy of the time fuelled the idea that creativity could be viewed as no longer the privilege of an artistic elite but a democratic right for all. Of all the Paris mime schools, the Lecoq School was probably the one that rose most convincingly to the challenge this shift in culture offered – allowing students to take ownership of their learning through the *auto-cours*, a part of the course given over to group project work. Basic but accessible venues, new touring circuits, an ideological rejection of materialism and a desire for political change acted as useful creative lubricants (Craig, 1980: 17) and helped give mime economic, political and aesthetic significance within theatre making over following three decades – these changes are dealt with in more detail in Chapter 3.

---

17 Adam Darius was a successful American dancer who turned to mime after watching Marceau perform. He co-founded the Mime Centre in Kentish Town, London, in 1978. His mime work was economical but informed by his dance training. His performances could be shocking – in his 1969 adaptation of Momoko Hosokawa's play *Narcolepsy* the male character is nude for most of the play and at one point performs a simulated sex act with his mother. Darius' wider impact on UK mime was limited, although he did work with the singer Kate Bush to choreograph some of the dance movements for her 1978 single *Wuthering Heights* (see *The Times* – Adam Darius: Obituary, 2017).

18 This was a period of student unrest in Paris and across France which lasted about seven weeks. It represented a spirit of liberation and collective political action.

19 Although Brook then moved to Paris, his influence was felt in the UK throughout the next two decades both through the tours of his Paris productions, including *The Ik* (1976), *Ubu* (1978), *The Mahabharata* (1988) and *The Man Who* (1994), and through the various books that were published on his work.

The idea of the rock or pop group grew to have a particular social and cultural power during the 1960s. Experimental theatre companies liked the association with an alternative lifestyle and a rejection of convention. As with rock bands, touring was relatively easy at this time; there were plenty of venues, it was cheap to get a van and travel, and there was, at least initially, the romantic allure of the nomadic life. The burgeoning 1960s and 1970s festival culture also meant that theatre, dance and rock music were regularly rubbing shoulders. The British Art Colleges played an important role, encouraging experimentation in performance art and music that fed into both alternative performance and popular music. Mime and popular music certainly both benefitted from these points of cultural cross-over and integration, which were to continue and develop during the 1980s (see Chapter 8). Positioning mime as part of the fabric of cultural activity during the late 1960s and the early 1970s enables us to place the work of other key practitioners born between 1930 and 1940 in a clearer context.

Lindsay Kemp

Lindsay Kemp (1938–2018) was one of the most influential mime artists to emerge from the dance lineage[20]. He studied dance under Hilde Holger and later trained in mime with Marcel Marceau. He started his own mime company in the 1960s in order to create an outlet for his artistic vision. Kemp spent a period of time in Edinburgh and his work was clearly influenced by the experimental companies and artists he saw at the Fringe and the Festival, including Jerome Savary and The Living Theatre. Kemp's blending of fictional and actual personas on stage was informed by the avant-garde work that was available in Edinburgh during this period.

Kemp met David Bowie (1947–2016)[21] in 1966, Bowie became a student with Kemp and performed in Kemp's show, *Pierrot in Turquoise* (1967). They became lovers for a period and Kemp certainly influenced Bowie's artistic development, in particular his interest in mime and Japanese Kabuki and the creation of Bowie's Ziggy Stardust persona[22]. He performed in some of the Ziggy Stardust concerts and can be seen dancing in the video made for Bowie's 1972 single *John, I'm Only Dancing*[23]. Kemp also explicitly or indirectly influenced a number of other important music artists of this period, including Marc Bolan, Mick Jagger, Vivian Stanshall and King Crimson. Throughout the 1960s and the 1970s, the public

---

20 An extensive online archive of material relating to Kemp's life and work can be found at: www.lindsaykemp.eu.

21 Bowie had a long-lasting fascination with mime, dance and physical theatre. In 1968 he had performed a mime act (apparently a version of the Chinese invasion to Tibet!) as an opener for Marc Bolan's Tyrannosaurus Rex. Bowie also performed a brief mime sequence, filmed in 1971 at Andy Warhol's studio in New York (www.dailymotion.com/video/x7ixb6). In 1988 he was involved in a collaboration with the Canadian dance company La La La Human Steps.

22 See Bowie in interview on the BBC Tonight programme on 12 February 1979. Available at: www.youtube.com/watch?v=JODbmaAfitg.

23 The video for *John, I'm Only Dancing* can be seen at: www.youtube.com/watch?v=lmVVyhpuFRc.

18 The moment of mime

FIGURE 2.2 'Dancing with an angel' Lindsay Kemp and David Houghton in *Flowers*, c. 1979–1981. By kind permission of David and Richard Houghton.

Source: Photo by Richard Houghton.

image of mime had been dominated by the white-faced Pierrot[24], an image of male sentimentality and pathos, and by the ubiquity of Marceau. Kemp was a significant force in challenging these stereotypes[25].

Over a period from the late 1960s Kemp experimented with versions of the production for which he is probably best known, *Flowers*, inspired by Jean Genet's 1943 novel *Our Lady of the Flowers* (see Fig. 2.2). The show eventually opened in London in 1974, transferring to the West End and touring internationally. The novel tells the story of a man's journey through the Parisian underworld. The novel combines drag, eroticism, explicit sex and masturbation all of which informed Kemp's theatrical adaptation. The production quickly became notorious for its decadent style and the provocative blending of identity between characters and performers.

---

24 The popular image of Pierrot, the white face with the tear, comes from the impact of the French nineteenth century mime Jean-Gaspard Deburau (1796–1846) (see Evans, 2015: 347). The look of Deburau's Pierrot – baggy white costume, white face and black skull-cap – became synonymous with this brand of silent pantomime. Deburau's work is celebrated in the 1945 film by Marcel Carné *Les Enfants du Paradis*.

25 Interestingly, both Bowie and the singer Leo Sayer made use of the Pierrot figure. Leo Sayer dressed as a Pierrot for his 1973 song 'The Show Must Go On'. Natasha Korniloff, who designed costumes for Lindsay Kemp, also designed the Pierrot costume that Bowie used in the 'Ashes to Ashes' music video (1980).

In 1977, Kemp collaborated with choreographer Christopher Bruce to create *Cruel Garden* for the dance company Ballet Rambert (Kemp had also studied with Marie Rambert), a dance/theatre work inspired by the writings of Frederico Garcia Lorca. However, from the late 1970s onwards the majority of Kemp's productions took place outside the UK, so that by the end of the century he was perceived as an international performance artist. There can be little doubt however that his passionate and personal vision of theatre, dance and mime and his commitment to creating work that was daring, provocative, sexually liberated and sometimes proudly camp were influences on many other UK companies. He wasn't afraid to tap into his own emotional truth as a person and a performer and had an almost painterly ability to construct arresting visual imagery on stage. His work can certainly be seen as a precursor for DV8, Stan Won't Dance and Volcano, as well as the work of performers such as Neil Bartlett. His interest in combining multiple influences – his own work drew on ballet, Kabuki, butoh, music hall, cabaret and flamenco – was more playful and iconoclastic than the work of many contemporaneous intercultural practitioners at this time.

Kemp was an inspirational teacher, many actors, artists and performers took his classes. Nola Rae recalls undertaking a mime class with him in the early 1970s, during which she was paired with the actor, Ron Moody[26]. Mime, in part as a result of Kemp's influence, began to move away from both the simplicity of the illusion and the opacity of performance art – it was starting to become part of popular culture and the culture of pop. In the hands of artists like David Bowie, it was used to express alienation, sexual ambiguity and an exotic/erotic physicality. Kemp opened up mime as a space for those who felt marginalised by the conventionality of 1950s and 1960s Post-War Britain:

> I always felt foreign in England, because I was always accused of being a foreigner. . . . They didn't really like arty types in England, certainly not when I was growing up in the 1950s. So I felt a bit of a loner. People used to come up to me and say, 'Are you a man or a woman?' But I'm not effete and I don't walk with a mince or anything. There was just something about my persona that people thought was rather alien.
>
> *(Kemp interviewed in Lewis, 2016)*

Pat Keysell

Pat Keysell (1926–2009) trained as an actress. In 1961 she set up the Royal National Institute for the Deaf (RNID) Mime Group, which became the British Theatre of the Deaf, and which she led until 1977 (see Chapter 7). She was also a lead presenter for the popular BBC television programme, *Vision On* (1964–1976). She

---

26 An actor who achieved international fame in the role of Fagin in the 1968 film *Oliver!* He also played a French mime artist, The Great Orlando, in the 1963 film *Summer Holiday*.

20 The moment of mime

trained in mime with Claude Chagrin and attended a short course with Jacques Lecoq in 1967. After British Theatre of the Deaf, Keysell took a course with Desmond Jones at his school in London in 1977. She went on to teach at Rose Bruford College (1978–1980) and to found the Electric Light Show, which explored mime and multi-media. In 1982 she was appointed as mime artist in residence at Brewery Arts Centre in Kendall. Her career reflects her passion for sharing mime with anyone who was interested, and as she wrote in her book *Mime Over Matter*, 'Art is not just for the elite, the trained professional. It is for everyone, and should be a natural part of everyday life, just as it was in the distant past' (Keysell, 1990: 4). In 1984 she launched the International Festival of Mime in Cumbria. In 1985 she became Mime Artist in Residence at Dunfermline College of Physical Education in Edinburgh, and also ran workshops in the Grampian, Highland and Central Regions of Scotland. Keysell founded and directed the Scottish Summer School of Mime from 1986 to 1989, and in 1987 she was the co-founder and director of the Festival of Mime and Mask at the Netherbow Arts Centre. She moved south to East Sussex in 1996, where she set up a community theatre company, Compass Community Arts. She died in 2009, leaving a substantial legacy as a great advocate for mime as an art form across several regions/nations/constituencies within the UK.

Julian and Claude Chagrin

From an early age, Julian Chagrin was interested in comedy. He worked briefly in a strip club in the West End of London as a curtain puller, where he used to cover for the comedians when they were tired, and later he joined the Fol de Rols[27] as prop boy. In the late 1950s he went to Paris with his parents and 'who should we meet outside the Odéon but Jean-Louis Barrault' (Chagrin, 2020):

> My father had conducted the incidental music for a play of [Barrault's] in London. And he said, '*On avait grand difficulté avec ce fils. Il veut être comique, mais on sait pas quoi faire*'. And he said, 'Jacques Lecoq', Barrault said: 'He's giving a demonstration tomorrow night, why don't you go and see it?' So, I went to see it, and I stayed for three years.
>
> *(ibid.)*

Julian studied with Jacques Lecoq from 1959 to 1962 (see Fig. 2.3). At the end of his studies, he returned to the UK to make work with two other ex-Lecoq students – his wife, Claude Chagrin, and George Ogilvie (1931–2020)[28]. The show that they created, *Chaganog*, toured England and eventually played in London. As a result, Julian became well-known as a mime and comedian, appearing on TV,

---

27 The company toured piers and pavilions in seaside towns, performing variety, Pierrot and summer shows. See: www.folderols.org.uk/articles/welcome.html.

28 On his return to Australia, Ogilvie was to become a prolific actor and theatre/film director.

FIGURE 2.3 Jacques Lecoq and Julian Chagrin at Ecole Jacques Lecoq, Paris, c. 1960. By kind permission of Julian Chagrin.

Source: Photo from Julian Chagrin's personal collection.

including with Spike Milligan. Claude also started to pick up work as a teacher and a movement director. In 1966, Claude and Julian performed a mimed tennis match[29] for the final scene in the iconic 1960s film *Blow Up*, directed by Michelangelo Antonioni.

Julian's work was influenced by cartoon comedy, and by English variety humour (see Fig. 2.3). He admired the work of Max Wall, whom he thought 'could dance brilliantly, the eccentric dance was his. Fabulous' (ibid.). He understood that what he was offering was a new kind of comedy mime at a time when the British public were used to balletic mime: 'They liked it very much. It worked well. And in my one man show, of course I was also speaking. I did not eschew the spoken word' (ibid.). Claude and Julian were alert to the opportunities that a more accessible

---

29 You can watch this extract of the film at: www.youtube.com/watch?v=4TYyhRbQBgs.

FIGURE 2.4 Julian Chagrin in performance. Date unknown. By kind permission of Julian Chagrin.

Source: Photo from Julian Chagrin's personal collection.

approach to mime offered. In 1974, they made a comedy mime film, *The Concert*, which won a first prize at the Berlin Film Festival[30]. In Julian Chagrin's opinion, his success was all about humour: 'I was funny. I wasn't stylised. I wasn't in any way nearly as talented bodily as Marceau. But I was very funny, you know, I had some great sketches, and people loved them' (ibid.). Claude took a different route. She had trained with Marceau as well as with Lecoq and was appointed by William Gaskill to become the movement specialist at the National Theatre, working on 17 productions between 1961 and 1974 (Tashkiran, 2020: 11–12). She had a significant success with movement direction for productions of Peter Shaffer's plays *Royal Hunt of the Sun* and *Equus*, both directed by John Dexter. Steven Berkoff recalls that 'Although John Dexter was a skilled director, she created the images that lifted the drama' (Berkoff, 2020). She also taught in London for several years, including at the City Literary Institute and Morley College, and ran short courses for the English Stage Company at the Royal Court. She was recognised by many who trained with her as a talented and inspirational teacher. Her work was not properly recognised

---

30 You can watch *The Concert* at: www.youtube.com/watch?v=XVPouJPJrp0.

until Ayse Tashkiran's recent book on movement direction in the theatre (2020), which locates Claude Chagrin as an important figure in the history of this field. In 1976 the Chagrins relocated to Israel; although this curtailed their impact on mime and physical theatre in the UK, their influence has been lasting and profound, as will become clear in other sections of this book.

Three other mime artists from this time, whose careers were influenced by the Chagrins, are also important to mention.

Steven Berkoff

Steven Berkoff was born in the East End of London and started acting in 1960 after training at the Webber Douglas Academy of Dramatic Art. Quite early on in his career he recalls that he went to see Marceau: 'I bought a ticket and went to see him. And then I saw something which was quite extraordinary, and seemed to go beyond acting . . . It was magical' (Berkoff, 2020). This experience helped motivate Berkoff to work on his body and his physical technique. He recalls:

> I took dance classes that seemed to help me think about the body as my instrument. I would go to the gym quite frequently. And then sometime in 1964 one of the great pupils of Jacques Lecoq came to London. Her name was Claude Chagrin and she was married to an English mime called Julian Chagrin. Claude was a phenomenal teacher. I saw, maybe in *The Stage*, mime classes advertised at the City Lit at Holborn. And so I signed up to do these classes with Claude Chagrin.
>
> *(ibid.)*

Inspired by Claude Chagrin's teaching, Berkoff attended Jacques Lecoq's Summer School in the rue de Bac, in Paris. On his return from Paris, he was offered a job as an understudy by Julian Chagrin, and then, in 1963, worked on a televised production of Hamlet as one of the troupe of players that performs for Hamlet and the royal family: 'Lindsay Kemp and I got a flat together. And we would work on mime together. We created the Players' scene in mime in the Japanese style of Kabuki with strong gestures and Lindsay choreographed them' (ibid.). Berkoff has written of his genuine admiration for Kemp's individuality, his ingenuity and bizarre talent (1995: 49–50; 1996: 258). He reflects, with a generous candour, how,

> Lindsay and I were always a little in competition with each other and sneakily envied each other's successes. In other ways we were like old dogs burying our ancient bones and digging them up from time to time – his bone being *Flowers* and mine *Metamorphosis*.
>
> *(1995: 50)*

Berkoff's breakthrough production as a director/theatre maker was indeed an adaptation of Franz Kafka's short novel *Metamorphosis*. At first, he struggled with the

24 The moment of mime

challenge of representing the beetle on stage, but after watching a student production at Oxford in which an actor portrayed the beetle, he realised it might be possible to represent the transformation through mime. Drawing on the ensemble mime work he had learnt at the Lecoq School, he created the theatrical vocabulary that was to inform so much of his future work: choral acting, muscular physicality, provocative text, bare staging (his production of *Metamorphosis* used scaffolding to present the Samsa's house), and a fiercely independent aesthetic (he raised the money to stage *Metamorphosis* himself). Since *Metamorphosis* he has created many landmark productions, including: *The Trial* (1970), *East* (1975), *Greek* (1980), *Sink the Belgrano* (1986), *Decadence* (1987) and *Salome* (1988). By the 1980s he had a successful movie career (starring in films such as *Octopussy* (1983) and *Beverley Hills Cop* (1984)) and consequently had less time to make theatre. In 1997 he was awarded a *Total Theatre* Lifetime Achievement Award. His theatre practice has influenced several generations of UK mime and physical theatre makers. In particular, his work demonstrates how mime, physicality and text might be blended together; it reintroduced expressionism, ensemble performance and physicality into UK theatre in productions that appealed to young theatre makers of the time. Whereas many of the other figures from this period developed careers as solo mimes, Berkoff, like Kemp, showed what could be possible with a larger ensemble of mimes. He demonstrated to those coming after him that it was possible not to be limited by mime training, but freed by it. His work was an antidote to the politely civilised mime of Marceau, and his humour offered a more robustly satirical take on the world. Berkoff was not afraid to allow passion its expression, and this willingness to take performance to the edge was to chime with the interests, desires and frustrations of some of the young artists to emerge in the next decades.

Geoff Buckley

Buckley (1932–2020) was a fellow student of Claude Chagrin and was inspired by her to go with Berkoff to study with Lecoq: 'She said, "If you want to do mime, you should go to Lecoq's", where she was trained. So, I did' (Buckley, 2018). Buckley tells of performing improvised mime with Berkoff on the streets of Paris – playful, short routines – and of how they both enjoyed the improvisations at the School. Lecoq encouraged students always to spend some time outside, to 'see what people are doing, how are they doing this, how are they doing that' (ibid.). For so many mime artists in this period, the street was an important place both to observe human behaviour and also to hone performance skills with minimum outlay. On his return from Paris later in the 1960s, Buckley took over Claude Chagrin's teaching at the Royal Court. Warren Jenkins then invited him to work at the Belgrade Theatre in Coventry as the resident mime artist and movement person; he also led classes at Birmingham Repertory Theatre and throughout the next few decades taught at drama conservatoires, including Bristol Old Vic Theatre School. Buckley's mime performances were largely based on the character of Pierrot; he spent 18 years touring in the UK and internationally. A gentle and down-to-earth man, passionate about mime, he always saw his art as something 'that was not about "me", it was about "that" – the thing that is being mimed, that's where the attention of the audience is drawn' (ibid.).

Ben Benison

Benison (1933–2019) was born in Wigan and worked as a pit boy and then as a mining surveyor. He was passionate about performing and whilst working took lessons in various disciplines including tap dancing and ballet, leading initially to a career in dance. He went to Paris and enrolled at the Lecoq School, but lack of money meant that he had to leave before the end of the first term. He returned to London to study with Claude Chagrin and ended up joining Julian Chagrin's performance troupe. In 1965, he took part in Keith Johnstone's show *Clowning* at the Royal Court, alongside Roddy Maude-Roxby[31]; this led to the launch of the Theatre Machine co-operative, an influential improvisation group that made imaginative use of mime, masks and puppetry. He also trained with Yat Malgram[32] and learnt mask work from George Devine[33]. He was probably best known to the general public for his regular appearances as a mime on the BBC children's programme *Vision On*, alongside Pat Keysall. He toured a one-man show, *Wigan Pierrot*, in the 1970s, and in the 1980s turned to writing and directing. He taught mime at RADA, as well as at Webber Douglas Academy, the Guildhall School of Music and Drama and in New York at the Stella Adler Studio; he also worked as a movement and comedy coach for the National Theatre, the Royal Shakespeare Company, English National Opera and on the film *Alien* (1979). He brought a distinctive energy to his work, which was always full of rich comic invention.

Venues: putting mime in its place

Initially, in the late 1960s, there was a chronic shortage of small alternative venues, but then,

> in the space of only three or four years, between 1969 and 1973, a large number of small, independent theatres came into existence, often taking over

---

31 Roddy Maude-Roxby was one of the UK's first performance artists, having trained initially at the Royal College of Art. He went on to work with masks and improvisation and was one of the founding figures of the improvisation company, Theatre Machine, along with Keith Johnstone and Ben Benison.

32 Malgram was an expert in Laban's approach to movement and character, and one of the founding directors of the Drama Centre in London.

33 George Devine (1910–1966) was a director, teacher and actor. He was a founding figure of the Old Vic Theatre School and became Director of the English Stage Company at the Royal Court Theatre, London. His classes in mask work at the Royal Court inspired Keith Johnstone's work on masks and improvisation (see Wardle, 1978).

26 The moment of mime

> disused premises or spaces such as the back rooms in pubs and converting
> them into rudimentary theatres.
>
> *(Malcolm Hay in Craig, 1980: 153)*

At the end of 1968 fewer than a dozen London fringe venues existed, by 1980 *Time Out* listed 40–50 venues each week. This change was vitally important to the emergence of mime and physical theatre. Instead of needing to fill larger buildings, emerging performers could create more experimental work and tour it more widely. A few venues are worth noting for their impact on the small-scale theatre touring circuit at this time. The Arts Lab was started by Jim Haynes, who had founded the Traverse in Edinburgh, in 1962. Although a very short-lived venue (1967–1969), it was hugely influential in establishing an ethos for such spaces – as a meeting place, a theatre venue, a space to view alternative films and see multimedia shows. The other venue that regularly presented the work of new theatre groups in 1968/69 was Oval House. Peter Oliver (1926–2007) was appointed in 1961 as Warden of Oval House, a sports-orientated Boys' Club. Under his leadership the sports facilities were converted into a 120-seat theatre, a smaller theatre, and a dance studio. Oliver allowed groups to rehearse for free, provided they performed at least once at the Oval and gave workshops to young people. A largely unrecognised figure – 'Peter Oliver was *so* important; where is there anything about him?' (Geraldine Pilgrim, 2020) – his support was enormously important for many of the mime, visual theatre and physical theatre companies that emerged after the 1960s.

The survival of these small theatres generally relied on, 'artistic directors and managements with the courage and conviction to take the necessary risks' (Malcolm Hay in Craig, 1980: 164), and was supported by a broad base of activities encouraging skills development for professionals and engagement for amateurs. The casual ambience appealed to a generation less interested in the rituals of traditional theatregoing and eager for creativity and involvement. Outside of London, networks of similar small-scale venues grew up. Birmingham Arts Lab, for instance, was set up in 1968, and although it struggled to find a permanent home through the late 1960s and the 1970s, nonetheless it was an important venue for new work and helped pioneer the idea of residencies for fringe companies. York Arts Centre was established in an old church building in 1968 and thrived throughout the 1970s and early 1980s. These venues owed their existence to and were closely linked with notions of alternativeness and community, catering to people who wanted something different. Their success led to a growth in studio spaces attached to regional repertory theatres, with 100–200 seat auditoria allowing for a more experimental and/or adventurous programme of shows. David Glass, who started his early career in the late 1970s and the 1980s when these venues and touring circuits were thriving, recalls 'rolling up to do a show to two people in 300 seat studio theatres . . . there were days we would have two people in the audience and one of them was asleep. Another day you'd have 300 people' (Glass, 2020). But failure back in those days didn't cost much: 'they probably paid me £200 and I'd do a week of work . . . we were given a chance to basically fail and fuck around' (ibid.).

The next generation: mime in the 1970s

By the time the next generation of mimes came along in the 1970s, there was, therefore, an infrastructure of venues to support and nurture their work. These were small venues that offered bare black box spaces – spaces whose very simplicity functioned to emphasise gesture, physicality and visual impact. The alternative to these venues was outdoor performance – on the streets, at festivals – that allowed access to new audiences and spoke to the counter-culture ethos of the time.

Nola Rae

Nola Rae (see Fig. 2.5) started as a ballet dancer. She attended the Royal Ballet School and then went to Sweden and danced professionally for a few years, including at the Tivoli Pantomime Theatre. While in Scandinavia she met Marcel Marceau, whom she knew was opening a school in Paris. Rae asked if she could attend, and that is where her mime journey began. After training with Marceau at the end of the 1960s, she worked in France for a year, learning how to perform on the streets, before coming back to England where she met up with the American clown Jango Edwards. They formed a company together, which became Friends Roadshow – a popular and influential mix of mime, clowning and music. She stayed with the company for three years (1972–1975) until leaving to form her own company, London Mime Theatre, in 1976.[34] Many of her early shows were produced with little or no subsidy, but she has enjoyed consistent popularity and for many promoters, artists and audiences she was and still is the face of British mime. Like many mime and physical theatre performers, she has spent a considerable amount of time touring internationally, in part because it has always been hard to make much money through mime in the UK: 'the venues don't pay much. In those days you had to pay for your own publicity, your own hotel, your petrol. By the time you've done all that the fee is 2s/6d' (Rae, 2020). Her international experience was an important factor in her contribution to the initiation of the London International Mime Festival. It is easy to forget the challenges of touring as a solo artist: 'We couldn't do grand performances. We couldn't do that, we didn't have enough funding. So, our shows were what they were – cheap!' (ibid.). It was a fragile existence for many, Rae did well because she had the talent to become well-known and the imagination to turn simplicity into a virtue. She continues to perform and in 1999 she was awarded a *Total Theatre* Lifetime Achievement Award in recognition of her contribution to mime. In the view of Joseph Seelig, 'Nola is an artiste, you know, she is exquisite – I don't think there's been anybody else of her calibre or stature as a mime/clown artist in Britain' (Lannaghan and Seelig, 2020).

---

34 At one point in the early 1970s she also briefly joined the international theatre company, Kiss, whose work was influenced by Grotowski.

28 The moment of mime

FIGURE 2.5 Nola Rae in *Upper Cuts*, c. 1980. By kind permission of Nola Rae and Matthew Ridout.

Source: Photo by Matthew Ridout.

Chris Harris

Chris Harris (1942–2014) trained at Rose Bruford College and worked in rep as an actor, before attending the Lecoq School. He went on to work with the Ladislav Fialka Pantomime Company in Prague and briefly at the Moscow State Circus School before returning to the UK, one of very few British performers to explore these Eastern European traditions before the end of the Cold War. From 1976 he toured his one-man shows in the UK and abroad, as well as acting in pantomime, theatre and on television. His most successful show was *Kemp's Jig*, which told the story of Will Kemp (a comic actor in William Shakespeare's company), who danced his way from London to Norwich. This was a show that tied together several of the historical strands of UK mime, blending foolery, clowning, mime and popular comic performance. Harris was interested in the history and traditions of physical comedy and his later career focused on writing, directing and performing in Christmas pantomimes.

Justin Case

Justin Case's interest in mime and physical performance came from seeing Julian Chagrin as a teenager. After putting on his own mime show at Leeds University in 1971, and travelling to Australia, where he met George Ogilvie (who had worked with Chagrin), Case decided to follow Chagrin's advice and go to the Lecoq School. He arrived at the School in 1972, at the same time as John Martin[35], one of the few other Brits at the School at that time. When he came back to the UK, he found it was,

> actually quite difficult to find other people with that background. . . . All the other mime performers wouldn't work together. So that's probably why I headed towards improv and people who are very different. I wanted to make films, so created a Video-Theatre show *Candid Case Affair* (1977) and from that grew The 2 Reel Co with Peter Wear, a physical-visual theatre about a filmmaking duo and then teamed up with The Wee Wees and formed the group Omelette Broadcasting Company, we toured UK and Europe with Mike Myers. We were pioneers in a totally un-American style of Improv – no rehearsals, no rules and no games, free-form comedy mayhem, taking mime, mask-work and theatre to a whole different level.
>
> *(Case, 2020)*

He identifies the Oval House as one of the important venues of this period – a 'melting pot of talent' (ibid.). This was a place where a wide range of mimes and comic performers would congregate, make work and perform, including Nola Rae, Ben Benison, John Ratzenberger[36] and Ray Hassett from Sal's Meat Market, actors Pierce Brosnan and Tim Roth[37], and comedians Mel Smith and Bob Goodie[38]. The Omelette Broadcasting Company, one of the first improvisation companies in the UK, had various members over its lifetime, including Jim Sweeney, Peter Wear, Steve Steen and Justin Case as well as occasional guests Johnny Melville, John

---

35 John Martin has, since 1986, been the artistic director of Pan Intercultural Arts, whose work is referenced in Chapter 6.

36 Ratzenberger went on to create the role of Cliff Clavin in the US comedy series *Cheers* (1982–1993).

37 Roth performed the role of Gregor Samsa in Berkoff's 1986 revival of *Metamorphosis*.

38 Goodie was a founder member of Shared Experience theatre company in 1975.

30 The moment of mime

Elk, Mike Myers, Neil Mullarkey, Lee Simpson and Alan Marriott. The company became regulars at Jongleurs comedy club in London and was part of the explosion of alternative comedy, paving the way for successful television shows like *Whose Line Is It Anyway?* (Channel 4, first broadcast 1988). Case's career marks important moments of cross-over with stand-up comedy and film during this period. Improvisation provided a meeting point for comics and mimes that caught the public imagination. Generations of earlier comics had honed well-rehearsed acts to tour the clubs and pubs around the country – this new approach, clearly influenced by Julian Chagrin's earlier example, brought a physical energy and an immediacy to comedy that challenged the conventions. Case was also able to use his mime, movement and mask skills in his role as the Scarecrow in the film *Return to Oz* (filmed in the UK in 1984, released in 1985)[39]. Case lived in Los Angeles for a while; he eventually moved to Australia in 1995 and has lived there ever since.

FIGURE 2.6 Justin Case performing his restaurant sketch in Budapest, Hungary, 1984. By kind permission of Justin Case.

Source: Photo by Jonathan Morse.

---

39 The rise in pre-digital special effects for films during the 1970s and 1980s meant that mime and movement skills were under high demand. Specialists such as Desmond Jones and Peter Elliott taught actors to mimic animal or pre-historic human movement (e.g. *Quest for Fire* (1981) and *Greystoke* (1984)). Anthony Daniels, who learnt acting and mime at Rose Bruford College, starred as C-3PO in the Star Wars movies (1977–2019), and other mimes were employed in the early films in the franchise to animate non-human characters.

Moving Picture Mime Show

Moving Picture Mime Show [MPMS] was formed by David Gaines, Toby Sedgwick and Paul Filipiak on their graduation from the Lecoq School in Paris in 1976. Sedgwick recalled seeing Marceau perform and being impressed, not so much by the style and content of Marceau's work, but by the way in which the emptiness of the stage was peopled by the imagination of the performer. As a teenager, he met Julian Chagrin and, like Justin Case before him, was excited by Chagrin's comedic imagination. He followed Chagrin's advice and went to the Lecoq School. This was a 'golden era' at the School – the teaching staff, in addition to Lecoq himself, included Pierre Byland[40], Philippe Gaulier and Monika Pagneux. MPMS' first show, *Seven Samurai*, came out of the *pantomime blanche* work in the second year. Early performances were on the streets in Paris, where they fine-tuned the company's fast-paced and energetic style. In the UK, the company found support from Battersea Arts Centre and soon received Arts Council funding. Nobody else was doing what they did; they hit on a style and content that was wacky, irreverent, high energy, funny and different. It's simple staging and use of cartoon idioms appealed to young people inspired by the do-it-yourself ethos of Punk culture in the late 1970s: 'It was extraordinary how quick you could take off then, if you had an idea and it was good' (Sedgwick, 2020). They were also one of the first groups to perform extended mask pieces – *Handle With Care* and *The Examination* (see Fig. 2.7) – using larval masks similar to those used at the Lecoq School. Their accessible style meant that the British Council funded extensive foreign tours, building them an international reputation. David Glass, who toured alongside MPMS in America, suggested that they 'were like The Police of mime. I mean, the band, you know' (Glass, 2020) – they acquired an almost legendary status in the UK mime world.

In Sedgwick's view, their mime appealed because, 'the audience is always engaged and their imaginations are always stirred. . . . We've always wanted to make the audience work a little' (Sedgwick, 2020). MPMS came to a natural end after 10 years; the company started to lose enthusiasm for touring and each wanted to follow other opportunities. MPMS was an important part of a period when mime helped to internationalise British theatre, to open it up to a different set of aesthetics: 'We created a huge potential for companies like Complicité, and all the other companies . . . not only in England, but in Europe. . . . I think we opened that window for a wider audience' (ibid.). See Chapter 5 for additional detail on their working methods.

---

40 Lecoq credits Byland with the initial introduction of the red nose mask of the clown to the Lecoq School.

32 The moment of mime

FIGURE 2.7 Moving Picture Mime Show (David Gaines, Toby Sedgwick and Paul Filipiak) in *The Examination*, 1978. By kind permission of Moving Picture Mime Show.

Source: Photographer unknown.

Street theatre, circus skills and counter-culture – Footsbarn and others

Jonathan Paul Cook and Oliver Foot founded Footsbarn Theatre in 1971, after having trained at the Lecoq School in Paris and the Drama Centre, London, respectively. Based in Cornwall, the company mirrored something of the ethos of Les Copiaus in Burgundy in the 1920s – communal living; blending theatre, masks, mime, movement and music; a commitment to devising and to developing a style that spoke to the local communities within which they were based.

> Cornwall was to be our laboratory. We were very clear and up front about this. We were going to research theatre in terms of the audience, a grass roots audience, and Cornwall was going to provide us with an unspoiled environment. We didn't want audiences with polite conditioned reflexes.
>
> *(Cook, n.d.)*

In the 1970s and the early 1980s, the company became well-established in the South West of England. Several other ex-Lecoq students joined the company during this period, and it developed a strong physical style. Footsbarn left the UK in 1984, becoming an itinerant company and eventually finding a base in central France in 1991. Their impact can be seen in the work of Kneehigh Theatre and the forging of a reputation in the South West for bold, imaginative physical theatre that was rooted in its communities.

Bim Mason, who founded Mummer&Dada, Peepolykus and Circomedia, recalls arriving in London in 1978 and being recruited by Kaboodle to perform acrobatics, clown work and open-air performances (Mason, 2020). For many companies, working on the streets at festivals, music gigs and arts events and using performance styles rooted in popular forms of entertainment was a way of connecting with audiences that would not otherwise be interested in mime and physical theatre. The whole alternative and counter-culture scene in the 1970s inspired physical theatre practitioners to be enthusiastically ambitious, visually challenging and often anarchically comic (e.g. Ken Campbell's 22-hour epic *The Warp*, produced at the ICA in London in 1979). Circus skills started to become popular as performers recognised the value of stilt-walking, unicycling and juggling, and found opportunities to perform at festivals and spaces such as Covent Garden Piazza. Mime was also relatively easy to learn, if you weren't looking to achieve technical precision; plus, it kept technical and design needs low. Organisations such as Ed Berman's Inter-Action (founded in 1968) acted as a model for the ways that this kind of work could be set up and supported within a community context.

International influences

All of the mime practitioners examined so far spent time studying and/or working on the European continent. It is important to recognise the European mime and physical theatre scene, and the extent to which it inspired and enabled UK mimes. Europe offered opportunities not just for study, but for experiment, collaboration, touring and the broadening of experience. Venues such as The Melkveg in Amsterdam were very supportive of mime and were welcoming to British artists and companies. The Festival of Fools, a regular European event, was 'a huge thing for the performers coming from all over the world' (Case, 2020). The Mickery in Amsterdam, run by Ritsaert ten Cate, was another venue that was very supportive of UK fringe theatre, mime and physical theatre. As well as hosting shows, they would offer residential workshop experiments, providing accommodation and expenses. Touring to Europe helped develop and sustain a strong visual style to UK artists' work – 'you emphasised the visual things because of the language barrier' (Case, 2020).

As well as the French mime tradition, and the impact of the schools run by Decroux, Marceau and Lecoq, there were several other important physical theatre traditions that influenced UK practice during this period – most significantly those from Eastern Europe, but also from the USA. The Cold War had meant that information about mime practitioners from Communist Bloc countries such as

34 The moment of mime

Poland (e.g. Henryk Tomaszewski) and Czechoslovakia (e.g. Ladislav Fialka, Bole-slav Polivka and Ctibor Turba) had been slow to emerge and difficult to access[41].

Vsevelod Meyerhold

In the UK after the First World War, the Workers' Theatre Movement (1926–1935) envisaged a break with conventional British dramaturgy and a rejection of conventional staging techniques. Their work adopted the same aesthetic as Meyerhold (1874–1940), seeking to transcend the written word through the use of physical movement and strong visual imagery. For UK socialist theatre makers of this time, the idea was that a new type of actor would emerge, inspired by the experience of modern industrialised life, and informed by 'machine movements, acrobatics and athletics' (Samuel, MacColl and Cosgrove, 1985: 42). Meyerhold's Biomechanics echoed the attempts of UK socialist theatre groups, such as Theatre in Action, a precursor of Joan Littlewood's Theatre Workshop, to reject naturalistic acting: 'We must train our actors so that they can do all the things with their bodies that a conjuror can do, or an acrobat, or a dancer, that any athlete can do' (in Samuel, MacColl and Cosgrove, 1985: 243). Drawing on popular theatre forms, these groups, like Meyerhold, were attracted to the raised platform stage (echoes of Copeau's *tréteau nu*) and the stereotypical and highly physicalised characters of the Commedia dell'Arte (Warden, 2012: 116–7). Meyerhold's techniques were widely publicised by Huntly Carter in his 1925 book on the European theatre. Littlewood and Theatre in Action would have reconstructed Meyerhold's practice from details of productions in books such as Leon Moussinac's *New Movement in the Theatre* (1931) and André van Gyseghem's *Theatre in Soviet Russia* (1943), rather than any direct experience.

For Meyerhold, who was influenced by Taylorism[42] and William James[43], movement came first and emotion was a product of the movement. This was in contrast to the psychological realism of Stanislavski's approach to acting, and to Rudolf Laban's movement practice, but a precursor to the ideas that would later underpin important aspects of some physical theatre practice. Little was known in the UK about Meyerhold's biomechanic work until Ted Braun's pioneering 1969 publication, *Meyerhold on Theatre*, and Mel Gordon's publication in 1974 of a series of descriptions of Meyerhold's études in the US journal TDR. In 1995, the Centre for Performance Research in Aberystwyth hosted a Past Masters workshop (see Chapter 6) with Gennady Bogdanov and Alexei Levinsky, who had trained with

---

41 Eastern European mime and physical theatre developed in part out of tactics to create non-textual productions that might avoid political censorship. Several articles on their work appeared in *Total Theatre*, see for example: Lang, 1994: 20–21.

42 A system developed by Frederick Taylor (1856–1915) that was designed to encourage labourers to complete work tasks as efficiently as possible.

43 William James (1842–1910) was a philosopher and psychologist who held that emotion was the mind's perception of our physiological reactions to stimuli.

Nikolai Kustov, one of Meyerhold's collaborators. Fern Smith from Volcano Theatre was one of the attendees at this workshop. However, the only physical theatre company identifiably influenced by Meyerhold during our period is TNT (see Chapter 5). The lack of further traction for Meyerhold's ideas is probably a reflection of the difficulty of accessing training outside of a few academic institutions, the difficulty in disconnecting the practices from their Russian and political context, and the gradual decline of interest in socialist political theatre in the UK during the 1980s.

Rudolf Laban

Dartington Hall in Devon was an important site for the influx of European and Russian ideas and practices during the 1930s and 1940s. The choreographer Rudolf Laban (1879–1958), fleeing Nazi Germany, arrived in Dartington in 1938 – whilst Michael Chekhov (1891–1955) established his studio and theatre company at Dartington from 1935 – and maintained a long connection, leading classes and residencies until the 1950s (a short section on Dartington College of Arts can be found in Chapter 6). While Laban did not directly affect the development of mime in the UK, he exercised an important influence on physical theatre and on practitioners' understanding of the relationship between character and physicality. Laban's influence on UK mime and theatre was most powerfully realised through his collaboration with Joan Littlewood, through the impact of his student and fellow émigré Kurt Jooss (1901–1979)[44] and through UK tours of the dance/theatre of Jooss' former student Pina Bausch (see Chapter 5). Laban, Jooss, and Bausch all draw on the aesthetics of German expressionism – an arts movement that focused on the experience of modern urban life and the solace potentially provided by nature; the naked individual as an expression of the condition of life; and the need to confront the devastating experience of violent conflict and a bleak post-war vision of human existence. Expressionism's influence can also be seen in some of the works of Berkoff (*Metamorphosis* and *Decadence*) and Théâtre de Complicité (*The Visit* and *Anything for a Quiet Life*).

Margaret Barr

Born in India in 1904, Barr trained in the Denishawn technique and with Martha Graham in New York. She brought this strong set of influences with her when she relocated first to London and then to Dartington (in 1930), where she taught dance-mime until 1934 (see Fig. 2.8). Her work sought to develop the student's ability to identify the movement impulse and find its most effective stylisation. Her practice typically involved large groups and is reminiscent of Laban and Jooss' work,

---

44 For example, Jooss' anti-war dance/theatre production *The Green Table*, and the founding, with Sigurd Leeder (1902–1981) of the Jooss/Leeder School of Dance.

FIGURE 2.8 *Dartington Dance School interior with Dance Mime Group, c. 1935.* By kind permission of Dartington Trust and the Elmgrant Trust.

although she apparently resigned from Dartington rather than work under Jooss. Along with Laban and Jooss, she can be positioned as one of the international pioneers of modern dance whose work also impacted on the aesthetics of UK mime performance in the mid-twentieth century and whose work represents a cultural shift at this time towards the importance of dynamic physical expression as a central element of a healthy society.

This rich strand of Central European dance and movement practice outlined earlier not only was influential in its time but also points forward to the politically engaged dance/theatre of the 1980s and 1990s that we examine in more detail in Chapter 5.

Tadeusz Kantor

Kantor (1915–1990) founded the Cricot 2 company in Poland in 1955. His work was first introduced to the UK via Richard Demarco, who brought Kantor's productions to the Edinburgh Festival several times, particularly in 1972, 1973 and 1976. Kantor created a substantial body of performance work, but in terms of his impact on UK mime and physical theatre his key productions are *Dead Class* (1975) and *Wielopole* (1980) – both of which toured to the UK. His work tackled themes of memory, history and myth, questioning the role of the artist in relation to twentieth-century history. He did not teach, but the impact of his productions was important. Although highly individual, his work does echo and address some of the ideas and practices developed by European practitioners of the early twentieth century, such as Edward Gordon Craig and his idea of the actor as marionette. Kantor shared with Jerzy Grotowski an interest in poverty as an aesthetic choice: 'I examine and express issues through base materials, the basest possible, materials that are poor, deprived of dignity and prestige, defenceless and often downright contemptible' (Kantor in Kitowska-Łysiak, 2022).

What Kantor's influence brought to UK mime and physical theatre is difficult to define precisely. In much the same way as the German choreographer, Pina Bausch, his impact was subtle and less to do with particular ways of performing than an attitude to the work, an ethos and a way of delving into and dealing with what it meant to try and exist and make art in post-war Europe. Kantor, for instance, adopted a role on stage as a conductor to the work of the ensemble and employed objects and puppets during the performance. His work has been particularly influential for UK practitioners such as Simon McBurney, who would sometimes both direct and perform in Théâtre de Complicité shows – for example *The Three Lives of Lucie Cabrol* and *Mnemonic*. *Mnemonic* is a particularly interesting example, given the way that puppetry becomes integral to the performance of history and memory, and in the ways that McBurney moves between the role of narrator and the role of a central character. Kantor's dream-like imagery and savage comedy are given contemporary echoes in the way that *Mnemonic* blurs the divides between past and present and between scattered locations.

Jerzy Grotowski

Grotowski[45] (1933–1999) is a significant figure in the European theatre, and yet his impact on performance practice within the UK has not been as enduring as one might expect. After 1971, Grotowski had become more interested in what he referred to as 'paratheatre' than in the creation of productions, although the Teatr Laboratorium that he had established in Wroclaw, Poland, continued to function until 1984. As the opportunities for performance work diminished, Grotowski's collaborators increasingly offered their own workshops on the methods they had developed (including in the UK). This meant that those seeking to make theatre after his example tended to base their own work on an understanding of his practice in the 1960s. Grotowski himself was reluctant to conceptualise his approach to performance and theatre making as a method: 'Grotowski was dubious of not only the efficacy of such methods, but also the impulse behind the desire for recipes and easy solutions' (Lisa Wolford in Hodge, 2010: 194). It was thus challenging for UK physical theatre practitioners to access this lineage – travel to study in Poland was likely to be difficult and expensive[46] and the training process arduous. The intensive nature of the transmission of such practice meant that the 'purity' of experience

---

45 For a more detailed history of Grotowski's work, see Slowiak and Cuesta (2007).

46 It was not until 1989 that Poland began its transition to become a democratic state. Previous to this period, Poland had been part of the Communist bloc that came under the influence of the Soviet Union after the Second World War. Between 1981 and 1983, the Polish leader General Jaruzelski imposed a harsh period of martial law and the country experienced economic decline.

38 The moment of mime

became an issue within this lineage. The longer-term impact of Grotowski, Barba and Staniewski within the UK owes much to a small number of people who sought out access to training and information about this work.

The heavily subsidised laboratories of Grotowski and Brook were largely seen as unaffordable and unattainable in the UK, during a period when arts funding was increasingly hard to get. The activities of Mike Pearson and Richard Gough at Cardiff Laboratory Theatre, and the Centre for Performance Research, positioned Cardiff and Aberystwyth as leading points of access for Grotowski-based work in the UK. Their location in Wales, outside the English mainstream and the largely metropolitan world of UK mime at this time, is significant. It speaks to a sense in which the alternative Welsh theatre scene offered a more accepting context for Grotowski's work. Further discussion of the impact of Grotowski on the making processes for physical theatre can be found in Chapters 4 and 5.

The Americans are coming!

Charles Marowitz (1934–2014) arrived in the UK in 1956 as an advocate of American Method Acting. He soon became embroiled in the experimental theatre scene in London, and in 1964 he was involved in Peter Brook's influential Theatre of Cruelty season at LAMDA, under the auspices of the RSC. This bold exploration of non-naturalistic approaches to acting, inspired by the writings of the French surrealist Antonin Artaud, emphasised the physical and visceral presence of the actor, and the power of movement and visual imagery over text in theatre making. The Open Space theatre on Tottenham Court Road, London, founded in 1968 by Marowitz and Thelma Holt, was one of the few examples of an English theatre laboratory – a space for experiment and risk-taking. It survived until 1976, when it was closed for redevelopment. Marowitz was one of the practitioners at this time who sought to pull psychological acting into a physical space. The Theatre of Cruelty season was hugely important in encouraging the re-discovery of Artaud and the emergence of physical performance, performance art, happenings and live art.

His arrival also marks a period in the 1960s when American influence on experimental and physically expressive theatre in the UK was at its strongest. The Living Theatre, led by Julian Beck and Judith Malina, visited the UK several times during this period. Their production of *Paradise Now* played at the Roundhouse in London in 1969 and they visited again in 1971. British alternative companies were influenced by the Living Theatre's group ethos, its political commitment and the rejection of fictional identity in performance. La Mama Theatre and Joseph Chaikin's Open Theatre also toured to the UK in 1967, providing additional examples of powerful ensemble creation and the use of strong and uninhibited physicality – initially picked up in the UK through the work of Freehold and Nancy Meckler. Though a long way from classic mime, this was work that enriched the theatrical soil from which British physical theatre would later emerge.

Conclusion

Mime and physical theatre emerged in the 1970s in a state of tension between discipline and freedom. On the one hand, the 1960s had created a more liberated cultural environment in which expressive movement could play a significant part. Improvisation, playfulness and comedy thrived as audience tastes changed and performers' imaginations were allowed freer rein. On the other hand, there was a significant increase in the training available for the performer's body. The leading mime schools offered sustained programmes of training that included the study of (sometimes) rigorous technique. The implication was that the physical performer had to be disciplined in order to achieve expressive freedom and give the performing body a structure. Situating the training outside the conventional institutions also gave it a mystique – further enhanced by the difficulty in writing about mime, the international nature of the schools, and the intensity of the training. The disciplined body might also be perceived as a white male construct – privileged in its access to training, implicitly rejecting bodies that were too playful, disruptive or unruly, and setting boundaries that established status and ownership. In Chapter 7 we examine some mime and physical practices that challenged such hegemony, and that renegotiated how technique and discipline could be used in the service of agendas around feminism, black life experience and disability.

The circles of connection and influence revealed earlier show how the run-up to our period was shaped by a confluence of individual passion and drive, opportunity and location. Stories overlap – many of the interviews we recorded reveal the importance of personal relationships and the ways in which the effects of work (performances, collaborations, meetings) rippled out across the various communities of practice. We also begin to see the ways in which geographic location, professional networks, funding policy and venue management influenced and shaped practice from the middle of the century onwards (to be expanded on in the next two chapters). The ways that mime and physical theatre have connected with the public imagination – through seminal performances and popular culture for instance – reveal the cultural complexity of the field and the need to understand the history of mime and physical theatre within its context. The following chapters develop these interconnections and influences in more detail.

3

CULTURAL ECONOMIES OF MIME AND PHYSICAL THEATRE: ECOLOGIES OF SUPPORT

Having considered mime's historical context in the UK and the early landscape of the 1970s to the mid-1980s, this chapter maps out the broad cultural and infrastructural conditions through which mime became more formally recognised, and then by the 1990s began to be reconstructed, re-thought and, perhaps, re-branded as physical theatre. This chapter further develops the central assumptions and premises of this book, the most central of these being that theatre – in all its myriad forms – is *of* society and not merely *in* it. The prepositional distinction here is far from being a merely arcane or academic one, as we contend that mime and physical theatre cannot be thought, understood, analysed, sensed, perceived, heard or positioned through form and aesthetics alone. Form and aesthetics are social, of the world, in conversation with that world and not simply *in* it. In dialogue with any close examination of such practices, the conditions whereby these practices were imagined, made, performed and received are crucial for any holistic account of the unfolding field of mime and physical theatre during our time. Consequently, Chapters 3 and 4 particularly respond to questions such as these:

- Where in the UK were mime and physical theatre made and performed?
- In what kind of spaces was this work performed?
- Who paid for this work to be made and seen?
- What were the cultural structures and institutions which enabled or inhibited the making of this work?

This chapter attempts therefore to provide an overview of the cultural economy, institutions and people who created the conditions in which mime and physical theatre were made and seen.

DOI: 10.4324/9780429330209-3

Political and economic landscapes

If we take our period to begin in the early to mid-1970s and to conclude in 2000, the UK experienced the Conservative Party in government under the leaderships of Edward Heath (1970–74), Margaret Thatcher (1979–90) and John Major (1990–97) and Labour Party administrations under Harold Wilson (1974–76), James Callaghan (1976–79) and Tony Blair (1997–2007). The defining political and chronological feature of this period has become known as the 11 years of 'Thatcherism', a shorthand for a range of radical – though profoundly inegalitarian – economic, social and political policies which are now seen to have ushered in the epoch of Neo-Liberalism[1]. Amongst its many pervasive influences on personal and public life Thatcher's neoliberalism had significant consequences for thinking and policies around funding of the arts. Apart from huge reductions in financial support for the Arts Council nationally, local authorities and regional arts association (or boards), Thatcherism ushered in and began to define a new paradigm for understanding and supporting the arts. In their introduction to a collection of essays entitled *The Glory of the Garden: English Regional Theatre and the Arts Council 1984–2009*, Kate Dorney and Ros Merkin write that since 1984:

> A series of significant shifts in ways of working, expectations, and language also shaped the life of these theatres and they have been faced with a barrage of new possibilities. Commercial terminology overwhelmed the subsidised theatre: plural funding, product, marketing, efficiency, cost effectiveness, business incentives, performance indicators, challenge funding, parity funding, incentive funding and a constant push for plurality in funding sources.
>
> *(2010: 5)*

We return to some of these issues, but at this point it is important to emphasise that while the production and performance of mime and physical theatre could hardly escape the consequences of neoliberal policies for the arts and cultural production, much of this work fell under the radar of funding and financial support. Nonetheless, these artists and their practices were inexorably touched and shaped by these cultural changes and the climate within which they were enacted. If companies did evade these imperatives, it was because they operated largely in a cultural economy of self-help (self-finance) and a bare subsistence level of existence. In an interesting,

---

1 Neoliberalism describes developments in capitalist liberal democracies which can be dated back to the 1960s and 1970s, a period continuing to the present day, but welcomed and nurtured by Margaret Thatcher in the UK and Ronald Reagan in the USA. Neoliberalism identifies competition and apparent freedom of choice as the defining characteristic of human relations. It identifies citizens as individual consumers or customers and maintains that 'the market' delivers benefits that could never be achieved by planning or collaborative effort. A key feature of neoliberalism is a celebration of the private as opposed to the social or public dimensions of human life. In the arts neoliberalism has been particularly manifested by policies which promote private sponsorship rather than local or national state funding.

42 Economies of mime and physical theatre

but perplexing way, small-scale production of mime and physical theatre was absolutely part of a market economy – it could not be otherwise – but was also underwritten through the state's personal 'subsidy' of unemployment and social security benefits and schemes such as the Enterprise Allowance[2]. By the end of our period, these survival strategies had become much harder to engineer for artists of any kind as they were subject to the constant requirement to prove that they were 'searching for work'.

Each of the 'new possibilities' identified earlier by Dorney and Merkin not only reshaped the conditions and criteria of funding (however tiny) for new or established artists and companies, but they also generated a climate of feeling and thinking which pervaded the economic, social and cultural worlds of the UK from the late 1970s. Although many artists were disinclined to sign up to these values they nonetheless informed and shaped the policies and structures of cultural production in which work was made and seen. The extent to which mime and physical theatre practitioners could ignore, sidestep, contest or mediate these values and imperatives is examined and reflected upon throughout the rest of this volume.

Alongside and within these explicitly political shifts in government policies, there were other, more productive, force fields at work which shaped the conditions of invention imposed upon or embraced by makers of mime and physical theatre. It is commonplace to identify the 1960s, and until at least the mid-1970s, as a period of radical cultural ferment of (second wave) feminist, racial, sexual, trade union and community politics. The impact and value of these movements and achievements have been regularly debated, with two camps representing often diametrically opposed views and positions. On the one hand, 'the Sixties' – and, of course, the myths and behaviours which apparently accompanied this epithet – were denigrated, largely by the right wing media, as being degenerate, amoral, undisciplined and selfishly hedonistic – an aberration and a diversion from the proper and serious tasks of rebuilding post-war Britain. On the other, the various movements and feelings for which 'the Sixties' appeared to speak represented a long overdue challenge to establishment privilege and norms which sanctioned various forms of inequality, sexism, racism and homophobia – a moment of liberation and the performance of truly democratic values and practices in relationships, the home, public life and the workplace. Here was a country attempting to modernise itself in terms of the human values it believed in. In an important, but often uneasy relationship with these tumultuous developments, various progressive

2 The Enterprise Allowance Scheme was an initiative set up by Margaret Thatcher's government which gave a guaranteed income of £40 per week to unemployed people who set up their own business. It was introduced nationwide in 1983, against a background of mass unemployment in Britain. It went on to fund 325,000 people and anyone wishing to claim money under the scheme was required to fund the first £1,000 out of their own funds, and also to produce a basic business plan. Admirers of the scheme believed that it would have a great impact on unemployment and support entrepreneurial activity. Critics, however, argued that it had little impact on unemployment figures since most of the start-ups were sole traders and that 1 in 6 of these businesses failed in the first year.

(but circumscribed) acts of parliament were passed by Harold Wilson's Labour Government between 1964 and 1970: the Race Relations Act (1965), the Sexual Offences Act (decriminalising homosexual acts in private between consenting adults – but not until 1980 in Scotland) (1967), the Abortion Act (1967), the Theatres Act (removing the Lord Chamberlain's powers of censorship) (1968), the Divorce Reform Act (1969) and the Equal Pay Act (1970). Although falling outwith the period of our purview these pieces of legislation marked some significant changes in the moral and ethical climate in which mime and physical theatre were to grow in the decades which followed.

Other parts of the 1960s and 1970s cultural and political tapestry which frames our book included the Civil Rights Movement in the USA, the Anti-Apartheid movement in South Africa and in Britain, the Campaign for Nuclear Disarmament (CND), debates about joining the European Economic Community (EEC) (later the European Union [EU]), housing collectives, squatters' occupations of empty properties, campaigns for industrial democracy, workers' control and socially useful production.

Clearly, the political and cultural milieu of Britain in the 1960s and 1970s was a perpetually contested one and the Thatcher project from 1979 was certainly achieved on the perception of a country socially out of control, underperforming economically and in the hands of particular vested interest groups (trade unions, left-wing Socialists, feminists, gay, lesbian and black activists). In addition, the end of the British Empire and the complex psychological, economic and social reverberations of 'winning' the Second World War all contributed to an intricate and dense web of felt possibilities, hopes, fears, resentments, aspirations, nostalgias, prejudices and identities. Britain's war against Argentina over the Falkland Islands for 10 weeks in 1982 was used by Thatcher as an opportunity to hark back to a sense of a country re-asserting its world position and standing up to a 'foreign dictator'. The most palpable challenge to the war from the mime and physical community was Steven Berkoff's *Sink the Belgrano* in 1986 (see also Chapter 3 footnote).

This was the cultural backcloth which framed and shaped the performance making of artists and companies who, by the mid to late-1980s (with certain stoical exceptions), had readily exchanged the mime appellation for that of physical and visual theatre. Whether or not the cultural ferment of the late 1960s substantially changed the country as a whole, it certainly inspired, shaped and nuanced the practices of physical theatre makers in the 1980s and 1990s.

Structures of support and funding

The centre

> The Arts Council has been talking about the same four things, I think, ever since it was invented: posh or pop; London or the rest; instrumental or aesthetic; and, rather more recently, public or private?
>
> *(Forgan, 2016)*

44 Economies of mime and physical theatre

In a witty and perceptive keynote speech to a conference entitled 'The Arts Council at 70: A History in the Spotlight' Liz Forgan[3] wryly summarised the issues facing the Arts Council since its creation in 1946. The support, development and funding of mime and physical theatre over the 25-year period covered by this book were critically inflected, in varying degrees, by the four binary choices identified by Forgan above. Of course, as Forgan would herself admit, these choices have never been simple 'zero sum' alternatives and can only be properly understood through a close attention to historical context and a forensic (and semiotic) investigation into the meaning of these terms. Her four sets of choices remain, however, a useful shorthand to aid thinking about the strategies and principles behind funding the arts and how mime and physical theatre engaged with these.

This section provides an overview of the structures which have been created in the post-war period to fund the arts and offers a summary of the strategic and philosophical thinking which have underpinned organisations charged with such responsibilities. The idea of a national body which shaped policies and provided funding for the arts can be traced to the 'post war settlement'[4] which embraced the belief that promotion of and support for the arts was a collective and national responsibility. In 1940, as an early measure of this thinking, the Committee for Encouragement of Music and the Arts (CEMA) was set up by the Royal Charter, and a year later economist, John Maynard Keynes, became its chair. By 1945, 46 art organisations were funded by CEMA and in 1946 CEMA becomes the Arts Council of Great Britain (ACGB). Over the following 75 years, its title has changed twice: in 1994 it devolved into the Arts Council of England and in 2003 became Arts Council England (ACE) after joining with the Regional Arts Boards. The 1994 date is significant in many ways, but particularly as it heralded the establishment of the National Lottery and the moment when the national Arts Council relinquished its UK-wide responsibility. At this juncture, the responsibilities and operating mechanisms of the Scottish Arts Council[5] and the Arts Council of Wales

---

3 Forgan was the first female chair of Arts Council England (ACE) and was appointed by the Labour Government in 2009, but subsequently did not have her contract renewed by the Conservative and Liberal Democrat Coalition Government in 2013 following her resistance to a huge reduction in ACE's budget.
4 'The post war settlement' (or consensus) describes the dominant political and social thinking – and, to an extent, cooperation – which informed the reconstruction of Britain when the Second World War ended in 1945. Drawing upon the thinking of radical Liberals such as John Maynard Keynes and William Beveridge in the 1930s, the 1942 Beveridge Report, and implemented by the Labour Government under Clement Attlee (1945–50), this 'settlement' was encapsulated by the National Health Service, the construction of the welfare state, acceptance of a mixed economy and a degree of nationalisation, strong trade unions and a retreat from empire. Although it is debated when this 'settlement' became dissipated, its final and categorical repudiation began with the arrival of Margaret Thatcher as prime minister in 1979. This consensus was, of course, always conditional, reluctantly embraced by the political right and criticised for being too timid and constrained by the Socialist and Communist left.
5 From 2010, the Scottish Arts Council reinvented itself as Creative Scotland.

were recalibrated and all three national bodies, along with the Arts Council of Northern Ireland (founded in 1964), became distribution channels for the Lottery.

In her 2016 keynote, Liz Forgan drily noted that the Arts Council – once a UK body but by then an English one – 'has essentially been the same institution all that time, although its style has morphed a bit'. This is true in the sense that the institution, from its foundation in 1946, has habitually wrestled with the principles and practical mechanisms whereby (always) scarce resources are distributed to individuals and organisations across the landscape of the arts. It is less accurate in that her statement disguises numerous – and often repeated – moments of soul searching, policy review and reporting around complex and changing perspectives on equity, excellence, diversity, access and innovation. Sources of funding and the London-based centre's relationship with the periphery (the regional arts organisations and local authorities) have also been a vexing and recurring object of policy making and debate. Since its inception the Arts Council has produced a startling amount of publications and reports and these have included major policy reviews and documents such as *The Glory of the Garden* (1984), the Cork Report into publicly funded theatre (1986), the Wilding Report (1989) and Naseem Khan's *The Arts Britain Ignores* (1976). Wilding and 'The Glory' reports attempted to address the vexed issue of inequitable funding between London and the regions, whilst Khan's investigation tackled for the first – but not the last – time the underfunding and lack of support for British Black and Asian artists. In direct and tangential ways all these had an impact on the developing world of mime and physical theatre. Outwith the aegis of the Arts Councils themselves, a seminal statement of aspiration and intention, and one which continues to provide a benchmark against which subsequent policy documents might be measured, was Jennie Lee's 1964 White Paper, *A Policy for the Arts: First Steps*. Lee was Arts Minister in Harold Wilson's Labour government and, astonishingly, it was the first and, to date, only White Paper on the arts produced by any political administration. The White Paper argued that the arts must occupy a central place in British life and be part of the everyday worlds of children and adults. Lee recognised that the arts needed to be embedded in the education system, that they should be valued as highly as any other industry, and that equality of access to and participation in the arts, wherever people lived, was crucial. Arguably, the popular appeal of early mime spoke to many of Lee's aspirations.

Underscoring all these debates, policy statements and developments during our period is an almost, it would seem, inexorable trend towards requiring potential clients, large or small, to seek and secure other sources of private and 'matched' funding. At the same time, in the name of public accountability, applicants for funding have been required to undergo increasingly complex and demanding initial form filling and reporting back after a project – or time period – is completed. Here, through the 1990s, we find an increasing requirement to match projects against criteria, leading to benchmark-driven funding decisions, rather than judgements based on the quality or nature of the work. All of these conditions provided particular challenges for practitioners working in the territory of the small scale.

46 Economies of mime and physical theatre

Regions or the 'periphery'

As has been suggested earlier, the relationships between the Arts Council as a national body based in London, the Regional Arts Associations (later boards) and local authorities have been at best perpetually uneasy ones and, at worst, matters of mutual suspicion and hostility. For most of the mime and physical theatre artists profiled in this volume their relationship – if they had one at all – would be with the regional rather than the national bodies. The exception here from 1994 was in Scotland and Wales where there were no 'regional' organisations as such. Only a small number of higher-ranked companies would receive funding from the national purse. How this ranking was decided and performed was then – and still remains – a contentious and divisive matter. Regional Arts Associations (RAAs) were set up from the mid-1950s as the Arts Council began to move away from organising its own arts' activities. By 1971 there were 12 RAAs[6] (including Greater London) and these organisations acted as a link between the Arts Council and the regions and were set up by local authorities or consortiums of local arts associations. The governing (policy making) boards of these RAAs were drawn from local councils and other arts associations and offered a degree of democracy and autonomy from the Arts Council in London.

In 1989 the Wilding report recommended that the RAAs be replaced by ten Regional Arts Boards (RABs)[7], as there were significant differences in distribution of funding between the regions. The RABs received most of their funding directly from the Arts Council rather than local sources. This further weakened the already fragile democratic link with local government councils and other bodies in each of these RAB regions. There is, therefore, a revealing arc between 1946 and 2001 which traces the foundation of the Arts Council as a national, London-based organisation, through various models, stages of autonomy and (semi-)devolved responsibility to the regions (as well as Scotland and Wales), to a point 55 years later when hitherto Regional Arts Associations or Boards became sub-offices of the cosmopolitan centre. The consequences of such fluctuations and variations have had real-life impact on the availability of financial support for the makers and performers of mime and physical theatre.

Forms of funding from RAAs and RABs for artists and companies have taken many shifting guises across our period. These have varied from region to region, on the rural-urban character of the area, on the ever-changing continuum of priorities between and within different art forms, on fluctuating grant aid from the Arts Council in London, on relations with local councils and on the types of funding

---

6 The 12 RAAs (1956–1990) were East Midlands, Eastern Arts, Greater London, Lincolnshire & Humberside, Merseyside, North West, Northern, South East, South West Arts, Southern, West Midlands and Yorkshire.

7 The 10 RABs (1990–2002) were Eastern Arts, East Midlands Arts, London Arts Board, Northern Arts, North West Arts Board, South East Arts Board, Southern Arts, South West Arts, West Midlands Arts and Yorkshire and Humberside Arts.

support deemed to be most appropriate at any one time or in any one place. In addition, the particular interests, enthusiasms and cultural backgrounds of the relevant officers in these organisations have inevitably been important. In Chapter 4 we offer a profile of the Northern Region and the significant support it offered over at least two decades for mime and physical theatre. Alongside the broader economic, cultural and political considerations which shaped and determined funding and its mechanisms, our extensive range of interviews revealed the importance of key individuals who were willing and able to champion – within certain constraints – mime and physical theatre. The complex inter-play between imaginative and energetic individuals and the contextual temporal, cultural and economic forces in which they operated has been particularly fascinating in this story. Such individuals may have been art form officers (Dance and Mime, or Drama) within RAAs and RABs, directors of art centres or small-scale theatres, festival organisers, teachers and community arts workers, and, of course, persuasive and charismatic mime and physical theatre practitioners themselves. The types of funding (directly or indirectly) for mime and physical theatre, and the activities for which they were applicable, varied according to the complex inter-weave of factors identified earlier. However, at any one time or place, these might have included:

- Project funding to support the making and rehearsal of a particular show. This might have covered or contributed to wages; rehearsal space hire; equipment, set, costumes and props; fees for writer, director, dramaturge, or composer; marketing, publicity, administration.
- Revenue or regularly funded organisation status (terminology varies between RAAs and RABs). This was funding for a very small number of companies whose perceived quality of work and prestige was deemed to deserve financial support for a full two- to three-year period. After this cycle was complete, funding would be reviewed and either continued or ended.
- Training fees on a regular or one-off basis.
- Attendance at appropriate conferences or meetings.
- Touring costs to venues within the region where the artist or company was based.
- Grants to venues to support performances, company residencies and festivals.
- Fees for writing reports and strategy documents.

Local authorities, the National Lottery and private sources of funding

At the beginning of our period, in 1976, under the chairmanship of Lord Redcliffe-Maud, an investigation into arts funding was published with the title, *Support For The Arts In England And Wales: A Report To The Calouste Gulbenkian Foundation.*

48 Economies of mime and physical theatre

Despite considerable backing for his proposals from across the arts the election of a Conservative government under Margaret Thatcher in 1979 undermined and effectively destroyed the practices and principles laid out in the report. Three key principles or recommendations of Redcliffe-Maud's report deserve quoting here as they frame the cultural debates, possibilities and contexts that emerging mime and physical theatre companies were to experience in the mid-1970s, but which were subsequently destabilised and challenged under Thatcherism:

- We must look to elected councils at district and county levels to become the chief art patrons of the long-term future.
- We must now decide to devolve wide decision-taking powers from the national level.
- The excellence of our artists, professional and amateur, and our increasing enjoyment of old and contemporary art depend in each case more on education than on anything deliberate arts patronage can do. A revolution therefore in educational policy over the next 10 years which brought the arts nearer the heart of the curriculum in British schools and teacher training institutions is what I would most dearly like to see.
(From the Redcliffe-Maud report in Forgan, 2016)

These three fundamental principles from Redcliffe-Maud's report identified the terms of a debate around organisational support for the arts which have remained contested and unresolved to the present day. Within our period from 1979, at least until 1997, reductions in national grant settlement for local government severely weakened any likelihood of these three tenets (quoted earlier) ever being realised. It also deserves noting that outwith our book's timelines (from 2010) the teaching of arts subjects in the school curriculum has been significantly eroded and reduced.

Local authority funding was subject to many of the same considerations that shaped the cultural economies of RAAs and RABs, although direct political considerations more obviously informed decisions to fund the arts in any area. Politically, with some exceptions, Labour-controlled authorities were more likely to allocate funds towards the arts than those led by the Conservatives. This, for example, was manifested in the Northern Region which was constituted for much of our period by predominantly Labour-led authorities across Cumbria, Northumberland, Tyneside/Wearside, County Durham and Teesside. Wherewithal and sympathy towards spending money on the arts in these authorities contributed, for example, to an extensive array of arts centres and small (and middle) scale theatres across the whole of this large and diverse geographical region. In addition, this sympathetic disposition enabled a much more fruitful relationship – both attitudinally and financially – between these authorities and the various policy manifestations of Northern Arts during this time.

Across the UK, local authority investment in the arts has been on a continuum between owning or subsidising buildings – theatres, art centres and concert halls – through partial funding of established theatre and dance companies (and orchestras) to the provision of grants (used to employ artists) for educational and other community purposes. Mime and physical theatre companies performing or running workshops in schools, for example, may have been paid from individual school budgets, grants from local education authorities or as a condition of their funding from RAAs/RABs and the national body. These relationships were not based upon any national geographical agreement around division of funding between local authorities and regional arts organisations, but rather on types of activity which may historically have been funded. In *The Arts Council at 70: A History in the Spotlight* symposium in 2016, Jo Burns, who worked for North West Arts for 11 years from 1979, makes this point in relation to Manchester:

> I could not get Manchester City Council to talk to me about the arts for ages because they did not put any money into the Arts Council organisations. They funded their own theatre, the Library Theatre, and their own gallery. They did it all themselves. . .. It took some time and some convincing to get Manchester to understand the relationship between the cultural organisations and the city's ambitions and aspirations, and to forge constructive partnerships.
>
> *(Ibid.: 2016)*

The scale and range of local authority funding of arts activities has fluctuated but within a diminishing curve over the last three decades of our period. This diminution of funding has been particularly noticeable in relation to supporting theatre work within the education sector.

National Lottery

From its inception in 1994, National Lottery funding for the arts was confined to 'bricks and mortar' and to equipment, vehicles and other materials. Whilst it could fund a radical expansion of existing buildings, or create new ones, the Lottery – in its early years – could not be used for a company or arts centre's production or running costs. One consequence of this was that new Lottery-funded buildings often did not possess sufficient and continuous revenue resources for overheads and to pay the wages of those employees who kept spaces operating on a day-to-day basis. The justification for this was to reassure artists that Lottery funding could not be used as an excuse to cut further state funding via the Arts Council or RABs. In the final six years of our period small-scale companies were beginning successfully to gain small but significant amounts of Lottery funding and from 1997 the Lottery *Arts for Everyone* (A4E) scheme allowed companies to apply for small amounts of project funding. Physical theatre company, Théâtre Sans Frontières (TSF), for example,

50 Economies of mime and physical theatre

based at the Queen's Hall Art Centre in Hexham (Northumbria), received lottery funding in 1995 which included costs towards equipment (lighting and sound) and a small van. This in turn enabled the company to develop its touring programme to schools in the region and beyond.

Private funding

Private and business funding of arts activities predate our period and versions of this are exemplified down the centuries by 'patrons' and philanthropy from wealthy individuals for artists, composers and writers. The Association for Business Sponsorship of the Arts (ABSA) was established in 1976 and based on a model developed by the millionaire, David Rockefeller, in New York. Two separate but inter-related economic force fields propelled this cultural shift, and both are significant dimensions of the emerging neo-liberal landscape. Firstly, as Conservative governments from 1979 were driven ideologically to reduce the role and function of the state, both nationally and locally, so a reliance on state funding for the arts was to be diminished and inhibited. Secondly, from the mid-1980s applicants for national and regional arts council funding were increasingly required, or encouraged, to seek 'matched' funding or, at least, contributions from local authorities or private and corporate sources. Underpinning and articulating these imperatives was the influential Cork Enquiry into the funding of theatre with its subsequent report entitled *Theatre is for All* (1986). Essentially, Cork diagnosed an acute cash crisis in British theatre at that time and argued that the only solution to this predicament was for a complete rethinking of funding for performing arts institutions, and for the people who ran them to become much more entrepreneurial and reliant on private and corporate resources.

However, for all but the middle range or well-established companies, corporate sponsorship was hugely difficult to attain as it was perceived that small companies did not reach significant enough audiences to justify such patronage. Nonetheless, many of the revenue or regularly funded companies such as Trestle (Sainsburys), DV8 and Théâtre de Complicité (Beck's Beer)[8] struck sponsorship deals and anecdotal evidence suggests that at regional level modest deals were also possible. TSF, for example, based in the Northern Region, received small sums from North East Water (owned by a French company) and Nestlé in the late 1990s. In addition to individual deals, certain companies ran competitions whereby productions could be nominated for awards. In the Northern Region, utility company, Northern Electric, ran an awards scheme during the 1990s in conjunction with Northern Arts and Tyne Tees Television to recognise excellence in the arts and promote sponsorship. TSF won one such award in 1994. At a national level, the Barclays New

---

8 A Théâtre de Complicité report provides these figures from private sponsorship (largely Beck's) over a 6-year period: 1986/87: £1,500; 1987/88: £3,000; 1988/98: £15,000; 1989/90: £12,000; 1990/91: £40,500; 1991/92: £15,000.

Stages Award for experimental theatre ran between 1990 and 1996. It is salutary to note, however, that many of these sponsorship deals were relatively short-lived and were responsive to the national economic climate and the changing profiles of the companies concerned. Théâtre de Complicité observes in a 1993 report:

> The current recession has seen a noticeable hardening of attitude to sponsorship in the arts. Throughout the period, we have been supported by Beck's Bier and we are the only company of our size to have retained a sponsor for six consecutive years. Beck's Bier's support has resulted in the Company receiving three BSIS Awards. In 1990/91 earned income increased by £52,000 over the previous year while grants increased by only £4,900.
>
> *(Théâtre de Complicité, 1993)*

Cultural industries: an emerging but dominant paradigm

The second key feature of this period in relation to the arts was the emergence of the 'cultural industries' paradigm, a dawning but increasingly explicit awareness that, even if most artists made little money from their practice, the arts as a whole were income generators and, as businesses, possessed huge economic value both nationally and internationally. This represents a perspective largely in tension with the personal, social and cultural value of the arts. It is impossible to underestimate the extent to which this 'structure of feeling'[9] began to dominate ways of thinking – and subsequent policies – about funding, promoting and organising cultural production. This was no mere academic abstraction but had a significant and practical impact on how applicants argued for (and justified) claims for funding and how arts organisations (RABs, the Arts Council, theatres and art centres, for example) strategised their work and future development. A measure of this increasingly hegemonic understanding of the arts as economically valuable production is in the number of reports and publications[10] to emerge from the Arts Council and other bodies during the second half of the 1980s. Together, these reports extolled and described the opportunities for artists if they were to become more actively sympathetic to this paradigm and learn how to position their practices in this way. Indeed, from this moment on artists had little choice but to consider matched and private sources of funding if they were successfully to raise resources for making

---

9 'Structure of feeling' is a rich and generative term coined by cultural theorist, Raymond Williams, (1977, pp. 128–135) as a way of understanding the 'world', or social phenomenon within it, which holds sway in any particular period. A 'structure of feeling' is an ideological collection of beliefs, feelings, understandings, behaviours and analyses which shape how we think about and act within our social and cultural lives. In linking structures with feelings, it challenges the habitual separation of the social from the personal.

10 Examples of these include: A Great British Success Story: An Invitation to Invest in the Arts (ACGB, 1985), Partnership. Making Arts Money Work Harder (ACGB, 1986), Better Business for the Arts (ACGB, 1988) and The Economic Importance of the Arts in Britain (John Myerscough for the Policy Studies Institute, 1988).

52 Economies of mime and physical theatre

and performing their work. It is an irony, that to survive, most artists have always been imaginatively and energetically 'entrepreneurial', but not in the business sense that appealed to governments of the time. Significantly, it is around this time that commentators began to start referring to and invoking the 'theatre *industry*' within the various discourses on theatre as an art form and its possible funding. For the emerging mime and physical theatre companies and artists of the period, this was the landscape they had little choice but to inhabit. Whatever their ideological disposition, most artists were faced with funding criteria and mechanisms which reflected the 'structures of feeling' identified earlier.

A home for mime

The accounts above offer an overview of the mechanisms, organisations and policies for supporting mime and physical theatre, and indeed all cultural activities across the nations of the UK, and within its regions, since the Arts Council was established by Clement Attlee's Labour Government of 1945–1950. Here, we have sketched out the complex and changing array of factors and considerations which shaped funding policies across the arts in general, from both local and national state agencies, and – increasingly – towards the end of our period from the private sector. In this section, we focus particularly on where and how mime (and later physical theatre) was positioned within these national and regional arts organisations.

As we have already noted, by the early 1990s, mime as a descriptive category for an art form had largely been replaced by various terms such as physical theatre, movement theatre or visual theatre, the former being the most prevalent towards the end of this period. In the first 15 years of our era, mime was a category which the arts councils, both nationally and regionally, accepted as an organisational given, even if the forms it described were becoming increasingly plural, uncertain and elastic. This ambiguity – and a degree of suspicion – around what practices mime described was epitomised and performed by indecision as to where it should find a home in the departmental structures of the Arts Council nationally and in the RAAs.

Before we examine the position of mime within the funding bodies it seems important to step back and note that even the status of dance as an independent art form was not acknowledged organisationally at the Arts Council until 1979 when, at the behest of Jane Nicholas, the organisation established an independent Dance Department. However, it was not until April 1986 that it was re-titled to become the 'Dance and Mime Department'. Prior to 1979, dance was located – perplexingly – as a sub-section of the Music Department. The rationale, such as it existed, was because the ballet companies had been funded under the umbrella of music. Nicholas became director of this new unit within the Arts Council until her retirement in 1989. During this period she not only was an energetic and skilful champion of contemporary dance but also became increasingly enamoured with the practices of some of the leading mime companies and artists who were beginning to receive recognition. In 1989/1990 mime was moved from Dance to the Drama Department following recommendations in the 1986 Cork Report.

For example, in the Northern region, Susanne Burns started her post at Northern Arts in 1985 as 'Assistant Dance and Mime Officer' and was still positioned within the Music Department there until the end of the decade when it moved to the Drama Department in line with changes in the national organisation (see profile of Northern Region in Chapter 4). In 2020 we spoke at length with Sue Hoyle who became the Arts Council's Dance and Mime Officer in 1986 under the leadership of Nicholas. When the latter retired in 1989 Hoyle became Director of Dance, mime having now moved 'sideways' to the Drama Department in that same year.

From our conversations with Hoyle and Burns, both admitted that mime had really fallen under the radar of the Arts Council until the arrival of Nicholas in 1979. Nola Rae was one of the first mime artists to approach the Arts Council for support in the late 1970s or early 1980s and Hoyle reflects that:

> The reason mime was in dance was because no-one else could think where mime should go. Mime artists were just knocking at the doors of the Arts Council and there was no letterbox, as it were. The Theatre Department didn't think it was text-based enough or it fitted into their criteria. But Jane knew that Nola had trained as a dancer and she said, 'OK, we'll give them a home'. Of course, Dance had a tiny budget, everything was low status. Jane didn't have the same ranking as the other art-form directors, the budget was miniscule, but, nevertheless, she had a very inclusive view of what dance was and she was happy to welcome Nola, and subsequently others, into the Dance Department. And it became the Dance and Mime Department.
>
> *(Hoyle, 2021)*

What is clear is that the acceptance of mime under the umbrella of dance was not the consequence of considered policy making but because Nicholas felt it was the right fit at the time and argued persuasively within the Arts Council for this to happen. By the time Hoyle had arrived at the Arts Council in 1986 a number of other mime and physical theatre companies were receiving varying amounts of funding; these included David Glass, Moving Picture Mime Show [MPMS], DV8, Théâtre de Complicité, Trickster, Trestle and the London International Mime Festival (LIMF), all from within the exceedingly modest overall Dance and Mime budget. Toby Sedgwick, founder member of MPMS, recalls that Jane Nicholas was a 'big supporter' (Sedgwick, 2020) and that Val Bourne of Dance Umbrella 'loved their work' (Ibid.). Early in her post as Dance and Mime Officer Hoyle remembers

> Complicite coming into my office for meetings. There were just the three of them, Marcello and Annabel and Simon at that stage. And gradually, as they made bigger shows, there were more of them coming in, because they were very much a collective. And at that stage, in the mid '80s, the grants those mime companies were getting were miniscule – £4000 was considered to be quite a big grant.
>
> *(Hoyle, 2021)*

54 Economies of mime and physical theatre

Graham Saunders in *British Theatre Companies 1980–1994* fleshes out Hoyle's remarks with some details:

> In 1985, Trestle, Trickster and Theatre de Complicite 'wrote collectively to the Secretary General, Luke Rittner, demonstrating how they were the poor relations in comparison to their drama colleagues by citing a series of statistics. They pointed out that less than 3 per cent of the Dance budget was allocated to mime and compared the 1984/5 funding allocation for Trestle (£2,500), Trickster (£10,000) and Complicite (£8,000) to the amounts given to small-scale touring companies Paines Plough (£65,000) and Avon Touring (£73,000) (ACGB, 1985, 41/45/7)'.
>
> *(Saunders, 2015: 110)*

The driving forces behind mime being moved into the territory of the Drama Department at the Arts Council – a course of action shortly followed within the RABs – are intriguing and complex. As we have noted 'there was no letter box' (Hoyle, 2021) for mime until the Dance Department explicitly became tagged as Dance and Mime in the early 1980s. Mime found a home under the aegis of dance in part because an early mime applicant for funding, Nola Rae, had trained initially at the Royal Ballet School. Another vocal missionary for mime, and an applicant for funding, David Glass, had been to the London Contemporary Dance School. Perhaps, too, that illusionary mime sometimes figured in ballet, and of course had an emphasis on communication through movement and the body, intuitively suggested a fit with dance. But, of course, companies such as Théâtre de Complicité and MPMS came out of the Lecoq School in Paris (then widely known as a mime school) and had no explicit base in dance. For artists such as these, we can only imagine that their flair, brio, energy and skill were enough to persuade Nicholas and Hoyle during the 1980s of the virtue of funding support, however small. There were, nevertheless, two other key factors: a/ the disinclination of the Drama Department to host mime: 'they didn't think it was text-based enough, or that it fitted into their criteria' (Ibid., 2021); and b/ the dogged, eloquent and insistent articulation of the case for mime made by a number of key figures and through the channels of the early Mime Action Group (MAG). We tell the story of MAG later. Ironically, it was the relative success of this advocacy to the Dance (and Mime) Department that enabled and encouraged the move to Drama in 1989/1990.

The advocacy of mime in the 1980s and early 1990s as an art form deserving of funding and as distinct from dance on the one hand and theatre on the other offers a fascinating case study of a small and select group of artists as cultural activists, parallels for which we believe are hard to find. Key figures in this (passionate but often angry) guerrilla warfare included Nola Rae, David Glass, Desmond Jones, Nigel Jamieson, Peta Lily, Pat Keysell, Helen Lannaghan and Joseph Seelig. By the late 1980s when MAG began to receive Arts Council funding and could thereby employ a full-time administrator, campaigning and arguing for mime became organised into the quotidian functions and activities of the organisation. The figure

Economies of mime and physical theatre **55**

of Desmond Jones, for example (see Chapter 6), stands out here as a charismatic, witty, eloquent and sometimes irascible proselytiser for mime. For Jones, like his teacher, Etienne Decroux, mime was not a branch of either theatre or dance, but a distinct and revolutionary art form, which at some point in the future would usurp the existing practices of the performing arts. A flavour of Jones' rhetoric was regularly to be found within the pages of *MAGazine* – later *Total Theatre*[11] – as this example from a 1985 issue illustrates:

> I do mime
> What do you do?
> Stand up and be counted.
> I am convinced that Mime will change the face of speaking theatre in the next 25 years. Maybe not mind-numbingly staggeringly, but significantly. People will come to us, are coming to us to learn our techniques. . . . We do mime. No pissing about. If we are strong people will come to us. We are going through an identity crisis, certainly. . . . Krakatoa was a squib compared to what has happened in mime in the last 9 years.
>
> *(Jones, 1985: 4)*

Beyond these rhetorical flourishes, a number of key figures (including Jones himself) patiently – or impatiently – attended committee meetings, sat on panels, spoke at conferences and wrote reports about the radical excitement of mime and why it should be recognised and more adequately funded. In our conversation, Sue Hoyle spoke warmly and enthusiastically of certain figures:

> By the time I joined the Arts Council in 1983, not only was it there as a label, but mime really did have a voice. Two members of the Dance panel, the national panel, were mime people, and two members of the projects committee were also from mime. . . . I think what was really important about the mime people on the panel is they were strategic thinkers, which meant, even though there wasn't much money, they could work tactically. Joseph Seelig was really important in that respect and another person was Kenneth Rea, who was teaching at the Guildhall and writing for *The Guardian*. . . . David Glass was also influential. The big mover and shaker in the funding system was Nigel Jamieson. Nigel was incredibly influential. He'd been running Trickster, which was really successful. Anyway, he got funding to animate things and then to set up the International Workshop Festival. . . . These people were strategic influencers. Kenneth in a quieter way. Joseph in his own special way. And Nigel Jamieson and David Glass . . . they were great.
>
> *(Hoyle, 2021)*

11 *Total Theatre Magazine* can be accessed at www.totaltheatre.org.uk and the *Total Theatre* Print Archive can be found at totaltheatre.org.uk/archive

56 Economies of mime and physical theatre

In addition to Burns and Hoyle, there was only one other dance officer with some responsibility for mime employed within the national or regional arts council structures and this was Lynn Maree at Greater London Arts. These posts were in part the beneficiaries of the growth and enthusiasm for contemporary dance on the one hand, and for modern mime – in all its multiple guises – on the other, during the early years of the 1980s. In turn, recognition of these movements fed into the evidence provided for the *Glory of the Garden* report (1984) which had little choice but to recognise that both dance and mime were hugely underfunded both nationally and regionally. Burns recalls:

> A lot happened because of *Glory of the Garden*. Dance was being valued for the first time, and mime benefited from this growth, or rather was an essential part of it. Problems started to arise as both grew in popularity. The money just wasn't there. I think it was at that point that the argument started to take place within the Arts Council about where mime should be placed. I remember a CORAA (Council of Regional Arts Associations) meeting in Liverpool where CORAA dance officers were saying we have to push for mime to be moved out of our portfolios and into drama. We simply haven't got the resources to support two growing art forms.
>
> *(Burns, 2020)*

We return to Burns' work for Northern Arts later, but the accounts above provide a register of the growing ferment around mime in the 1980s, both nationally and regionally.

Mime Action Group: for and of its times

We debated where to position our account of Mime Action Group (MAG) in this volume, sensing it could legitimately be placed in any one of several chapters. We have alighted on this one, since MAG for the last 16 years of our time period was an absolutely central feature within the 'ecologies of support' for mime and physical theatre. It was, however, much more than simply a *support structure* and was a significant player in the ecology itself. We consider at the end of this section the extent to which MAG was a wholly responsive or reactive organisation, and how much it actually initiated and led some crucial developments in the unfolding story of UK mime and physical theatre between 1984 and 2000.

The first newsletter of MAG, wryly titled *MAGazine*, was published in the autumn of 1984 and this marked the 'coming out' of MAG to a wider public beyond the small gang of mime activists who had been gathering in Helen Lannaghan's flat in East London to scheme, plan and organise around the future funding and profile of mime. In correspondence with us – and reiterating Hoyle above – Lannaghan recalls that:

Early movers and shakers I remember from those early years included David Glass, Nigel Jamieson, Penny Mayes and Toby Wilshire (Trestle), Peta Lily, Nola Rae and Matthew Ridout, Ben Keaton, Andrew Dawson and Gavin Robertson (MTP Productions) and Molly Guilfoyle from Intriplicate. There were of course more, but those are ones I specially remember. The first meeting was held at the office of GLAA (Greater London Arts Association) in Bloomsbury, with the huge support of Linda Dyos, the Dance and Mime Officer who was so supportive in those early years. If you ask me who were the dominant voices in that group, definitely Nigel Jamieson and David Glass, but it was specifically Nigel who wanted to move 'mime' from the dance to the theatre department at ACE, where budgets were potentially bigger and where he felt there was more legitimacy for work that was drawing sizeable audiences.

(Lannaghan, 2021)

Some years later in the 1990s, during a period of extended – and to a certain extent, interminable – debate on the pros and cons of a new name for MAG, Mhora Samuel[12] remembers a board member at the time sardonically remarking that MAG 'sounded like a small terrorist group' (Samuel, 2020). We sense that the early MAG activists and missionaries assembling in Lannaghan's flat would not have been displeased with that description. The first newsletters were photocopied on monochrome stapled pages and for a £5 cheque (sent to Lannaghan) you were invited to join the organisation. By 1984 MAG had its own bank account and described itself 'as a recently formed organisation which aims to promote the Art (sic) of Mime and related disciplines' (*MAGazine*, Autumn 1984: 1). This was to be achieved, and we quote these aspirations in full, through:

- Increasing public awareness and understanding of the wide and important areas of theatre represented by mime based work.
- Improving the financial status and the level of public subsidy for those working in the field of mime.
- Acting as a resource and information pool for both those working in the profession and other interested parties.
- Acting as a forum in which to discuss common problems and to determine ways of solving them.
- Campaigning for the improvement in training opportunities and related skills.
- Improving the image and understanding of mime through and in the press and media.

(Ibid.)

---

12 Mhora Samuel was Administrative Director of MAG/Total Theatre between 1992 and 1998.

58 Economies of mime and physical theatre

We felt it was important to reproduce these goals verbatim as they clearly remained the yardstick of MAG's purpose even when it metamorphosed into 'Total Theatre: the UK umbrella organisation for Mime, Physical Theatre and Visual Performance' in 1997, and to the simpler, but ill-defined 'Total Theatre Network' only three years later in the autumn of 2000. But, what is in a name? Evidently, a considerable amount. In 1984 we find not a hint of 'physical theatre' or 'visual performance', by 1997 mime remains in the strap line but in partnership with physical theatre and visual performance, and by 2000 all three descriptors have vanished, at least at headline level. In 1984 mime is proudly and unproblematically stated, although with just a hint of uncertainty in the final aspiration as possible doubts seem to creep in through 'improving the image and understanding of mime' (Ibid.).

Before considering the unfolding work of MAG it is important to mark its structural and spatial evolution over this 15-year period. Lannaghan notes that she produced the early issues of *MAGazine* virtually single-handedly until managing to secure the first grant of £5,000 via Sue Hoyle at the Arts Council's Dance and Mime Department. At this juncture, in early 1988 the MAG baton was handed to Deborah Barnard and Alicyn Marr who had replaced Pat Keysell as (job share) mime animateurs at the Brewery Arts Centre in Kendal. By the end of 1989, although MAG remained MAG, *MAGazine* had become *Total Theatre* and in 1990 the organisation returned to a London base at the Battersea Art Centre under the administrative leadership of David Ryan. By March 1992, Mhora Samuel replaced Ryan who had departed to Australia, and the MAG office had moved across the Thames to an office in Sadler's Wells. Samuel had been working at Chisenhale Dance Space in East London and was to become an energetic and key strategic player in the 'maturing' of MAG throughout the rest of the 1990s until she left, early in 1998, to be replaced by Annabel Arndt in June the same year. Throughout this period MAG was to receive enough Arts Council and Greater London Arts financial support to employ both Samuel and also, for a few years, Tina Ellu, as the organisation's (part-time) assistant and finance officer. These grants paid for the administration of MAG, but not, by and large, for projects initiated by the organisation. These would have to be funded either by separate awards or through partnerships (co-productions, as it were) with, for example, art centres, local authorities and regional arts boards or associations.

The 'governance' of MAG became more elaborate and systematic as the decade unfolded and as a stronger sense of democratic accountability to members became embedded as a consequence of the organisation's growth and maturity. From Lannaghan's time MAG had a *de facto* – and later more formalised – editorial committee which curated and managed the production of *MAGazine* and then *Total Theatre*, but until 1990 no formal executive group either to guide or to take responsibility for the organisation. By the spring of 1993, Mel Jennings (then Marketing Officer for Talawa Theatre Company and previously Administrator for Black Mime Theatre) had been elected chair, with Alistair

Spalding[13] and Simon Murray as her vice-chairs. During these early years of the decade there is a sense that the Editorial Group – of which Samuel was always a member – became more (properly) independent from the overall management of the organisation and its Executive Committee. We may note, too, that with the arrival of Samuel, *Total Theatre* moves from its short-lived broadsheet format, pioneered by Ryan, back to A4, but now with a higher-quality gloss finish. The journal remained in this format until it went purely online after 2006/07. It also became longer and longer, so that by 1997 it is often running to 28 pages. In 1995 this small team was joined by John Daniel as Information and Publications Officer and Melissa Alaverdy as magazine designer. Later Daniel was to become the overall editor of *Total Theatre*.

In our interview with Samuel (July 2020) she remarked upon the regular – and often meanderingly inconclusive – discussions on the executive committee and editorial group about the organisation's name. As with many such debates about titles the conversations were both arcane (to many) *and* deeply felt. By the mid-1990s there was an increasing groundswell of opinion from paid-up members of the organisation that the word 'mime' in its title was too restrictive, probably misleading and perhaps irrelevant. By this time 'physical theatre' and/or 'visual performance' had a significant degree of common currency, even if most people were hard pressed to define exactly what practices these terms actually defined and embraced. At the 1997 AGM MAG became 'Total Theatre: the UK umbrella organisation for Mime, Physical Theatre and Visual Performance'.

Debates about naming always reflect profounder issues around form, content, style, lineage, ownership and possible reception. Indeed, the pages of *MAGazine/ Total Theatre* over this 16-year period implicitly – and occasionally quite explicitly – speak of these shifting positions, practices, dispositions and tensions. We know from the early issues of *MAGazine* that certain key players at the time – Desmond Jones, Nola Rae, Pat Keysell and David Glass, for example – had strong views about protecting mime from what they regarded as dilution, erosion and enfeeblement. In turn, these understandings and opinions reflected powerfully held beliefs about whether mime represented an autonomous and potentially transgressive art form, distinct, for example, from theatre and dance, or whether as practice it stood in for a portfolio of movements and tendencies which aspired to shift theatre's centre of gravity away from the dominance of text and the spoken word, firmly and unequivocally towards action, movement, gesture and embodiment

Scanning issues of *MAGazine/Total Theatre* it is clear from the outset that the landscape was never circumscribed by a pure and tightly bounded notion of 'mime'. However, by the second half of the 1990s the range and variety of practices – particularly, for example, 'new circus' – which are being described and reflected upon

---

13 Alistair Spalding at that time was on the MAG executive committee and Programmer for the Hawth Art Centre in Crawley, West Sussex. Since 2004 he has been Artistic Director and Chief Executive of Sadler's Wells Theatre in London.

seem hugely diverse and cover almost anything which fell outwith text and play-based drama. Whilst this tendency represents editorial choices made by a group of MAG aficionados and volunteers, it also reflects complex uncertainties and disagreements as to what might constitute modern mime, physical theatre and visual performance, both in academia and in the professional world of theatre. As Murray and Keefe discuss in their book (2016) the signage applied to these performance practices was – and remains – as much to do with marketing and promotion as it did with clearly and confidently held self-definitions amongst artists as to how their practices and dramaturgies might be described and analysed.

An almost complete set of *Total Theatres* from 1984 to the end of our period (and beyond) now exists in digital form (http://totaltheatre.org.uk/archive/). This project was championed and executed by a later editor of *Total Theatre*, Dorothy Max Prior.

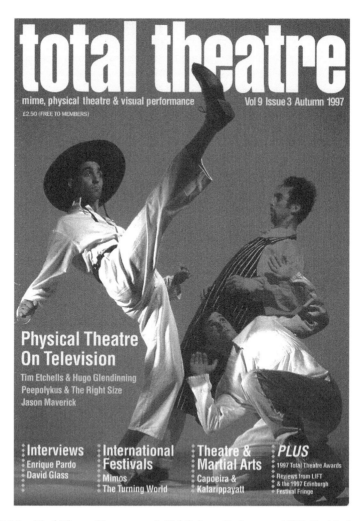

FIGURE 3.1 *Total Theatre* (Front cover), Vol 9, Issue 3, Autumn 1997. By kind permission of Aurelius Productions & *Total Theatre* Magazine.

The archive offers a fascinating measure of the structures of feeling from this corner of cultural production and the performing arts landscape and is a project worthy of doctoral research. In our volume, however, we cannot do justice to the detail and richness of all this material and how (and what) it signifies. Nonetheless, what follows is an attempt to distil and capture the thematic tropes and tendencies within the journal over these 16 years and to discern the assumptions and thinking behind those who led the organisation, either as paid staff or as editorial (and other) volunteers. Essentially, the contents of the journal over this period maybe divided into the following loose and overlapping categories:

- Editorial opinion and strategies.
- Notice of and reports on a variety of training and education events and experiences (workshops, conferences, summer schools, seminars, university and private theatre school programmes and courses).
- Profiles of artists, programmers, producers, companies, significant venues and regions.
- Profiles of art form sectors or categories: for example, puppetry, circus, live art, dance, new writing.
- Reports on policy initiatives from governments, the arts council and regional arts boards or associations.
- Funding information: available sources, categories and reports on awards made.
- Notice of and reports from festivals within the UK and beyond.
- Obituaries: Lecoq, Barrault, Decroux, Grotowski and others.
- Company news, venues and touring information and schedules.
- Provocations, debates and letters.
- Performance and book reviews.
- Listings of performances and advertisements for various schools and courses.

If one was to distil these categories even further we might suggest that the journal could schematically be summarised as delivering advocacy, debate, factual information (e.g. touring schedules and workshop details), profiling and current news. It is important to note that the publication never aspired to be an academic periodical, although it has certainly been an excellent source of information and debates for scholars and students over the years. Moreover, from time to time a few university academics would contribute short discursive and reflective pieces for its pages. Inevitably the quality of the writing was variable and, quite regularly, strong opinions – thoughtful, informed or otherwise – were expressed, axes ground and disagreements aired. All these, at best, contributed to a capacious sense of the landscape of mime and physical theatre – and the temper of its times – as the years passed. However, the single largest category of contributions throughout the 1990s was factual information, and by the middle of the decade between one-third and a half of the

62 Economies of mime and physical theatre

total pagination of each issue was regularly devoted to company touring schedules, information on training and workshop opportunities, company updates (changing personal, new locations, etc.), bursaries and funding opportunities, awards given, festivals and publications. Without detailed readership research it is impossible to gauge whether this information was used instrumentally, but of course, it is salutary to remind ourselves that this is still the pre-internet age and therefore what was on offer here was the most comprehensive calibration of factual details available. Certainly, scanning these back pages provides a resonant sense of a thriving and busy ecology, but equally disguises personal and collective precarity, an uneven distribution of scarce resources and a patchy geographical supply of performed work.

Beyond its publishing wing, MAG/Total Theatre was an arena for, and animator of exchange, debate, sociability, campaigning and the organisation of events, often in partnership with other organisations. Under Samuel's enthusiastic administrative leadership the organisation increasingly planned and led seminars, discussion groups, symposia and facilitated meetings between artists, programmers, funders and – sometimes – politicians.

Most of MAG's non-publishing projects could properly be defined as educational, and, as such, we identify some of these in Chapter 6. In September 1994 MAG organised its most elaborate and ambitious event ever: a seven-day workshop and symposium in Manchester entitled *Moving into Performance* (MIP). The scale and internationalism of the six-day programme was reflected in the statement that it was a collaboration between:

- Mime Action Group
- European Mime Federation
- Theater Institute Nederland
- Mime Centrum Berlin
- Manchester Metropolitan University School of Theatre
- Physical State International
- International Workshop Festival

We examine MIP, the details of the programme and its aims, ambitions, controversies and participants in Chapter 6. Together, these events gave notice that MAG was keen to be seen to engage with provocative and discursive issues within the (by then diminishing) field of mime and the more expansive one of physical and visual theatre. Certainly, through MIP, MAG also announces the feasibility and desirability of wider European engagement and partnerships. In reality, there was little of MAG's work which was not educational in the sense that its founding mission was to support and promote these art forms and to persuade and inform various constituencies (publics, funders, artists, promoters, arts boards, local authorities and venues) of their importance. To these interconnected ends, MAG also commissioned a number of reports and publications during the 1990s, the most significant of these were:

Blueprint for Regional Mime Development. This was launched at the Hawth in November 1992 with a performance and workshop from the Gamboling Guizers and contributions from Jac Wilkinson (author of the report), Alistair Spalding and Toby Wilsher (Trestle). Funding for Wikinson's research and writing, and printing the report itself, came from the Arts Council and South East Arts.

UK Mime and Physical Theatre Training Directory. Published in 1993 this was a collaboration between MAG and Neil Blunt (researcher/writer) of the Arts Training Programme at De Montfort University. The Directory contained factual details of regular workshops, university courses, private theatre schools, practitioners and companies, art centres and other organisations involved in various aspects of training. It was sold at £5.95.

Guide to Mime in Education. Published for £3.50 in 1994, this was researched and written by Jac Wilkinson. Wilkinson at the time of writing the report was Education Officer at the University of Warwick's Arts Centre and had been a mime animateur in Luton during the late 1980s. She was also a performer and director. The Guide was completely directed towards the teaching of mime in schools and with youth groups and contained practical teaching exercises and case studies.

Moving into Performance Report. Published by MAG in June 1995 for £4.00, the publication was compiled and written by John Keefe. Keefe's report documents the workshops and symposium and captures the debates and controversies therein.

Mime in Schools. A report (1996) into the mime and physical theatre education requirements of schools in the London, South East, West Midlands and Northern Regions, written by Anna Ledgard.

The Mime, Physical Theatres and Visual Performance Project: A Report from Mime Action Group to Northern Arts Board. Published in August 1995, this was researched, compiled and written by Simon Murray. Northern Arts commissioned MAG for this project who employed Murray to undertake the work. Murray was advised by a steering group consisting of Alan Lyddiard (Northern Stage), Frank Wilson (Dovecot Arts Centre), Sarah Kemp (Theatre sans Frontières), Mhora Samuel (MAG) and Mark Mulqueen (Northern Arts). His report contained a large number of recommendations to sustain, develop and promote mime and physical theatre practices in the Northern Region and was based upon an extensive range of interviews and meetings with practitioners, venue promoters, teachers and officers from Local Arts Development Agencies (LADAs).

64 Economies of mime and physical theatre

Threading across this period MAG undertook a series of interviews with key figures. Understandably, these were largely practitioners and teachers – Nigel Charnock, Ken Campbell, Keith Johnstone, Tim Etchells, Wim Vandekeybus and John Wright, for example – but also with Peter Brook who was then Conservative Minister at the Department of National Heritage in 1993. Whether political 'balance' was a consideration, a year later a rather more dynamic conversation took place with Brook's shadow minister, the Labour Party's Mo (Marjorie) Mowlam. All these interviews were subsequently written up in the pages of the journal. From the outset MAG had not been shy to perform as both vehicle and conduit for strongly felt messages to the Arts Council and other bodies with regard to funding. The very first issue of *MAGazine* (Autumn, 1984) began with a draft of Nigel Jamieson's letter to Jane Nicholas at the Arts Council which was essentially a critique of *The Glory of the Garden* report. Jamieson – and by association MAG – argued that the report largely ignored (only 'fourteen lines') the value of mime as an art form. This letter also began the argument that mime should be moved from the Dance to the (larger) Drama Department. Two years later in the summer of 1986 David Glass, following Jamieson, took up the cudgels for enhanced mime funding in a paper – 'Mime – A Poor Theatre' that he had prepared for the Arts Council's Dance and Mime Projects Awards Committee. Issue 8 of *MAGazine* reproduced Glass's paper in full, and here he eloquently argued the case for enhanced support for what he termed the 'poor theatre' of mime, and cogently explained the different forms and technical training traditions from which modern (in the 1980s) mime springs.

Another significant activity to be noted at the end of our era was an initiative MAG took in 1997 to establish the Total Theatre Awards at Edinburgh's International Fringe Festival[14]. In the Spring 1997 issue of *Total Theatre* the purpose of the awards was identified as being 'designed to bring attention to the success of physical and visual theatre companies in the Fringe' (*Total Theatre*, 1997: 20).

Retrospective thoughts: from MAG via Total Theatre into Total Theatre Network (1984–2022)

Today (2022) we note, with a slightly elegiac wistfulness, that at the foot of the stylish website for the Total Theatre Network, it states that: 'TOTAL THEATRE' IS THE TRADING NAME OF MIME ACTION GROUP, REGISTERED IN ENGLAND AND WALES, COMPANY NUMBER 53966643 CHARITY NUMBER 1052358. Under Mhora Samuel's stewardship MAG officially became registered as a company in December 1995 and as a charity in January 1996. That the Total Theatre Network still has the trading name of Mime Action Group strikes us as salient and resonant for an organisation that was formed 38 years ago out of indignation and frustration at the absence of respect and recognition for mime.

---

14 A full list of the nominees and winners in different categories can be found in *Total Theatre* Volume 9, Issue 7, Autumn 1997

Although our period ends in 2000 the endless dance around names and the art forms represented by the organisation under its various signages has continued into the twenty-first century. The current information on the *Total Theatre* Awards – now the main activity of the organisation – expresses the breadth and multiplicity of practices embraced and extolled by the Total Theatre Network:

> Resisting too narrow a definition of the term 'total theatre' the awards focus on artists and companies leading innovative work beyond the classical cannon and new writing – working within the fields of devised theatre, live art, visual performance, mime, puppetry, physical theatre, experimental theatre, dance, clown, circus, street, immersive, outdoor, site specific performance and more. The process also places a special emphasis on exploring difficult issues and the spaces in between established performance forms where innovative new creative practices, approaches and models are emerging.
>
> *(Total Theatre Network, 2021)*

So, mime still figures, but although this statement falls well outwith our period, the tectonic plates of the landscape it describes were already shifting when Helen Lannaghan and her gang of cultural bandits were passionately articulating the case for mime in 1984. Regardless of how we might assess, let alone measure, the role, impact and function of MAG between 1984 and 2000, its work and profile speaks evocatively of the temper of the times, or certainly the temper of the times within the territories of an experimental performance world which refused to be driven and defined by play-based drama and the spoken word.

If we might speak of this period as the 'first phase' of MAG/Total Theatre it was a time which drew upon and harnessed the transgressive cultural energies of the late 1960s and 1970s. The 'action' in Mime Action Group reflected various dispositions which were not peculiar to theatre or the performing arts. Perhaps, the most important of these temperaments was that if, out of a sense of discontent and outrage at a particular state of affairs, one wished to make changes then the way to do this was to organise through collaborative action and to articulate goals and aspirations in this way. We and others (Heddon and Milling, 2006) have already observed that if devised – and hence in this case mime and physical – theatres are children of the cultural and social movements of the 1960s then MAG is also part of that progeny. However, beyond MAG's early years of explicit campaigning, the organisation appears to have followed a developmental arc not dissimilar to other organisations which began with comparable impulses. From 1988 when the organisation finds an institutional – if temporary – home with mime animateurs, Deborah Barnard and Alicyn Marr at Kendal's Brewery Arts Centre, through to a permanent move to London with grant funding to enable the appointments of administrator-directors and other part-time staff, there is an unfolding process of formalisation occurring. From the early 1990s, under Samuel's administrative regime, structures of accountability are put in place, membership systems established, executive, editorial committees and working parties are formed and annual general meetings held. The

66 Economies of mime and physical theatre

collaborative nature of so much of MAG's work was always politically and culturally desirable, but also inevitable given that the organisation never had enough funding to resource its own singular initiatives.

Our account of MAG has been constructed from two sources. Firstly, from memories of personal experience with the organisation, particularly, perhaps, from Murray's perspective as a board member and co-chair of the executive. However, both authors were occasional writers for *MAGazine/Total Theatre* and participants in a range of seminars, symposia and workshops during the 1980s and 1990s. Secondly, we have drawn upon almost all issues of the journal over this 16-year period. These have been a dizzying, though hugely rich and valuable, source of information, mnemonics, ideas and thoughts. We conclude this section with some (unanswered and, perhaps, unanswerable) questions about MAG and what its story might tell us about mime and physical theatre during these times.

- To what extent did MAG drive and shape agendas and the performance practices of artists, and how much was it a reactive organisation, serving the needs, passions and interests of the sector?
- How useful – in an instrumental way – was the organisation and its publishing wing? Or was the value of MAG and its journal largely appreciated as a cultural and discursive backdrop to the work which was being made and performed?
- To what extent did MAG influence in a positive way the funding and support levels for mime and physical theatre?
- What does the prevalence of events, writing and information around training opportunities tell us about the landscape of mime and physical theatre during these times? Is there a subtext to this preoccupation with training which suggests that the quality of UK-generated work was perceived to be lacking, inadequate and under-realised?
- Which diverse constituencies of interest are under-represented in the actions of MAG and though its prolific publishing activities?
- Did the range of performance practices embraced and supported by MAG lead to a dissipation of mime and physical theatre, or did it represent a necessary and rich extension to our understanding of work available?
- What did the identification of multiple young – and often short-lived – companies in the pages of journal tell us about the cultural economy of the sector?
- Why did university drama and theatre departments feature relatively rarely in the journal, and in relation to the projects organised by MAG?
- To what extent did MAG – its activities and writings – have any long-term influence over modes of acting and dramaturgies within the performance of play and text-based dramas?

We hope, however, that this whole volume provides – implicit or explicit – responses to these questions.

Festivals as vehicles for community, conviviality, collaboration and cultural production

> festival (n.) 1580s, 'a festal day, appointed day of festive celebration,' short for festival day (late 14c.), from Old French festival (adj.) 'suitable for a feast; solemn, magnificent, joyful, happy,' and directly from Medieval Latin festivalis 'of a church holiday,' from festum 'festival, holiday,' neuter of festus 'of a feast' (see feast (n.)). The English word returned to French 19c. in certain specialized senses.
>
> (www.etymonline.com/word/festival)

Historically, the meaning of 'festival' seems to possess a number of qualities, but for our purposes, a day 'suitable for a feast; solemn, magnificent, joyful, happy' (Ibid.) may convey some of the characteristics which those marketing performance events signed as festivals seek to promise. Through many lenses, a festival suggests an aesthetic, spiritual or social event which is more than the sum of its parts, is bounded in time, although often recurring, and which offers a degree of conviviality and camaraderie for the participants involved. Perhaps, the rise of festivals and the development of MAG is serendipitous since both speak of the ideals of camaraderie and social bonding: at best, a degree of solidarity amongst practitioners in such events. However, arts festivals are also cultural commodities – modes of cultural consumption – and as such are spaces where our idea and experience of art is played out, performed (in various modes) and sometimes debated and contested. They also may have a strong spatial identity where what the festival offers is tightly linked in proposition, experience and memory to the landscape (urban or rural) where it is sited. In this, and other senses festivals may be transformative both experientially and in that they re-shape places – if only temporarily – from the quotidian to the special and unfamiliar (Waterman, 1998). In this section, we consider how festivals became a popular structuring mechanism in the 1980s and 1990s for key figures organising mime and physical theatre performances, residencies, seminars and workshops, and for enhancing the public appeal of these art forms. Waterman well encapsulates the multiple ways in which festivals may perform themselves:

> Although people ostensibly attend festivals to participate in an aesthetic event, their attendance can also be seen as a group celebration of shared mythologies and values through managed interaction among performance, audience and place at which they share in the production and consumption of artistic performances and creations by artists. The arts festival here is a 'cultural framework' reflecting the world view of a distinct socioeconomic section of modern society.
>
> *(Waterman, 1998: 59)*

68 Economies of mime and physical theatre

The festivals we consider here range from deeply embedded and repeated events of considerable longevity – the London International Mime Festival (LIMF) or the Edinburgh Festival, for example – through much shorter-lived occasions, to experiences which are never signed as festivals but which have a 'sense' of the festival about them. We particularly focus on LIMF, the Northern Festival of Mime, Dance and Visual Theatre at the Brewery Arts Centre in Kendal, the Riverside Festival at the Dovecot Arts Centre in Stockton upon Tees and a number of less ambitious and shorter events across the UK. The very significant International Workshop Festival (IWF) is alluded to here, but since it is a *workshop* festival we reflect upon its scope and importance in Chapter 6. Each of these festivals has different histories, contexts and topographical features, but share a common goal in aspiring to gather together a greater number of spectators to see work than would have been the case if these performances had not been corralled spatially and temporaneously into one place and period.

London International Mime Festival (LIMF)

Beyond the factual information available on its elegant and extensive website (https://mimelondon.com/), the pages of *MAGazine* and *Total Theatre* and the authors' personal memories, our intelligence about LIMF has been mined from the lengthy, funny, insightful and occasionally scurrilous conversation we had with Joseph Seelig and Helen Lannaghan in June 2020. LIMF has many notable features, but the two most startling reside in its longevity and its name. The first ever LIMF was held at the Cockpit Theatre in 1977 and even 45 years ago was titled the 'Cockpit Festival of Mime *and Visual Theatre*'. Significantly, from 1980 it has simply been the London International Mime Festival, although always referencing 'visual theatre' in the Festival's gloss. From 1977 the driving inspiration behind LIMF has been Joseph Seelig, who was then working as a programmer-manager at the Cockpit in North West London. In 1987 Seelig was joined by Helen Lannaghan and since then these two have been the energetic creative and organisational force fields behind all the festivals. If durability has been one extraordinary quality of LIMF, the other is that Seelig and Lannaghan have proudly, unashamedly – and perhaps recklessly – kept the Mime word at the epicentre of its name. We return to this act of heroic stubbornness below.

At the beginning of our conversation, Seelig and Lannaghan explained their personal journeys into this 45-year project. At the Cockpit, Seelig largely programmed fringe theatre of the day. He elaborated:

> One of the artists we often booked was somebody call Nola Rae. Nola Rae was the only mime artist that meant anything other than Marcel Marceau. She really was an artiste, and we did okay, but wanted to get better audiences for Nola in particular. She spoke to me one day. She had been to a festival in Germany – a festival of clowns, mimes, visual theatre, all that sort of thing. And she said, 'Why don't we try something like that here?' I thought it was a

very good idea. I had a theatre. She had some contacts. . . . We went to the Arts Council and asked for a little grant, and they've given us a grant every year since 1977 . . . except one year. The idea really had been that if you call something a festival, you'll get some press interest, especially in January when there's not a lot else going on in the theatre in London. Anyway, we started this in 1977 and it was an amazing success. Every night was sold out. And we thought, blimey, we'll do this again. Not every show was wonderful. Some of them were quite terrible actually. But those shows that were reviewed were reviewed very well. And it caused a great deal of interest.

(*Seelig and Lannaghan, 2020*)

Three points seem resonant here. Firstly, the connection with Nola Rae; secondly the festival as a device to gain press interest, and hence enhanced audiences; and thirdly, the importance of timing – January, a hitherto 'dead' period in the London theatre scene. The name of Nola Rae re-occurs throughout this book and such is the extent of her enduring relationship with Seelig, Lannaghan and LIMF that we discovered she was scheduled to conduct a workshop ('Broaden Your Mime') in January at LIMF 2022. Lannaghan had attended LIMF performances throughout its early years and during the early to mid-1980s had been the driving force behind setting up MAG. Lannaghan summarised her story for us:

So my roots . . . I used to go to those early festivals. I think the first one is about 1979 and my route . . . you could say that I got involved in mime because of David Bowie. Bowie was a huge influence on my then boyfriend, who was the front man in a rock band. He wanted to learn mime in order to be like David Bowie[15]. So, he went to study with Ronnie Wilson at the City Lit, as many did. I ended up touring with John Mowat[16] in the back of his van. And then, producing *The Intimate Memoirs of an Irish Taxidermist*, a one-man show by Ben Keaton, which went on to win the Perrier award in Edinburgh in 1986. And that was the year when Joe was possibly going to stop completely[17], but I think it was David Glass who said, why don't you get someone to help you. And he (Joseph) asked me . . . it wasn't my life's intention to get into mime. But nevertheless, that was the net effect of it.

(*Ibid.*)

These brief biographical sketches tell us something beyond purely personal anecdotage, since they shed light on the complex warp and weft of both the lives of those working in this corner of the cultural landscape, and the multiple webs of

---

15 See Chapter 8 for mime and popular music section.
16 See Chapter 2.
17 1983 and 1986 were the only years between 1977 and 2022 (apart from COVID-induced lockdown in 2021 when the whole Festival went online) where there was no London International Mime Festival.

70 Economies of mime and physical theatre

influences and practices which helped to construct the world of mime and physical theatre during this period. In all this, we see a process – a dynamic – which is very much about encounters, friendships and being part of a loose community- a 'gang' perhaps – that shared opportunities with each other. It might, conversely, also be experienced as maintaining a kind of informal 'closed shop' which was sometimes hard to break into.

LIMF's website contains some fascinating archive material with the facsimile of every programme since 1977 reproduced page by page (https://mimelondon.com/archive/) – like the multiple issues of *Total Theatre*, a gold mine for any researcher. From the outset, through name and deed, LIMF was always an international event, and the balance between UK-based companies and those from overseas varied from festival to festival; but this sample, spread across our period, provides an indication of the distribution – and the names of home-grown artists – in the following years.

> *LIMF 1979.* International: 6; UK: 3 (Ben Bennison, Edwina Dorman Theatre, Moving Picture Mime Show)
>
> *LIMF 1984.* International: 8; UK: 7 (Moving Picture Mime Show, Peta Lily, Theatre de Complicite, Johnny Melville, Trestle, Peter Wear and Nola Rae.)
>
> *LIMF 1992.* International: 9; UK: 5 (Linda Kerr-Scott, Leicester Haymarket Company, Talking Pictures, The Right Size and Trestle.)
>
> *LIMF 1996.* International: 7; UK: 11 (Scarlet Theatre, Black Mime Theatre, Clod Ensemble, Academy Productions, Improbable, People Show, Ralf Ralf, Lee and Dawes, Rejects Revenge, Stephen Mottram's Animata and Circus Space Cabaret.)
>
> *LIMF 2000.* International: 10; UK: 6 (Stan's Café, Johnny Melville, Stephen Mottram's Animata, Les Bubb, Faulty Optic, Ridiculismus)

In almost all years, international contributions outnumbered UK-based ones, but it seems important to note the London-centric nature of this global exposure. However, a few of the companies and artists from Europe and beyond might also have performed at venues outwith the capital (Coventry, Birmingham, Cardiff, Bury St Edmunds and in Yorkshire, for example) and at the Riverside (Stockton), Brewery (Kendal) and Edinburgh festivals. Scanning all the programmes between 1977 and 2000 reveals a heterogeneous array of practices from within the UK. These, unsurprisingly, represent a diverse range of training, aesthetic and dramaturgical influences and speak of Lannaghan and Seelig's disposition to embrace a multiplicity of forms, moods and performance worlds for their festivals, notwithstanding their unyielding commitment to mime. In addition to the names identified earlier in those festival years, these UK-based practitioners and companies – not an exclusive list – were invited to perform at LIMF within our time period, and some of these on a number of occasions:

David Glass, Desmond Jones, Annie Stainer, Glee Club, Dereck Dereck Productions, Brouhaha, Katie Duck, Natural Theatre Company, Intriplicate Mime, Julian Chagrin, John Mowat, Lindsey Kemp Company, Trickster, Gavin Robertson, Andrew Dawson, Josef Houben, Ra Ra Zoo, Mick Wall, Alan Heap, Toby Sedgwick, John Lee, Bim Mason, Rick Zoltowski, Ben Keaton, Told By an Idiot, Kneehigh and Peepolykus.

LIMF has also regularly offered a series of workshops, and occasional talks, films and performances for children in conjunction with the main festival. One of the most significant developments towards the end of our timeline, and a sharp measure of LIMF's success, has been a move towards hosting many of the performances in large-scale and high-status venues. From 1980 (until 2011) LIMF was presenting shows annually at the Institute for Contemporary Arts (ICA), but by the end of the 1990s was also using the Royal Festival Hall, the Purcell Room (300 seats) and the Queen Elizabeth Hall (1,000 seats) in the South Bank Centre, as well as some of its more habitual smaller locations. Into the 2000s this list was extended to include one of the Barbican's theatre spaces and Sadler's Wells. For Seelig and Lannaghan this move into some (much) larger venues indicated the commercial imperatives of increasing income by selling more seats. In addition, however, it also spoke of the multifaceted and changing perceptions of mime which audiences have when they sign up to see a performance at a high-profile event called an International *Mime* Festival. At these larger venues, Seelig suggests that 'there's a huge bond of trust' (ibid.) with audiences at, for example, the Barbican, Sadler's Wells and the South Bank Centre, because even if they have little sense of what mime is, or its histories, they trust the judgement of both the Festival curators and the venue managers who welcome in this work.

We sense that Seelig and Lannaghan have had a complex relationship with mime, one that is both principled and pragmatic. We sense a cheerful and stubborn bloody-mindedness in persisting with the project as a mime festival even when by 2000 there was little of the traditional stuff around, and when visual or physical theatre seemed a more fashionable, if vague and imprecise, descriptor for the work they wanted to programme. Today the debate around whether mime still serves as a useful signpost to particular kinds of physical practice is – thankfully – long dead, or at least regarded as immaterial; but back in the 1980s and 1990s it still resonated, certainly in the pages of *Total Theatre*. In the 1991 Spring and Autumn Issues of *Total Theatre* Desmond Jones wrote a two-part essay on LIMF. It was a typical Jones piece: witty, irreverent, perceptive and hugely committed to defending mime from cynics, detractors and naysayers. He wrote:

> Joseph has a constant battle with our image. In the States it is common amongst mimes to say that Marcel Marceau is the worst thing that has happened to the art (and Decroux would probably agree). He gave it an image that the rest of us are still trying to crawl out from under. When I put this to Joseph he replied, quick as a flash, 'absolutely untrue'. Like me, he agrees it is the job of other performers in other areas of mime to be as good as Marceau; to touch the public sensitivity

as subtly as he can, but in a different way, with a different style. Too many people try to knock him down instead of trying to build themselves higher.

(Jones in *Total Theatre*, 1991: 9)

We give the final word to Seelig who, in conversation with us, captured not just his thinking on mime, but also the secret of LIMF's extraordinary longevity. His words, echoing those of some of the artists quoted in Chapter 1, express the paradox of holding on to mime whilst at the same time refusing to be confined by it, the importance of letting go:

> We've always wanted to stay loyal to the word mime, but we wanted people to know that there was more to it than that – hence 'visual theatre'. We've never really used the term physical theatre, because I think all theatre is physical unless you're sitting in a chair. So we use the term *visual theatre*, but we didn't want to drop the word mime. Although, honestly, it has been at times quite a heavy cross to bear. From very early on, we've been telling people mime is more than what you think it is. Mime is more than just somebody pretending to climb up and down stairs. But actually, we all know what mime is, it's what Marcel Marceau did. That's what mime is. We have managed to convince ourselves that it's a great big umbrella term where what you see is more important than what you hear. So it's been very important to convince the public, or try to, that there's more to this word than you think. It's a useful umbrella term.
>
> (Seelig and Lannaghan, 2020)

FIGURE 3.2 *Twin Houses,* Compagnie Mossoux-Bonté, London International Mime Festival 1996, by kind permission of Manon Dumonceaux.

Source: Photographer: Mikha Wajnrych.

Economies of mime and physical theatre 73

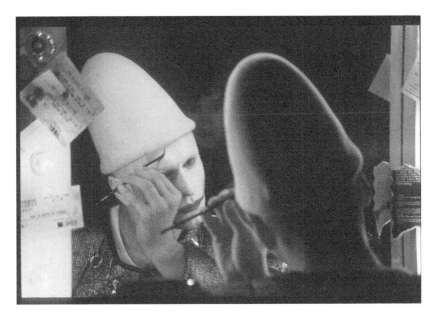

FIGURE 3.3   *Sur La Route de Sienne*, Theatre le Ranelagh, featuring Stanislav Varkki, London International Mime Festival, 1997, by kind permission of Helen Lannaghan.

The Riverside, the Brewery and other festivals

The story of mime and physical theatre festivals during our period is diverse, geographically uneven and often driven by dedicated and charismatic individuals. The pages of *Total Theatre* contain regular notices of festivals but clearly these are hugely variable in size, aspiration and purpose. Many are understandably concentrated in one area, or, indeed, in a single venue, but others spread across regions and towns. The Summer/Autumn 1992 issue of *Total Theatre* contains a short account by Ellis Rothenberg described as 'Southern Arts Marketing Consultant'. We learn that a festival, *Larger than Life*, which lasted between October and February, was distributed across four English counties in the towns and cities of Oxford, Salisbury, Poole, Plymouth and Swindon. Apparently, 'attendances were not insignificant: over 1,500 people in 5 cities attended 25 performances of what, in a national context, is considered to be a developing art form' (Rothenberg, 1992: 5). Regardless of the pleasures experienced by audiences at any of these performances, we speculate about the extent to which *Larger than Life* was actually experienced by audiences or performers as a 'festival'. It seems hard to imagine that a festival so geographically dispersed and held over five months could engender much sense of a community of audiences and the *joie de vivre* which such events aspire to generate. Significantly, the register of Rothenberg's short account suggests that this festival was driven largely by the tasks of audience development for the venues involved. Whilst this motivation is not dishonourable, it does reflect a motivation where celebrating and raising the profile of these art forms was secondary to – or at least, alongside – income generation. The

74 Economies of mime and physical theatre

tenor of Rothenberg's writing certainly reflects this disposition and is couched in the language of commercial accountancy and business management:

> It is important to foster innovative small-scale work regardless of the size of potential audience, i.e. in commercial terms, it should be regarded as a 'loss leader' product, funded on a venture capital basis with no apologies.
>
> *(Ibid.)*

A rather different articulation of 'festival' can be seen over a number of years at the Hawth Arts Centre, led in the early/mid-1990s by Alistair Spalding. Spalding ran a number of *Beyond Words* mime festivals at the Hawth and in the Summer/Autumn 1992 issue of *Total Theatre* wrote about his approach and the experience, and we quote him at length here as his words offer that blend of commitment, pragmatism and daring which we have already noted with Lannaghan and Seelig in LIMF:

> Every time I mention the Mime Festival to our Publicity Officer he becomes ashen-faced and has to sit down for a while. Who can blame him? It does seem a reckless idea in these times of cutbacks, but I think there is enough method in my madness to make it successful and hopefully an annual event.
>
> Firstly, I've tried not to be too precious about what is included in the festival, my main criteria being the inclusion of work where the predominant means of communication is not words.
>
> Secondly, I firmly believe that there isn't just one mime audience, each company attracts a different audience for different reasons and so diversity is of key importance. . . . So I think we have a formula for a successful if small-scale festival and the seeds of a larger event next year.
>
> *(Spalding, 1992: 5)*

Spalding's imaginative 'formula' also included the strategy that his festival should become a focus for practitioners as well as spectators and, to that end, the first *Beyond Words* event ran a seminar in association with MAG on the future of regional mime development. Partnership events with MAG became a notable signature of the Hawth under Spalding and one feels his acute sense (both strategic and aesthetic) of the qualities and possibilities of modern mime for contemporary audiences. Indeed, as we have already noted, Spalding was vice-chair of MAG for a time in the 1990s and, after leaving the Hawth, went on to take up leading programming and administrative leadership roles at the South Bank Centre, and later Sadler's Wells. Spalding seems a salient example of one of a number of key characters populating this book who energetically, intelligently and cannily embraced and promoted mime and physical theatre during our period and beyond.

We finish this section by returning to the Northern region of England to offer brief profiles of two remarkable festivals – the Stockton **Riverside Festival** and the **Festival of Mime, Dance and Visual Theatre** in Kendal – already alluded to above. Frank Wilson (profiled in more detail in Chapter 4) was Director of

Stockton-upon-Tees' Dovecot Arts Centre (and then its lottery-funded replacement, ARC) for over a decade from 1986, and as such became a key player in the mime and physical theatre ecology of the Northern Arts Region. Wilson reflects that the Riverside Festival started 'almost by accident' (Wilson, 2021), when, in the summer of 1988, he brought in an animal-free circus with its big top, largely as a reaction to the lack of activity within the Dovecot over the months of July and August. The event was popular and attracted new audiences and so from this moment Wilson began to develop the festival dimensions of his work both within and outwith the Dovecot. However, Wilson stresses that:

> The Festival was very much for me a continuation of the kind of work I was interested in. In some cases, it was a continuation of the same artists – companies like Natural Theatre and others who had made indoor work for me also offered work outdoors as well. Another example was Gob Squad, and programming *Super Night Shot* enabled me to do that thing of literally bringing the festival into the building, and it was hilariously successful when they went off into the town centres of Stockton and Middlesbrough. They hit McDonalds and other fast food places and had surreal conversations with typical Stocktonians. Absolutely fantastic.
>
> *(Ibid.)*

The Riverside Festival did not simply please the funders and bring in spectators, but it also allowed him to continue programming the work he loved – mime, physical theatre and dance – but on a larger and more ambitious scale. Wilson ruefully noted that audiences for this work 'remained stubbornly small' (Ibid.) in the Dovecot theatre itself. The Festival clearly allowed him to expand his programming repertoire into work at scale, into new circus and street theatre. Wilson recalls 'a light bulb moment was when IOU's *Journey of the Tree Man* played to an aggregate outside audience of 800+ despite being wordless and surreal' (Ibid.). After briefly working at the newly opened ARC, and before it went dark for nearly two years due to funding cuts, Wilson left to start up his own independent company, Event International and continued to run the Riverside Festival until stepping down in 2012. The Festival, however, continues and is, at the time we write, publicising its plans for 2022.

As with Spalding, Wilson's combination of staying power, curatorial imagination and energy has made him a vital figure in developing, promoting and sustaining this broad range of non-text-based theatre forms through the vehicle of both a building-based art centre and a (largely) outdoor festival on Teesside. He ended our conversation by reflecting:

> I cannot stress enough it was actually wonderful for me to get into the festival world. I've done so much traveling, met so many wonderful people, and got an MBE for services to festival arts in the North East. I don't regret a moment of it.
>
> *(Ibid.)*

76 Economies of mime and physical theatre

We conclude this section on festivals by considering what, in the vernacular of the day, was often known as the 'Kendal Mime Festival'. In a different way from LIMF, the Mime, Dance and Visual Theatre festivals hosted and curated by the Brewery Arts Centre in Kendal are almost as extraordinary an achievement as the London event. If running a mime festival in one of the world's great capital cities is not totally surprising, organising its equivalent in a small market town in the English Lake District is possibly more remarkable. In terms of dedicated and passionate curatorial teams, if LIMF had Lannaghan and Seelig, the Brewery had Pat Keysell, Deborah Barnard and Alicyn Marr.

Keysell (who also features in Chapters 2 and 7) was one of the first mime animateurs in the UK and from 1982 worked at the Brewery Arts Centre. Employed on Arts Council funding through Northern Arts, Keysell had a strong outreach role in Cumbria but was also instrumental in bringing mime performances to the Brewery and organised the first festival there in 1982/1983. Barnard had graduated from the Charlotte Mason Teacher Training College – just up the road from Kendal – in 1984 and became Keysell's 'assistant' later that year. She recalls:

> As a student I had joined the mime group at the Brewery Arts Centre with Pat Keysell. That's how I got involved. Pat said when you finish college instead of doing your first year in education, how would you fancy doing an apprenticeship with me. And I just thought, brilliant. And that was it. I got a grant from the Arts Council of £4000 to last me for a whole year. What I didn't realize was that I was part of her succession plan and when Pat moved on, the Brewery offered me her job.
>
> *(Barnard, 2020)*

When Keysell moved to Scotland in 1986, Barnard began a job share at the Brewery with Alicyn Marr. This working partnership continued until Barnard left to join Walk the Plank Theatre Company in 1990. Although the Mime Festival became the epicentre of Barnard and Marr's working year, their labour extended across the whole of Cumbria and within the Arts Centre as a whole. Barnard remembers:

> With a brief to animate Cumbria, there were several strands to our work: from community outreach initiatives – you might be delivering a project in a school, or workshops with stroke patients in hospitals – to running public classes as well as programming the festival. We'd have to raise money for the festival as well and you'd always have X number of months in the year where you'd be going to other festivals such as the Edinburgh Festival, always trying to find the next new thing.
>
> *(Ibid.)*

Economies of mime and physical theatre 77

FIGURE 3.4 Festival of Mime, Dance, and Visual Theatre, Brewery Arts Centre, Kendal. Brochures for 1986 and 1989, by kind permission of Deborah Barnard.

Barnard shared with us festival brochures for 1986 and 1989 and scanning these we are reminded of the ambition of the programmes and the range of work performed there. Murray, then a mime and physical theatre practitioner based in Newcastle upon Tyne, attended most of the festivals during this period and participated in many of the shorter workshops. He remembers a vibrant sense of 'festivalness' and conviviality each year, with performers and spectators enjoying each other's company, especially every evening in the Brewery bar. The schedule for each festival, in addition to evening performances, was an afternoon workshop led by the company or artist who had performed typically on the previous evening. However, perhaps the key feature which defined the Brewery Festival was a week-long residential course led by practitioners of high repute and status. The presence of students

78 Economies of mime and physical theatre

signed up for these residential workshops meant that the Festival could almost guarantee a critical mass of participants present for the whole week. Of course, there were many additional visitors, either local or from across the UK. In 1986 the residential course was led by Peta Lily and David Glass, whilst in 1989 there were two such workshops led by Monika Pagneux ('Awareness through movement') and Leah Hausman with Alan Scholefield ('Melodrama: the devising and directing process'). Barnard noted that ticket sales for the festival were enhanced since, in addition to the range of professional practitioners, there would often be community performances as an integral part of the program. In this context, she recollected with pleasure that:

> One of my proudest moments was Monika Pagneux watching the Brewery Youth Mime group. We did a show called *The Big Sneeze*. It would go down really well today because it was all about contagion. There was a song 'We are the Snotties' and she loved it and kept referring to it in the workshop because of the innocence of children performing.
>
> *(Ibid.)*

In the process of programming the festival Barnard and Marr had a productive relationship with Lannaghan and Seelig at LIMF; 'we used to swap intelligence and top tips. . . . They used to come up to our festival. So it was a real two-way street' (Ibid.). We asked Barnard about companies she was particularly pleased to host at these festivals and she identified the following as significant: Faulty Optic, Théâtre de Complicité, Mime Theatre Project, Nola Rae, Adventures in Motion Pictures, Trickster, Moving Picture Mime Show, Ralf Ralf and Wissel Theatre (from Ghent in Belgium). Those companies with a greater profile would be programmed to perform in the Kendal Leisure Centre which had a much greater seating capacity than the theatre at the Brewery.

The Brewery's Festival never had the longevity of LIMF but in certain ways stands out as an exemplary beacon for the excitement that mime and physical/visual theatre could generate at that time. However, there was, unsurprisingly, some local wariness and suspicion, especially when Barnard and Marr began to programme some challenging and demanding work. She wryly encapsulates the degree of scepticism from some quarters:

> There was a lot of cynicism: hang on, hang on guys, this is Kendal, this is sheep country . . . you're not in modern London, or the metropolis of Manchester. What we managed to do well was get our local audience. They began to trust what we programmed and an appetite genuinely built up for stuff that was a little bit off-beam, or had a little bit of a physical theatre flavour. Against the odds, you know!
>
> *(Ibid.)*

For this relatively short period the 'Kendal Mime Festival' with sensitive, judicious but also daring programming seemed to find the perfect chemistry for a highly successful event. For Barnard, this was particularly a blend, or meeting point, between carefully nurtured local enthusiasm and professional practitioners from across the UK (and beyond) finding the work, the stimulation and the conviviality of a week in rural Cumbria absolutely to their liking. As well as the art and the sociability, Barnard perhaps nails the pragmatics of its success in this way:

> People wanted to stay for the whole week . . . it was brilliant because the Brewery had a youth hostel right on site. So it could be as cheap as chips and folks used to turn up in camper vans and stayed in the car park. We didn't quite anticipate the number of artists who actually wanted to be there. It was a great environment, and the bar afterwards was great fun. You got to meet the artists because it was small. It wasn't London where people scatter at the end of an evening.
>
> *(Ibid.)*

Festival reflections

Festivals became a significant and increasingly popular feature of the cultural landscape in the 1980s and 1990s, continuing unabated into the twenty-first century. This section has, for obvious reasons, focused upon those with an explicit bent towards mime and physical theatre, but the festival as phenomenon begins to span most art forms during this period. At its most unsophisticated the festival is merely a rather crude marketing device constructed in the hope of making a collection of performances appear more attractive and eye-catching than they would do if promoted singly. As we have observed, the semiotics of 'festival' suggest a gathering of people and events with a sufficient degree of (consciously) shared interests and enthusiasms, and always – whether born out or not – with more than a hint of sociability and conviviality in prospect. There is not, however, an in-principle contradiction between festivals satisfying commercial interests, congenial cordiality and aesthetic purpose, but it remains productive to identify the dominant driver behind any one event.

An obvious and explicit omission in this account is the Edinburgh Fringe (Festival) which, in any given year, will contain multiple examples of physical and visual theatre work from all over the world. We have deliberately omitted an account of the Edinburgh phenomenon, not because it is unimportant, but since it is too huge, multifaceted and international to be examined at any level of productive detail in this chapter. The Edinburgh Fringe has its own ecology, but serves a useful function in providing an accessible showcase for small companies, not necessarily selected for a more focused mime festival.

Moreover, for similar reasons and given the purview of this book, we have not written about other European festivals but should note, however, that with almost every new issue of *MAGazine/Total Theatre* notices and reports appeared about mime and physical theatre festivals in France, Germany, Holland and Italy, for example, during the period under investigation. In conclusion, as a rhetorical addendum, we would suggest that there are other projects which never sign themselves as 'festivals' but which possess many of the qualities we have identified earlier. The most resonant examples of this phenomenon are, perhaps, the wide-ranging events (symposia, conferences, seminars, performances and laboratories; see Chapters 4 and 6) organised by Richard Gough and Judie Christie for the Centre for Performance Research (CPR), often in Aberystwyth and other Welsh towns and cities. In these, alongside discursive educational activities and performances, the celebratory conviviality of eating and drinking together has always been a dynamic and crucial element of such projects.

After-words

This chapter has sought to identify the main institutional mechanisms – cultural, economic, social and relational – which supported or inhibited the growth of these art forms in our period. These forces in often explicit, but sometimes oblique ways, began to construct an infrastructure – the conditions of invention, production and reception – for modern mime and physical theatre as they began to grow in the UK from the late 1970s until the turn of the century. Our next chapter drills down into these developments in the English regions, Scotland, Wales and Northern Ireland.

4

MIME AND PHYSICAL THEATRE BEYOND THE CENTRE

A detailed factual inventory of unfolding mime and physical theatre events and structures over this 30-year period could only be contained within a volume of encyclopaedic proportions. This chapter attempts to provide a *sense* of the myriad and multiple activities in the English regions (with a more detailed profile of the Northern Region), Scotland, Wales and Northern Ireland as they grew, morphed, mutated and declined over the period covered by our volume. As in other chapters, our sources here have been a blend of found material from publications (journals, reports, policy documents, books and articles) and the accounts of certain key players whose voices and stories seemed crucial to us right from the initial stages of planning and imagining the book. These voices have provided rich – and sometimes surprising – insights into the four geographical and performance landscapes of the four countries which constitute the UK. Accounts from these figures are extensive, generous and thoughtful, but they can never tell the complete or whole story. And neither can we. So this chapter blends detailed information with speculation, informed generalisations, personal reflections, anecdotes and tentative conclusions. It is neither encyclopaedic nor is it an inventory, rather a collection of fragments which together, we believe, offer a strong and grounded *feel* or *sense* of these landscapes and these times.

Mime and physical theatre in the English regions

By the late 1980s, structures enabling the making, teaching and performing of modern mime and physical theatre – were beginning to be embedded in the English regions, but in a geographically disparate and unequal way. By the mid-1990s evidence suggests that these events were beginning to reach a peak and it is the years between 1992 and 1994 which are the focus of this section. Although the 1980s witnessed selective and limited funding of certain key artists and companies,

DOI: 10.4324/9780429330209-4

82 Mime & physical theatre beyond the centre

and the development of a range of support and facilitating structures, it was a period of imminence, a decade of possibility and promise. Paradoxically, from the early 1980s to the arrival of a Labour Government in 1997, this was also a period of wide-ranging cuts to arts funding and to local government. These, of course, affected Scotland, Wales and Northern Ireland as much as they did England. It is difficult, however, to generalise about the effects of these losses in local and national spending for mime and physical theatre. On the one hand, this work was inevitably framed by the Thatcherite economic climate and the difficulties it generated for all artists, but, on the other, the groundswell of excitement and enthusiasm for these practices meant that much more financial support was being made available than in the past. Nonetheless, in relation to those theatre companies, usually housed in permanent buildings, and occupying the text-based mainstream of the theatre landscape, these budgets remained small by comparison.

Much of the evidence which furnishes this section, and indeed the whole chapter, has been extracted from issues of *Total Theatre*, as well as interviews and official reports. Even a light scanning of the pages of this journal suggests hectic activity amongst 'young' companies, dozens and dozens of venues booking this work[1] – although not on a regular and systematic basis – and an ever-increasing array of festivals, conferences, training workshops and forums where these practices were relentlessly discussed and feverishly – sometimes angrily – debated. The life of many companies was short-lived; starting up and disappearing a few years later. However, a significant number of practitioners worked across several companies, exchanges enabled less by formal auditioning and more by shared training experiences and social networks. One might be forgiven for feeling that by the mid-1990s mime and physical theatre had indeed successfully stormed the citadel of text-based drama across the UK and that the spoken word was in retreat. Our point here is that, for all the evidence of burgeoning activity during this period, the practices of mime and physical theatre remained largely on the fringes of the mainstream. In so far as this work implicitly or explicitly represented an 'assault' on the formal word-bound conservatism of most professional theatre, this was how many artists and companies wanted it. For many companies and artists there was a self-conscious and palpable sense of working against the grain of what were perceived to be the hegemonic and exclusionary conventions of a lifeless, bodily inert, text-based theatre. Existing in the margins, however, also often meant surviving on tiny and sporadic grants, signing on and off with various unemployment and social security benefits and living a life of considerable financial insecurity and precarity.

---

1 For most of the smaller venues – studio theatres, art and community centres, pub theatres – booking a show with a company whose profile was modest usually meant offering a box office split with the groups in question. Sometimes, if venues were in receipt of RAA/RAB grants, a modest fee of – for example – £200/£300 might be given. For the larger and better established companies this might be a significantly higher figure.

Rowan Tolley, mime animateur in Yorkshire and Humberside put it like this in a profile of the region where he was working in 1992/1993:

> You try to survive while you battle against the pressures, the deadlines and the cold bare realities of the 'arts' world. . . . The 'Total Theatre' sector exists through the enthusiasm of the performers dedicated to their work. There is no doubt that the biggest subsidy for the work comes from the artists involved – underpaid and undervalued. But it can be wonderful work, immensely satisfying and challenging.
>
> *(Tolley, 1993: 12)*

A salutary postscript – and a sign of the times – to Tolley's reflections comes in the same issue of *Total Theatre* where Mileva Drljaca of Yorkshire and Humberside Arts notes that 'Rowan Tolley's post came to an end prematurely due to massive overspends in one of the key partner local authorities' (1993: 13). One imagines that Tolley wrote and filed his article before Drljaca. However, the larger, better established companies such as Théâtre de Complicité, Trestle, David Glass Ensemble, Kaboodle, Black Mime Theatre, IOU, Forkbeard Fantasy and The Right Size were, to an extent, exceptions to this pattern, at least for certain time-limited periods when they received three-year franchise funding (see *Total Theatre*, 1994, Volume 6, No 2: 22.).

What follows offers a snapshot of the landscape for supporting, making, performing and debating mime and physical theatre during the middle period of our timelines within the English regions. Here, we consider places, people, venues, touring, animateurs and the interventions and initiatives from some of the RAAs and RABs. A more detailed profile of the Northern Region follows along with separate sections on Scotland, Wales and Northern Ireland.

RAA/RAB initiatives and profiles

As we have noted in Chapter 3, the Regional Arts Associations (RAAs), first established in the 1950s, were replaced in 1990 by Regional Arts Boards (RABs), following the Wilding Report of 1989. This altered the boundaries of some of the RAAs and reduced their overall number from 12 to 10. It also changed the funding mechanisms for the newly formed RABs, making them more directly accountable to the central Arts Council in London. By the early 1990s, most of the RABs would have had designated Dance and Mime officers with varying responsibilities and interest in supporting and developing mime and physical theatre. When mime was moved to the Arts Council's Drama Department in 1989/1990 it took some years for all the RABs to follow suit.

Monitoring the pages of *Total Theatre* from the late 1980s to the mid/late 1990s we can identify particular initiatives from – or within – Yorkshire and Humberside Arts, Southern Arts, South East Arts, South West Arts, West Midlands Arts and

84 Mime & physical theatre beyond the centre

North West Arts in particular. As a product of fruitful and imaginative collaboration between venues, companies, artists and funders certain specific places became hubs of activity: Liverpool, Coventry, Dartington, Bristol, London and Kendal are just some examples. Northern Arts was also significant in its championing of mime and physical theatre, but we deal with this RAB in a separate profile below. Here, under 'Fragments from the regions' we provide examples of mime and physical theatre activities which offer a sense of the wide-ranging events that were taking place during this period. The selection of these regions also should not suggest that mime and physical theatre activities and support structures were absent in other parts of the UK.

Fragments from the Regions (1): North West Arts

- Resident companies: Talking Pictures, Doo Cot, Third Estate (Manchester); Loudmouth, Kaboodle, Rejects Revenge (Merseyside).
- Liverpool's Unity Theatre, under the artistic leadership of Graeme Phillips, actively promotes physical theatre, 'a cornerstone of our programme' (Phillips, 1992: 10)
- The North West Circus Network supports circus practitioners through teaching or play-related activity from Merseyside through Great Manchester to West Yorkshire.
- Physical State International (Manchester), under the direction of Rivka Rubin, offers a wide range of training workshops in dance, movement, (physical) theatre and multi-disciplinary practices.
- Liverpool's Everyman Hope Street Actor's Centre offers workshops and classes. It 'has opened people's eyes to the vast horizons beyond the sanctity of the text and cerebral interpretation' (Phillips, 1992: 10).
- *Moving into Performance*: European Mime and Physical Theatre workshop Symposium (Manchester, September 1994). A hugely ambitious event organised by MAG/Total Theatre with Manchester Metropolitan University School of Theatre and the European Mime Federation. Explored more fully in MAG section, Chapter 3.
- Mime and Physical Theatre residency (March 1996) organised by The Unity Theatre with Hope Street Actor's Centre, Liverpool Institute of the Performing Arts (LIPA), Liverpool John Moores University and local arts officers and teachers. Workshops, discussions and performances by Commotion, Rejects Revenge, John Wright, Andrew Dawson and Sally Cook.
- *Chasing Shadows* workshops and *Mind the Gaps* conference organised by the Centre for Performance Research (CPR) and Lancaster University (July/ August 1994).
- Venues include: Burnley Mechanics, Leigh Drama Centre, Alsager Arts Centre, Blue Coats Arts Centre, Priestley College, Unity Theatre, Arden School of Theatre.

Fragments from the regions (2): South West Arts

- Dartington College of Arts (1961–2010), Totnes. Within the performing arts this specialist college offered degree-level programmes and particularly generated work in physical and dance theatre and live/performance art (see Chapter 6). Also, the ground-breaking dance summer schools of the 1980s.
- John Lee appointed Mime in Residence (October 1988-April 1989). With special emphasis on the Fool, Lee was based at the Exeter and Devon Arts Centre, but worked across the region. Funded by SW Arts and the Arts Council.
- Chris Harris: Lecoq trained clown, based in Bristol and toured in the 1970s and 1980s.
- South West Festival of New Mime and Circus Theatre. (April 1989)
- Bristol circus schools: following the demise of Fooltime, Bim Mason and Helen Crocker open Circomedia in 1994. (Murray and Keefe, 2016: 193–6)
- Resident companies: Kneehigh (1980–2020), Kaos, Mummer&Dada (1985–1989), Footsbarn (1971–1984)
- Exeter, Bristol and Plymouth universities all providing theatre degrees with elements of practice through movement and physical theatre
- Dartington Theatre Papers, now part of the University of Exeter Digital Archives, edited by Peter Hulton (ex-Director of Theatre and Principal at Dartington College of Arts and Research Fellow at the University of Exeter). The series between 1977 and 1984 reflects, in its selection of subject matter, an increasing preoccupation with body and movement in theatre making.
- Physical theatre performance forum. First meeting in Exeter, 1993.
- Venues include: Merlin Theatre (Frome), Brewhouse Arts Centre (Taunton), Dartington Hall (Totnes), Barbican Theatre (Plymouth), Stert Arts Centre (Liskeard), Falmouth Arts Centre, The Acorn (Penzance), St Austell Arts Centre, Truro arts Centre, Bridgewater Arts Centre.

Fragments from the regions (3): Southern Arts

- Mime Skills Exchange (September 1993) hosted by Jonathan Kay in Winchester.
- Resident companies: Attic Theatre, Bouge-De-La, Jane Watson and Company
- Venues include: Salisbury Playhouse, Oxford Playhouse, Havant Arts Centre, Theatre Royal Winchester, Pegasus Theatre (Oxford)
- Southern Arts increases funding for mime in 1992/1993 to include support for Black Mime Theatre, Jonathan Kay, The Right Size and Jane Watson and Company.

86 Mime & physical theatre beyond the centre

- *Larger than Life* mime and physical theatre festival with work performed in Oxford, Poole, Salisbury, Swindon and Plymouth (1991/1992).
- *Talking Mime*, day conference to raise awareness of mime and physical theatre with performance from The Right Size in association with Salisbury Playhouse and Salisbury college of Performing Arts (March 1993)

Fragments from the regions (4): South East Arts

- *Beyond Words* Mime Festival at the Hawth Arts Centre in Crawley (November 1992)
- Mime Development Forum meeting at the Hawth (May 1993). South East Arts pledges to appoint a/ a mime development worker, b/ fund two mime festivals and c/ fund strategic residencies in schools and the wider community.
- David Glass Ensemble residency (Early 1990s)
- Resident companies: In Toto, Bodily Functions
- Venues include: Horsham Arts Centre, Hawth, Trinity Arts Centre (Tonbridge Wells), Old Town Hall (Staines), Northbrook Theatre (Worthing), Zap Club (Brighton), Gardner Arts Centre (Brighton)
- MAG 'Critical Practice' seminar (Hawth, November 1993).
- Travelling Mime Roadshow (July 1994). A three-week tour of mime across Surrey, Sussex and Kent with Trestle, Facepack and Phil Gunderson.
- *Voices Off* – Festival of Mime, Dance and Physical Theatre (March 1994), Trinity Arts Centre.
- Tom Leabhart residency in Lewes (May 1995), organised by Bodily Functions (Phil Gunderson) and Maureen Salmon, Dance and Mime officer for SE Arts.
- SE Arts is assembling funds to support creative work around mime and physical theatre in three phases: research and development, production and major investment (Summer 1996).

Fragments from the regions (5): Yorkshire and Humberside Arts

- Mime and Physical Theatre Forum meeting (April 1993) discusses promotion of work and considers making a video of practices from artists and companies in the region. Also discusses Birmingham *Women in the Arts* Symposium and prepares for a presentation from Mhora Samuel (MAG) at next meeting in July 1993.

- Mime and Physical Theatre Forum re-named Live Art Forum at July 1993
- Leeds Street Theatre Festival September 1993
- Rowan Tolley. Mime animateur (1992/3)
- Practitioner networks or forums: Kirklees, Sheffield/Rotherham, Yorkshire Dance Centre (Leeds)
- Venues include: Square Chapel Arts Centre (Halifax), Alhambra Studio (Bradford), Huddersfield Art Gallery, York Arts Centre, Spring Street Theatre (Hull), Ferens Art Gallery (Hull)

Fragments from the regions (6): West Midlands Arts

- Regional companies/artists: Snarling Beasties, Triangle (Carran Waterfield), Metaphysique (Jane Sutcliffe), Stan's Cafe, Foursight, Pathways, Talking Birds, Bare Essentials, Talking Pictures, Mick Wall.
- MAC (Midlands Art Centre, Birmingham), under the artistic leadership of Dorothy Wilson, promotes mime work and has its own mini festival (Moving Parts) which includes work from the London Mime Festival. Jane Sutcliffe is based at MAC and offers regular mime classes.
- Lesley Moss is appointed as mime animateur in Coventry at the end of the 1980s.
- Geoff Buckley (teacher and performer) based in Leamington Spa.
- Coventry Centre for the Performing Arts (CCPA) offers a series of regular workshops and residencies co-ordinated by Mark Evans, with companies such as: Volcano Theatre, Black Mime Theatre, Trestle, Théâtre de Complicité, Julian Crouch, Frantic Assembly, Snarling Beasties, David Gaines (Moving Picture Mime Show).
- CCPA offers training courses (HND and BA) that include modules in mime, movement, mask-work and a physical theatre production led by members of Volcano Theatre.
- Warwick Arts Centre programmes physical theatre productions by a range of international, national and regional companies including Volcano, Frantic Assembly and DV8.
- Jac Wilkinson appointed as Education Officer at Warwick Arts Centre and employed by MAG to write a number of reports including 'Guide to Mime in Education', which features several Midlands case studies.
- In 1994, Coventry hosts Odin Teatret's first whole company visit to England for a residency that includes performances, workshops, lecture demonstrations and panel events at the Belgrade Theatre, CCPA and Warwick Arts Centre.

88 Mime & physical theatre beyond the centre

- Teatr Biuro Podróży, a physical theatre company from Poznań in Poland perform Carmen Funebre in Coventry in the mid-1990s and are commissioned to create a new version of the Mystery Plays for the Millennium in 2000.
- Venues include: MAC (Birmingham), Arena Theatre (Wolverhampton), Warwick Arts Centre and Belgrade Studio (Coventry).

The Northern Region – a profile in time

We offer here a more in-depth case study of this region, which until 1990 was covered administratively by the Northern Arts Association and then by the Northern Arts Board (henceforward, simply Northern Arts). As we have indicated earlier, this change signalled an adjustment in the relationship to the Arts Council nationally and, in some cases, a re-drawing of the geographical boundaries of these constituencies. In 1990 Northern Arts lost Cumbria to North West Arts leaving Northumberland, County Durham, Tyneside, Teesside and Wearside within its geographical and cultural portfolio. Simon Murray lived and worked as a mime and physical theatre practitioner/teacher from a base in Newcastle upon Tyne during much of the period covered by this book and thus experienced first-hand the realities of being part of a network of performance makers in the Northern Arts region. Authorial investment in this particular narrative apart, the Northern Arts region from the mid-1980s to the end of our period can lay claim to have been particularly fertile ground for nurturing and enabling the practices of mime and physical theatre.

As we have already noted (Chapter 3), in 1985 Susanne Burns became the first Regional Arts Association dance officer outwith London. In fact, her official title was 'Assistant Dance and Mime Officer', and as had been the case previously within the national Arts Council itself, dance was positioned within the much larger – and better funded – Music Department at Northern Arts. Burns notes that when she arrived the total budget for dance and mime was around £60,000. Mime was only added to her job title, she suggests, since the region possessed the first mime animateur in the country at that time: Pat Keysell at the Brewery Arts Centre in Kendal (Cumbria). Burns moved on from Northern Arts in 1988/1989 for freelance and other work, but during her time in the post made a significant impact on developing what she chooses to call an 'ecology' for and of mime in the second half of the 1980s. Burns identified her role as being proactive rather than simply responding to requests and proposals as they came in. In our conversation in 2020, she reflected that what she did was 'put the right people in the room at the right time' (Burns, 2020). And by the 'right' people she was referring to artists, educators and venue managers/directors. From Murray's recollection, this was an unduly modest description of the energetic and imaginative role played by Burns. Alongside, but in conversation with, spaces full of the 'right people at the right time',

RAA officers then had art form panels of advisors who not only would provide feedback on performances, but would also be accomplices in discussing strategy and policy. Today these arrangements no longer exist, but then they offered a sense of constructing a shared project with the arts officer in question. Such projects felt informed not simply by the 'expert' personnel employed by the arts boards, but by a range of interested parties, all with an investment in promoting and championing the work in question. Today we might label such people as 'stakeholders'!

During the period of Burns' time at Northern Arts the constituency was both very rural (Cumbria, Northumberland and parts of County Durham) and highly urban and industrial – or rather declining industrial – as in Tyneside, Wearside and Teesside. However, across these diverse areas, the region was blessed with a significant number of arts venues and community centres that hosted theatre and performance activities, and these became a communicative network of touring locations for mime, dance, music and more mainstream theatres. The most significant of these were: the Dovecot Arts Centre (Stockton upon Tees), Queen's Hall (Hexham), Gulbenkian Studio Theatre (Newcastle), Live Theatre (Newcastle), Brewery Arts Centre (Kendal), The Customs House (South Shields), Stanwix Art Centre (Carlisle) and the Rosehill Theatre (Whitehaven). Although all these venues were independent of each other and conducted their own programmes, there would often be collaboration between many of them to form a *de facto* touring circuit for mime and, later, physical theatre companies. Penny McPhillips, Director of the Gulbenkian Studio in Newcastle chaired a touring group of venue directors/promoters to consider and plan small tours of the work they considered to be attractive and suitable. Burns remembers:

> I would bring to that touring working group the product that I felt that we could afford and they would make decisions. So it was actually those promoters who were deciding to take, for example, Gambolling Guizers, David [Glass], Trestle.
>
> *(Burns, 2020)*

We asked Burns why there was an interest around this time in booking mime companies, and she responded:

> It was accessible. It was storytelling. You know, at that point I think dance was seen as being very abstract and this work was telling stories, albeit physically. It was about access. It was about the fact that they knew they would get an audience for it. Just like they knew that they would get an audience for Phoenix Dance Company because it was five guys and they were incredibly acrobatic.
>
> *(Ibid.)*

There is an interesting interrelationship here between the size of most of these venues – and hence their economics – and the scale of work that could be brought

90 Mime & physical theatre beyond the centre

in. Moreover, some of these spaces did not have sprung floors and hence could not safely programme dance. Many of the venues identified earlier only had seating capacities of between 100 and 150 and hence calculations on budgets and income streams were gauged on the relationship between the potential sale of tickets and the size and ambitions of productions and their casts. When, for example, David Glass's company or Théâtre de Complicité became ensembles in the early 1990s with casts of between five to ten performers they had become too big and too costly to be engaged by these small art centres. Hence, by the late 1980s, companies performing or touring into the region either were often solo artists or had minimal casts of two or three. Touring schedules published in *Total Theatre* around this time, for example, seem only to identify Attic Theatre, Les Bubb, Mark Saunders, John Mowat and Nola Rae – in addition to those artists identified earlier.

As part of her strategy for mime and dance, Burns was keen to support and engineer projects where selected artists built connections with certain venues, and their constituencies, beyond one-off performances. These took the form of residencies, usually with a strong educational and training dimension to them, and where sometimes the artists devised, rehearsed and premiered a new work at the venue in question. These residencies seemed to be very much a 'child of the time', and helped to shape a connection and degree of loyalty between companies and parts of the region which would not otherwise have been the case. For Burns, it was also a matter of economics and better value for money. Peta Lily, David Glass and the Gambolling Guizers all had a regular presence in the region through such residencies. In this way the Guizers had a relationship with the Dovecot Arts in Stockton through educational activities on Teesside, David Glass worked on and premiered *Solaris* at the Gulbenkian Studio and Peta Lily did likewise with her solo performance of *Piaf* at Stanwix Theatre in Carlisle. From the early 1990s (until 2016), Théâtre Sans Frontières, was based at the Queen's Hall Arts Centre in Hexham. The Brewery Arts Centre's International Mime Festival (see Chapter 3), enthusiastically supported by the Centre's Director, Anne Pierson, in the mid-1980s, regularly incorporated artists' short teaching residencies (including, for example: John Wright, Frankie Armstrong, Rick Zoltowski, Gerry Flanagan, Monika Pagneux, and Trickster) as part of its annual programme.

Another dimension to her work as an officer with Northern Arts – and actively continued by one of her successors, Mark Mulqueen, in the 1990s – was to build up the skills and experience base of emerging mime and physical theatre artists living and working within the region. In addition to offering grants for individuals to participate in conferences and training workshops outwith the region – for example at the annual International Workshop Festival, often in London – Northern Arts helped to fund a residency for David Glass in Peterlee (County Durham) in 1989.

We spoke at length with Frank Wilson, who began working at the Dovecot Arts Centre in 1986. Wilson collaborated productively and enthusiastically with both Burns and Mulqueen in championing this work and later developed the highly successful Riverside outdoor festival in Stockton (see Chapter 3). The Dovecot had been adapted into an arts centre with a 120 (retractable) seated theatre from an old

YMCA building. The theatre was the original gymnasium and above was a small bar where poetry readings and scratch nights occurred and, above that a workshop and making space. Stockton Borough Council and the Arts Council were the main institutional funders and at first Wilson was one of three members of a skeleton staff but then became Artistic Director in October 1986. He had done an English degree at Leeds University, initially aspired to be a playwright, but at the same time had been very influenced and impressed by the work of Impact Theatre Cooperative[2] and the Pip Simmons Theatre Group[3]. We asked what prompted him to lose interest in word-based theatre.

> I think partly it was exposure to the very visual and impactful work of Pip Simmons and later to the early work of Impact themselves. And partly, I suppose, disappointment with the kind of *cul-de-sac* I had put myself into by wanting to be a playwright. I wasn't making any headway and was not impressed by the work of my contemporaries quite honestly. While I was writing I was thinking about stage direction more than the text because I was interested in the visual possibilities of theatre.
>
> *(Wilson, 2021)*

Wilson and the Dovecot were key players in the small-scale touring jigsaw within the Northern Arts region for ten years between 1986 and 1996. We have elaborated on festivals in Chapter 3, but here it is important to note the relationship between the London International Mime Festival (LIMF) and productions which would tour in the Northern Arts region (and, of course, others too). With the support of Burns and Mulqueen, and as Wilson's appetite for programming mime and physical/visual theatre increased, he would spend time at LIMF, the Brewery and the Edinburgh festivals to check out artists whom he could afford and whose work appealed and suited this small theatre space. The touring traffic from LIMF to the Dovecot and other venues in the region became increasingly significant. By the early 1990s Wilson was visiting selected European festivals to spot work which appealed to him for the Riverside Festival. In the period until 1996, in addition to Glass, Lily, Trestle and the Gambolling Guizers, Wilson also programmed companies such as The Gob Squad, Goat Island, Forkbeard Fantasy, Splinter Group, Wall Street Productions, Kneehigh, Théâtre Sans Frontières (TSF) and, within the realm of disability arts, Candoco, Graeae and Mind the Gap.

---

2 Impact Theatre existed between 1979 and 1986 and was based in Leeds. Its experimental work melded the languages of the visual, the physical, text and live art. The Company's final performance, *The Carrier Frequency*, (1985) has assumed almost mythic status in the landscape of visual and physical performance.

3 The Pip Simmons Theatre Group was formed in 1968. Initially based in London, much of its devised experimental work was made and performed in mainland Europe, especially in Holland. The company's practice specialised in highly physical performance and often fused rock music with agit prop techniques to generate a visceral and immersive experience for audiences.

92 Mime & physical theatre beyond the centre

From around 1990 it was felt that larger premises were needed and a major National Lottery bid was assembled. The original Dovecot was demolished in 1996 and with the planned new build two and half times larger, the ARC was completed in 1999, four months late and with a massive capital budget overspend. With no cash in the bank and not enough funding to support a programme or staff to run the building, the ARC closed in 2000 and remained dark until 2002. Wilson left in 1999 and set up his own dedicated outdoor performing arts event company which he ran and programmed until 2012.

We provide this brief snapshot profile of Frank Wilson and the Dovecot in the late 1980s into the 1990s, as it offers a sense of the cultural currents and force fields which contributed to the conditions of invention and public performance (and reception) of mime and physical theatre at that time. Wilson's journey into enabling and promoting these practices was both singular but also part of a wider 'structure of feeling(s)' (see Chapter 3) of that moment. The story of ARC and its Lottery funding felt then – and now – like a parable for the times: huge amounts of money for bricks and mortar or equipment, but little or nothing to pay for recurring overheads, programming budgets and staff costs. Part of the rationale behind Lottery funding at this time was that better facilities could mean higher ticket prices, attract audiences and thereby raise sponsorship. Beyond this, the story of the Dovecot also stands in for the larger narrative of the decline of the small-scale touring network, not only in the Northern Region but across the UK as a whole. This was regularly evidenced in many of our interviews. Even if audiences for mime remained small, venues like the Dovecot offered a stage for emerging companies and, with a bit of touring subsidy, the finances, one must assume, just about stacked up. When the original Dovecot was replaced by the ARC with its 450-seat theatre the economics became very different. Wilson reflects:

> Frankly, the ARC was built on the strength of my success at running the Dovecot and the Riverside festival, which was attracting huge audiences – single audiences in 10s of thousands. But the economics of putting on the work changed quite radically when you go from 120 seats to 450 . . . it's no longer a question of losing 100 quid on a production which doesn't quite cut the mustard with the audience, because now it's losing potentially thousands as you've scaled up the programme.
>
> *(Wilson, 2021)*

Whilst middle-scale 400–500 seater venues offered the better-established companies, with larger casts and higher fees, an opportunity to perform their work, it was a big step up for the smaller ones since they were now unlikely to be offered two nights. The financial risk for both the company and the venue was substantially higher as well. Ironically, the upgrading, or replacement, of small venues (by larger and flashier ones) led to their own decline. Towards the end of our conversation, Wilson looked back to the days when he ran the Dovecot:

The region was exciting and unusual – a number of quite small venues actually had a commitment to this innovative, not for everyone, strand of work. We were going over to Kendall for a meeting at the Brewery Arts Centre, the Queen's Hall in Hexham, or the Darlington Arts Centre and formed a fantastically strong network. We were mutually supportive and actually it wasn't happening in Newcastle, Sunderland or Middlesbrough. It was happening in these kind of smaller towns. It almost feels in hindsight that in the three years from when the Dovecot closed in '96 and ARC opened in '99 the network no longer seemed to exist.

(Ibid.)

The trajectory of Wilson's time at the Dovecot/ARC and as director of a very ambitious festival, is a revealing and illustrative one for our narrative.

In addition to bringing in productions from other parts of the UK, and, occasionally, abroad, there were a number of smaller groups of varying longevity with a working base in the Northern region, whose work broadly fitted the profile of mime and physical theatre. From the mid/late 1980s 'indigenous' companies, with varying theatrical styles, training legacies, audiences and aspirations, included: Splinter Group Mime, Slap, Eezy Trapeze, Puppets and People, Wyrd Arts, Wall Street Productions, Jack Drum, Really Deep Company, Dodgy Clutch, the Bruvers, Cleveland Theatre Company (CTC) and Théâtre Sans Frontières (TSF). In addition to these small groups there were the 'County Companies', five larger and better-funded organisations based in different parts of the region, but usually with little explicit interest or claim to engage with physical or visual dramaturgies. However, the distinctions and boundaries were sometime fluid, as was the case with, for example, Northern Stage and CTC. Northern Stage became the resident company based in Newcastle upon Tyne's Playhouse Theatre and Gulbenkian Studio in the late 1980s. Initially working on the traditional repertory model, with the appointment of Artistic Director, Alan Lyddiard, in the early 1990s the company aspired to become an ensemble of actors in the mould of the great European theatres and to make and promote work within the frame of our book. Two of Northern Stage's most successful productions in the 1990s – *Animal Farm* and *Clockwork Orange* – were firmly within a physical theatre tradition but it hosted performances from the companies of Peter Brook and Lev Dodin, as well as Théâtre de Complicité, DV8, Volcano, the Market Theatre of Johannesburg, Robert Lepage's company, Ex Machina and Yukio Ninagawa. CTC metamorphosed from being Teesside's 'county company' to one that only made theatre for young people, and within this trajectory, artistic director, Paul Harman, particularly embraced physical approaches to acting and highly visual performance styles. At one point, Harman brought in Simon Murray as an actor with a strong disposition towards and skill base in mime and physical performance. Murray performed in intensely physical productions of *The Odyssey* and *The Rime of the Ancient Mariner* and ran training sessions with the other actors. As an indication of this commitment, Harman invited Murray to chair the CTC board for several years in the mid-1990s

94 Mime & physical theatre beyond the centre

Splinter Group was co-founded as a collective in 1985 by Murray with actors, Anna-Marya Tompa and Joy Lawson. In the early 1990s, Murray established a new company called Wall Street Productions for a physical theatre version of Herman Melville's short story, *Bartleby* with textual adaptation by writer and dramatist, Lee Hall. *Bartleby* subsequently toured across the UK and received small project and touring grants from Northern Arts and the Arts Council. Murray had spent a year training with Philippe Gaulier and Monika Pagneux in Paris (1986/1987), for which he had received a grant towards his fees, and the style of work generated by both these companies reflected – although not exclusively – this experience. Dodgy Clutch and the Bruvvers all made highly visual, sometimes outdoor work, through the process of devising. The latter company, founded and led by the charismatic Mike Mould (1939–2020), was steeped in the popular political theatre traditions of Joan Littlewood at the Theatre Royal Stratford East. TSF arrived slightly later in 1991 and was set up by Sarah Kemp, John Cobb and Adrian Norman. Kemp and Cobb remain the company's artistic directors to this day[4]. The company's work is deeply rooted in the teaching of Gaulier and Pagneux and many of the actors who work with Cobb and Kemp have also been exposed to these training influences. From the 1990s to the present day TSF has become a successful and highly regarded company working from a base in Hexham's Queen's Hall Arts Centre until 2016.

After initially slow encouragement from Northern Arts, by the mid-1990s TSF began to receive some financial support in 1993 and, following advocacy from Mulqueen, a national touring grant of £12,000 from the Arts Council for its production of *Candide*. In 1994 the company was commissioned by the Brewery Arts Centre to create a new show, *Notre Dame de Paris*, for the Mime Festival of that year. The production went on to win the Northern Electric Award and it is significant to note the international nature of the Company at this juncture with a cast of performers from Britain, Japan, Spain, Germany and Brazil and choreography by Canada's Yellow Rabbit Theatre Company. By the end of the 1990s TSF work was supported by small grants from Northumberland and Cumbria County Councils and by 2001 Northern Arts' support had grown to a point where it had become a Regularly Funded Organisation (RFO).

Over the period from 1986 with the arrival of Susanne Burns, through the 1990s when Mark Mulqueen took responsibility for mime and physical theatre, the Northern Arts Region seemed to offer a supportive, complex and multi-faceted ecology for this work. Both Burns and Mulqueen saw their role as proactive and strategic, occupying positions where, within organisational and financial limitations, they could create supportive frameworks and generate thinking and discourse around strengthening the profile of mime and physical theatre in the Northern Region.

---

4 The TSF website describes its work thus: 'TSF creates a rich and diverse theatre which explores and celebrates cultural exchange. Dedicated to creating a European theatre of excellence, the company produces and tours plays by world authors in their original language. Since 1991, TSF has produced over 50 shows in English, French, German and Spanish and toured extensively to theatres, arts centres, schools and colleges throughout the UK and in recent years to festivals in Tunisia, Egypt and China. TSF is renowned for its vibrant and visually-driven productions which are made accessible to all through mime, mask, puppetry, clowning, dance and live music' (TSF: 2021).

Mime & physical theatre beyond the centre **95**

FIGURE 4.1 *Contes Mauriciens*, Théâtre Sans Frontières, 1999. Featuring Rebecca Jameson and Helen Iskander. By kind permission of Théâtre Sans Frontières.

Source: Photographer: Sarah Kemp.

A measure of this strategy was exemplified by Mulqueen's commissioning of MAG to undertake an applied research project (see Chapter 3) which would 'investigate the role, support and development of modern mime, physical theatre and visual performance with the Northern Region' (MAG, 1995). Murray, who was awarded the contract to undertake this work, and who wrote the subsequent report (published

96 Mime & physical theatre beyond the centre

in 1995), reflects that his proposals were probably too multiple and overly ambitious. A brutal but partially fair reading of the report paints a picture of artists struggling to survive and to get their work seen, of productions often being regarded as 'difficult' to promote and sell, and of uneven relationships and communications between companies and venue promoters or directors. Murray's sense of the report some 25 years on is that it provided not only an honest profile of how mime and physical theatre was being made, performed and received in the Northern Region in the mid-1990s, but also a set of observations, reflections and conclusions which might equally apply to all regions across the UK at that time. Nonetheless, that Mulqueen thought it important to commission such a report and to seek an honest discourse between artists, funders and promoters, is a measure of the seriousness with which the Northern Arts Board regarded the future sustainability of these practices.

In practice, Burns and then over a longer period of time, Mulqueen pursued a two-pronged approach which generated a variety of support structures for regionally based artists and promoters on the one hand, and which sought to encourage companies from outwith the area to bring their work into this geographically and socially diverse constituency on the other. At best, these two goals were inter-related and mutually reinforcing. This is not to suggest that the money flowed liberally into the bank accounts of venues and emerging companies, but that there was a culture of enthusiasm and interest around these practices and how best to support them. A combination of Northern Arts officers who performed as intelligent 'critical friends' to the artists they funded, a network of small-scale touring venues with some imaginatively cooperative and well informed promoter/directors, a nationally and internationally renowned mime festival at the Brewery Arts Centre in Kendal and a culture of combining educational and outreach work with professional production, all blended to help generate an environment sympathetic to mime and physical theatre. This work across the Northern Region reflected and responded to wider cultural currents across the whole of the UK, but also made a significant contribution to these force fields.

As an epigraph to this section it seems fitting to conclude with a quote from a local newspaper which perhaps encapsulates many of the attitudes, misunderstandings and difficulties which have surrounded public perceptions of mime. A short news item in Newcastle's Evening Chronicle marked Burns' appointment with Northern Arts in 1986 offering the strapline, 'Susanne doesn't say a word' and went on to inform its readers that 'Former Washington English teacher Susanne Burns is miming her way through a new job, but she is doing it for real' (Burns, 2020).

Scotland

For our profile of mime and physical theatre in Scotland we recorded conversations with four key players in this particular part of the Scottish landscape during the 1980s and 1990s: Mark Saunders, Alan Caig Wilson, Ian Cameron and Stewart Ennis. Apart from the light that these interviews shed on the macro developments of mime and physical theatre in Scotland, how each of them arrived as performers and theatre makers offers a revealing insight into the varied (and eccentric) pathways, histories and backstories not untypical of so many practitioners in this field.

The configuration of developments in Scotland during our period, unsurprisingly, follows many of the contours of what was happening in England, but breaks with these in certain significant respects. If there is a degree of singularity about the Scottish narrative it lies in the urban/rural topography of the country, the dominance of Glasgow and Edinburgh as magnets for resources and audiences, the establishment in 1991 of the Scottish Mime Forum (SMF), the role of the Edinburgh Festival, the relationship between the Royal Scottish Academy of Music and Drama (RSAMD)[5] and the pedagogy of Jacques Lecoq, and the cultural-political issues around Scottish nationhood and independence.

The Scottish Arts Council (SAC) had existed as a semi-autonomous body since 1967, but was reconstituted in 1994 following a restructuring of the Arts Council of Great Britain. Unlike in England, there were no Scottish Regional Arts Associations or Boards and so the national body in Edinburgh administered all grant arrangements and applications from across the country. Of course, city, district and regional councils also had, in varying degrees, budgets for the arts. However, most of the issues facing emerging mime and physical theatre artists in Scotland were very similar to those in any other parts of the UK: resources/funding; recognition in terms of both the art forms more generally and, more specifically, Scottish companies and their output; relations with promoters; and attitudes towards these practices not only from more mainstream and text-based companies but also from groups with a palpable agenda of agitprop and political theatre. From the accounts of our interviewees, disinterest, disdain and suspicion from other theatre constituencies about *mime* – and indeed *physical theatre* – as signposts or descriptors of apparently trite, fey and politically lightweight theatre practices seemed particularly in evidence in Scotland during the 1980s and early 1990s.

We spoke with Caig Wilson and Cameron together, since their working lives as practitioners in Scotland had overlapped and intertwined over a ten-year period and they remained good friends. Caig Wilson had spent a year with Lecoq in 1984/1985 and, significantly, received a SAC bursary to study in Paris. In his early exposure to mime we noted that he had seen the ubiquitous figure of Julian Chagrin (see Chapter 2) perform at Stirling University. Caig Wilson commented 'I was astonished by what he was letting me see. I was having visions when I was watching him. And I thought, this is great' (Caig Wilson, 2021). Of his early life, Cameron said:

> I went to art college to study painting. Which I still do. I had not imagined I'd go into theatre at all. But I had seen the film *Les Enfants du Paradis*[6] and loved the way that Jean-Louis Barrault moved. I said, I want to move like

5 The Royal Scottish Academy of Music and Drama (RSAMD) was renamed the Royal Conservatoire of Scotland (RCS) in 2011, and is a conservatoire of dance, drama, music and film in the centre of Glasgow.

6 *Les Enfants du Paradis* is an iconic film made in occupied France during the Second World War and directed by Marcel Carné. It featured Decroux-trained mime, Jean Louis Barrault, as Baptiste Deburau. Decroux himself also acted in the film. The film has often been claimed to be one of the greatest movies of all time.

that. Some friends said there is someone called Desmond Jones who is offering classes. This was not long after Desmond had come back from studying with Decroux so he was teaching pure classical mime at that time. He changed later on. So I studied with him over a period of three years.

(Cameron, 2021)

Cameron and Caig Wilson moved (separately) to Scotland in the mid- to late 1980s and both remarked on the lack of mime and physical theatre activity at the time: 'what I did notice, coming back to Scotland was that there was precious little going on up here' (Caig Wilson, 2021) and Cameron endorses this feeling:

> When I came up here it was a very strange feeling of going back into the past as far as mime and physical theatre was concerned because I'd been involved in everything that was going on down south and in London. But up here it was like a sort of backwater. There was only Pat Keysell who was funded by the Scottish Arts Council to promote physical dance theatre and mime. And she was really the main thrust behind this sort of work up here.

(Cameron, 2021)

However, by the turn of the decade, Cameron and Caig Wilson suggest that things were beginning to shift a little. The SAC was making sympathetic statements about further supporting these art forms, and identifying small pockets of money from the Dance budget to help realise such aspirations. Nonetheless, the picture remains opaque about the extent of SAC support for mime projects in the 1980s. Through these official bodies, mime was on the radar across this decade, but attitudes from the professional theatre community were, at best, mixed, as Caig Wilson's story here indicates. Perplexingly, Caig Wilson was advised by a professional actor to remove any reference on his CV to having studied with Lecoq, presumably as it might raise doubts and suspicions with potential employers. This anecdote may be very singular but it is revealing in that it perhaps betokens little understanding – and indeed mistrust – at this time of Lecoq's teaching, which, if registered at all, was assumed to be only mime, clowning and mask work. Such wariness was not peculiar to Scotland, and, of course, this was by no means a coherent or hegemonic position as Scottish Art Council bursaries, the presence of Pat Keysell from the mid-1980s as mime teacher/animateur and the closeness between the RSAMD and the Lecoq School all testify.

Mark Saunders has been a significant player in the Scottish mime and physical theatre landscape for almost 40 years. Saunders, having trained with Lecoq (1977–1979), was a ubiquitous performer both of his own solo work and with other Scottish theatre companies. He was also an active participant in the Scottish Mime Forum (SMF) (from 1991) and then an influential tutor at the RSAMD/RCS until his retirement in 2017. These multiple experiences gave Saunders a perceptive overview of the Scottish scene. After graduating from Durham University in the mid-1970s – he formed a mime group there and was deeply influenced by

Marceau – he arrived in Scotland which, as he says, was a cheaper alternative to the 'hippy trail to India' (Saunders, 2020). He quickly found work at Edinburgh's Theatre Workshop (an arts centre) and then:

> In about 1976 I saw Lindsay Kemp's *Flowers* in the Edinburgh Festival at the old Traverse and that completely blew me away. This was a type of physical theatre I just had not seen before. You know, with The Incredible Orlando[7] and goodness knows what they were doing, but it was fantastic. And lots of semi-naked young men wondering about doing outrageous things, you know. And also around that time I saw a good Grotowski-based theatre company called RAT theatre, with Pete Sykes and Mike Pearson.
>
> *(Ibid.)*

Saunders returned permanently to Scotland after Lecoq and throughout the 1980s was prodigious in making and performing his own solo clown/mime shows, working with actor, John Matthews, as physical comedy duo (Tony and Derek) or acting with other companies such as Communicado. He reflected:

FIGURE 4.2 Lindsay Kemp, St Nicholas Graveyard, Aberdeen, 1971.

Source: Photographer: Jamie Taylor.

---

7 The Incredible Orlando was the stage name for Jack Birkett (1934–2010). He was a British dancer, mime artist, actor and singer, best known for his work on stage as a member of Lindsay Kemp's theatre company, and in the films of Derek Jarman. Most of his best-known work was done when he was totally blind.

100 Mime & physical theatre beyond the centre

> Tony and Derek were our clown personas, and we created full-length shows. We started off with mock epics. It was the idea of two people trying to do an epic. And so first of all, we did all of Wagner's *Ring Cycle* in an hour and a half. And then we did the life of *Lawrence of Arabia* and then we did the *Trojan Wars*. . . . It was very physical and visual.
>
> *(Ibid.)*

That there were some funds available in the 1980s is evidenced by Saunders, who noted that he received small grants for touring and making solo work, and for the Tony and Derek duo. He was an artist in residence at Moray House College of Education in Edinburgh during the mid-1980s for a couple of months and this was paid for by the Scottish Arts Council. Saunders had also worked with Pat Keysell on a children's show for the London Mime Festival in 1980, so when she arrived in Scotland in 1985/1986 there was an opportunity to open a wider front for the advocacy (and performance) of mime. Keysell remained in Scotland for about ten years and initially was employed as a mime animateur in Fife working from a studio base in Dunfermline. A third figure in this trilogy of mime 'workers' was Sue Mitchell, who had been Mime Development Officer for Great London Arts. Mitchell subsequently moved to North East Scotland and for a period was Dance and Mime Animateur for Banff and Buchan but by 1995 was Education Coordinator at Peterhead prison. One assumes that her education work with those 'detained at her majesty's pleasure' in Peterhead was suffused with elements of mime and physical theatre.

In 1984 Saunders curated and organised what he calls 'a short modest mime festival' (Saunders, 2020) in Glasgow at the Third Eye Centre, now the Centre for Contemporary Art (CCA). He recalls:

> They paid me to organize a mime festival. So I invited a couple of groups up from down South. One of them was called Mivvy Mime. And then there were the two lads who did *Thunderbirds* – Andrew Dawson and Gavin Robertson. I also got Annie Stainer who was a solo dance mime performer and had worked with Lindsey Kemp.
>
> *(Ibid.)*

As a snapshot of one mime practitioner's 'career' Saunders' illustrates not only the eclectic variety of work many similar artists might chose – or be obliged – to undertake, but also the mad ambition of distilling epic works of opera or literature into a live performance of 90 minutes. One might propose that such apparently crazy tasks were only made possible through an imaginative and highly skilful use of the tools of modern mime and physical theatre. It is not too fanciful to suggest, perhaps, that work like this presages much larger scale but highly physical work such as the National Theatre of England's *Warhorse* (2007) and the National Theatre of Scotland's *Black Watch* (2006).

Although the presence of mime in Scotland across the 1980s was modest, despite the activities of Keysell, Saunders, Caig Wilson and Cameron, three theatre

FIGURE 4.3 Mark Saunders: *The Clown and the Jockey*, Traverse Theatre, Edinburgh, 1984. By kind permission of Mark Saunders.

companies – 7.84 (Scotland, 1973–2008), Wildcat (1978–1998) and Communicado (1983) all might be examined through the lens of physical theatre in the sense that their work was boisterously physical, energetic and visual. None of these companies, however, were in the least interested in claiming the physical theatre appellation, let alone the mime one. The iconic 7.84 Scotland and its offshoot, Wildcat, were passionately political but chose to subvert any crude sense of agitprop by the exuberant delivery of song, dance, humour and various modes of audience participation. Communicado's website tells us that:

FIGURE 4.4 Mark Saunders, *The Chaplin Obsession*, 1988. By kind permission of Mark Saunders.

Source: Photographer: Michael Siebert.

> Communicado was formed as an actors' company, and has always sought to engage the energies and attributes of the ensemble of actors in speech, song, music making and physicality in order to tackle the demands of theatrical story telling. Our repertoire is Scottish and International. We believe that the audience is at least as important as the artist in the creation of theatre.
>
> *(Communicado Theatre Company, 2021)*

Again, we are confronted with the complexities and vagaries around 'labelling' and (self) identification. This was exemplified by Saunders' account of working in 1987 with the Big Bang Orchestra – an offshoot of Communicado – in a show called *Strangers in Paradise*, a cabaret style parody of the Old Testament. This was a significant, if small, example of cross-fertilisation between theatrical forms and companies since two of the early members of Théâtre de Complicité, Celia Gore-Booth and Annabel Arden, were also in this production: Communicado and Théâtre de Complicité joining forces across two different training and theatre lineages. In the summer of the same year, Gore-Booth and Arden performed in Philippe Gaulier's bouffon play, *No Son of Mine*, at the Traverse Theatre during the Edinburgh Festival. At around this time, Saunders also remembers the Scottish Arts Council funding a week-long laboratory/workshop which allowed him, dancers Malcolm Shields and Frank McConnell, and Gerry Mulgrew (Director of Communicado) to 'play around' (Saunders, 2020) and improvise together.

In reflecting on the 1980s Saunders and Caig Wilson also noted the presence of Scottish Mime Theatre (SMT) which was founded in 1978 by Fay Dummer (later Prendergast) who had trained with Claude Chagrin and had been inspired by her participation in the Polish International Mime Workshop. In the pre-internet age so much information on small theatre/mime companies was lost, or indeed was never archived or collected. SMT is a good case in point, since between 1978 and 1984 it was evidently one of the most significant players in Scotland's mime landscape, receiving regular annual funding from the Scottish Arts Council[8]. Like David Glass, Moving Picture Mime Show, Desmond Jones, Pat Keysell and Nola Rae at that time, SMT had little hesitation in describing itself as a 'mime company' and its members had variously received training with Jacques Lecoq, Claude Chagrin, Carlo Bosso, Desmond Jones and Lindsay Kemp. Between 1979 and 1983 SMT toured extensively, not only across Scotland but also in Northern Ireland and Europe. Significantly, any internet investigation of SMT revealed virtually nothing, and our intelligence on SMT came exclusively from Saunders and Clare Brennan, theatre reviewer for *The Observer* newspaper, who furnished us with facts and figures.

In October 1991, Caig Wilson and Keysell launched the SMF from a base in Edinburgh. For some time they had discussed the need for an advocacy and representative organisation for Scotland that performed a similar role to London-based MAG. MAG aspired to be a UK-wide platform for mime and physical theatre, but its home in the (English) capital inevitably meant that Scottish preoccupations were distant and largely unreported. SMF was an entirely independent body but had good sisterly relations (and formal affiliation) with its much bigger relative in London and also with the European Mime Federation in Amsterdam. Saunders and

---

8 1978–1979: £8,370; 1979–1980: £10,246; 1980–1981: £19,000; 1981–1982: £19,000; 1982–1983: £24,000 (Arts Council Annual Reports).

104 Mime & physical theatre beyond the centre

Cameron also quite rapidly became involved too and the latter furnished us with some illuminating historical documentation on the development and activities of the SMF between 1992 and 1996. In an editorial for the organisation's newsletter for April 1995, which raises the continuously vexed question of funding, Caig Wilson writes:

> Let's be clear about what we are. The Mime Forum is a developmental organisation that: creates training and network opportunities for Mime and Physical Theatre practitioners; provides a public platform for contemporary Scottish work for promoters and other potential employers of practitioners; advocates the art-form, creating a higher public profile and awareness in general.
>
> *(Mime Forum Scotland, 1995)*

Clearly, but unsurprisingly, SMF offered a very similar prospectus to MAG. With slim funding, it organised, facilitated or curated an impressive series of events between 1992 and 1996, the central thrust of these was to bring respected practitioners to Scotland both to perform and to run workshops or mini residences. To this end, Cameron's documents include notice of the following:

- *TAKE ACTION* at the Traverse Theatre: demonstrations from six Scottish companies followed by panel discussion with key practitioners including Annabel Arden and Gerry Mulgrew (April 1993)
- Showcase of new work at the Eden Court Theatre in Inverness (November 1993).
- *MORE ACTION* at various Edinburgh venues over 10 days and in conjunction with the Traverse Theatre and the Richard Demarco Gallery. Performance and teaching from Odin Theatre (Eugenio Barba and Julia Varley), David Glass and Enrique Pardo[9] (May 1994)
- *MIME IN THE COMMUNITY.* A week of workshops led by Keysell, Caig Wilson, Cameron and Mark Hamilton (September 1994).
- Professional master class with Claire Heggen of Theatre du Mouvement at Edinburgh's Dance Base (September 1994).
- *MOVING MUSIC*, a four-day masterclass led by Jos Houben and Micheline Vandepoel at Tramway, Glasgow (March 1995)
- THE BODY OF WRITING, a research event exploring writing for physical theatre with Pete Brooks and Geraldine Pilgrim at Traverse, Edinburgh (July 1995)

---

9 Enrique Pardo is the co-founder of Pantheatre in 1981. He worked with the legendary Roy Hart theatre company and his practice focusses on myth, the voice and corporality. Throughout our period he regularly ran workshops in the UK.

Apart from such a striking assembly of events and European practitioners, the SMF, like MAG, provided a range of informal networks for this small number of key artists to share experiences, knowledge and to strategise around increasing the profile of mime and physical theatre in Scotland. One senses that its most energetic years were between 1992 and 1996, and it eventually closed in 1996/1997 around which time Keysell, disillusioned about the possibilities of deepening the mime/physical theatre ecology in Scotland, had relocated to Eastbourne, and Cameron's work increasingly took him south of the border and into continental Europe. Caig Wilson taught 'pure' mime technique at Queen Margaret College for three years from 1994, but in 1997 embarked on training to become a professional Feldenkrais teacher. Saunders' investment was by now largely consumed by teaching full-time at the RSAMD. In our conversation, we asked Caig Wilson and Cameron to reflect, with the wisdom of hindsight, on the SMF and what it achieved. Their responses were honest, nuanced differently but essentially slightly doleful. Cameron reflected:

> I think in terms of what initially we wanted, I don't think it did. However, in terms of bringing artists to Scotland – the quality of the people who had never been here before – that was a good thing. In retrospect, when you look at today's situation, it was amazing.
>
> *(Cameron, 2021)*

Caig Wilson went further and elaborated:

> I might be a bit more measured, I would say that the aim of trying to develop a marriage between Scottish performance and physical theatre, no that didn't happen. I think that Ian and I have gone on to place our mime and physical theatre work through other people and what they do. Either through teaching, or making, which is in keeping with what Lecoq wanted from us anyway. He didn't want us to be Lecoq performers. He wanted us to develop into something else as artists. I don't think we succeeded in making career opportunities or livelihoods for Scottish based mime and physical theatre performance. But if you soften that aim a little and suggest that we wanted to create a space for mime and physical theatre work to happen in Scotland then I think we did. . . . I would say that we failed, but honourably. I feel very sad for Pat because when she left Edinburgh her mood was very low. She felt that the work she had put into Scotland had not achieved what she hoped it would do.
>
> *(Caig Wilson, 2021)*

Before concluding this account of Scotland, it is important to acknowledge both the arrival of Benchtours as a highly regarded Scottish company formed in 1990 and the enduring role of the RSAMD and its links to École Jacques Lecoq in Paris. Benchtours' practice was, initially at least, strongly shaped by the experience of company members having trained with Philippe Gaulier in Paris or London. In

106 Mime & physical theatre beyond the centre

conversation with Stewart Ennis, he traced the way in which the company was in thrall to Gaulier's working methods and ideas:

> He was very, very present in the rehearsal room with us. We would be invoking his name like an Indian guru. In rehearsal we used neutral mask, clown, melodrama, and chorus and *le jeu* to create characters and to forge a kind of ensemble playing style. By this point I had been there (to Gaulier) so I was now able to talk the language and had joined the Gaulier Masonic Lodge! Our first Scottish Arts Council funded show (1991) was called *The Splitting of Latham* – a kind of Victorian melodrama clown piece – which was both very old fashioned and quite new. But it also had its roots in melodrama, in music hall and those old larger than life theatrical styles. I enjoyed farce.
>
> *(Ennis, 2020)*

Later in the conversation Ennis goes on to record how, after several more productions, Benchtours loosened its apron strings to Gaulier and began to take on board other dramaturgies and inspirations. That this is of more general interest is because it traces the kind of trajectory common to many companies that have a degree of longevity. Initial and perhaps dominating influences may dissipate, are refined and begin to jostle and co-exist with different forces as companies become exposed to new stimuli and develop greater 'maturity' and confidence. Ennis remembers:

> I think by the fourth show that we did, which was a very first adaptation of Salman Rushdie's *Haroun and the Sea of Stories*, Gaulier was still there but he wasn't such a presence in the room. Following this we ended up in a fairly lengthy series of collaborations with Pete Brooks from Insomniac. That was an interesting collaboration because his aesthetic was really different. I mean, working with Pete, we were in danger of becoming quite cool for a short period. We had never been cool. There was something about our work that he really liked. We created three shows over a period of four years. The first was called *Limbo* and then, *Carnivale* and finally, *Peep Show*. There were recognizable Pete Brooks tropes in those productions. Each of them had movie references and gangsters but those were interesting because by that time we had really moved quite a distance from Gaulier and he wasn't at that point being invoked at all in the rehearsal room. However, he was still there in the playfulness. Confidence in our own ability to create work meant that we didn't have to draw consciously on him anymore.
>
> *(Ibid.)*

Benchtours continued until 2009 and in the 1990s increasingly became a signature Scottish company that one may legitimately assign to the physical theatre portfolio, although, like many others it did not choose to promote itself with this epithet. During this period they became a regularly funded 'client' of the Scottish Arts Council, touring widely across rural and urban Scotland and beyond to the rest of the UK and continental Europe. Their success and longevity reinforces the Scottish connection with the lineage and training traditions of Jacques Lecoq and Philippe Gaulier. Significantly, Mark Saunders chaired the Benchtours board for about ten years. We return to, and elaborate upon, Lecoq and the RSAMD in the subsequent chapter on education and training.

In conclusion, we might say that the 1980s and 1990s represented cycles of repeated 'waxing and waning' for mime and physical theatre, a rhythm perhaps little different from other parts of the UK. The establishment of the SMF in 1991 by energetic champions such as Cameron, Keysell and Caig Wilson seemed to promise a sturdy infrastructure of support and activity for this work but its demise after only four years suggests unfulfilled ambitions. Caig Wilson's rueful observation that its attempt 'to develop a marriage between Scottish performance and physical theatre . . . didn't happen' (Caig Wilson, 2021) was exemplified by a story he told us which seemed to epitomise, at best, the disinterest and, at worst, the deep suspicion in which mime and physical theatre were held by the theatre establishment. During Odin Theatre's residency in May 1994, based at Edinburgh's Traverse Theatre and DeMarco Gallery, the artistic director of the former had been scheduled to meet Eugenio Barba, one of Europe's most respected theatre directors and makers. At the last minute the Traverse director announced that he had to go to a meeting in Glasgow and Caig Wilson wryly, but regretfully, notes that 'he declined to meet Eugenio in his own theatre so that connection was never made' (Caig Wilson, 2021). This, I sense, for Caig Wilson, Keysell and Cameron – the driving forces behind the SMF – spoke volumes about the daunting tasks facing mime and physical theatre in Scotland. And yet, and yet, the picture is almost certainly more nuanced than this little anecdote suggests. As previously noted, the presence of the physically skilled, politically committed and highly energetic companies of 7.84 (Scotland), Wildcat and Communicado during much of our period offers strong evidence that Scottish theatre was not uncomplicatedly rooted in and confined by the play text. Furthermore, the performance work of Saunders, Cameron and Caig Wilson, the residencies with high-profile visiting artists, the community and college teaching led by the indefatigable Keysell (and others), Lecoq's influence within the RSAMD (and well beyond) and the arrival and sustained impact of Benchtours, all suggest that – inevitably – the picture is complex and nuanced. And beyond these, and each deserving accounts in their own right, the presence of the National Review of Live Art (NRLA) in Glasgow intermittently between 1988 and 2010, Glasgow venues such as the Arches and the Tramway, and the Highlands and Islands small-scale touring circuit, all might be considered to have contributed to the Scottish performance ecology we are considering during this period. The NRLA often featured body-based and highly corporeal performance whilst the Tramway, saved from demolition by Peter Brook's *Mahabharata* (1988) and Glasgow's City of Culture status in 1990, has continued to host dance and physical theatre work from across Europe and beyond. In conclusion, therefore, Scotland's profile in terms of mime and physical theatre during these two decades suggests a diverse and unevenly flourishing ecosystem of practices.

108 Mime & physical theatre beyond the centre

From Scotland into Wales

In constructing this partial and selective profile of Wales and its relationship to mime and physical theatre it has been impossible not to reflect on comparisons with Scotland and, whilst facile point scoring is of no interest to our project, certain significant differences and preoccupations suggest themselves. As we have observed, the particular influence of Jacques Lecoq and Philippe Gaulier on Scottish companies, on the RSAMD, and the missionary zeal with which Pat Keysell pursued mime in Scotland for ten years from the mid-1980s, was not replicated in Wales. However, for Lecoq and Gaulier we might read Jerzy Grotowski and Eugenio Barba, and the account which follows traces the ways in which these two practitioners hugely influenced the work of Richard Gough and Mike Pearson and thereby gave shape and direction to a significant amount of physical theatre making from the late 1970s to the early 2000s.

Wales had no equivalent of the Scottish Mime Forum, but it seems likely there were other priorities and networks at play through, for example, the Cardiff Laboratory Theatre (1974–1988) and later the Centre for Performance Research (CPR). South Wales had RAT Theatre, Paupers' Carnival, Moving Being, Brith Gof, No Fit State Circus, Volcano, and (initially) Frantic Assembly, whilst, over roughly the same period, Scotland was home, for example, to 7.84 (Scotland), Wildcat, Communicado, Scottish Mime Theatre, Tony and Derek and Benchtours. What each country reveals in these snapshots is that emerging practices, preoccupations and interests are forged by a shifting web of influential artists and companies stamping their impress on what kind of work is made, valorised and seen by audiences. In turn, these activities and passions are moulded and framed by wider cultural and economic forces and, as part of a dialectical process, shape them back.

We had a lengthy and engrossing conversation with Richard Gough in October 2020, and this section on Wales draws heavily upon this and on previous conversations Simon Murray had with Mike Pearson[10]. Gough has been a substantial player in shaping the currents of experimental and visual/physical theatre over four decades, particularly in Wales, but also across the UK and Europe. He joined the Cardiff Laboratory Theatre (CLT) as a performer and director in 1975 and has subsequently been an energetic and charismatic curator, producer, teacher, animator, writer, editor, publisher and one-man pivot for a huge range of projects, some of which we identify later. In particular, his invention and leadership of the CPR stands out as a long-lasting achievement. We briefly examine the educational work of the CPR in Aberystwyth in Chapter 6.

At school in Hereford, Gough had organised what he says was a 'rather subversive' (Gough, 2020) group called the Spider Arts Movement and organised regular trips to Cardiff to see experimental theatre companies such as Moving Being[11]. In these early years, he was influenced by the likes of the Pip Simmons Theatre

---

10 Mike Pearson was to die in May 2022 during the final stages of writing this book.
11 Moving Being (1983–1993) was an influential, but loosely structured, company (see Chapter 5) whose members largely drew on their own training practices. Mark Evans recalls being introduced to mime, Meyerhold's 'shooting the arrow' étude and dance and circus skills during workshops with Moving Being company members.

Group, The People Show and, from the USA, the Living Theater, Bread and Puppet Theater and Meredith Monk. After leaving school Gough told us that he 'ran away', not to join the circus, but to CLT whose Manifesto he had read in the Cardiff *Echo*. Mike Pearson had been the main author of the Manifesto and he and Gough were to work together in the CLT between 1973 and 1980 and in other capacities thereafter. Gough remembers the Manifesto:

> It was outrageous in many ways because it outlined what the grandly titled Cardiff Laboratory for Theatrical Research was going to do and how it was going to function in the studios, how it was going to document research, show work in progress, and organise debates and conferences. I've often joked that a lot of what I've done in the last 40, almost 50 years now, is to try and achieve what I imagined that that manifesto would realize. But I very rapidly discovered that actually none of it existed and that it was truly utopian in the sense it was Mike's idea. It was wholly aspirational.
>
> *(Ibid.)*

By the mid-1970s CLT had established a base in the Chapter Arts Centre – already home to Moving Being – and Pearson and Gough began working together on a number of productions. The semiotics of the company's title – Cardiff Laboratory Theatre – is intriguing and, as Gough remarked, 'the pretension is in the name in some ways. It was extraordinarily audacious' (Ibid.). 'Laboratory' as a descriptor for a theatre company and its processes has deep roots in Stanislavski, Meyerhold and (Michael) Chekhov, but for Pearson and Gough in the 1970s the name particularly gestured towards Grotowski, to the Teatr Laboratorium in Wroclaw and, and increasingly, towards Barba. There are differing inflections of what laboratory theatres mean in practice[12] but at the centre lies a sense that research, training, creation and rehearsal are – or should be – an integrated and inseparable process. Furthermore, for Meyerhold, Chekhov, Grotowski and Barba, the epicentre of laboratory theatres' research and training processes lay in the performer's body, its action and its gestural range and expressiveness. For Pearson's practice as performer and maker with RAT (Ritual and Tribal Theatre), CLT and then with Brith Gof between 1981 and 1997 these deeply embodied practices became the propelling force fields for all his work. It is interesting to note that Pearson has never been shy to embrace 'physical theatre' as a broad sweep appellation for his practice. It is, of course, much more than this, too. As the 1970s decade unfolded both Gough and Pearson became more and more engaged with Odin Teatret as Barba was developing his ideas around 'Third Theatre'[13]. In 1977 all CLT members attended

---

12 Bryan Brown's book a *History of the Theatre Laboratory* (Routledge, 2018) explores different models of theatre laboratory.

13 Eugenio Barba attempted to define Third Theatre like this: 'The Third Theatre lives on the fringe, often on the outside or on the outskirts of the centers and capitals of culture. It is a theatre created by people who define themselves as actors, directors, theatre workers, although they have seldom undergone a traditional theatrical education, and therefore are not recognised as professionals' (Barba, 1986: 193)

```
THEATRE LABORATORY FIRST STATEMENT

What follows is an initial document setting out proposals for the founding of a
theatre laboratory in Cardiff. It is designed to draw essential comment, suggestions
and criticism.
The theatre laboratory will come into being early in 1974. It will function as a
body for intensive long-term research into theatrical methodology, with performance
and documentation as the application for a newly created language.
It will work essentially in the field of physical expression, developing a style
of performance which synthesises a variety of techniques into a language of bio-
energetics.
The laboratory will have a two-fold function.
Firstly, it will concentrate on research, even for the sake of research, without the
restrictions of performance dates and rehearsal schedules. A permanent performance
group will apply the fruits of research to experimental theatre pieces. Performances
may be extended over a period of time, perhaps one per week for several weeks so that
organic development may occur.
Secondly, it will have a major teaching role to make completed research more widely
available. Workshops will be arranged whenever required, preferably in a permanent
home, if the laboratory succeeds in finding one. Week-end and week-long courses will
be available in conjunction with other organisations. Thus, the research will have a
practical application in servicing the sadly neglected field of experimental theatre.
Documentation will be of the utmost importance in supplying an ideological base
for this type of work. There will be a quarterly publication of work from inside
and outside the laboratory, recording workshops, seminars, and performances and
presenting articles on methodology.
By necessity, the laboratory will be initially ephemeral, with workshops and
performances in a variety of locations. Obviously, such a venture will eventually
require a permanent home, a small plain space to fulfil the following functions:
    1) Training, rehearsal and research work in a stable atmosphere.
    2) Performance by members of the laboratory to small numbers of initially
       sympathetic public. These will be experimental in setting, subject matter and
       delivery.
    3) Public demonstrations of technique. Regular workshops open to the public.
    4) Seminars concerning the development of experimental theatre.
    5) Guest performances and workshops by other groups and individuals working in
       the field of physical theatre.
    6) A meeting place and forum for those concerned about the future of theatre.

Mike Pearson
October 1973
```

FIGURE 4.5 Cardiff Theatre Laboratory First Statement, Mike Pearson, October 1973.
Source: CLT/CPR Archives.

the second meeting of the International School of Theatre Anthropology (ISTA) in Bergamo in Italy, organised by Barba, and Gough notes the importance of this event for his practice and future thinking:

> The gathering at Bergamo was extraordinary in that Eugenio managed to bring together 30 or 40 very young companies – in fact they were hardly companies, much more like clubs, loose associations or gangs from all parts of

Europe. It was at that meeting that I first encountered the work of Odin and we (Cardiff Lab) became fans at that point, like groupies we stayed on in Italy and followed them to Genoa for a week. The experience had a profound impact on me and I became interested to see how we could bring Odin's work to Wales. I suppose I was acutely aware of lacking any training at all, so I began to organize workshops and sessions with different teachers – a wide range of skills, partly to teach us as an emerging company, but also then to open it up to the profession. I had the idea to bring the whole of Odin to Wales and to organize a month-long residency. A hugely complicated project which we finally realised in August 1980.

(Ibid.)

After Odin's visit to Cardiff in 1980, with differing trajectories and aspirations, Pearson and Gough amicably parted company, with the former moving much more into performance and production and the latter into organising, curating and animating international exchanges and residencies within the compass of CLT. In 1981 Pearson, with Lis Hughes Jones, formed Brith Gof, which for almost 20 years was to become (with Volcano arriving later in 1987) Wales' signature physical theatre company. Rooted in Artaud's Theatre of Cruelty, shaped by Grotowski and Barba, Pearson's project had been to define, develop and use through practice a basic vocabulary of physical training exercises he called *All Languages*. Working at scale in both urban and rural sites in Wales and

FIGURE 4.6 *Origin of Table Manners* (Director: Richard Gough), Cardiff Laboratory Theatre, 1985.

Source: CLT/CPR Archives.

112 Mime & physical theatre beyond the centre

FIGURE 4.7 Odin in Wales: Barter Evening (publicity leaflet), Cardiff Laboratory Theatre, 1980.

Source: CLT/CPR Archives.

across Europe Pearson's physical dramaturgy was never intentionally virtuosic but always highly committed, both politically and through his performers' investment in action and gesture, sometimes angrily and hugely stated, sometimes finely sensitive, delicate and complex. In an early issue of *Performance Research* Pearson

Mime & physical theatre beyond the centre **113**

begins an essay entitled 'My Balls/Your Chin' by saying, 'I want to tell you about Antonin Artaud and me'. Later, in what amounts to a kind of manifesto for his theatre, he writes:

> I want to find different arenas for performance – places of work, play and worship – where the laws and bye-laws, the decorum and learned contracts of theatre can be suspended. I want to make performances that fold together place, performance and public. I want to make 'hybrids' – of music, action, text and site – that defy conventional labels. I want to make slippery, sliding performances that are not a mirror of some social issue or a simplification but a complication, which defies instant scrutiny.
>
> *(Pearson, 1998: 40)*

We suggest there is something distinctive in these examples of Welsh physical theatre that is also about a search for cultural identity, and perhaps more specifically, a suspicion of English and London-centric formations of character. An emphasis, perhaps, on place and space, but also a relationship with language and Celtic culture (poetry and song). A trajectory also shared by Moving Being and Scotland's 7.84 Company. An important similarity with Scotland, we sense, is a facing outwards towards Europe for influence and connection rather than towards England and London.

From the late 1970s throughout the 1980s, until the demise of CLT in 1987, Gough took productions to Odin's base at Holstebro in Denmark and organised and curated a number of very ambitious residencies and exchanges back in Cardiff, across Wales and other parts of the UK. These included the Akademia Ruchu (The Academy of Movement) from Warsaw in 1979, a Kathakali/Balinese project in 1980 and the Popular Entertainer Festival in 1985. The first Odin residency in August 1980, based at Chapter but which included events across Wales (in Blaenau Ffestiniog and Bala, for example), was followed by a 'Ten Years On' sequel in 1990, where the company did a complete exposition of its work (both indoors and street based), ran workshops and a programme of talks led by Barba.

In 1981 Gough invited Grotowski to Cardiff. Noting the genesis of this residency, he recalls

> Eugenio ringing me up on my birthday and saying, Richard I have a gift for you. Sensing something mischievous I asked cautiously what it was, and he said, I'd like to give to you Grotowski: 'Can Grotowski come and stay with you in Cardiff for 4 weeks'. This was at the time when Grotowski was exiled from Poland and was moving between Haiti and California and needed somewhere to stay and rest and recuperate. We organised a conference around him and one year later the whole of Grotowski's company came and that was the last time they were all together before the dissolution of the Polish Lab. I think they ran nine parallel workshops.
>
> *(Gough, 2020)*

114 Mime & physical theatre beyond the centre

FIGURE 4.8 Grotowski's Teatr Laboratorium Workshops (publicity leaflet), Cardiff Laboratory Theatre, 1982.
Source: CLT/CPR Archives.

Undoubtedly, the most ambitious project which Gough was to organise in the 1980s was a three-month tour of the Peking Opera signed as 'Peking Opera Explorations' and he contextualised this in terms of his burgeoning interest in world theatres, both at a scholarly level – building a library, for example – and in terms of introducing these Eastern dramatic forms to Welsh, and indeed, UK audiences.

Initially imagined as a modest project to bring over a small company to perform and run workshops in 1986, the whole venture mushroomed into a second tour the following year (1987). On this occasion the company and associated artists numbered almost 60, performed at the Edinburgh Festival, and then, as a co-production with Sadler's Wells, the London Palladium was hired for two weeks. Notwithstanding popular reception for the work in Edinburgh and South Wales, the huge London Palladium theatre only played to half-full houses and lost a considerable amount of money, resulting in the insolvency and final closure of CLT late in 1987.

Gough and Judie Christie had established the CPR as a resource centre of CLT in 1985 and after the dissolution of the latter it became an independent entity in 1988. Initially based at Cardiff's Chapter Arts Centre, the CPR moved with its founders to the University of Wales Aberystwyth in 1995 under the umbrella of the University's Department of Theatre, Film and Television Studies, where an archive, library and resource centre were established. Gough became a member of the teaching staff at this juncture and was to be joined by Mike Pearson two years later in 1997. The presence and impact of both CLT and CPR in Wales has given this country a defining signature within particular histories and lineages of experimental and body-based theatre.

Our conversation with Gough regularly skirted around questions of whether the range of work he had successfully made, curated, programmed and written about in and for Wales over a 40-year span constituted physical theatre, or indeed, mime. One senses that labels were of little concern to Gough, but that throughout many and eclectic projects he was driven by a range of factors and forces which particularly included:

- A huge curiosity for experimental performance work from other cultures.
- An awareness – certainly in the 1970s and 1980s – that such practices were undoubtedly hardly seen across the UK and, at that time, were treated with some disdain and disinterest by university drama departments and established theatre institutions.
- A compulsion not only to bring such work to Wales, but to help cultivate it on home soil.

Of the work made by CLT and the numerous projects he organised, Gough observes:

> There was a sort of clear visual aesthetic, but I was very well aware that we were doing something a bit different in Cardiff. As far as I recall, we didn't call it physical theatre, we would just call it experimental theatre, but it was very strongly physically based, but also vocally and musically. We did a lot of work with music and song. But it was always with a strong physical training in contrast to Moving Being who continued in the multimedia way of working. My interest in how physical theatre emanates in other cultures has always remained a preoccupation. In the early days of being in Aberystwyth

116   Mime & physical theatre beyond the centre

as the CPR, we were still producing some quite unusual work. We brought over one of Alan Platel's early works from what we now refer to as the Flemish Wave, and in that work it is difficult to distinguish physical theatre from dance. Of course, in the UK we were more familiar with DV8 and that was a company which began to interest me a lot. When I began to see their work, I appreciated that Lloyd Newson was realizing what I'd always had an ambition for, but never managed to create in my own work. There was a sort of an athleticism and dynamic and vision to that work which I then saw in Platel's Ballet C de la B . . . I'm still proud of this very strong decentralized policy at that time, we really felt it important to bring work to Wales first.

(Ibid.)

We drew Gough on his thoughts on mime, and these reflect not only a perceived schism between practices apparently represented through the lineage of the French mime tradition and those of Grotowski and Barba, but also the views of many theatre and performance studies academics at the time, and perhaps still today. He remarks that 'we didn't open ourselves up to the Lecoq tradition' (ibid.) which, we sensed, seemed to represent for Gough a dominant cosmopolitan London hegemony. Nonetheless, he was to host a week-long workshop with Philippe Gaulier at Chapter in 1985, and much later became enamoured with Decroux-trained Swedish mime performer, Ingemar Lindh's (1945–1997) 'poetic physicality' (ibid.). Indeed, as part of the 'Past Masters' series on Etienne Decroux in 1997, when the CPR had moved to Aberystwyth, Lindh was to have performed and presented at the event. That this did not happen was due to Lindh's untimely and early death a few weeks before the Decroux project was to take place.

We close our profile of Gough by quoting his wry, and only slightly bashful, thoughts on mime during our conversation. Humour aside, his feelings, though somewhat on the extreme end of a continuum, perhaps represent views and suspicions held by other practitioners, promoters and academics during our period. Gough reflected:

I'm afraid I have an aversion to mime and I'm very badly behaved. In theatre if we go and see a show I'll sometimes lean to my wife and say, oh dear, he's had mime. I see mime as a sort of disease like amoebic dysentery, or something that you know you never quite get out of the system. . . . Sometimes you see a performer and you can see that he or she has had a very bad bout of mime! Of course, I say it lightly, but there is something about the particular training that I didn't know at the time – something about the exactitude of the training that does produce those sort of physical traits. I really disliked anything that was illustrative, whether that was in American acting or in mime. And I remember early on in my collaboration with Mike (Pearson) I proposed in one of our outrageous statements that we should proclaim ourselves as illiterate on purpose.

(Ibid.)

We conclude with a brief reference to Volcano (see also Chapters 5 and 7). Formed in 1987 and working from a base in Swansea, the company has figured in the same spatial and temporal landscape as the work we have identified from Gough and Pearson. We sense that out of choice or circumstance their respective worlds did not significantly overlap or encounter each other. There is little sense that Volcano was a product of exposure to either Grotowski or Barba, rather from the dance theatre wing of the physical theatre lineage (see Chapter 5). The company's web page reveals a prolific output of productions since 1987, many of which take classic and contemporary – but not necessarily dramatic – texts as their starting point. Tony Harrison, William Shakespeare, Karl Marx and WG (Max) Sebald are but four examples. DV8 and solo performer, Nigel Charnock directed two Volcano shows: *L.O.V.E.* (inspired by Shakespeare's Sonnets) in 1992 and *Macbeth – The Director's Cut* in 1999/2000. The Company revived L.O.V.E. twice more in 2003 and 2013 and their final version is described as a 'highly-charged and athletic classic that helped define the term "physical theatre"' (Volcano Theatre, 2021). Whilst physical theatre as a tag evidently holds no embarrassment for Volcano, the range of its work – performance, education and conferences, for example – and its willingness to find a meeting point between texts, dance, narrative and action suggest yet another strand in the formal taxonomy of physical theatre.

Welsh after words

This short snapshot of multiple practices around physical and visual theatre, made or brought to Wales over a 30-year period, suggests a number of questions and issues which, of course, reflect and speak to the subject matter of this volume. These profiles of mime and physical theatre practices in Scotland and Wales reveal two key dispositions or patterns which need to be grasped in all their messy elusiveness: deeper currents and groundswells of change occurring in UK cultural life and live performance and their conjunction with dedicated, inspirational and often charismatic figures who have chosen to work within or against the grain of these broader movements. If, in a highly conditional and partial way, we are prepared to acknowledge the impress of Grotowski and Barba in Wales and Lecoq and Gaulier in Scotland it is to acknowledge that cultural production is a complex and complicated 'structure of feeling', blending economic impulses, individual agency and the forces and shapes of cultural production.

Northern Ireland

We had a productive exchange of correspondence with theatre studies colleagues, Tom Maguire (Ulster University) and David Grant (Queen's University Belfast) regarding mime and physical theatre in Northern Ireland during our period. Maguire and Grant have worked as university teachers and inhabited the professional (and amateur) theatre landscapes in Northern Ireland for several decades. Both Maguire and Grant confirmed our hunches that the presence of mime and

118 Mime & physical theatre beyond the centre

physical theatre in Northern Ireland during our period was less explicitly focused, practised and claimed than in either Scotland or Wales. However, once again, their helpful accounts raised slippery and complex questions as to what constitutes physical theatre, and, to a lesser extent, modern mime.

Any reflections on cultural practices in Northern Ireland during the last three decades of the twentieth century have to be contextualised and understood by the intervening and destructive factors of the 'Troubles', those tensions and conflicts between Catholic and Protestant communities and the role of the British and Irish Republic. Our narrative can only acknowledge an awareness of these huge social and political factors in the sense that the turmoil must have inhibited, repressed and constrained the material conditions of invention which were generative of physical theatres in other parts of the UK. Another elusive factor mentioned by both Maguire and Grant was – and remains – the dominant weight of the Irish literary tradition in the production and validation of theatre forms across the whole of the island of Ireland.

If our two correspondents had a shared perspective on the lineage and presence of mime and physical theatre from the 1970s until 2000, it was especially around the importance of popular political theatre forms and circus. Grant observes that in the 1970s 'there was a strong burlesque physicality evident in popular vernacular theatre of the time' (Grant, 2021). They both note the importance of the Charabanc Theatre Company, founded in 1983 (disbanded in 1995) and driven by the frustration of five Belfast-based actresses about not only the lack of work for women at that time but also the dominance of text-based theatre and the narrow range of dramaturgical possibilities apparently available. Maguire notes the influence of variety and agit-prop on the company's early productions, epitomised perhaps by director, Pam Brighton, with whom Charabanc worked on several occasions. Maguire identifies some of the qualities of the company's work as follows:

- Co-creation by actors within an ensemble, using a range of approaches including devising and improvisation.
- Cross-gender roles and casting
- Developing characters quickly and through physical gestures
- Creation of *mise-en-scene* through the performers rather than naturalistic sets
- Acknowledging the complicity between performers and spectators

(Maguire, 2021)

For Maguire, Charabanc in the 1980s marks 'the high point for physical theatre in Northern Ireland . . . they were inspirational for many practitioners who followed in their wake such as Paula McFetridge at Kabosh' (ibid.). Kabosh, founded in 1994, evidently is proud to engage strongly with the social and political histories of the country. The company's home web page states:

Through blending new writing and unusual locations every production is unique. The company gives audiences a theatrical experience that encourages them to reimagine a space, a person or a moment in history. We aim to break down barriers to access the arts and maximise participation for all. Kabosh work with an ever-changing ensemble of actors, playwrights, designers, technicians, film makers and musicians.

(Kabosh, 2021)

Whilst signalling new writing, sited work ('unusual locations') and participatory practices, nowhere on Kabosh's website does the company invoke physical theatre or similar. Of course, this proves nothing in relation to whether we might be disposed, as Maguire hints, to describe Kabosh as physical theatre. After all, Théâtre de Complicité has never claimed any ownership over the term. Rather, as we intimated earlier, the phrase is less than precise in identifying particular practices as physical theatre, and, perhaps, more (or only) useful as a marketing and publicity device to point to an orientation or a direction of dramaturgical travel.

Maguire writes about a 'separate lineage of development' (2021), which in our analysis certainly overlaps with the popular and political theatre route, being located through the influence of Steven Berkoff and, to a lesser extent, Dario Fo. Significantly, Maguire identifies the economies of cultural production, burgeoning teaching of theatre studies in the university sector, and the appeal of devising and improvisation from and during the 1980s, as contributory reasons for the appeal of Berkoff:

The widespread availability of Berkoff texts from which to work and the relative economy of mounting work in that style made a deep impression across the university drama sector throughout the UK during the 1980s/1990s – an emphasis on ensemble devising and improvisation also opened up a space for creative theatre-making in those departments distinct from conservatoire training.

(Maguire, 2021)

Berkoff's chutzpah and skill has been influential in the university sector and beyond, perhaps as a consequence of making work which confronts and excites in equal measure.

Connectedly, Grant also pointed us to the importance of the now semi-derelict, but still functioning Crescent Arts Centre in Belfast which, he suggests, should remind us of the possible place of youth and community theatre practices in our enquiry. In the early 1980s, Crescent Arts was the home of the Fringe Benefits Theatre Company and the short lived, Belon Puppets, but:

the longest-lasting legacy of this period was undoubtedly the Belfast Community Circus, established in 1985 by an Australian practitioner called Mike Maloney, who went on to champion prison arts in Northern Ireland. The

120 Mime & physical theatre beyond the centre

> Community Circus made a huge impact on community arts practice generally, introducing a form of performance that avoided sectarian categorisation and attracted a very broad social mix of participants. By 1991, it had become so well established that the TV advertisement for a big cultural promotion that year used stilt-walkers and jugglers as the main theme in attempt to find an image of Belfast which was unaligned to either side of the community.
>
> *(Grant, 2021)*

This scant profile of Northern Ireland reinforces the difficulty in distilling or reducing any country or region within the UK to a series of dominating, clear and categorical forms and styles of mime and physical theatre. It would be tempting to assign Scotland to Lecoq and Gaulier, Wales to Grotowski and Barba, and Northern Ireland to popular political theatre and circus. Whilst there may be an inkling of truth in these simplistic generalisations they fail to acknowledge both the unfolding hybridity of influences on theatre forms and artists, and do little justice to the obvious fact that customs and practices characteristic of a particular place are likely to change quite significantly and rapidly during any one time span. This mutability is further seasoned by the continual precarity of the lives of most theatre makers and the complex political, economic, social and cultural configurations of these three geographical sites.

A note on traffic across the seas

The extent to which the subject matter of this book is categorically bounded and proscribed by its (self-imposed) title *Mime into Physical Theatre: a UK Cultural History 1970–2000* is debatable. Being an island, albeit containing four distinct countries, evidently defines a degree of geographical immutability but the cultural and artistic boundaries of influence, lineage, exchange and travel are fluid and porous indeed. As with all discourses about origins, roots and pedigrees, theatre is a delightfully mongrel beast, and perhaps physical theatres are more than usually hybrid and tangled. As we have seen in this chapter there is little purity of form or influence in the physical theatre practices developed and nurtured in the UK over the three decades covered by our volume. Possibly, the practices defined by the Decroux-based techniques are an exception to this claim. For some, this multiplicity – or perhaps excess – of influences over UK practices revealed certain compositional and dramaturgical weaknesses, whilst for others, such diversity illustrated cultural richness and an exciting abundance of possible styles and training lineages. Whatever one's position on these critical issues there is evidence that Lecoq, Gaulier and Pagneux were the most dominant – but still unevenly distributed as the case of Wales indicates – forces in the UK landscape of physical theatre in the final two decades of the twentieth century.

Our chapter on education and training (Chapter 6) of necessity identifies recent and deep historical training ancestries from outwith the UK: the French corporeal mime of Decroux and Marceau; the physically and corporeally sensitive and alert

bodies fashioned by Lecoq, Gaulier and Pagneux; the laboratory theatres of Polish Grotowski and Danish Odin with its Italian director, Barba; the German tanz-theater of Wigman, through Laban to Bausch; and the Soviet etudes of Meyerhold, all find their marks and traces in contemporary UK mime and physical theatres. This chapter (and Chapter 5) explores these strands of influence in more detail, and in particular the extent to which the significant growth of the short (1–5 day) workshop contributed to an internationalisation of training lineages.

Without extensive statistical analysis it is difficult to ascertain whether traffic to and from continental Europe during our period was more heavily weighted towards artists coming in or to those leaving these shores to perform and display their work. Scanning listings within *Total Theatre* from the mid-1980s to the turn of the century suggests more tangible evidence of companies coming here to perform and teach. The ubiquity of festivals (see Chapter 3), whether longstanding, such as the London International Mime Festival (LIMF), the International Workshop Festival (IWF), the Edinburgh Fringe Festival and Stockton's Riverside Festival, or those of much lesser heft and longevity, all identify a regular roll call of companies and artists from across Europe and beyond. Indeed, one might suggest that an explicit purpose of both LIMF and IWF, for example, was to fulfil this internationalisation function for cultural, political and ethical reasons. During the January 1991 LIMF, 19 companies or artists are listed and 10 of these were from outwith the UK. Of these 10, three were from Italy, two from France, and one each from Spain, Israel, the USA, Australia and Brazil (see Chapter 3). Many of these companies went on immediately to perform in other UK towns and cities such as Coventry, Bristol, Swindon, Norwich, Hemel Hempstead and different London venues. The work of LIMF and IWF are considered in more detail in Chapters 3 and 6 but the internationalism – unsurprisingly, given the title of the organisation – of IWF is made manifest in the list of countries represented through workshop teaching between 1988 and 1998. In IWF's 10th anniversary report Dick McCaw, who had taken over from Nigel Jamieson in 1993, identifies the following:

> Algeria, Armenia, Australia, Belgium, Benin, Brazil, Canada, Chile, China, Cuba, Ecuador, Egypt, Eire, France, Germany, Georgia, India, Israel, Italy, Jamaica, Lithuania, Nicaragua, Nigeria, Philippines, Peru, Poland, Romania, Russia, Sierra Leone, Senegal, South Africa, Spain, Switzerland, United States of America and the former Yugoslavia.

Beyond well-established organisations such as LIMF, IWF and the Edinburgh Festival, there are countless other examples of imaginative and risk-taking promoter-curators bringing companies from Europe and beyond during our period. We reflect upon Richard Demarco in Edinburgh first inviting Tadeusz Kantor and Richard Foreman's Ontological-Hysteric Theater to the UK in the 1960s and 1970s, Glasgow's Tramway securing the (self-) exiled Peter Brook's production of the *Mahabharata* in 1988, Sadler's Wells bringing Pina Bausch to London audiences, Richard Gough's relationship with Eugenio Barba's Odin Teatret, Grotowski and

122 Mime & physical theatre beyond the centre

Beijing Opera, Alan Lyddiard at Newcastle's Northern Stage championing Lev Dodin's Maly Theatre of St Petersburg, and the Centre for Performance Research in Aberystwyth's Past Masters symposia and other international projects. There were many more.

It is less easy to identify UK-based companies which had travelled abroad to perform, but by the early to mid-1980s the larger or more established artists and companies such as Nola Rae, Théâtre de Complicité, Trestle, Moving Picture Mime Show, Trickster, Frantic Assembly and DV8 were already beginning to perform their work in continental Europe, usually under the promotional and financial wing of the British Council. Apart from the obvious desire of artists to have their work recognised internationally, and of producer-promoters to expose UK audiences to a range of potentially exotic and unusual work beyond home-grown products, there were wider cultural and economic reasons for the opening up of this landscape. As the 1960s progressed out of post-war austerity there was an increasing appetite – and wherewithal – for foreign travel, with younger people especially finding such possibilities an exciting expansion to their horizons. In 1985 the Schengen agreement[14] enabled almost unhindered and visa-less movement between most EU countries and thereby further encouraged and facilitated touring arrangements for both young and better-established companies. At the same time, this was further enhanced in the 1990s by the opening of the Channel Tunnel (1994) and the beginning of the era of low-cost flights, although many artists' European travel arrangements were facilitated more through transit vans than jet engines. Furthermore, we surmise that mime and physical theatre is perhaps much more portable and mobile than mainstream realist dramas, with less reliance on props and sets. Finally, we note the perception – not always an accurate one – that these gestural, body-based theatre forms had an almost inherent universal internationalism to them, rendering them more open to touring across language barriers. Here, perhaps, the spoken word was deemed no longer to be an obstacle to comprehension and enjoyment. Of course, such claims and assumptions are open to considerable debate and disagreement!

Over the three decades of our study, it may not be too fanciful to suggest that the making and performance of mime and physical theatre was no more or less susceptible to the forces of globalisation than other sectors of the economy. Certainly, market forces were (and remain) one of the driving factors in the production, distribution and exchange of work which, in order to be paid for, needed to be seen and consumed as widely as possible. There is a market 'logic' to the economics of such globalisation but this – often uneasily – co-exists with the more principled and human desire to communicate across borders and to resist a defensive retreat into parochialism and 'little Englandism'. The pages of *Total Theatre* from the mid-1980s regularly mark this edging towards a more open-minded embrace

---

14 The UK only opted into the Schengan Agreement in 2000, and even then only accepted parts of the provision.

of internationalism – for example, a whole feature in Volume 7, number 4, Winter 1995, entitled 'International Connections: collaboration, exchange and performance' – whilst at the same time, a company such as Théâtre de Complicité is proclaiming its internationalism by virtue of their performers being drawn from a diversity of geographical backgrounds. A paradox and – we hope – creative tension within our book resides in the fact that, despite the (deliberate) limitation of placing 'UK' in our title, any attempt to describe and analyse these practices purely within the geographical frame and constraints of a single country are constantly exceeded, fractured and transgressed.

We end this 'Beyond the Centre' chapter, with its gesture towards escaping the national boundaries of the UK, by a wittily provocative – yet insightful – comment from Enrique Pardo.

> I see 'physical theatre' today as a particularly British phenomenon: the grand-children of Stephen (sic) Berkoff stomping about the stage, at best an anguished and poetic rebellion against literary theatre.
>
> *(Pardo, 2001: 9)*

5

MAKING MIME AND PHYSICAL THEATRE

The rise of physical theatre and modern mime has a close, significant but complex relationship with the recent history of devised theatre. Almost all mime and physical theatre from the 1970s onwards was produced through various types of devising processes, including adaptations of prose or poetic texts and whether working with a writer, director or choreographer. Relatively few books on devising for theatre were published during the last decades of the twentieth century, despite its prevalence within the experimental, educational and alternative theatre sectors in the UK. Many of the books available focused on the use of improvisation (Barker, 1977; Boal, 1992; Clements, 1983; Johnstone, 1981; Ritchie, 1987); only a few examined approaches to devising that emphasised the physical and the visual (Frost and Yarrow, 1990; Grotowski, 1969; Hunt, 1976) or devising within the performance, dance and live art sector (Etchells, 1999; Hunt, 1976; Savran, 1988; Tufnell and Crickmay, 1990). The two academic texts published during the 1990s that focused most extensively on devising were Anthony Frost and Ralph Yarrow's *Improvisation in Drama* (1990) and Alison Oddey's *Devising Theatre: a practical and theoretical handbook* (1996). Oddey's book examines the work of a number of companies across a range of theatre forms – including mask work, performance art, visual theatre and live art. It includes studies of companies such as Trestle, Forkbeard Fantasy, Lumiere & Son, IOU and Forced Entertainment. Frost and Yarrow review the wider history of improvisation within theatre making and performing, referencing several forms of mime and physical theatre, including: Meyerhold and constructivism; Copeau, Saint-Denis, Keith Johnstone and the use of masks; the US improvisation movement; Grotowski and paratheater; and Jacques Lecoq's approach to mime and clowning. Together with Thomas Leabhart's *Modern and Postmodern Mime* (1988), which largely focuses on the leading French and American mimes, these books probably represent the most detailed analyses available during this period of the ways in which mime and physical theatre performance was made.

DOI: 10.4324/9780429330209-5

Dee Heddon and Jane Milling (2006), similarly to Oddey (1996), do not focus in detail on most of the companies and artists that this book sets out to investigate. What they do offer are indicators of the influences, forces and pressures that shaped devising practices. Dymphna Callery (2001) compiles an exhaustive guide to physical theatre exercises and devising strategies, and draws on the work of many of the key companies from the 1990s. Beyond the introduction, however, the focus of her book is on the doing and not on the contextualisation. Murray and Keefe (2016) do not directly address the processes of devising within physical theatre; instead, they suggest a number of thematic concerns which inform such processes, for example: the formation of a physical vocabulary; the engagement with space and objects; the use of masks; the exploration of ambiguity, uncertainty and transformation, coupled with a general rejection of realism; the use of risk and danger; movement/stillness; and, collective authorship. These thematic concerns are broadly represented in the structure of this chapter. Heddon and Milling (2006) propose some common features of devised theatre practice and process: the human scale of the work, the generation of content and images through physical improvisation, and the use of storytelling mechanisms and/or choreographic techniques as a structure for the work. They suggest that the body emerged in the 1960s as 'an authenticating expressive tool of itself' (2005: 189). Furthermore, they propose that 'the rhetoric that surrounds the devising of physical theatre companies is that the gestural and spatial interaction of bodies provides a different language from that of words, for the audience to decipher' (2005: 189). Their notion of 'deciphering' is interesting in its suggestion that the meaning is somehow more hidden and/or opaque than in text-based theatre – we will examine this in a bit more detail later in this chapter and in Chapter 8. They also recognise the importance of shared training as 'the acquisition of the "common language" that performers will share, and which will form the foundation of the physical "vocabulary" with which they will communicate story or meaning to the audience' (2005: 189).

A particular challenge for this chapter is that devising processes were largely unrecorded. Devising meant that scripts didn't usually exist, and if they did the chances of them being published or surviving over time were slim. In many respects this was a condition of practice that matched the nature of mime and physical theatre – its ephemerality was intrinsic to its appeal. Video recording was also relatively basic during this period and VHS recordings from the time tended to be unsatisfactory, with poor resolution and often filmed only from the back of an auditorium or rehearsal space[1]. Rehearsal and devising processes were seldom written about, and if they were the words struggle to capture the sheer messiness and uncertainty of the process, its rhizomatic complexity, the often intuitive nature of devising, and of course the tensions and disagreements (creative or personal) so often involved. Processes also

---

1 One notable exception to this was the 1992 BBC *Late Show* episode documenting the creation of Théâtre de Théâtre de Complicité's *Street of Crocodiles* – unfortunately this is not freely available and copies are hard to track down.

126 Making mime and physical theatre

repeatedly cross-fertilised from one company to another as performers moved to work with different companies or set up their own groups.

If we look at content as well as process, we can build a picture of the ways in which mime and physical theatre were used to represent the world we lived in over this period. A broad overview might indicate an interest in: clowning and tales of absurdity and surreal humour; revisiting cultural icons (films, books, history, myths), often with humour or irreverence; critiquing middle-class angst; and, interrogating issues around gender and personal identity. Themes that might emerge from such an overview include: identity in its various forms, crises of modern life, gender politics, the nature and value of physical risk/danger, and authenticity. All of this indicates the cultural expression of a society seeking to re-evaluate the relationships individuals might have with their sense of self, identity and stability. In the face of the socio-political certainties that Thatcherism sought to impose between 1979 and 1997 (nationalism, market forces, individuals rather than society), artists reacted with pastiche, physical risk, comedy, transformation and ensemble creation. Most mime and physical theatre did not address the macro politics of the times head on (e.g. class, party politics, world affairs), but resisted it obliquely[2].

The economics of devising

As we have seen in Chapter 3, funding was not easy to access for mime and physical theatre during the 1970s and 1980s. This meant that group devising was often under-funded with limited access to research and development, prolonged devising periods, or work on the show after it opened. It also meant multi-tasking within companies – with performers taking on administrative roles, as well as attending to dramaturgy, music, design, prop or mask making, stage management, and get-ins and get-outs. If a set could be afforded it would have to be tourable, and it would need to be constructed at the start of, if not within, the devising process. Uncertainty around funding would inevitably affect the time available to devise and the resources to support the process (space, cast size, materials). Annabel Arden's memories of her early work with the 1982 Company reveal how financial realities influenced the company's ethos and spurred their creativity:

> For example, the 1982 Theatre Company which preceded [Théâtre de] Complicité is very important. . . . We met a full year before we intended to start and our plan was, since we really didn't have much funding if anything, to work as many jobs as possible in 1981 in order to fund ourselves for 1982. Of

---

2 A couple of notable exceptions from the 1980s might be: Steven Berkoff's *Sink the Belgrano!* (1986), which openly criticised Margaret Thatcher's decision to sink the Argentinian warship Belgrano, during the 1983 Falklands War; and Trickster's production *Memory Gate* (1986), which dealt with the Miners' Strike (and was incidentally the company's final show).

course, we did have supplementary benefit, those of us who were British. . . . We had no electronic stuff. And I think that's a major, major thing – because if you wanted to just forget the world and go into your rehearsal room and go into your creative process, you could. Nothing was pulling you out. . . . You could just become an obsessive with great ease. And the other thing was – Neil [Bartlett] said to me, and I've never forgotten it . . . I said, 'But Neil, there's just no money', and he said, 'No', he said, 'We must learn to be poor'. I think that's really interesting, and we could then for a while. . . . It seems more challenging today.

(Arden, 2021)

It is important to acknowledge that although many artists survived and even flourished within an 'aesthetics of poverty', there were many others who could not sustain their work under such austerity. This inevitably meant that some careers were short-lived as a result of a paucity of funding and not a lack of training, talent or commitment.

In the 1970s, short sketches became prevalent because they suited the performance opportunities available – street theatre, small arts centres and cabaret/variety. These were environments that worked against the development of longer complex work. Justin Case (2020) recalled in interview how his early performances tended to be composed of a series of sketches that would be linked thematically and were predominantly comic in nature. For solo artists, the challenge of moving beyond short sketches was simple – how to develop a prolonged narrative with only one person on stage. The breakthrough to more sustained pieces started with some of the productions staged by Julian Chagrin, Lindsay Kemp and Steven Berkoff in the 1960s and 1970s, and was sustained by the later work of Nola Rae, Moving Picture Mime Show, Trestle, Trickster, Black Mime Theatre and Théâtre de Complicité. The opportunity to apply for Arts Council funding was clearly important in supporting the development of longer and more complex productions. Nola Rae's process moved towards longer and more complicated shows from the start of the 1990s, with *Elizabeth's Last Stand*: 'I decided to tell a story and not to change character – so it would be a story with one character throughout' (2020). For many of the other companies, the significant breakthrough came with the chance to apply for regular funding.

The spaces in which work was made would also vary according to funding and company support networks – school halls, community centres, back rooms and bedrooms, all sorts of ad hoc spaces, sometimes serendipitously shared with others. On occasion, such spaces would inform the making of the show – Frantic Assembly recall a plastic Wendy House left in a rehearsal space that found its way into their show *Zero* (Graham and Hoggett, 2014: 20). They also recall that posh studio spaces could even work against creativity – stifling the messiness, noise and unruliness that are sometimes needed. Spaces need to allow and encourage transformation, play and risk. Rehearsal environments could provide spaces where people meet people and share work, as could festivals (see Chapter 3), workshops

128 Making mime and physical theatre

or bars. Work created in more rural settings (for example parts of Wales (Brith Gof) or the South West (Footsbarn and Kneehigh)) seemed to come from a slightly different aesthetic – more interactive, playful and rough-edged. Small and intimate performance spaces, where the performers and the audience were in close proximity or sharing the same space, helped generate a sense of shared creativity between actor and audience. Often toilet and bar facilities were shared as well, making for very direct communication and building strong relationships with audiences: 'in the early days, people used to come to the [Théâtre de Complicité] shows, and we would always ask them to talk to us in the bar afterwards, because we wanted to learn what they thought' (Arden, 2021). Unconventional spaces were often cheaper and more accessible for audiences who might be intimidated by large theatres (as largely middle-class, white institutions with poor disabled access at this time) or even who were ideologically opposed to mainstream theatre.

Improvisation – the body and soul of devising

A rapid and enthusiastic increase in the use of improvisation within the education, alternative and experimental theatre sectors during the 1970s and the 1980s prepared the ground for young mime performers eager to devise their own work. Until the Theatres Act 1968, which abolished censorship of theatre in the UK and removed the requirement to submit a text to the Lord Chamberlain's Office for approval, it was very difficult to create a production through improvisation. After 1968, there was an explosion of devised theatre making, with practitioners attracted by the excitement of spontaneous creation; the empowerment of the individual creative voice; the possibility of exploring non-linear narrative, surreal imagery and physical expression; and, the democratisation of the making process. As well as the use of improvisation in the devising of material for performance, it is worth noting the growing interest in improvised performance created spontaneously on the night, from a provocation provided by the company, the director or the audience. By the 1990s, spurred on by the popular success of television programmes such as *Whose Line Is It Anyway* (Channel 4, 1988–1999) and the work of practitioners such as Keith Johnstone, Theatre Machine and Justin Case, a number of physical theatre companies such as Spike Theatre[3] (Liverpool) and Improbable[4] (UK touring company) also explored long and short form improvised performance.

---

3 Spike Theatre was formed in Liverpool in 1993 by Glenn Noble. In the early 2000s the company developed a show, *Hoof!*, with Reject's Revenge, based on extended improvisation that then continued to tour for the next ten years – it was of course a different show wherever it went.
4 Improbable were formed in 1996 by Phelim McDermott, Lee Simpson, Julian Crouch and Nick Sweeting. Live improvisation on stage was a key part of the company's work from the beginning: 'Really we never rehearse, we only make theatre. Rehearsals are making theatre all the time' (Lee Simpson in interview in 2004, in Heddon and Milling, 2006: 186). Their work is influenced by Philippe Gaulier, John Wright, Keith Johnstone and Michael Chekhov. Their shows are playful and sometimes game-based; for Improbable improvisation was also about recognising that the audience have a role in the creation of the show.

Denise Wong (Black Mime Theatre) neatly articulates the nature of the devising process and the benefits of using improvisation as she experienced it in the 1990s:

> It was a case of having an open ear all of the time, in the rehearsal room. It wasn't that I was dictating to the actors. It was a collaborative devising process, where I have an idea, I may initiate and start it, but the actors would always at some point come back with their own ideas. It was great to give them the opportunity to put those ideas into practice. Or they did something . . . maybe I'd wanted something to be created in the space, and they did the exact opposite, 'That's not what I meant!' But it was brilliant, and it was like, 'OK. We'll go with that.' It wasn't a case of I was a dictator in the space wanting them to do it my way. More to the point, it was a collaboration based on achieving excellence. The process created trust and the willingness to explore, go beyond what we knew, past the clichés. Whatever was the best, we would create on stage . . . and that's what we did. It was a wonderful experience.
>
> *(Wong, 2020)*

It is important to recognise that even by the end of the 1990s, this kind of practice – improvisation, devising, physicality and collaboration – was a challenge to the nature of conventional British theatre, which emphasised text and voice, used traditional power structures and hierarchies, and embodied patriarchal politics within its rehearsal rooms. For Black, disabled and female performers, an alternative to these repressive and exclusionary structures was especially important (see Chapter 7). For many young male performers, these authoritarian and didactic strategies for making work were also acutely unpalatable. Devising offered the opportunity for a more democratic creative process, recognising multiple voices and life experiences within the making of theatre. Nonetheless, it is important to recognise that the rhetoric of democratic collaboration was not always performed in practice and that devising can also involve traditional power structures unless closely monitored. Funding constraints would make it hard for companies to act as a creative ensemble throughout the year. They would more often work on a project-by-project basis, which meant that core members would end up with more responsibility and more input, but also that new members would keep arriving to re-invigorate company processes.

Auto-cours: *a model for group devising*

As noted earlier, UK mime during the 1960s and 1970s seems largely (with a few exceptions such as Steven Berkoff's London Theatre Company and the Lindsay Kemp Company) to have been about making sketches and solo acts. This was undoubtedly influenced by the availability (or not) of funding and the expectations of venues and audiences, but also by the nature of the training available. Where they were available, classes and workshops would sometimes provide opportunities

130 Making mime and physical theatre

at the end of a session for students to make short pieces to share. Steven Berkoff recalls how, when he and Geoff Buckley were studying mime with Claude Chagrin in the 1960s, she would invite the students to create a performance:

> And so we would get together for 10 minutes and quickly think out a scene. Geoffrey and I would work. And that was so exciting. We found something which was quite unusual and quite stimulating and made the actor more like an author than an interpreter, creating your own work.
>
> *(Berkoff, 2020)*

But it was only really with the instigation of the *auto-cours* at the Lecoq School in 1968 (see Chapter 2) that any mime training began to insert a part of the curriculum that offered students the chance to learn how to devise. The *auto-cours* allowed a period of time each day when students would work in groups to devise their own creative responses to a provocation or theme supplied by the teachers. Enabling the students to discover their own theatrical voice within the experience of the School, the *auto-cours* naturally became a model for the ways in which graduating companies/artists would create their own work[5]. The *auto-cours* also grew out of Lecoq's fascination with the creative possibilities offered by the chorus. Berkoff, who attended a summer course at the Lecoq School in the mid-1960s, recalls that,

> it was the group exercises I found most fascinating. And that became in some way the core of my work as a director. It was a simple idea, so simple. A man goes to sit on the chair. Where are you? You may be in a cafe, you might be working in a bank, you might be sewing, being an old tailor, you might be painting, you could be sculpting. So soon as you start, the group of twelve come into the scene. You may be then having a café, 'un café, s'il vous plait, eh', and then everybody will come in . . . 'je desire un croissant avec . . .'. Suddenly it is a great Café, it's exciting. People all talking, overlapping, making relationships, communicating. And then, as soon as somebody wants to change it . . . you don't appoint it, or you could . . . so another person within the group might change it. Suddenly he's in the trenches in the war, after eating it becomes a gun, everybody's in . . . suddenly it's become a war scene. Of such invention, such danger, such fear; people hiding and being wounded and crying. It's something I'd never seen before in my life.
>
> *(Berkoff, 2020)*

This kind of work helped Lecoq's students to develop confidence in using improvisation and devising to make extended group performance work. Initially, graduates

---

5 It is also interesting that the *auto-cours* implicitly became a model of working for many of those who had never been anywhere near the Lecoq School – a kind of osmosis created by increased awareness of the School's pedagogy and its dissemination by companies such as Théâtre de Complicité.

from Lecoq who returned to the UK tended to work predominantly as individual artists (e.g. Julian Chagrin, Geoff Buckley, Chris Harris and Justin Case). However, from the late 1970s onwards, as more UK students attended the School and as changes in freedom of movement within Europe facilitated the arrival of non-UK graduates, small international companies became the norm. Théâtre de Complicité is a high-profile and well-documented example of a company founded on just such a basis; even today, when working on texts, Complicité still begins with a collaborative and devised approach. Philippe Gaulier's *Stages* at his Schools in Paris and in London have also offered a similar introduction to devising, influencing companies such as: Peepolykus, The Right Size, dereck dereck, Gloria and Spymonkey. Other schools and practitioners have developed their own approaches to group devising, but these all owe a significant debt to the influence of Lecoq's *auto-cours*. The training offered by Decroux and by Marceau at their own schools in Paris placed more emphasis on the development of individual technical mastery than on group creativity. Consequently, the majority of mime artists working in the UK from this tradition continued to practice as solo artists (e.g. Nola Rae) or duos (e.g. Theatre de L'Ange Fou – Steven Wasson and Corinne Soum).

Solo artists – improvising on your own

Solo performers were successful in the 1970s and 1980s, but this success often necessitated side-stepping the economics of devising. In the early years of this period, artists such as Nola Rae or John Mowat could create shows with little or no funding because they only had to fund themselves. They could then tour extensively but at low cost across the growing network of small-scale, and sometimes mid-scale, venues which had emerged. But if the financial model was different, the process was still the same. John Mowat, who has performed as a solo mime since 1980 as well as directing visual theatre shows for others, preferred to take time to create a show, as much as 'two to three months' (Mowat, 2020). This included time to 'play and just explore and experiment and try things, regardless of whether I'm working from a story, a script or whatever . . . I have to find it in the workroom, with the people I'm working with' (ibid.). For Nola Rae, the process of making mime is also a process of elimination:

> That's what mime does. It knocks out everything you don't need to tell a story. So, you get to the essence of something physically, without using extraneous things. . . . That's why I like mime – you can get to the seat of your argument in as few moves as possible.
>
> *(Rae, 2020)*

Her approach is underpinned by one of the central tenets of illusionary mime – the simple and direct communicative power of gesture. She sees mime as a process of simplification and communication: 'The audience doesn't have to struggle with words and what they mean – because words can mean different things – whereas the

132 Making mime and physical theatre

gesture means one thing . . . A gesture is a gesture, it's got no hidden meaning about it' (ibid.). Although one might contest the assumption that gestures do not have hidden meanings, this statement is also about the importance of encouraging the audience to use their imagination. For Rae, there is an initial decision about the nature of the show – the story or theme that drives it – and then a decision about the style and feel of the show, for example does it have a twist, will it include music. For *Elizabeth's Last Stand* (1990), Rae had help in the devising process from Simon McBurney.

> I put in front of him all sorts of mimes and bits and pieces I was working out, and he said, 'Yes. Very rich.' And then he tore everything up and threw it in the air. 'What you've got to do is this, you've got to do that, you've got to do this'. You've got to start with a character you know – so my grandmother – you've got 20 minutes to draw the audience in, otherwise you've lost them . . . A lot of research went into the show. . . . You start very big and then you narrow down – this is the essence of mime.
>
> *(ibid.)*

Rae's process of creation and reduction demonstrates the principles at the heart of most mime performance – consistent simplification and the distillation of gesture and story to its essence. The two most important elements are generating initial material and then the editing process:

> I would write a story, then a director would come in, and he would say no this doesn't work, why don't you try that. But I would have something for him to see. I don't go in with a director, trying to develop things – I don't have the time usually. So I write a story, then I try to do it.
>
> *(ibid.)*

Much is already decided for Rae by the time that she presents her ideas to a director: 'By the time I put them in front of a director, I've decided what the set's going to be, I've decided the costume . . . I've decided on the props, I've made things. So it's quite well developed' (ibid.).

Play, creativity and 'le jeu'

From the 1960s onwards there was an intense interest in the nature of creativity. The figure of the (usually male) individual genius was increasingly critiqued and people were inspired to recognise and celebrate their own individual creativity. There was a movement towards cultural democracy, in which diversity was recognised and accepted. Linearity and rational logic were also increasingly challenged by the concepts of play and transformation, what Sean Foley (founder member of The Right Size) calls 'the invitation to playfulness' (2021). The idea of a transformative playfulness that functions both as a core attitude towards the work for the actor/deviser and as something that draws in the imagination of the audience was

Making mime and physical theatre **133**

a central tenet in the training provided by Lecoq, Gaulier and Pagneux[6]. As such it deeply informed the processes of all the artists and companies who emerged from those schools. Annabel Arden sums up a common process for such companies when she describes how, 'There isn't initially much discussion amongst Complicite [sic] actors; we just kept trying things out' (in Luckhurst and Veltman, 2001: 4). David Glass also highlights the importance of the playful quality of the ensemble: 'Working with people who have the imagination for something they haven't yet seen but they feel is out there somewhere, is the key' (Glass in Olsen, 1997: 11). This playfulness is a process that creates scary and unsettling moments for an ensemble or an artist – great resilience is required and a high level of trust in each other.

> In the process you have staging posts where it is complete crap. . . . They are as important as the good things. The reason you have bad stuff is to know what not to do. Beautiful, simple things usually occur only at the beginning and very end of the rehearsal process. In the middle is just rubbish. . . . I know when someone is doing something wrong, but I don't necessarily know when they are doing something right. Right has not been decided yet. There is no right.
>
> *(Glass in Olsen, 1997: 11)*

Playfulness also helped to de-centre authority in the making process, as Bim Mason describes it: 'you just sort of prime the group up and tell them the sort of journey it's going to go on, or just give them key words, and then just let things happen and material kind of comes out of that' (2020). There is a common conception embedded in such practice of 'the collective head' (Foley, 2021). As director and teacher John Wright states,

> I try to find the game and make it meaningful. That's fundamentally what I'm trying to do. Looking at what do we like. Because I'm not going to say, oh we're doing this and we're doing it this way, and it means this, and you need to do this, this and this. It's not like that, we *find* everything.
>
> *(Wright, 2020)*

The following three case studies look at examples of practice deeply informed by notions of play.

John Wright

Wright is a key figure in the development of this playful approach to improvisation and physical devising in the UK. Inspired as a teenager by seeing one of Julian Chagrin's mime performances, Wright, unable to afford the Lecoq School in Paris,

---

6 Although only briefly mentioned in *The Moving Body*, it thoroughly informs Lecoq's writing. For a more extended discussion of *le jeu*, see Murray (2018: 65–69 and 2010: 221–223).

134 Making mime and physical theatre

initially trained as an actor at the New College of Speech and Drama (now Middlesex University). After a period of professional work, he returned to teach mime, mask and improvisation at New College. The course structure allowed him to explore ways of using improvisation across disciplines, and to investigate the use of masks in improvisation. It was out of this work that Trestle Theatre evolved. Another inspiration was the work of Philippe Gaulier and Monika Pagneux; after attending a workshop in London in 1984, Wright worked with Gaulier whenever he was able, eventually teaching at Gaulier's school in London in the 1990s. From Gaulier he took the idea of the 'game' and pleasure in the game, and from Pagneux the pleasure and value of physical attunement – themes that have since deeply informed his practice. After his early work with Trestle, Wright later founded Told by an Idiot in 1993, with Hayley Carmichael and Paul Hunter. He still teaches today.

In an interview, Wright explained how, within his work, he was trying to get to something like the playfulness that had inspired him in Julian Chagrin's work.

> I'd seen quite a lot of work, been influenced by people who had worked with Marcel Marceau and Etienne Decroux – but this work did not appeal to me. This was conceptual, very aesthetic, which was not the way I wanted to go. I wanted something more impulsive, more playful, more fun.
>
> *(Wright, 2020)*

His approach is collaborative and open-ended, requiring frankness, openness and mutual respect. Initially, the work is divergent, exploring a number of different routes and paths, seeing what catches, what might take off or go in an interesting direction.

> I say, 'OK. You like that. Has anyone got a response to that?' And that means, you come up with your image. Don't tell us about it, just do it. There's always that response. The only question is what do we like.
>
> *(ibid.)*

At a certain point, the work converges, things start coming together. For Wright, this is also something that's collaborative.

> Once you say 'What do you like?', 'We like that'. OK. We will keep that. For the moment we keep it. For the *moment*, we keep it. Let's see where it goes. It doesn't mean to say you are committing your life to it . . . for the moment, we've got that, and we see where it goes. And the same process continues. The thing is, we all want to centralise things, we all want to know where it's going.
>
> *(ibid.)*

This is a process that clearly depends on the group and its willingness to work in this way. In the case of Trestle and Told by an Idiot, these were, at the start, groups of actors who had been trained by Wright (and in Told by an Idiot's case also had ten years or so of previous experience). For Wright, the time it would take to create a show would depend on the group.

> If you have a skilled group, you could get a remarkable long way in a few days. If you have a group where someone . . . it only needs someone who is deeply uncomfortable with this freedom and you have a disaster. It just won't work. So, you have to find the right group.
>
> *(ibid.)*

Moving Picture Mime Show

Moving Picture Mime Show's work grew out of the *auto-cours* assignments they had worked on during the second year of their course at the Lecoq School. Toby Sedgwick (2020) recalls how:

> We wrote *The Seven Samurai* when we were there [at the School]. It came out of the *Pantomime Blanche* exercise, doing a famous film. I think David [Gaines] did a version of it, *The Seven Samurai*, first, and then we thought this is a really good theme, why don't we work on it. So, we got together . . . we didn't think we were going to do anything more.

Lecoq would set students a project to combine *pantomime blanche* techniques, storytelling and the visual imagery, ambition and rhythmic pacing of cartoons to create a mimed version of a classic film. If the styles used drew from their shared experience at the School, the ideas for content came from observing the world around them. Sedgwick recollects that ideas for shows 'came out of extraordinary places really' (ibid.). He recalls how the work fell into two different forms, 'There's the mask work, and then there's the non-mask' (ibid.), indicating the different dynamics and technical requirements of working with or without masks. In ways that echo the work of other companies that used masks, such as Trestle, Sedgwick identifies mask work as needing a very specific devising approach – 'The character of the mask would be the first thing' (ibid.).

> The whole idea of *Handle with Care*, started from an improvisation around one very comfortable arm chair and one ordinary chair. It was an improvisation that was played out about who got the chair, then who had to go and get the other chair. Then just seeing them sit there, we thought, 'God, they look like two people in the corridor of an old people's home.' And then we thought, 'Well that's a good starting point. Old people's home. Let's do a piece about old age.' Then what the idea was, was to show that people shouldn't be thrown away, they still have a mind of their own, and the nurse who never has enough time for them. So basically, it then almost became a political, well not political, but a very strong idea – literally out of that one idea of an arm chair.
>
> *(ibid.)*

136 Making mime and physical theatre

With a group of three, this would involve two improvising and one watching, sharing responsibility for creating, evaluating and refining the work as it developed. The *auto-cours* model is ideal for this, encouraging both ensemble creation, constant peer critique and constructive criticism, based on observation and shared vocabulary.

> That was the way we worked. Very much like the way we always worked at Lecoq. All the decisions were made on a two-to-one basis. Three is a magic number, we never wanted four – that would have been mayhem.
>
> *(ibid.)*

It is also a process that provides for constant renewal and revision, as Sedgwick reveals:

> A piece was never finished really. Even with the *Samurai* we used to change bits that we weren't happy with. *Creatures from the Swamp*, we were always working on that as well. We'd change bits, or we thought bits weren't very clear or we'd make them better.
>
> *(ibid.)*

The company's work drew heavily on the transformative potential of the mime taught at the Lecoq School – anything could become anything, through the physical technique of the performer. This enabled the company to create wild flights of imaginative transformation – as Sedgwick puts it, 'one of the aspects of doing mime, the audience is always engaged and their imaginations are always stirred' (ibid.). This would enable them to devise shows that would move easily from character-driven narrative to broader images that would set context or offer juxtaposition. An example of this process might be the way they structured *Passionate Leave*:

> We did a short sequence within *Passionate Leave*, it was just a moment. The story would stop, and you would see the whole history of how the Coliseum was created. There were three parts – one part was an airport, was the whole thing about the phenomenon of travel, another one was the touristy aspect of an Italian city, and the other part was placing the audience in Rome, what it means, the whole background about tourism and the importance of the historical background to the history of the world basically.
>
> *(ibid.)*

This process was further encouraged by their spell of collaboration with Ken Campbell, one of the leading figures in UK alternative theatre and a true master of the surreal and absurd. It was Campbell who suggested a scene in *The Complete Berk* in which Sedgwick conjures up an image of bacon being fried – his whole body transformed into a sizzling rasher!

Théâtre de Complicité

Although the work of Théâtre de Complicité has been extensively covered elsewhere (e.g. in Fry, 2015; Heddon and Milling, 2006; Murray, 2018; and, Wisniewski, 2016), it is important to acknowledge the significant impact that they have had on physical theatre practice over the 1980s and 1990s. The company was founded by Simon McBurney, Annabel Arden, Marcello Magni and Fiona Gordon in 1983[7]. McBurney, Arden and Magni remained at the core of the company over the next decade or so. Their work has always been informed by the training they undertook in Paris at the Lecoq School (McBurney and Magni) and with Philippe Gaulier (Arden). Throughout the 1980s, their work was almost entirely devised. Tapping into a general cultural enthusiasm for comedy, improvisation and playfulness, they created a series of highly successful shows (including *A Minute Too Late, More Bigger Snacks Now* and *Anything for a Quiet Life*) before bringing their physical inventiveness and comic imaginations to a landmark production of Friedrich Durrenmatt's *The Visit* in 1989.

Lecoq's sense of *le jeu*, central to their training experiences in Paris, infuses all of their work throughout this period. Initial warm-up games would provide starting points to launch into improvisations, exercises would morph into more structured work that might develop into a scene. The inter-play (*complicité*) between company members as they played during the warm-ups would be something the company consciously aimed to maintain in the devising process and performance. The success of their productions and their willingness to offer workshops to schools and colleges (see Chapter 6) meant that interest and enthusiasm for this way of working grew and spread quickly. The company's move towards using texts and addressing more serious themes in the 1990s indicated how play and improvisation could be used to produce work closer to the mainstream. It is important to recognise that this was a company that never set out to be a mime company – they wanted, in the spirit of the Lecoq School, to create the kind of theatre that they could not see around them: physically expressive, interdisciplinary, challenging and international. Our enjoyable and productive interview with Annabel Arden, and our extensive use of verbatim quotes from this conversation, is testimony to the importance and huge impact that this company – and its leading figures – have had on the landscape mapped by this book.

What was particularly noticeable about the work of Moving Picture Mime Show and Théâtre de Complicité was the way that it tapped into the cultural energies of the time – comic irreverence and a kind of punk ethic of physical energy and of making work simply and with commitment. Their work used the energy and freedom of devised theatre making to push back against the rather quaint image of the classic French mime, as epitomised by Marceau.

---

7 Fiona Gordon left the company after the first production.

138 Making mime and physical theatre

The etude and physical scoring

Jerzy Grotowski's work represents a different approach to improvisation, devising and performing – one that draws on the concept of the *étude*, a term that encapsulates both training and performance and suggests the use of technique to inform structure and composition[8]. His work also emphasises the profound impulses of the actor as revealed through physically engaged performance. At the heart of this approach is the *via negativa*, an approach that works by 'taking away, eliminating resistances (such as self-consciousness or fear), finding impulses/reflexes/reactions, not getting blocked by self-judgement' (Allain, 2022)[9]. He also employed improvisation as one of the ways to re-work and invigorate existing (often classical) text. Grotowski's influence on UK physical theatre can be seen most vividly in Peter Brook's Theatre of Cruelty season at the LAMDA Theatre Club (1964) and the subsequent production of *US* (1966) at the RSC, as well as in the work of a number of fringe theatre companies such as Freehold, Triple Action and TNT in England, and Cardiff Lab Theatre, RAT Theatre and Brith Gof in Wales (see Chapter 4). The devising processes used by Grotowski and those influenced by him focused on a strong ensemble, the use of song, and movement generated from inner impulse. They also invoked the indivisibility of training, devising and rehearsing within the laboratory theatre structure. The work might be thematically driven, with the performers generating their own physical scores in response to provocations offered by the themes. Workshops available at the time with people who had worked or trained with Grotowski often offered UK practitioners opportunities to learn 'core' exercises, such as The Cat and dip into the process for a day; but such exercises were not the real heart of the practice. Exercises such as The Cat had only evolved as contingent and necessary means through which Grotowski would challenge the actor to achieve their own authenticity – something much harder to undertake second-hand. Inevitably this led to various misunderstandings of the nature and focus of Grotowski's work.

Events such as Grotowski's visit to Cardiff Laboratory Theatre in 1982, Odin Teatret's residencies in the UK in 1980 (Cardiff) and 1994 (Coventry[10]) and Gardzienice's UK tour in 1989 meant that more UK practitioners had the opportunity to observe demonstrations and performances and to take part in longer

---

8 Pablo Pakula's unpublished doctoral thesis, *Jerzy Grotowski's influence on British theatre 1966–1980 (histories, perspectives, recollections)*, (University of Kent, 2011) is an excellent source for more detail on this strand of influence.

9 *Via negativa* is a widely used but often misunderstood term. Grotowski's approach is, for instance, distinct from the pedagogy of Jacques Lecoq and Philippe Gaulier, who are sometimes also credited with using a *via negativa* approach in their teaching. However, Lecoq never used the term *via negativa*, the challenges for the student arose out of the improvisation tasks. Gaulier would reject a student's offer within class in order to provoke their creativity and stimulate the quality of their relationship with the audience.

10 The Odin residency in Coventry ran from 9 to 18 May 1994. It involved performances of *Kaosmos, Judith, The Castle of Holstebro* and *Itsi Bitsi*, as well as numerous work demonstrations, training sessions, a barter session and public discussions. It was hosted by the Belgrade Theatre, Warwick Arts Centre and Coventry Centre for the Performing Arts.

workshops that illustrated how performance material might be developed. The limitations on the spread of this approach and its traction on physical theatre making in the UK came largely from the difficulties in accessing opportunities to learn how to work in this way, the rigour and commitment required, the length of time needed to develop a full understanding and the lack of intensive training opportunities in the UK. John Wright suggests that what motivated many young performers at this time was a desire to 'make theatre' – they weren't interested in extended training, but in how to 'make compelling visual images' (Wright, 2020). Those who wished to pursue Grotowski or Barba's work method further were required to travel to Denmark (Odin Teatret), Poland (Gardzienice or the Grotowski studio in Wroclaw) or Italy (Grotowski Workcenter, in Pontedera) and to study/work there for prolonged periods. As a result, the number of UK practitioners working in the Odin/Grotowski tradition in the UK in the 1990s was very small: for example, Carran Waterfield (Triangle Theatre) in Coventry, Melanie Thompson in Glastonbury, Paul Stebbings and Phil Smith (TNT) in Bristol, Jonathan Grieve and Para Active Theatre in East London, as well as Cardiff Laboratory Theatre, RAT Theatre and Paupers' Carnival in Wales, and Triple Action in Mansfield. As with other approaches to physical theatre practice, only a very limited number of UK university drama/theatre departments offered any focus on making theatre in this way (for example Paul Allain at Brunel University College and Goldsmiths, Mike Pearson at Aberystwyth, Nigel Stewart at Lancaster, Nick Sales and Sandra Reeve at Exeter, and Gabriel Gawin at Manchester Metropolitan). This, of course, was driven in part by the lack of work – 'there probably wasn't the place for them in the theatre profession and industry' (Allain, 2020). The work of Odin and Gardzienice is arguably more well-known now than that of Grotowski, in part because of Eugenio Barba's extensive publications ('Barba has written so well about the work, it's so accessible and it's so much easier to get to' (ibid.)) and also because of the publications by academics focusing on their work (Allain, 1997; Watson, 1995; and Turner, 2004). Cardiff Laboratory Theatre, led by Richard Gough, also hosted important residencies and masterclasses (see Chapter 4). In the 1990s, Gardzienice's work became well-known in the UK as a result of a number of productions by Katie Mitchell at the RSC, which were informed by its work. A closer examination of the work of two UK companies influenced by Grotowski follows.

Freehold and Triple Action

Freehold emerged out of Wherehouse La Mama in London in 1969 and stayed together until 1973. Freehold were a disciplined ensemble – 'a long time was spent in workshop before the group played publicly' (Chambers in Craig: 106). For Chambers, 'The distinctive quality of their work (apart from offering strong roles for women) was the creation of non-naturalistic images through gesture and movement to present a story' (ibid.). There is little evidence that Grotowski influenced Freehold's work directly, although the company clearly knew of and was inspired by his practice. The company's devising process involved explorations of movement and voice through improvisation, guided and directed by the director, Nancy Meckler.

140 Making mime and physical theatre

The work placed a profound emphasis on process – a short scene could take several days to work on, with great attention paid both to the visual composition of the scene and to the precision of the physical and emotional score. The work started from the actor's impulses, not from their intellect. However, the work was not anti-intellectual or undisciplined, a misunderstanding that may have undermined the work of some trying to explore this approach. Rather it was about centring the actors' energies, aligning their impulses and challenging themselves to delve beyond habitual responses. The process was arduous and demanding, and sometimes the fatigue of the actors was intentionally used to push them beyond intellectual responses and towards physical freedom. These were processes that take time, and the other challenge for companies such as Freehold and Triple Action was the lack of funding to support the kinds of extended devising and rehearsal periods required. Where companies struggled to find the time to commit fully to the process the work could fall into cliché, becoming overly reliant on style over content, strained emotions, and a mechanical repetition of poorly understood exercises.

Although Freehold's approach placed a significant emphasis on the centrality of the actor to the process, it also gave considerable power to the director. Whilst the devising process was often collaborative and ensemble-based and the performers would sometimes be left by the director to work on their own for extended periods, the director was always the central figure who would act as the outside eye, empowered to make the ultimate selection of material or to provoke the performers to greater authenticity. For Freehold this role was taken by Meckler, while for Triple Action it was Steve Rumblelow, who had previously worked at the RSC and been inspired by Peter Brook. Meckler also provides an important link with the US avant-garde theatre scene, through her connections with La Mama Plexus and Richard Schechner (with whom she had studied in New York).

Freehold and Triple Action tended to focus on classical texts that had something of a mythical element to them[11]. Pakula points out that this interest in universal myths corresponds with the interest at the time in brotherhood, shared humanity, the collective unconscious and communion with an audience (2011: 158). The approach to the texts was however by no means reverential – the texts would often be re-worked into a textual montage that refined the focus both on the themes identified as important and on the emotional core of the play.

Another point of inspiration from Grotowski was the use of space and visual dramaturgy. Grotowski's productions, in particular those featured in *Towards a Poor Theatre*, carefully considered the spatial relationship between actors and audience and the visual elements that constructed the overall experience. Although UK venues did not tend to be flexible enough to accommodate profound changes to seating arrangements, both Freehold and Triple Action sought to develop a strong visual style and to make bold and innovative use of the spaces that they had – Triple Action's 1972 production of *Hamlet* 'took place on a rope-web suspended above

---

11 Rumblelow directed Triple Action productions based on Byron's *Manfred*, *Oedipus*, *Faust* and a number of Shakespeare tragedies (Cohn, 1975).

Making mime and physical theatre **141**

the audience's heads' (Pakula, 2011: 174). Both companies shared a 'poor theatre' aesthetic, with the stage space stripped back to enable the focus to fall on the actor and with minimal lighting and set design.

TNT

TNT (The New Theatre) was started in 1980 by Paul Stebbings and Phil Smith. After studying at the University of Bristol, Stebbings undertook some training with Grotowski's Labatorium in Poland and both Stebbings and Smith attended workshops with Eugenio Barba and other members of Odin Teatret. In addition, they were inspired by the work of the Russian director Vsevelod Meyerhold, and attracted to popular forms of theatre such as Commedia dell'Arte. They had worked with Triple Action for a short period, but were interested in making work that was more widely accessible. They describe their work as underpinned by several key questions:

> is it possible to make experimental theatre while avoiding the obscure modernist path to a niche audience? Is it possible to apply a physical theatre training to performances with intelligent texts on serious themes, without becoming bogged down in gymnastic or abstract theatre? And, if the answers to the first two questions are 'yes', how far and in what ways can such an aesthetic – combining experiment with popular forms – travel, develop and engage with a changing world.
>
> *(Stebbings and Smith, 2020: 9)*

They describe some of the key principles that informed their process for making work as follows:

- 'We always aspire to move not to a statement, but to music. Not to a mobile manifesto, but to the rhythm of unfolding ideas, Images, actions and abstract un-explainable sounds and motions' (Stebbings and Smith, 2020: 59)
- 'The rehearsal process should be kept open in its treatment of material, text and performance – so that profound changes can be introduced late on in rehearsals' (ibid.: 59)
- 'the set should be like a motor or an engine, a vehicle that can be ridden' (ibid.: 59)
- 'the actors . . . must have open, dilated bodies and an emotional warmth' (ibid.: 60)
- 'our poetics are those of "the grotesque". We make connections on stage that do not usually occur in daily life' (ibid.: 60)
- 'we are against the bureaucracy of the stage . . . scene changes or any utilitarian action that is not part of the performance's theatrical world' (ibid.: 61)

142 Making mime and physical theatre

Their work marks an interesting project to create popular performances within the Grotowski and Meyerhold tradition. TNT continue to make work and perform, both in the UK and abroad[12].

Objects and masks

As part of the broad landscape of improvised and devised practice, the use of masks, objects and puppets necessitates the development and use of some different, though aligned, skills and some specific approaches to devising. The use of masks in the making of devised performances has a long history in theatre, reaching back at least until the Commedia dell'Arte players in Renaissance Europe. More recently Jacques Copeau and Suzanne Bing developed approaches to devising theatre with Les Copiaus in Burgundy in the late 1920s that have profoundly influenced practitioners since then. Both Lecoq and Gaulier include training in mask work as a central part of their pedagogy (variously including neutral, larval, utilitarian, full-face and half-face mask training, plus Commedia and clown), and Keith Johnstone's influential book *Impro* (1979)[13] includes a chapter extolling the virtues of mask work for the development of spontaneity and imaginative transformation in performance. Masks have been central to the devised work of a number of UK companies and practitioners over the last 40 years, including Moving Picture Mime Show; Trestle; John Wright; Trickster (see Fig. 5.1); Ninean Kinear-Wilson (1953–2013; mask-maker from Liverpool); Michael Chase (The Mask Studio); Trading Faces (founded in 1987); and Olly Crick (teacher and performer).

Mask work shares much with the improvised devising processes described earlier. It requires similar attitudes and approaches and enables comparable flights of imagination and transformation. Its specific demands also function to clarify and simplify the development of character, gesture and narrative – the typical restrictions on the performer's eyesight mean that the whole head must turn to look. The performer's body has to respond to the physicality that the mask is offering (or play very deliberately against that physicality), and with full-face masks, the inability to use dialogue means that exchanges become more deliberate and their sequence needs to be clear and uncluttered.

Trestle's mask work drew heavily on the early members' shared experiences of studying with John Wright at Middlesex Polytechnic. Wright conceives of the devising process as akin to a planned improvisation. Joff Chafer, a former member of the company, recalls that:

---

12 A detailed history of the company can be found in Stebbings and Smith (2020).
13 Johnstone acknowledges the influence of Copeau through Michel Saint-Denis, George Devine and William Gaskill on his work on masks.

FIGURE 5.1 Trickster Theatre (Mary Stuart, Rachel Ashton, Michele Hine, Roger Ennals, Mark Hopkins and Robert Thirtle) in *Mantu*, 1983. By kind permission of Tessa Mulgrave and Trickster Theatre.

Source: Photo © Tessa Mulgrave.

> his teaching style . . . was very much that thing of anything is possible. Give it a go. Also very much on pushing things further and further and further, even if they went way off the text. Hunting the joke down, if there was a joke there.
> *(Chafer, 2021)*

In disguising the individual performer, mask work enables the devising process to be significantly more ambitious. In the early Trestle shows, three or four performers could play between 15 and 20 parts (Oddey, 1996: 66). The process could start from the simplest of notions.

> In 'Plastered' (1985), the group decided on two locations, a pub and a hospital, devising what happened in the pub that ended in the hospital. The performers needed to devise characters, so they built a pub set and made a collection of masks. The masks were then 'liberated', and out of 'auditioning' the various bunches of characters, a cast was assembled. The group tried out various improvisations with the masks from which a thread of action was established. Then with painstaking choreography, the group attempted to clarify the story, so that the audience could seize on the action immediately.
> *(ibid.)*

144 Making mime and physical theatre

FIGURE 5.2 Trestle Theatre Company (Toby Wilsher and Thomasina Carlyle) in *Top Storey*, 1987. By kind permission of Trestle Theatre and Joff Chafer.

Source: Photo by Joff Chafer.

The role of the director was to adapt the process to the needs of the show and its themes, and then to note what was working and what needed further development as the process unfolded:

> [John Wright] was very much that outside eye, feeding back to you what you're doing. And then pulling out, going, 'It actually looks better if you do it that way, or try this one first, or that and that'. So, he had quite a directorial role, but the whole thing felt very collaborative.
>
> *(Chafer, 2021)*

There would then be a dramaturgical process whereby the montage of scenes and characters created could be written into a narrative structure. As Oddey observes, this kind of process 'depends on relationships and chemistry between people, which means that the feeling of the group must be maintained' (Oddey, 1996: 66). This dynamic becomes more challenging as company membership changes and new people join, requiring the core process to be rerun.

A typical Trestle production would start from the initial idea, which might involve some rough ideas for characters and place. Then the company would go off and make masks (sometimes alone, sometimes together) to bring back, share and explore. Whoever made each mask would have the chance to try the mask out first, although they could also be shared around if others had ideas for how a mask might work. This process would create a selection of characters and their inter-relationships, and elements of the storyline that connected them. A specific challenge to working with full-face masks was the lack of speech and the subsequent difficulties in dealing with certain plot points within the narrative where speech would normally be required. This would inevitably place constraints on the devising and require careful planning around how to move the story along in a suitable manner. It is, however, in Chafer's opinion, the very restrictions imposed by the mask that create its particular appeal for audiences.

> [It's] that sense of how something moves you in a way that you don't quite fully comprehend and don't necessarily want to fully comprehend. You know, the way it takes you on a journey or moves you in a way that you're not expecting.
>
> *(Chafer, 2021)*

Trestle's work was enormously successful in popularising mask work within the UK, and for several decades they were the leading mask-based physical theatre company in the country[14]. However, mask performance has declined in popularity since 2000, and is now more likely to be experienced as part of an outdoor

---

14 By 1994, Trestle were giving, on average, 300 performances a year to around 50,000 people in the UK and abroad (Chafer and Wilsher, 1994: 2).

146 Making mime and physical theatre

performance piece or a physical theatre training regime. In the early days, Trestle masks seemed to be largely based on the white larval masks from Basle and European featured full-face and half-face masks (Lecoq's Caucasian-featured neutral mask was designed for training rather than devising or performing). As awareness of cultural diversity developed, a wider range of masks became available – Joff Chafer recalls Trestle working to develop masks that used a variety of colours and facial tones, and consulting over the prototypes of these masks with Denise Wong from Black Mime Theatre. Other than the work of Trickster, there is little evidence of the exploration of non-western traditions of masked performance in UK theatre (e.g. East Asian or African masks).

Masks are largely used for and associated with comedy – Peter Hall's National Theatre production of Aeschylus' *Oresteia* in 1983 is one of the very few UK examples from this time of the use of masks to perform tragedy. The classic Italian form of masked comedy, Commedia dell'Arte, also experienced a number of revivals during this period. Its inclusion in the training offered by Lecoq and Gaulier evidences its value as a training tool, but it has failed to become widely established as a form of professional theatre performance in the UK[15]. The training for Commedia is demanding – the actor is required to combine athleticism, acrobatic prowess, physical stamina and precision, improvisation skills and characterisation within set storylines. Few companies have explored how Commedia might be modernised for a contemporary UK audience, with the exception of Moving Picture Mime Show (*Passionate Leave*). The notion of archetypal characters which broadly underpins most mask work has also increasingly seemed out of tune with a more nuanced and complex understanding of identity and agency that has evolved in contemporary culture.

Objects can also be conceived of as a form of mask. The puppet or the manipulated object is an inanimate object that is given life and meaning through the way that it is used by the performer. A number of mime and physical theatre companies have made direct use of objects and puppets within their work – Théâtre de Complicité for instance animated a chair to create the image of a 5,000-year-old 'ice-man' buried in a snowstorm on the alps in *Mnemonic*, as well as using chairs to create a forest and books to create a flock of birds in *Street of Crocodiles*. Bouge-de-la (Aurelian Koch and Lucy O'Rorke), inspired by their training at the Lecoq School

---

15 There were a limited number of Commedia companies and practitioners in the UK during this period, such as: Olly Crick's Old Spot Company, Bim Mason's Mummer&Dada, Geoff Beale and Howard Gayton's Ophaboom, and I Gelati (formed in 1984 by Andy Crook, Carolyn Wroughton, Malcolm Tulip, Mladen Puric and Arabella Lyons, and directed by James Macdonald). Several established theatre companies also explored the use of Commedia in key productions, for example: Clifford Williams' Commedia-inspired production of *The Comedy of Errors* for the RSC in 1962; Mike Alfred's 1980 production of *The Merchant of Venice*; the Belgrade Theatre's *The Servant of Two Masters* (1993), with movement and mime direction by Mick Wall; and Oxford Stage Company's *Love is a Drug* (1995), directed by Antonio Fava.

Making mime and physical theatre **147**

and the LEM[16] also sought to integrate objects and structures into the scenic and plastic design of their productions. The use of objects in this way might be taken to include interactive sets, the use of structures, and the manipulation of everyday objects. Heddon and Milling's comments on Improbable's 1996 production *70 Hill Lane*, are revealing. They describe the design, indicating how the production was:

> based on a series of interlocking narratives about a poltergeist from Phe-lim McDermott's childhood, the house was marked out on stage using steel poles with Sellotape stretched between them. The Sellotape became vari-ously an architectural feature, rays of light holding objects as if in mid-air, and a sound-effect of a threatening presence, before being scrunched up and animated as the poltergeist and – in a final image – a luminous moon.
>
> *(Heddon and Milling, 2006: 187)*

It is of course the theme of imaginative and often playful transformation that links this kind of work with many of the other practices described in this chapter.

Dance, choreography and choreographic building blocks

In the late 1980s and the early 1990s, dance in the UK faced a number of challenges that drew some choreographers towards physical theatre. The impact of Contact Improvisation, coupled with an interest in the use of words and text within dance, and the perceived need to deal with more complex and contemporary content, all operated to encourage several UK dance practitioners to resist the abstraction that was deeply embedded in British contemporary dance and to explore territory closer to theatre. A number of influential European practitioners also helped inspire this transformational shift, including: Pina Bausch, Anne Teresa Keersmaeker, Alain Platel and Wim Vandekeybus. Here was dance that was theatrical, iconoclas-tic, provocative, sexualised, political, confrontational and sometimes female-led, but that also acknowledged the traditions it was coming from. Bausch's work[17] was characterised by the use of everyday movements, repetition, extreme physicality, physical risk, an emphasis on authenticity, and challenging use of sets/sites and of text/sound/music. She declared herself as 'not interested in how people move but what moves them' (Bausch, 2007). Contact Improvisation was a form of dance that emerged in the USA in the 1970s, and arrived in the UK later in that decade as various practitioners came over to work in the UK as teachers and performers (e.g. Mary Fulkerson at Dartington College of Arts). Its key characteristic was the development of movement dialogue between performers created through touch,

---

16 The Laboratoire d'Etude du Mouvement (LEM) attached to Lecoq's School (see Evans, Koch and Russell, 2023).

17 More detail on Bausch's work and its impact can be found in Murray and Keefe (2016: 87–91) and Climenhaga (2013 and 2018).

148 Making mime and physical theatre

lifting, the flow of movement and the sharing of weight regardless of gender (conventionally dance involved men lifting women). The impact of this work on UK theatre is best represented by the work of companies such as DV8, Volcano, Frantic Assembly, V-TOL, Featherstonehaughs/Cholmondleys, Charlotte Vincent Company and The Kosh. This small group of companies proved to be very influential over this period (indeed nearly all of them continue to operate over 20 years later – DV8 formally ceased in 2022), so much so that in 1996 Ana Sanchez-Colberg sought to position physical theatre as uniquely located in the intersection between avant-garde theatre and dance (1996: 40–56). Such a small community of practice meant that in the early years many of the performers would move between companies and there was a high degree of cross-fertilisation. Several of the personnel involved in the early years of this form of Dance/Theatre spent time working for Ludus Dance and Extemporary Dance, companies that focused on creating accessible dance performance and on group devising. Lloyd Newson worked for Extemporary Dance before founding DV8. Liam Steel, whose early career after graduation involved working closely with Ludus as an animateur, has subsequently worked with DV8, Volcano, Frantic Assembly and The Kosh, as well as performing with Théâtre de Complicité (for more detail on Liam Steel, see Chapter 7); and Wendy Houston, who also worked with Ludus, also went on to work with DV8, Charlotte Vincent Dance Company and, more recently, Forced Entertainment.

DV8, Volcano and Frantic Assembly

As well as drawing on the contemporaneous interest in devising within alternative theatre and mime, this new form of physical theatre was also influenced by what was happening in performance art at this time. As Liam Steel notes, 'part of the ethos was about blurring the boundaries between the performer on stage and reality' (2020). A lot of the work 'was about pushing the human body to its limit, sometimes over extended periods of time. There was a lot of risk taking . . . both physically and in terms of what we would talk about onstage' (ibid.). The work aimed to have a visceral effect on the audience, creating a different kind of relationship than that normally experienced during dance or theatre shows. In some instances, the risk was visible and palpable:

> I remember with Volcano, there was a section [in *L.O.V.E.* (1992)] where Fern [Smith] had a knife. It was a real knife and she used to put the point of the blade on my heart and then slam her hand down, and stopping just above the hilt. She then continued to put it down the crack of Paul's [Davies] arse and stuff. And because the audience had seen her use this knife to cut through our clothes (she sliced through our vests on stage), they knew it was a real, very, very sharp knife.
>
> *(ibid.)*

This was about creating a level of authenticity that subverted conventional notions of theatrical pretence and artifice. It asserted the realness and newness of the performance, its physicality and immediacy. It made the politics of what was being done with bodies on stage more tangible. Pina Bausch's work also inspired these companies to create strong visual images that embodied the tensions and conflicts within the themes of the productions: 'images were as important in the work as the movement vocabulary. Sometimes the simplest of images could allow us to express what was at the heart of it' (ibid.). Devising was an important part of the way in which work was made since it enabled the blurring of boundaries between who the performer was as a human being and the role they played within the performance. Together with the level of physical risk, this enhanced the audience's sense that the performances were bringing into play 'real emotions and life experience in terms of telling stories' (ibid.).

The importance of DV8 within this particular strand of work in the UK cannot be overstated. They were one of the first companies to use the words 'physical theatre' in their title. Like Berkoff, Lloyd Newson was unafraid of being controversial and challenging. The programme notes to DV8's *If Only . . .* (1990) state, 'The company's work is about taking risks, breaking down the barriers between dance, theatre and personal politics, and above all, about communicating new ideas directly, clearly and unpretentiously' (in Shank, 1996: 9). DV8's work methods have informed the practices of many other companies and inspired generations of students and aspiring performers. At the heart of the processes used by companies such as DV8, Volcano and Frantic Assembly and artists such as Nigel Charnock, Liam Steel and Wendy Houstoun is the notion of the 'task': 'It was task-based work . . . we'd come up with ideas that were based around very specific creative tasks' (Steel, 2020). This is very similar to what Frantic Assembly refer to as 'building blocks' (Evans and Smith, 2021:70–73), and is an approach also used by other performance companies, such as Forced Entertainment, who eschewed notions of 'acting' as traditionally understood and practised. At the heart of this process would be something simple – a phrase, an image, a gesture, a word – and the task would aim to create a set of responses out of which would emerge sequences that captured the theme and its human consequences. The beer glass in DV8's *Enter Achilles*, for instance, acts as the focus for a task to move through space with a particular point of contact:

> The pint glass being the symbol of masculinity. It was dangerous, it was fragile, it was transparent. The pint glass itself also became very much the choreographic tool in a lot of the tasks that were set up. It could be something as simple as keeping it away from someone else, or trying to get someone's glass without the other person knowing.
>
> *(Steel, 2020)*

Once the essence of a relationship or a story or a theme had become clear, tasks would be set to physicalise that essence. In *Enter Achilles*, for example, the relationship between the characters Liam (Liam Steel) and Rob (Robert Tannion) was eventually expressed through a sequence in which Liam's head had to remain stuck to Rob's body:

> It was always about stripping away and finding what was at the essence of the relationship. What was the essence of what you wanted to say? . . . you had

150 Making mime and physical theatre

the choreographic essence of the whole piece and then the essence of each scene, and then each specific relationship. How could each one be expressed? It was always about stripping everything away. Stripping everything back until the essence was found.

(ibid.)

In this way, the audience sees, feels and knows instinctively what is happening on stage, because of the power and immediacy of the image.

The task-based approach also creates a sense of co-ownership for the performers:

You invest in it because you feel you have ownership of it. You have a voice in that work. . . . The more you can get people to bring their own life experiences into the project the more it's going to speak to people on the outside.

(ibid.)

These were all approaches that Steel brought to his own work as choreographer and co-director with Frantic Assembly on their production of *Hymns* in 1999. This was a production that pushed that company further into its exploration of the relationship between movement and text, drawing on Steel's work with DV8 and Volcano. For Frantic, this was an important production that marked the point from which they started to work with more established writers.

The blending of performer and character/performance persona became integral to the work of DV8, Volcano and Frantic Assembly – reflecting both the strong sense of each company as a kind of 'gang' of performers and the desire for the work to feel authentic and personal and not abstract or 'pretend'. As Newson states,

There's only one person who does the role and the piece is built around them – around their improvisations, their personalities, the way they look, how they speak. . . . The style of the company will vary depending on the amalgamation of those performers. None of us move in the same way: I want to acknowledge the differences and what they mean, not eradicate them.

(Newson, 1994: 51 and 1999: 110)

For these companies, style and form are ways of looking at the world and exploring how people interact physically with each other: 'I'm always looking for different ways to see and train the body' (ibid.: 111). Over time the work of these companies developed, becoming more focused and precise. Newson describes his interests at the end of the 1990s:

I might want to work on the physicality of 'greeting' . . . perhaps from shaking hands to patting. I explore what happens to the changes in rhythm. What happens if the action remains the same but the speed or quality changes? What are acceptable and unacceptable places to touch when greeting and why?

(ibid.: 110)

Sian Williams – The Kosh

Trained as a dancer, Sian Williams also worked with Ludus Dance at an early stage in her career. As with the others in this section, she was clearly inspired to find ways in which dance could be integrated with other art forms including theatre. Her productions with The Kosh (which she co-founded in 1982) could start from very simple ideas, from which the company would improvise: 'Our method of working was we'd take an idea . . . and then start improvising around those themes and the relationships' (Williams, 2020). As with DV8, Volcano and Frantic Assembly, collaboration, co-creation and content were key aspects of the making process for The Kosh[18].

> The collaborations that we repeatedly had were with designers and new composers. . . . That was again another fascinating aspect of it, to work with those artists and devise really, devise the ideas. I would coordinate those improvisations, but the company that we formed were very much the collaborators in that. So, we'd create it from their responses to the information. Build the piece. We were passionate about the narrative, the idea that the physical expression would tell you something.
>
> *(ibid.)*

The other feature of devising work with little text is that the work can continue to develop for a considerable period as it tours. The Kosh could take eight weeks to produce a show and might then tour it for several months or even years. Williams remembers that with their show *Endangered Species*, 'we kept on developing it, there were only two of us in that production and we would work over and over on re-honing the ideas that came from the original creation of it and just keep developing it' (ibid.).

Of additional interest is The Kosh's collaboration with the veteran tumbler and acrobat Johnny Hutch (1913–2003). Hutch had performed across the music hall circuit and possessed an encyclopaedic knowledge of comedy and tumbling routines. Sian Williams recalls how,

> *Endangered Species* was inspired by a story Johnny had told us about a couple in the Variety days. The styles of the pieces we put together for that were very much taken from the acts that he'd seen; and we developed it ourselves through working with him.
>
> *(ibid.)*

The blurring of boundaries between forms of performance was part of the excitement in making this kind of work: 'sometimes the best way to express what's

---

18 There is an interesting documentation of the processes and education practices used by the Kosh during this period in Jenkins, Legge and Palmer (1988). This document records the company's work during a period in residence at a school in Leamington Spa. Unfortunately it is very hard to obtain.

FIGURE 5.3 The Kosh (Mark Hopkins and Siân Williams) in *Endangered Species*, 1990. By kind permission of Siân Williams.

Source: Photo by Mark Tillie.

happening in a scene is to do some tumbling' (ibid.). This kind of approach helped performers to develop new skills and also opened up the accessibility of the work for audiences. It also demonstrates a growing awareness amongst practitioners that their work had its own (marginalised) histories and traditions, often with roots in popular performance.

The influence of visual and live art on devising

As indicated earlier, some forms of theatre making that emerged at this time were shaped and influenced by what was happening in the art world, in particular within the performance art and live art sectors. This work took inspiration from the avant-garde movements of the early twentieth century (Surrealism, Dada and the Bauhaus, for example), but by the 1980s and 1990s, the processes and practices of performance art and live art were also influenced by feminism and by postmodern or post-structuralist theory. Historically, this influence can be seen in the devised performance work of Albert Hunt (1928–2015) at Bradford College and the work of companies such as IOU, Hesitate and Demonstrate, Lumiere & Son and Welfare State International – all of which were strongly shaped by the art school training and the political interests of their founders. These companies helped to shape the early landscape and to promote approaches to making work based on aleatoric methods and devising processes inspired by spaces, objects, atmospheres, moods, lighting, sounds, the performative, the non-linear, the de-centred and the conceptual. Their work often had a focus on musicality and rhythm, and/or on visual coherence over text, characterisation, meaning and sense. Sometimes this involved exploring the role of the subconscious in devising – introducing the surreal into the performance event.

Oddey suggests that one of the earliest companies to devise visual theatre productions was The People Show, who started working together in 1966. She quotes Mark Long as describing how: 'We are working around visual structures. A series of visual images is worked on beforehand and then we embroider these – with our bodies, with our words and with our reactions – to enlarge the images for the audience' (Long in Oddey, 1996: 5). Long also identifies the important role that the relationship between the performer/deviser and the audience plays in their work – often the nature of the show only becomes clear when it is performed to an audience.

As we noted in Chapter 3, the London International Mime Festival has for a long time preferred the term visual theatre to physical theatre in its general marketing. Though art-based theatre was not originally closely or explicitly aligned to mime and physical theatre practices, the gap closed as performers, designers and technicians from both sides worked across the boundaries. Peta Lily recalls the invaluable input of fine artist Tessa Schneideman, a fellow early member of Three Women Mime, who 'was delighted by the spatial canvas' mime afforded (Lily, 2020). Schneideman would make props and objects for the company, but would also push ideas for devising that were very visual (in a piece on emotional eating – a woman is herself eaten by a giant sweet bun). Her visual creativity inspired a piece where a hung drape made only the feet of the performers visible; as part of which, puppeteer-trained Claudia Prietzel created a mother lunging slowly, her down-at-heel shoe dragging a row of children's shoes behind it. The later integration of visual performance under the umbrella of Mime Action Group/Total Theatre also facilitated the sharing of ideas, information and practices over the last decades of this period – bringing to attention a shared fascination with liveness, embodiment and space.

154 Making mime and physical theatre

John Ashford outlines some of the key aesthetic concerns underpinning the development of performance art and these make for interesting comparison with the nature and processes of mime and physical theatre: 'an emphasis on process rather than product' (Ashford in Craig, 1980: 99); 'a rejection of the art commodity market. A performance cannot become an artefact bought and sold for profit' (ibid.: 100); 'an interest in kinetic sculpture' (ibid.); small companies that reject the notion of the director as central to the creative process; the rejection of text and literary devices and structures, instead borrowing from visual imagery and film techniques; use of spaces not conventionally designed or equipped for theatre; and working across disciplines – dance, music, word, image – to 'heal the breach between disciplines' (ibid.: 102).

Geraldine Pilgrim: Hesitate and Demonstrate

Geraldine Pilgrim remembers how important the freedoms allowed at art college were in enabling her to develop her practice and her processes: 'Basically Jeff Nuttall, John Darling, John Fox, would say, well, what do you want to do, go and do it' (Pilgrim, 2020). In some respects, this is a freedom that seemed to permeate the whole sector at that time and that in large part grew out of the post-war belief in people's inherent creativity that we have already discussed. Ideas, opportunities, challenges and resources were made available and students explored and experimented to find their own voices. One of the inspirations for Hesitate and Demonstrate (1975–1986), the company that Pilgrim formed with her colleague Janet Goddard, was the work of the photographer Eadweard Muybridge: 'our movements that were based on Muybridge . . . I can't describe it, but it definitely wasn't slow motion and it definitely wasn't mime. It was like freeze-frame' (ibid.). Exploring how to replicate the deliberate illustration of movement created in Muybridge's photographs, Pilgrim and her colleague, Janet Goddard, realised that this mix of observing, hesitating and demonstrating provided them with both a name for the company and also a guiding principle for their work method[19]. They drew additional inspiration from the everyday activities around them and would spend long periods talking, making notes and churning ideas around. They would go to shops and department stores to watch people going about their everyday activities:

> we would often go downstairs to the basement, where out of work actors would be demonstrating machines that chop up vegetables or how to polish glass, which means you never have to polish it again. And most importantly of all, the perfumery department where the women in white coats with painted faces would come towards you with a perfume spray and whisk you

---

19 Mark Evans recalls a Hesitate and Demonstrate workshop in the early 1980s which focused on the slowing down of action to focus attention on gesture and atmosphere, creating greater awareness of the potential resonances and emphasising work that was suggestive and quietly dramatic.

Making mime and physical theatre 155

FIGURE 5.4   Hesitate and Demonstrate (Janet Goddard and Geraldine Pilgrim) in *Points of Departure* at Oval House Theatre Upstairs, London, 1977. By kind permission of Janet Goddard, Geraldine Pilgrim and Michael Bennet.

Source: Photo by Michael Bennett.

off, make you up and throw you out. We realized that they were not acting. They weren't pretending to be someone else. They were performing, and that was our basis for performing. You were not pretending to be someone else, you were yourselves, but more so . . . depending on what world you were inhabiting. Hence Hesitate and Demonstrate.

(ibid.)

This is a process that heightens the performers' and the audience's awareness of what is going on: 'we wanted to create a super reality, and make people be more aware of what they were seeing' (ibid.). The emphasis on the visual did not preclude text, although perhaps because of the importance of what was shown/seen, there was less concern about using written text rather than devised text: 'we would take text . . . and incorporate it and write a bit of our own text. We did use text – not very much but we never improvised' (ibid.). At the heart of much of this work was the notion of experimentation – 'I think in the late '70s, very early '80s, it was experiment. You were allowed to fail. It was exciting' (ibid.). This excitement and experimentation were shared features of mime, physical theatre and visual theatre – there was a common emphasis on creating a specific, immediate and visceral experience with the audience: 'Documentation, for us, was completely irrelevant. It was about it being live' (ibid.).

156 Making mime and physical theatre

Other important and influential art-based companies during this period include:

Moving Being (1968–2013) – founded by Geoff Moore. The company created multi-media shows that combined dance, performance, text, image, film and video. Although it was founded in London, the company moved to Cardiff and was for many years based at Chapter Arts Centre[20]. The company lighting designer, Peter Mumford, left the company in the late 1970s and became a leading lighting designer in the UK dance sector. A leaflet for their 1978 production *The Influence of Moons on Tides* states that, 'Like most activity initiated in the late Sixties, the impulse of Moving Being's work has been towards inclusiveness. Both socially and artistically, that period urged the breaking of boundaries, the merging of categories, and a redefinition of forms'.

Lumiere & Son (1974–1992) – founded by actress Hilary Westlake and writer David Gale. The company explored work that blended spectacle, language and choreography and sought to explore the surreal. It also spawned Circus Lumiere, which became part of the emerging alternative circus scene during this period. Westlake directed *Wounds* for Three Women Mime in 1982. Peta Lily recalls that,

Hilary proposed that 'the only thing that separates women from men is that they bleed'. At the time, Hilary was working with these stamping dances and rhythms and gestures, and so we dressed in pure white costumes and moved in abstract rhythmic patterns, and at various moments blood would come from somewhere. The first blood came from a mouth, then a breast, from between the legs, and finally Claudia put up an umbrella and blood rained down on her. It was bold, perhaps disturbing, but uplifting.

(Lily, n.d.)

Westlake also directed a ten-day workshop for invited practitioners at the British Summer School of Mime and was one of a group of directors contributing to the Magdalena Project in 1987.

IOU (1976–) – founded by David Wheeler, Steve Gumbley, Di Davies, Lou Glandfield and Liz Lockhart. IOU (International Outlaw University) was formed as a group of artists that split from Welfare State International in 1976. Based in Halifax, they created small scale indoor shows and larger outdoor and site-specific productions:

Ideas always start from what something will look like, an object or an environment, and what someone wants to make. Someone has an idea of an object they want to make without really knowing how it will be used.

---

20 See Chapter 4 for a fuller discussion of Chapter Arts and the Welsh physical theatre scene.

The same applies to characters. It starts from a visual idea into which the performer feeds. The progression of the scenario is controlled by the object and the music. Dreaming of the ideas which fit into that happens at the same time, so that the narrative gradually reveals itself. We enjoy making. Quite often the performers on the stage have made the object they're working with.

(Wheeler in Dawson, 1994)

Station House Opera (1980–) – founded by Julian Maynard Smith, with the aim 'to make work that brings together theatre and the visual arts in a single unified vision' (Station House Opera, n.d.). From 1985 to 1989, Station House Opera produced a series of performances, including *A Split Second of Paradise* (1985), *Piranesi* (1988) and *The Bastille Dances* (1989), all of which included a company of actors and large numbers of concrete blocks used to make constantly changing sculptural and architectural constructions. During the 1990s the company also made a number of touring performance works; including *Black Works* (1991), in which a downpour of flour turned a black box theatre into a site for a series of marks, body shapes and drawings that covered the floor (Station House Opera, n.d.).

Forced Entertainment (1984–) – founded by Tim Etchells, Robin Arthur, Richard Lowdon, Claire Marshall, Cathy Naden and Terry O'Connor. Although the focus of their work is on the tensions inherent in live performance and the presence of an audience (*Speak Bitterness*, 1994), the productions also always have a strong visual aesthetic, combining mess and order and exploring the challenges in simplistic readings of scenic design. As with many of the companies formed at this time, Forced Entertainment often draws inspiration from the contemporary cultural references around them:

our work shifts approach from project to project, taking influence from movies, internet, stand-up, dance, bad television, performance art, music culture as well as from theatre itself. What ties the various strands of our work together is that the projects always strive to be vivid and original, demanding a lot from audiences.

(Forced Entertainment, n.d.)

The performance style of companies such as these, and of later companies such as Reckless Sleepers (1988–) and Stan's Cafe (1991–), was inspirational for those working in mime and physical theatre and encouraged bolder design and more experiment with form and content. Over the 1980s and the 1990s, many mime and physical theatre companies started to collaborate regularly with designers who could bring visual impact to their work – for example, Julian Crouch (Trickster and Improbable), Rae Smith (see later) and Alice Power (Trickster and The Right Size). Often these designers would contribute actively to the devising process, working within the rehearsal room rather than in their own studio – building the

158 Making mime and physical theatre

look of the show as part of the making process. Nigel Jamieson, for instance, is clear that design was always at the heart of Trickster's work:

> the other principle . . . was that the company would have a full-time designer, which for a small co-op at the time was kind of unheard of. So, Ali [Alice Power], who was a founder of the company, was a designer. The idea was that design was central to the company from the outset.
>
> *(Jamieson, 2020)*

Popular performance

Mime and physical theatre's historical roots in popular performance (Commedia dell'Arte, street entertainers, circus and variety performance, clowning, melodrama, cabaret, pantomime) are well recorded elsewhere (Leabhart, 1989; Lust, 2000; and, Rolfe, 1979) and touched on in Chapter 2. Several of such forms provide the bases for dramatic territories within the second year of training at the Lecoq School and some of the *stages* offered by Philippe Gaulier. For several companies, these histories provided important inspiration for the ways in which work was made and performed.

Mummer&Dada

Bim Mason's company Mummer&Dada (1985–1990) was inspired, as the name suggests, by English folk theatre traditions and by the Surrealists. Drawing on Mason's own experience of popular and street performance, and his experience of training in mime and Commedia dell'Arte at the Lecoq School in the mid-1980s, the company played largely outdoors, on streets and at festivals. Mason's description of the making process for the company reveals many of these connections, and is worth quoting at length:

> So, for the Mummer&Dada process, for example, the way that would work is that I would come up with a scenario, bearing in mind the Lazzi that already existed, the Lazzi that we knew we had in the company. So, not acrobatic routines, but there might be even a whole scene or something like that. They'd be building blocks which I would place in a scenario and then cast people according to what they would be good to play, because I know the performer. It was very much based on the Commedia dell'Arte model and that thing that the routines continue throughout the years, and you can recycle and re-form material. Then with that scenario, I offer it to the company. It's a really short rehearsal period – we'd often be two weeks or something like that, 10 days or 14 days. Not only to make the main show, but also to make a cabaret that would go alongside it. So, people just bring in their routine. Speed is important to the process. . . .. Time was always pressured, and I really liked that because there's a kind of energy and focus.
>
> *(Mason, 2020)*

FIGURE 5.5 Mummer&Dada (Ana Vasquez, Gregoire Carel, Kevin Brooking and Bim Mason, with Lee Beagley on percussion) street performance in Covent Garden, London, 1986. By kind permission of Bim Mason.

Source: Photographer unknown.

At its best, this approach helped develop immediacy, physicality and an openness to the audience that would become hallmarks of much of UK mime and physical theatre. It would also be part of bringing mime and physical theatre to the wider public and developing an audience. Of course, the interest in popular forms also reflected something of the financial precarity of many working in the field at this time – work would require short rehearsal periods, instant audience appeal and flexibility around where and when it could be performed.

Trickster

Ken Rea, in a MAG/*Total Theatre* article, praised Trickster's work for its 'extraordinary visual flair and bold imagination' (1994). Their work was very popular with mime and physical theatre audiences and attracted generous Arts Council support – £10,000 in 1985–1986, more than Trestle, David Glass or Théâtre de Complicité. Trickster was formed at the start of the 1980s by Rachel Ashton, who, along with Nigel Jamieson had studied with Desmond Jones. One of the company's longest running shows, *Charivari* (1984), made use of a range of acrobatic and mask performance techniques, as well as striking visual design. Their work sought to capture something of the wonder of the circus and of mask work – transporting audiences into imaginative worlds created through design and movement (see also Chapter 7).

FIGURE 5.6 Trickster Theatre (Roger Ennals, Robert Thirtle, Mark Hopkins, Maria Stengard, Mary Stuart and Rachel Ashton) in *Charivari*, 1984. By kind permission of Coneyl Jay and Trickster Theatre.

Source: Photograph by Coneyl Jay.

There was, as noted earlier in this chapter, a genuine fascination amongst mime and physical theatre performers for performance styles and modes that were part of popular culture, for example rock music (see Chapter 8), cartoons, hip-hop, dance, storytelling, music video, film, acrobatics and tumbling, juggling, stand-up comedy, street theatre and song. The making of mime would often reflect the influence of these forms – either directly, as in the Moving Picture Mime Show interpretation of *The Seven Samurai*, or indirectly through the challenge posed by its cultural impact. Peta Lily remembers the shock of seeing Quentin Tarantino's films: 'I remember thinking, how can mime even measure up?' (2020) – in response, Lily created a filmic visceral-psychological horror show: *Beg!* (directed by David Glass). The devising processes of early Théâtre de Complicité shows were influenced by the rise in alternative stand-up comedy in the 1980s, promoting the importance of improvisation, rapport with the audience, and a wacky and irreverent playfulness.

The cartoon movie acted as an important stimulus for this popular and visual approach to theatre making, offering and normalising a different kind of imaginative and kinaesthetic engagement for the audience. Cartoons, like mime, reject the assumption that art mirrors life; instead, they project dreams and fantasies, they deconstruct the world around us, showing us how it can be changed and reveal the possibility for imaginative transformation. In this respect, we can read Sandy

Craig's analysis of alternative theatre in this period as equally applicable to mime and physical theatre. It is

> a theatre which dismantles the world in order to demonstrate the possibility of creative change, a theatre which engages the audience in a shared creativity and unplugs them from a history pulped out in head-lines and news-flashes freeing them from a reality which seeks to defeat them.
>
> *(Craig, 1980: 29)*

It is worth noting that at certain moments this work has been in tension with processes that have sought to resist, undermine and/or challenge popular forms of making and performing. Radical theatre artists have sometimes drawn on these forms as part of their palette (e.g. the work of Emil Wolk in particular, who worked with The People Show, Freehold, Pip Simmons Company and The Kosh). However, from the late 1980s onwards some companies have been more influenced by contemporary cultural theory and have consequently deliberately sought to be more intellectually challenging in their work and in their citation of popular forms. Companies such as The Wooster Group in the USA and Forced Entertainment and Volcano in the UK created work that took a more critical view of popular culture and employed it with a sense of detachment, irony and playfulness. Academic interest in work that appears to be more conceptually dense is understandable, but it has meant that the work of companies such as Mummer&Dada and Olly Crick's Old Spot Company has either been ignored or it has fallen to the directors themselves to record the work and write about it.

From collaborator to director and back

Contemporary training for theatre directors was barely in existence at this time (see Kenneth Rea's 1989 report *A Better Direction*), and revolved largely around the needs of the larger subsidised theatres (e.g. the Regional Theatre Young Director Scheme). Directors within mime and physical theatre had to learn on the job. Working with others who shared the same training clearly made that learning process easier. Directors such as Annabel Arden, Simon McBurney, John Wright, Nigel Jamieson and David Glass clearly benefitted from early opportunities to work with like-minded performers with whom they already had some affinity. The use of improvisation allowed the production to emerge, rather than be shaped and formed by the director's vision alone. It also allowed for the possibility that the production would remain in a constant state of evolution. Heddon and Milling point out that early Théâtre de Complicité shows 'were conceived and designed to be unfinished before the first night' (Heddon and Milling, 2006: 180), as 'the ethic was one of continuous work rather than designed product' (McBurney, 1994: 16).

In the early Théâtre de Complicité shows, McBurney would be devising alongside the other performers, however as the work progressed and his role became more directorial, he would also sometimes leave actors to resolve tasks in his absence and

162 Making mime and physical theatre

come back to observe and comment on the work created: 'sometimes I leave the actors to prepare something which we then look at; it can be tremendously liberating for actors to work without the director' (McBurney in Giannachi and Luckhurst, 1999: 75). This kind of task-based approach draws on Lecoq's idea of the *auto-cours*, but also resonates with the working methods of dance-based physical theatre companies (see earlier). As Oddey (1996) observes, devising can centre around the director, but it can also pivot around the designer, the performer(s) or in some cases the music or the text. It can offer multiple points from which work can emerge and to which it can refer. Devised performance meant access to the means of production for all performers, an openness of process, democratic decision-making (sometimes!), and a new degree of control over the work for all involved. Colin Chambers celebrates this as an important moment when actors become 'workers in a team' (in Craig, 1980: 105), no longer seen as 'dilettantes, aristocrats or rabble, isolated from each other and their audience' (ibid.: 106), and by extension, directors also joined the team and relinquished significant portions of their status and control. We look at the work of David Glass below, as an interesting example of a director whose process emerged and developed very much within this kind of context[21].

David Glass

David Glass grew up within a family steeped in European and American film production. His grandfather worked as Fritz Lang's assistant until leaving Germany in 1935 for Switzerland. His mother worked in Los Angeles for Disney before leaving for Mexico. He was born in Switzerland and grew up in Los Angeles – surrounded by the artistic community of the time. In 1971 the family left the USA to come to England. Glass briefly started a degree at Cambridge but hated it, and instead went to Paris and enrolled to study circus and mime at the Nouvelle Carre. Whilst in Paris he also trained with Decroux, did a summer school with Lecoq, and performed on the streets of Paris when his money ran out. He returned to England and trained in dance at London Contemporary Dance School and with Alvin Ailey. After devising and performing solo work for a period, he formed the David Glass Ensemble in 1988.

Amongst the many notable shows that the Ensemble has created, perhaps the one that most stands out is *Gormenghast* (1992), the production for which Glass won the Martini/TMA Regional Theatre Award for Best Director. Glass' approach to his mime and physical theatre practice is both eclectic and personal. A maverick and a magpie, Glass took the various elements he had learnt, seen and experienced and 'broke those things up' (Glass, 2020) in order to create his own language. He describes the key stages of his process as origination and manifestation:

> Origination is about finding the relationships, not managing anything: finding the relationships between things, the connectedness of them, how are they connected, and from that, finding the meaning. And story is really the

---

21 There is additional detail on David Glass' work and significance in Chapters 3 and 6.

Making mime and physical theatre **163**

FIGURE 5.7 David Glass in *The White Woman*, directed by Rex Doyle, 1982. By kind permission of David Glass.

Source: Photo by Douglas Robinson

structure of finding meaning in a condensed time. The fourth stage we teach is manifestation. This is when all the bits come together to make something more than it is, usually. And also the quality of manifestation is an intensification of lots of time in a very short amount of time, which is special.

(ibid.)

164 Making mime and physical theatre

Gormenghast

Gormenghast is based on a trilogy of books by the author Mervyn Peake: *Titus Groan*, *Gormenghast* and *Titus Alone*. Written during the 1940s and 1950s, these books became cult classics of fantasy fiction – celebrated for their iconic imagery and strange characters. Glass' original production included Hayley Carmichael, who was also in Théâtre de Complicité's *Street of Crocodiles* in 1992 and went on to co-found Told by an Idiot with Paul Hunter and John Wright in 1993. John Constable, who had worked with Glass on *Bozo's Dead* (1992), was commissioned to adapt the text. Rae Smith, who also designed *Street of Crocodiles*, designed the set[22]. Constable saw the size and scope of the trilogy as being an advantage – it threw the emphasis onto the spine of the plot, and onto evoking the atmosphere of the book (Peake, 2006: 7). The production aimed to create a physical theatre piece that integrated mime and melodrama with elements from Kabuki and Chinese theatre (Glass in Giannachi and Luckhurst, 1999: 40).

The chosen style helped develop a dream-like logic for the production – using recurring motifs and heightened performance styles. The design focused on spatiality as a way of conveying the claustrophobia of the world of the book; it included seven doors – 'too many for the audience to absorb at once' (Glass in Giannachi and Luckhurst, 1999: 41). The heightened staging, design and acting created a symbolic language for the production, the chorus of performers representing the castle and its brooding presence. Constable describes how

> The work has a rhythm, like a musical score. In rehearsals, David refined the score, breaking down the scenes into even smaller units. Everything was strictly choreographed to serve the theatrical illusion. Yet within this discipline, the cast had enormous freedom to explore the world of the play and discover their own characters.
>
> *(in Peake, 2006: 8)*

Glass was undoubtedly influenced by Shared Experience's adaptation of *The Arabian Nights* (1975) and *Bleak House* (1977) directed by Mike Alfreds[23], and was no

---

22 Smith went on to design several other productions for David Glass Ensemble, including: *Shameless* (1993), *Mosquito Coast* (1995). In addition to *Street of Crocodiles*, she also designed *The Visit* (1988) and *Help I'm Alive* (1990) for Théâtre de Complicité. More recently she designed the National Theatre production *Warhorse* (2007).

23 Mike Alfreds directed adaptations of *The Arabian Nights* (1975), *Bleak House* (1977) and *Gothic Horrors* (1979) for Shared Experience, using physical storytelling techniques, some mime and minimal staging (see Alfreds, 1979). These were seminal productions in the development of a physically dynamic and expressive ensemble acting style in the late 1970s touring theatre industry. Celia Gore Booth, who had trained at the Lecoq school from 1968 to 1970 was one of the founding members of Shared Experience. Alfreds was later invited to lead one of the British International Summer School of Mime Theatre events, which gave a new direction to UK mime practitioners, steering them a little closer to the conventional theatre world. Alfreds also collaborated with David Glass on a stage production of *Les Enfants du Paradis* in 1994, and directed *Trouble in Paradise* for the physical theatre company Talking Pictures.

Making mime and physical theatre 165

FIGURE 5.8 David Glass Ensemble (Hayley Carmichael, Richard Atlee, Peter Bailee, Paul Hamilton, Neil Caplin, Di Sherlock, Sally O'Donnell) in *Gormenghast*, 1992. By kind permission of David Glass.

Source: Photo by Graham Fudger.

166 Making mime and physical theatre

doubt also pushing against the large-scale spectacle of the RSC's internationally successful adaptation of *Nicholas Nickleby* (1980).

It is significant that both David Glass Ensemble's *Gormenghast* and Théâtre de Complicité's *The Street of Crocodiles* happened in the same year. These two productions mark an important moment for the development of physical theatre in the UK. Both productions were remarkably successful in finding a physical staging for books that might have otherwise seemed unstageable. Both productions lifted the profile of the two companies and of their directors – reaching wider audiences than the earlier devised work and pushing them to extend their theatrical vocabularies. This moment felt like the cumulative impact of the relocation of Mime into the Arts Council's Drama Department, which had opened up larger funding opportunities and placed more emphasis on the theatrical and textual quality of the work.

Conclusion

Writing a chapter on the making of mime might imply that there was always method and structure to this work. While methods have certainly emerged over the years, an important feature is the level and amount of experimentation that was involved in getting to this place. For many mime and physical theatre companies their process evolved out of much trial and error. While training could provide some answers and the opportunity to make mistakes in private, for others the processes emerged through doing:

> So, you just do it. You might not know what you're doing. You're coming from a place of . . . I was going to say conviction, but conviction seems too certain . . . but almost like beautiful ignorance, coming from that place.
>
> *(Smith, 2020)*

Or as David Glass puts it, 'you don't know what you're doing in your 20s, you're just desperate to do something' (2020). Performers working with practitioners or companies would cross-fertilise working methods as they moved on to their next job. Making a show could link closely to training, with a new production requiring the learning of new skills with new company members. This kind of gathering of embodied experience might create stylistic coherence where all performers shared the same training, or it might generate a dramaturgical approach akin to collage, in which interesting elements and processes would be brought together as needed:

> We just tried lots and lots and lots of stuff, and we could see the connections. I think there was something about the lateral connections that we were making, that it doesn't matter if there's not a narrative connection here. There is something maybe about the pulse of energy which goes through this.
>
> *(Smith, 2020)*

For many companies, this meant that the early years would often involve developing what Smith refers to as 'a magpie sensibility' (ibid.), a frame of mind and a way of working that would be about borrowing, trying things out, being inspired by whatever looked interesting around you and whatever would solve the creative challenges you faced. This was an approach that was especially necessary if training together had been unavailable and/or unaffordable. But even companies built on the experience of a shared training eventually wanted to distance themselves from that experience and forge their own path: 'There were things we had learnt from our teachers, but we modified and changed and reshaped them, and were constantly changing them and reshaping them' (Arden, 2021). Process, in this respect, becomes a two-edged sword. It identifies a company, gives them coherence and represents what they do, how they do it and why. But it also, unless constantly challenged and reviewed, can pigeon-hole them and their work: 'we used to get uncomfortable because people would talk about the Complicité method or the Complicité technique, and there's no such thing. Absolutely not' (ibid.).

It is also clear that text and voice were not rejected outright. For a number of companies during this period, text would be important as a source of inspiration for material: for example, Théâtre de Complicité's productions of *The Street of Crocodiles* (1992, from a book of short stories by Bruno Schulz), *The Three Lives of Lucie Cabrol* (1994, from a story in *Pig Earth* by John Berger) and *Out of a house walked a man . . .* (1994, from short stories by Daniil Kharms), and Volcano Theatre's productions of *V* (1990, from a poem by Tony Harrison), *Medea: Sex War* (1991, from the Greek tragedy), *L.O.V.E.* (1992, from Shakespeare's sonnets), *Manifesto* (1993, from the Communist Manifesto), *How To Live (Ibsenities)* (1995, from the plays of Henrik Ibsen) and *The Town That Went Mad* (1997, from Dylan Thomas' radio play *Under Milk Wood*). It is important to note that both companies chose texts with a certain poetic, imagistic quality to them, texts that also appealed to their political and cultural interests, and texts that reflected the richness of European literary traditions. There are many other examples across the mime sector during this time, from companies large and small[24].

There was an overarching sense of community that drove the processes and practices. A sense of 'gangs' of performers bound together by shared aesthetics, shared politics, shared experiences, shared training, shared friendship, shared suspicion of other practices or lineages, or any combination of the above. As Fern Smith states, 'there was a sense that if you're going to have a really good party, who would you want there, what music would you like, what should the lighting look like, what kind of space do you want?' (2020). This created a camaraderie that audiences could perceive and identify with:

---

24 David Glass Ensemble produced *Popeye* (1990, based on the American cartoons), *Gormenghast* (1992, based on the novel by Mervyn Peake), *Mosquito Coast* (1993, based on the book by Paul Theroux), *Les Enfants du Paradis* (1994, based on the Michel Carné film) and *La Dolce Vita* (1995, based on the Fellini film of the same name). Kneehigh Theatre produced *Stig* (1988, based on Clive King's children's novel *Stig of the Dump*) and *The Red Shoes* (2000, based on the Powell and Pressburger film). Wall Street Productions (Simon Murray) produced *Bartleby* (1993, an adaptation of a short story by Herman Melville).

168 Making mime and physical theatre

> you could tell that they loved seeing the way that we were together . . .
> people would say, 'Well, you look like you're having such a lot of fun', or,
> 'We always wonder if anyone is sleeping with anyone, because you look so
> intimate'. And then they would come and see the next show, and would
> go, 'It's so nice to see you in this, because in the last show you did the thing
> where you did that', or you know, 'Marcello's different in this show. I've seen
> Marcello in every show'. The audience came partly to see 'the gang'.
>
> *(Arden, 2021)*

Work, in various complex ways, is always about identity; the identity of the company was constructed from the personalities of the company members and the common reference points of training. Although scripts of some shows were published[25] the nature of the show was always closely linked to the performers who had created that show. In some cases, characters in productions have names that reflect the actor who played them (for example in DV8's *Enter Achilles*). Even when companies have revived shows, it has proved as important to maintain the ethos of the original process as to recreate the words and moves. This close identification between actor and character emphasises that the meaning is somehow operating on a more personal, authentic and immediate level.

Finally, we have pleasure in quoting Annabel Arden's description of the ensemble physical theatre actor, a suitable summation of the qualities physical theatre practice demanded of a generation of performers – an appropriate statement to end this chapter.

> You need incredible stamina as an ensemble actor; you work with the same
> group of people all the time and the rehearsal room resounds with many
> voices and many concerns. You have to be generous and able to abandon
> ego. You also need a strong visual sense, which you acquire by doing, making, and acting as each other's mirror. Over time, you develop an interior eye
> and you begin to know what your movement looks like from a spectator's
> perspective. You also develop a physical memory and have a sense not just of
> where you are in the space but what your spatial relationship is to everyone
> else. You must be able to do, to make.
>
> *(in Luckhurst and Veltman, 2001: 5)*

What comes through clearly is that making mime and physical theatre is fundamentally about making meaningful, sometimes visceral, connections that start from the body and from movement; connections between performer and performer, performer and space, and performer and audience. The ways in which training might best prepare performers for working in this way brings us to Chapter 6.

---

25 For example, Complicite (2003) and McBurney (2008).

6

FROM SCARCITY TO ABUNDANCE: TRAINING, EDUCATION, DISSEMINATION AND DEBATE IN MIME AND PHYSICAL THEATRE

Landscape, provision and discourse

Any overview of the landscape investigated by this volume would highlight recurring and insistent preoccupations with training and education. Scanning the 30-year period covered by our book and the myriad artists, companies, funding/support organisations, festivals, art centres and small to middle scale theatres featured therein, we return again and again to what at times seems like an almost obsessive concern with *training*. This chapter explores the multiple dimensions and shapes of training not only for professional artists and theatre makers but also through their educational work in community contexts and schools. Beyond the activities, the programmes, the projects, the institutions, the workshops, the seminars, the conferences and the numerous channels for communicating these events, we also reflect on the possible reasons for this proliferation. On the one hand, such apparent abundance may seem like a healthy democratising impulse within the body of these 'young' mime and physical theatre art forms in the face of paucity and historical lacunae. However, on the other, it is possible that this profusion may also speak of a sense of deficiency or weakness – real or perceived – in the quality of the work produced, and a felt lack of confidence in the practices generated across the UK over this period. Impulses also, perhaps, driven by the apparent absence in the UK of substantial European pedagogic figures such Decroux, Lecoq, Pagneux, Gaulier[1], Grotowski and Barba.

From the outset, when tackling this chapter on training and education, we have been faced with certain paradoxes and tensions. Any acknowledgement – or indeed celebration – of the proliferation of workshop training activities identified earlier has to be tempered by a growing sense of unease which seems to develop into the 1990s,

---

1 Philippe Gaulier, however, transferred his school to London in 1991, returning to Paris in 2002. At the time this seemed a very significant move, especially as Gaulier was given some financial support from the Arts Council.

DOI: 10.4324/9780429330209-6

170 Training: from scarcity to abundance

at which point a whole set of reflections are being raised, often though the activities of MAG and *Total Theatre*. This disquiet may be articulated through a series of questions such as these: what sort of training is required and who defines such needs; how much training; can one be over-trained; what issues of access are inhibiting the realisation of training for a diverse set of students; is the ubiquity of the workshop model at the expense of more sustained and in-depth provision; what models of financial support are required for students; and the recurring issue of whether there should be a national school of mime and physical theatre? Whilst MAG wrestled with these questions through a variety of events, the Arts Council had already partially embraced the challenge by commissioning Naseem Khan (1939–2017) to investigate the training needs of mime practitioners. Khan's thorough and radical report was published in 1990 and clearly identified the current state of training provision, whilst also identifying 'Ideas for Change'. These were summarised by John Keefe in an article for *Total Theatre* in the autumn of 1991 and we reproduce them here since they represent an agenda which was to be relentlessly debated and returned to throughout the 1990s.

Ideas for Change

- That the proposed Regional Dance Agencies (see Devlin Report; 'Stepping Forward') should provide one-year foundation courses in physical theatre, mime and circus as well as dance.
- That the number of specialist independent schools be increased.
- There should be a strengthening of the training element in physical theatre festivals.
- There should be a strengthening of mime courses in drama schools.
- The forming of apprenticeships with established mime companies.
- There need to be bursaries and grants for students and trainee animateurs.
- Financial support for workshops that meet the criteria of having considered their market, of avoiding clashes of dates, and of structuring their work in an accumulative evolving manner.
- Improvement of international links between companies, animateurs and trainees.
- The development of a system of trainee credits gained by the structured accumulation of physical theatre/workshop skills, and supervised by a mime centre or council.
- Finally and most importantly the establishment of a mime and physical theatre centre that can offer extended training, co-ordinate national and regional activities and initiatives, liaise with other overseas centres, and produce resource and library material and a magazine (an extending and developing of MAG's *Total Theatre*).
- The ACGB should as a priority commission a feasibility report on the establishment of a British School of Physical Theatre.

(Keefe, 1991)

Keefe concludes his summary by stating:

> It is MAG's intention to use the full report as background material for MAG's work in developing its own training initiatives, venue provision and work in establishing the Centre for Physical Theatre.
>
> *(Keefe, 1991)*

Before embarking on a broad taxonomy of 'training' provision within the UK during our period, it seems important to reflect briefly on some of the philosophical and semantic elements contained within a term – covering multiple and heterogeneous practices – loaded with contested and contestable meanings. In the section on Dartington College of Arts (DCA) at the end of this chapter we particularly note how the institution regularly wrestled with the pedagogical ethics of training and 'anti-training'. In their essay, provoked by the closure of DCA, in the *Theatre, Dance and Performance Training* journal, John Hall and Simon Murray offer a pithy definition of training:

> *Training*. A teleological process with practical knowledge at the end of it and possibly a licence to trade.
>
> *(2011: 63)*

The extent to which the thousands of training workshops offered by mime and physical theatre practitioners over these three decades delivered a 'licence to trade' is, of course, debatable. Indeed, the term has a wryly perverse ring to it when applied to artists 'trading' their skills and talents. Nonetheless, in so far as a workshop enhanced the competencies and skill levels of participants then it has to be assumed that in their creative work as practitioners, selling performances in a cultural market place, such training contributed somehow to their 'licence to trade'. We might also note that this 'trade' would include selling of what had been learnt: a trade in workshop practices perhaps. The forms of pedagogy delivered in workshops (and other structures) were shaped both by context (see later) and – crucially – by the training and performance lineages embodied in the teachers concerned. A workshop or course in Decroux-based mime technique, for example, would look and be experienced very differently from those classes taught by practitioners steeped in the pedagogies of Jacques Lecoq or Philippe Gaulier on the one hand or Jerzy Grotowski and Eugenio Barba on the other. Over our period and beyond there developed a slippery and fluid vocabulary around training which offered, for example, apparent distinctions between 'preparation' and 'skill', or between somatic techniques and attitudinal dispositions. The obligatory 'warm up' which (properly) began every workshop or class, in the hands of an experienced and sensitive teacher melded muscular exercise with an invitation to embody and embrace that emotional or psychological openness – play, lightness, *complicité* and *disponibilité*, for example – so important for effective ensemble performance. Although distinctions between preparation,

172 Training: from scarcity to abundance

technique and composition are perhaps schematically and conceptually useful, in any particular teaching experience most workshops would slip up and down such a pedagogical continuum, with actual divisions eliding and blurring in the lived reality of the moment. The brevity of the workshop experience also enabled the participant to assimilate the practice in the context of their own attitudes, beliefs and practices, whilst a longer training experience might have moved them away from this and drawn them further (for better or worse) in to the belief systems underpinning the techniques and exercises they were studying.

In considering the training of UK-based practitioners between the 1970s and 2000 we are obliged to direct our attention towards three distinct but sometimes overlapping models of provision: (i) the workshop or laboratory, (ii) the universities and (iii) the conservatoires[2] and the private theatre schools. During our period, these latter were largely independent institutions, but since the 2000s have become incorporated into higher education structures with attendant regulatory obligations around funding, fees, accountability, 'quality control' and research. In the 1980s and 1990s these conservatoires received varying and irregular degrees of finance from the public purse, but were independent from the more formal university funding mechanisms.

Alongside the conservatoires, and in an uneasy relationship with them, there were a number of private (sometimes constituted as charities, though more often as businesses) theatre schools which specialised in mime and physical theatre. These were often established by charismatic and energetic individuals with a 'mission' to teach their own distinct approaches to such modes of performance. Within our timelines, these included:

- Philippe Gaulier who relocated his school from Paris to London between 1991 and 2002.
- Desmond Jones' School of Mime and Physical Theatre (1979–2004) (profiled below).
- Theatre De L'Ange Fou International School of Corporeal Mime, run by Steven Wasson and Corinne Soum, which transferred to London from Paris in 1994 before shifting to the USA in the early 2000s.
- The London School of Mime and Movement launched by Anja Dashwood in 1990 and based in London's Oval House Theatre.
- The School of Physical Theatre (London) run by Lecoq-trained, Ron East.
- The Mime Centre founded by Adam Darius and Marita Crawley in 1978 (London).
- Fool Time (1986–1993) founded by Richard Ward; and Circomedia run by Bim Mason and Helen Crocker from 1994 (Bristol).

---

2 Graham Marchant's article 'The funding of drama student training in Britain' (2001) contains many details about how funding worked at that time.

We should also note the existence of two circus schools: (i) Circus Space in London (established in 1989, later to be re-named in 2014, the National Centre for Circus Arts) and (ii) Bristol's Fooltime which by 1993 had become Circomedia (led by Bim Mason and Helen Crocker)[3]. Another phenomenon which merits more attention than we can give here was the biennial Arts Council-funded, week-long British Summer School of Mime throughout the 1980s and variously led by Jacques Lecoq, Daniel Stein, Théâtre du Mouvement, Mike Alfreds and Hilary Westlake.

Beyond London, Paris was self-evidently a training locus for (usually) young early career practitioners in the form of École Internationale de Théâtre Jacques Lecoq, École Philippe Gaulier et Monika Pagneux in the 1980s, Etienne Decroux who ran his school in Boulogne-Billancourt from 1962 almost until his death in 1991, and Marcel Marceau who established his own school, École Internationale de Mimodrame de Paris in 1978. Of these, although the teaching of Decroux was highly significant for Desmond Jones, it was the pedagogies of Jacques Lecoq, Philippe Gaulier and Monika Pagneux which emerged as the most significant in shaping and moulding the work of UK mime and physical theatre practitioners in our period. In charting these influences we have to note that no understanding of the practices which feature in this book can ignore the fact that so many UK actors, performers and theatre makers travelled to France to experience the teachings of these seminal figures. Having been largely ignored by academic writer-researchers until 20 years ago there has been a relative spate of publications on Lecoq and his school (Murray, 2018; Evans and Kemp, 2016; Lecoq [Patrick], 2016; Murray and Keefe, 2016; Murray, 2002; Murray in Hodge, 2010; Chamberlain and Yarrow, 2002; and Evans' Introduction to Jacques Lecoq's *The Moving Body*, 2020). Gaulier has published some of his own books (2006 and 2008) and there have been brief essay contributions on his teaching in Murray and Keefe (2016) and Murray in Hodge (2010). Apart from a collaborative writing exercise with Robert Golden entitled *Inside/Outside: theatre/movement/being* (2012), sadly, little has been published on or by Pagneux, although Golden's video of her work (https://vimeo. com/253941723) is a wonderfully illuminating and engrossing insight into her teaching. Now in her 90s, Pagneux is a hugely important figure in twentieth- and twenty-first-century European performer training and deserves the kind of attention and appreciation which has latterly been given to Lecoq. Given the UK parameters of this volume, the plethora of writings identified earlier, and despite the fact that Lecoq taught short classes in Britain over our period, we have decided not to add any further description or analysis of his Paris school here. We return to Gaulier and Pagneux in the section on workshops immediately below.

---

3 A more detailed account of circus training can be found in Murray and Keefe (2016), 192–198.

174 Training: from scarcity to abundance

A time of workshops

In one of the Festival brochures, Dick McCaw, director of the International Workshop Festival (IWF), poses the question, *what is a workshop?*

> The word does create problems so it would be wise to define what we mean by it. An IWF workshop is a short course led by an outstanding figure in the performing arts and lasts between a weekend and two weeks. It might be an open-ended exploration of a theme or problem where the teacher follows and guides rather than leads, or it may be a very tightly structured course. A workshop offers professionals a chance to brush up on old skills, to learn new ones, to find out about new directions and figures in dance and theatre. A workshop can be a port in a storm, an oasis, a pit-stop, a shot in the arm, a shot in the dark, a kick in the pants, a window on the world. A workshop can help you out of a creative block, set you off on a new path, or reaffirm your belief in yourself or your career.
>
> *(McCaw, IWF brochure extract, undated)*

McCaw's expansive characterisation of a workshop, is, of course particularly grounded in the IWF project which we examine in more detail later, but it also serves as a more generic set of propositions entailed in the offer of attending a workshop, whether conducted by an artist of international repute and status, or by an early-career and, as yet, little known practitioner. If, as we have observed in the opening remarks to this chapter, training is perhaps the most dominant and prevailing feature in the 30-year unfolding of UK mime and physical theatre, the workshop is certainly the most clamorous and ever-present mode of delivery within the multiple possibilities which could be designated as *training*.

Scanning the back pages of *Total Theatre* issues from the late 1980s through the 1990s we can regularly find up to as many as three pages advertising training opportunities through workshops. The picture, however, is also intriguingly blurred by the presence of events which are alternatively signed as 'programmes', or 'courses', or 'master classes' or even occasionally (theatre) 'laboratories'. Semantically, at least, there are significant differences between a workshop, a master class and a laboratory, even if in practice they might be found to contain overlapping qualities, behaviours and pedagogies.

However, in terms of the 'what' and the 'how' of the examples identified in *Total Theatre*, any coherent definition of what job of work a workshop could or should do becomes increasingly opaque and elusive. Historically, the Anglo-Saxon 'workshop' or the French 'atelier' is a phenomenon from the Middle Ages under the control of medieval guilds – a building or place where apprentices learn a craft skill from a 'master' (almost always male) and make things, create 'stuff' (Matthews, 2012: 349–361). In contemporary contexts, therefore, an artist-led 'workshop' is a loose and not very revealing metaphor, in contrast to the specificity of its medieval counterpart.

In trying to understand the workshop phenomena we might be guided by the following questions:

- What happened in workshops?
- Who ran them and in what contexts?
- How were they paid for?
- What matrix of cultural and economic conditions gave rise to workshops?
- What were the 'qualifications' of workshop leaders/teachers?
- Did the workshop as the dominant prototype for the delivery of training displace or deflect energy, resources and attention from other possible models of provision?
- Is it possible to attempt an evaluation of workshop provision for the quality of professional mime and physical theatre practice in the UK during our period?

Depending on context, purpose and participant population, workshops could last anything between three hours and two weeks and would target (broadly speaking) three types of constituency: i/ non-professional community and school groups; ii/ a mix of students, amateur/professional actors/theatre makers and enthusiasts; and iii/ purely professional performers/directors/designers/choreographers/dramaturges and writers. We return to the school and community groupings below and, in reality, the boundaries between the second and third categories were often blurred and porous.

The purpose and content of workshops would be multiple and, even in retrospect, are difficult to delineate into some neat and watertight classification. Skilled and confident workshop leaders, understanding the nature of their 'contract', would quickly gauge the aspirations, expectations and level of experience of a group and calibrate their pedagogies accordingly. Aims and purpose would variously be defined by the venue/organiser, the practitioner, the funders or, indeed, the participants. In contrast to acting, there was perhaps a perception that anyone could quickly learn a few simple mime techniques. Even with Lecoq's pedagogy, there are exercises that can be run at almost all levels of expertise and from which participants can take some immediate knowledge. The short workshop, at its most simplistic, decontextualises these skills and it takes longer exposure to a Lecoq, a Gaulier, a Barba or a Pagneux, for example, to build these into a developmental pedagogic journey rather than a loose assemblage of disconnected tricks and dispositions.

Workshops for professional theatre makers and performers

The appetite for professional training through workshops from the late 1980s seemed almost insatiable and for many emergent theatre makers with an orientation towards mime and physical theatre, it was the primary affordable route into acquiring new skills and extending their practice. Unwilling or unable to make the commitment for a year or two in Paris or to the protracted laboratory theatre training required by, for example, Eugenio Barba's Odin Theatre or the Polish

176 Training: from scarcity to abundance

Gardzienice company, a variable diet of workshops seemed to be both a pragmatic and a desirable solution to perceived training needs. It also perhaps felt like a strategy for keeping in touch with respected and admired practitioners and for being seen, for being noticed.

At this point, it is important to note that for practitioners working in mime and physical theatre, training through workshops represented a very different route from that available to actors working in mainstream theatre. The dominant model for preparing an actor for the industry remains professional training courses (undergraduate or postgraduate) at a drama school (LAMDA, Rose Bruford, Guildhall, RADA, RCS and RCSSD, for example). Despite these boundaries becoming more porous and unstable, for the aspiring mime and physical theatre practitioner the cultural economy of training in the UK since the 1970s remains significantly divergent from the mainstream.

From the authors' own experience (as professional performers and theatre makers) of participating in numerous workshops, and occasional master classes, the nature of these events varied considerably according to the artist/performer pedagogues, their personalities, their training, and the proposition entailed in the offer. As such, whilst almost all such events would entail 'warm-ups' – both action-based and dispositional/psychological – they might differ hugely according to the presence, or otherwise, of skill and technical training, exposure to the compositional and devising strategies of the pedagogues (constructing a physical or vocal score, for example), engagement with varying theatre genres (clowning, mask work, tragedy, melodrama, farce, mime, physical theatre, somatic practices and bouffons), play and improvisation. The tonal register and texture of these events would vary along a continuum between authoritarian and highly didactic modes of teaching through to openly collaborative forms of student-centred learning where the workshop leader played the role of enabler, mentor, provocateur, facilitator and/ or curator-animator.

Many of the teachers and practitioners we interviewed admitted to also devouring a diet of workshops in the early stages of their careers, and indeed continued – perhaps more selectively – to refresh their skills in this way. Franc Chamberlain (performer, teacher and writer) identified a tapestry of practitioners whose training he experienced, initially as a student at the University of East Anglia and then over many years after graduating. For Chamberlain the range of these influences was not untypical of practitioners embarking on a working life in the mime and physical theatre sector in the 1980s and his workshop training spanned contemporary (Greg Nash and Rosemary Butcher) and classical Indian dance (Barbara Vijayakumar and Kalamandalam Krishnakumar), Polish theatre (Rena Mirecka of Włodzimierz Staniewski's Gardzienice Theatre Laboratory), story-telling (John Martin of Pan Projects, and Hugh Lockton of The Company of Storytellers), mime (Geoff Buckley, Justin Case and Mark Saunders), voice work (Helen Chadwick) and with Théâtre de Complicité and Philippe Gaulier. Denise Wong (Director of Black Mime Theatre) was initially exposed to mime through courses at Rose Bruford College where she was a student (see Chapter 7), and later undertook workshops with Shared Experience, Gardzienice, Steven Berkoff and Mladen Materić, who had been brought over from Serbia by the IWF. Wong was particularly influenced, she says, by Materić. David Williams (performer, dramaturg, writer and teacher) continued to engage in an eclectic array of workshops and short courses throughout his career including: Grotowski's Teatr Laboratorium (at the Cardiff Lab), Bruce Myers, Toshi Tsuchitori and other members of Peter Brook's Centre Internationale de Recherche Théâtrale (CIRT), members of Ariane Mnouchkine's Théâtre du Soleil, Roy Hart Theatre, Peter Schumann's Bread & Puppet Theatre, Hesitate & Demonstrate, Joe Chaikin's Open Theater and Théâtre de Complicité. The arc of Williams' exposure to such training opportunities reflects an explicitly international and cross-cultural disposition and an openness that positions him largely outwith mime training in any sharply defined sense. Nonetheless, Williams' trajectory speaks of a commitment to hybrid practices – all deeply embodied and corporeal – and a willingness to experience different 'trainings'. In this way, he is similar to many of the practitioners we spoke to, although we might locate his interests within an arena of interest close to the work of Richard Gough and the Centre for Performance Research. Both Simon Murray and Mark Evans also engaged in a diversity of training opportunities throughout the 1980s and 1990s. Murray, in addition to spending a year in Paris with Philippe Gaulier and Monika Pagneux (1986/1987) took workshops with: Adam Darius, Peta Lily, David Glass, Yoshi Oida, Eugenio Barba, Mladen Materić, Simon McBurney, Trestle and Trickster theatre companies, Forced Entertainment, Carlo Bosso (Commedia mask making and performance), Enrique Pardo, Rose English, Jacky Lansley, Rosemary Butcher, Desmond Jones, Geraldine Pilgrim, Frankie Armstrong, Hilary Westlake and Mark Sakharov. Evans was in Paris at L'Ecole Jacques Lecoq (1982–1983) and with Philippe Gaulier and Monika Pagneux (1984) but beyond this, experienced courses or workshops with: Steve Rumbelow and Triple Action Theatre, Patricia Bardi (voice and movement), Moving Being, Mike Alfreds (Shared Experience), Yoshi Oida, Welfare State, Geraldine Pilgrim (Hesitate and Demonstrate), Sheryl Sutton (Robert Wilson Group), David Gaines (Moving Picture Mime Show), Eric Mallett and Mick Barnfather (Théâtre de Complicité), Trestle, Julian Crouch (mask-making), Frantic Assembly, Volcano, Liam Steel, Desmond Jones and Black Mime Theatre.

Reflecting on this rather startling litany of training opportunities experienced by Chamberlain, Wong, Williams, Murray and Evans it remains difficult to interpret or discern conclusions from such a bewildering lexicon. This multiplicity and diversity certainly speaks of the 'temper of the times', when these practitioners were part of a culture which fed an appetite for and openness to workshop training and which generated an economic marketplace to enable it to happen. There was also perhaps a need not to miss out, to appear 'in the know' and to be seen and noticed within this changing landscape. For Murray, his hunger for these opportunities feels, in retrospect, rather indiscriminate and profligate. In so far as there was a through-line to his choices it lay in a rather ill-defined focus on embodiment, physical action, experimentation and the exoticism of the contemporary avant-garde. However, like others identified earlier, his choices seemed to eschew 'hard' skill training and the mastery of particular technical prowess. For better or worse, this diversity of options and choices made by practitioners seems

178 Training: from scarcity to abundance

also to speak as much of a wider curiosity about new, different and international performance practices, cultures and impulses as it does of a channelled and focused desire to acquire additional skills. The complexities of the workshop phenomenon and diverging viewpoints as to its value were rehearsed in the pages of *Total Theatre* (Winter 1995 and Summer 1996) in a rather waspish exchange between Rivka Rubin (founder of Manchester's Physical State International) and Dick McCaw (as Director of the IWF in London). We return to this debate later.

For companies and artists whilst on tour there was often an obligation to teach workshops as part of the funding package they had received from the Arts Council, a regional arts board or a local authority. Many of these were directed towards school and community groups and were embraced with varying degrees of enthusiasm by companies when, after a demanding performance and an ensuing late night, they were faced with a class of sceptical or exuberant school kids in a cold hall or gymnasium the following morning. However, some of these training events, especially in larger conurbations, were deliberately angled at young or early career professional theatre makers and actors, or performing arts students in local universities, polytechnics or colleges. During our conversations with two highly experienced and respected practitioners, Annabel Arden (co-founder of Théâtre de Complicité) and David Glass, both testified to the importance that teaching has always had for them. Arden wryly, but passionately observed:

> Basically, you didn't get the gig if you didn't offer a workshop. You didn't have a choice, so you had to do it. We used to complain. 'Bloody hell. 10 o'clock in this school, 2 o'clock in another school and then we have to re-rehearse the bit that didn't go well last night, and then we've got to play the show'. We worked very hard and did an enormous number of workshops. But I think it's a measure of how much we loved our teachers that actually we did find – bit by bit – a huge joy in all of that teaching. And it was really joyful, it was really, really wonderful to see how you could inspire people and you could make them play and move, and how hungry they were. And also how much we learned through teaching. This was very clear to us, that if you really want to know how to make something you've got to be able to teach it. In teaching it, you refine your whole perception of what it is that you're trying to communicate.
>
> *(Arden, 2021)*

Arden's point about it being 'a measure of how much we loved our teachers that actually we did find – bit by bit – a huge joy in all of that teaching' (ibid.) seems significant and a reflection of how much respect and affection many practitioners held for such influential figures as Lecoq, Gaulier, Pagneux, Brook, Bausch and Barba, for example.

For David Glass, the educational dimension of his ensemble's work has always been pleasurably and existentially central to his practice. For Glass, teaching has never been a reluctant 'add-on' to performance but always a space to try out new ideas, often to expose workshop participants to themes and challenges from a production he was rehearsing at that time and to experiment with emerging forms and techniques.

Training: from scarcity to abundance **179**

We asked Glass about the role that teaching has played in his practice over four decades and he responded thus:

> I made it up when I was young, just made it up to make a living. And I loved it. But . . . you know this . . . the best way to learn is to teach. Something comes out of your mouth and you go, 'that didn't sound too bad', and it seemed to have had an effect. I now think learning is absolutely central to any creative act. Without learning, we don't have creativity. You certainly don't make anything that is not basically from within a very controlled situation. So learning has always been a central part of the Ensemble's process. And that means listening and then going again, which is very Lecoq. You watch, you listen, you go again.
>
> *(2020)*

Glass and his Ensemble, like a number of companies in the mime/physical theatre arena, seem almost to have dissolved the boundaries between training, devising, composition and rehearsal. In 1987 whilst rehearsing the *Dinosaur of Weltschmerz* under the direction of Rex Doyle, Glass ran a residency/workshop for emerging mime and physical theatre practitioners in Peterlee in County Durham. Murray was one of about 10 performer/theatre makers from the North East who participated in this Northern Arts-funded event and remembers it as very productive, not only in terms of learning skills and making strategies, but also as a generative exercise in collaboration between professional artists based in the region. In retrospect, the event seems like an exemplary and imaginative partnership between Susanne Burns (Northern Arts Dance and Mime Officer), a well-respected practitioner, David Glass, and a gang of enthusiastic early career mime and physical theatre professionals. (See Chapter 4 and Burns' efforts to build networks within the region.)

In the 1980s and 1990s, from Murray's experience of training with him, a Glass workshop would typically be a blend of movement preparation – indeed, 'technique' – and creative and playful improvisation. Harnessing the language of his dance training, over a week-long workshop, for example, the day would always start with at least an hour's worth of 'class'. Here, participants would be required to endure the discipline of various somatic exercises: stretching, lengthening, isolations, fixed points, rhythm, texture, tension and relaxation, shifting weight and balance, breathing, and exploring these both singly and in collaboration with the whole group. In the early 1980s Glass also took a summer school with Jacques Lecoq. Murray particularly recalls Glass's own signature to the Yoga 'salute to the sun' routine which was always repeated on a daily basis. Following this repertoire of movements, a Glass workshop session would progress into improvisation, comedy, play, clowning, work with text and objects, exploring space, and a range of creative exercises designed to generate the engines of corporeal ensemble: listening, noticing, touching, *complicité* and *disponibilité*. Murray cannot recall whether Glass explicitly used these latter terms, so essential to the goals of Lecoq's pedagogy, but they were certainly the dynamic qualities, dispositions and sensitivities which he was seeking in his students. In our conversation with him, Glass reflected:

I knew that the body had to be trained. I love the training of that. And Decroux is a very, very rigorous training. It's a very 'armoured' training though and it creates great tension in the body. But I always felt that the clarity of physicality was important for the actor, for me as a performer. And it was also the robustness that helped me have a solo career . . . In fact, over this break [2020 Covid pandemic UK lockdown], I've started giving myself class every day and Decroux is still part of it. So it's still there in my body.

(2020)

International Workshop Festival (IWF)

The workshops exemplified earlier, and so extensively advertised through the pages of *Total Theatre*, were often projects organised by art centres/small-scale theatres with companies or solo artists whilst on tour or undertaking residencies in different parts of the UK. However, a significant proportion of these were also part of the provision of particular organisations established purely for the purposes of promoting and offering short training experiences. The most significant of these, in terms of both the sheer quantity of its 'output' and the breadth and internationalism of its annual programme, was the International Workshop Festival (IWF) which ran between 1988 and 2001. The very existence of the IWF, and the ambition which lay behind it, speaks eloquently – sometimes tacitly, sometimes explicitly – about the force fields which shaped cultural production within the territories of mime and physical theatre during our period. Like much of the work profiled in this book the IWF seems in retrospect to be very much 'of its moment' and by this, we refer to its cross-culturalism, its eclecticism, its daring and – in a sense – its arrogance in terms of deliberately aiming to challenge and provoke the insularity of much of the training offered by drama schools and, to a lesser extent, universities.

In December 2020 we interviewed Dick McCaw, who took over from Nigel Jamieson as Artistic Director of the IWF in January 1993 and remained in this position until the organisation closed in 2001. McCaw had established and performed with the Actors' Touring Company and the Medieval Players in the 1980s but became Associate Director to Jamieson in 1989. Jamieson, as we have seen in Chapter 5, had worked as director with the Trickster Theatre Company and latterly as Mime and Circus Animateur for Greater London Arts (GLA). According to McCaw, when GLA asked Jamieson to write a report on his animateur work, he declined and proposed instead to run two festivals: a 'New Circus' festival and a 'Workshop Festival'. In a retrospective celebration of the IWF '10 years on' in 1998, Jamieson is quoted from a statement he made when launching the first-ever festival ten years earlier. His words capture the main impulses which would continue to drive the project:

> Behind the Festival lies the belief that if theatre is to play a vibrant role in our society then we must train our performers in a wider range of disciplines, drawing on the roots of theatre and reflecting the multi-cultural society we live in. . . . The last ten years has seen an explosion of interest in performance skills and physical theatre forms that has been spectacularly successful

at drawing new audiences for theatre. It has seen the renaissance of mime, mask work, Commedia dell'arte and clowning, the growth of Street Theatre and New Variety, the development of Circus Theatre and the determination to draw on the vast richness of non-western theatre forms.

(Jamieson in IWF, 1998)

Later in the document, Clive Barker (Chair of the IWF in 1998) elaborates on Jamieson's aspirations of a decade earlier and (re)articulates a radical prospectus for the IWF which positions the organisation as continuing to offer an antidote to the narrow and – by implication – inward-looking character of much existing training, whilst at the same helping to usher in progressive theatre forms more appropriate to the late twentieth century and the early twenty-first. Barker is unambiguous about the direction he wants the IWF to take:

> At the present time it is more than ever vital that the theatre escapes the chains of past forms and practices and finds new ways to face up to the competition of other media and the new communication technology. The training of actors in this country is still rooted in the past, which is a strength and as a basis for technique, but a weakness if that training is rigidly aimed at a theatre which no longer exists or is, at best, slipping away. What is needed are new ideas and an infusion of new methods and approaches to training which will create the flexibility to respond effectively to the demands which will be made on the actor and dancer to measure up to the new forms, from wherever they come.
>
> *(Barker in IWF, 1998)*

Jamieson, writing at the launch of the whole project in 1988, sees the work of IWF both as a response to new developments in UK theatre and as a progenitor of them. In the extract above he speaks of 'the renaissance of mime' which, again, obliges us to reflect on the currency of the mime word at that time and into the 1990s. We discussed this with McCaw during our interview and he acknowledged that by the early to mid-1990s, although remaining wedded to the practices, he had become increasingly reluctant to use the term in publicity. He reflected:

> I don't know how it happened or why it happened but physical theatre or a theatre of images, visual theatre all those words came in to that space, which had previously been occupied by the word mime. Jacques [Lecoq] said, I don't care what you call it, I just want new theatre. I want vital theatre. I want to see theatre that is alive. . . . Physical theatre was always pretty much centre stage for the Workshop Festival.
>
> *(McCaw, 2020)*

Figure 6.1 is a startling visual lexicon and record of the breadth, diversity and internationalism of IWF programmes over their 13-year history. Each name in each particular time frame and context tells its own singular story and disguises a

182 Training: from scarcity to abundance

Since 1988, 189 teachers

Mike Alfreds	Enrique Pardo	Solaris Lakota Sioux	Gabor Tompa	Carlotta Ikeda
Johnny Hutch	Theatre de Complicite	Germaine Acogny	Silviu Purcarete	Koffi Koko
Frankie Armstrong	Donato Sartori	Alan Bolt	Andrei Serban	Elsa Wolliaston
The Bhavaiyars	Grigor Belokian	Kalrwat Dance Theatre	Lam Kam Chuen	Georges Appaix
Desmond Jones	Monika Pagneux	Barney Simon	Edward Clarke	Patricia Bardi
Barry Grantham	Frankie Armstrong	The Gardzienice Project	Jayachandranl	Zygmunt Molik
Ivor Dembino	Charabanc	Augusto Boal	Sathyan Arayanan	Richard Armstrong
John Wright	Mouth Opera	Wolfgang Stange	Sylvia Bazzarelli	Enrique Pardo
Complicite	G. Yanovskaya	Comediants	Lam Kam Chuen	Patsy Rodenburg and
Shikisha	Robert Sturua	Simon McBurney	Annette Leday	Antonia Franceschi
Jacques Lecoq	Mark Sukharov	Donato Sartori	Garet Newell	Grzegorz Bral/Anna
Mas Soegeng	Anatoly Vasilev	Nancy Meckler	Henry Smith	Zubzycka
Ecole de Mime	Christopher Hampton	Flora Lauten	Naohiko Umewake	Jonathan Lunn
Lloyd Newson/DV8	David Edgar	Phelim McDermot &	Rosemary Butcher	Shi-Zheng Chen
Pierre Byland	Gennietta Yanovskaya	Guy Dartnell	Ken Campbell	Grisha Coleman
Monika Pagneux	Lev Dodin (Maly Theatre)	Peter Badejo	Edward Clark	Jonathan Stone
Lam Jup	Adriano Iurissevich	Johnny Hutch	Rick Zoltowski	Amel Tafsout
Ninian Kinnear-Wilson	Garet Newell	Sean Gandini &	Marie Chouinard	Andrew Dawson
Saily Brooke	Heather Robb	Gill Clarke	Dominique Dupuy	Stephen Powell
Carlo Boso	Johnny Hutch	Rosemary Butcher	Claire Heggen	Venice Manley
Natsu Nakajima	Rose English	Bobby Baker	Keith Johnstone	Garet Newell
Philippe Gaulier	Dalia Ibelhauptaite	Lionel Newton	Garet Newell	Jos Houben
Nakamura Matazo	Paos Dance Company	Wierszalin	J P Perreault	John Wright
Yoshi Oida	Ranjabati Sircar	Liza Mayer	Slava Polunin	Niamh Dowling
Patsy Ricketts	Cristina Castrillo	Shiro Daimon	Gennadi Bogdanov	Agus Bima Prayitno
Clive Barker	Theatre du Mouvement	Luanda Childs	Mandala Theatre	Alan Herdman
Julia Bardsley	Daisuke Yoshimoto	Nava Zukerman	Anatoly Vasilev	Wilson Pico
Shobana Jeyasingh	Station House Opera	Zygmunt Molik	Peter Schumann	Andrei Serban
Jos Houben	Gicely Berry	Annu Furakawa	Teatro Potlach	Wendy Houston
Mladen Materic	Alekienda Sumarti	Gog i Magog	Tim Etchells	Joe McGinley
Suraya Hilal	Cumbre Flamenca	Giovanna Marini	& Hugo Glendinning	Lillis O'Laoire
Ken Campbell	Kit Summers	Foorpaul	Maria Abramovic	Benoit Amy de la
Peter Badejo	Liu Fu-Sheng	David Freeman &	Helen Chadwick	Breteque
Francis Batten	Jean Palacy	Lokendra Arambam	Ellen Lauren	Houria Aichi
Richard McDougal	Franki Anderson	Koffi Koko	Wolfgang Stange	Stepanida Bonsova and
Sistren	Sean Gandini	Beija Flor	Andrew Dawson	Jun Spindanov
Zofia Kalinksa	Aboriginal and Islander	Carlotta Ikeda	Julian Crouch	Morag MacLeod
Dele Charley	Dance Theatre	Salidummay	Shiro Daimon	Edischer Garakanidse

from 35 countries have led workshops for IWF

ALGERIA	CHINA	INDIA	PERU	SWITZERLAND
ARMENIA	CUBA	ISRAEL	POLAND	UNITED STATES
AUSTRALIA	ECUADOR	ITALY	ROMANIA	OF AMERICA
BELGIUM	EGYPT	JAMAICA	RUSSIA	FORMER
BENIN	EIRE	LITHUANIA	SIERRA LEONE	YUGOSLAVIA
BRAZIL	FRANCE	NICARAGUA	SENEGAL	
CANADA	GERMANY	NIGERIA	SOUTH AFRICA	
CHILE	GEORGIA	PHILLIPINES	SPAIN	

This page background photo: Gennady Bogdanov

FIGURE 6.1 Since 1988, 189 teachers: International Workshop Festival, (centenary publication, 1998). By kind permission of Dick McCaw.

huge amount of planning, administration, publicity, marketing and 'negotiations' with the artists themselves, participants, funding bodies and venue managers. Over its lifetime the IWF developed in at least two distinct but inter-related ways. After 1988 'London' was dropped as a prefix for International Workshop Festival and from 1989, though remaining anchored in Britain's capital city, a number of the workshops began to be distributed across a handful of major UK cities: Birmingham, Coventry, Bristol, Londonderry, Belfast, Edinburgh, Glasgow, Newcastle, Leeds, Nottingham and the Scottish borders. Between 1988 and 1994 the IWF was a biannual event interspersed with smaller themed projects in alternate years. Over these six years, IWF-commissioned workshops included those from Clive Barker, Ken Campbell, Lucinda Childs, Lev Dodin (of the Maly Drama Theatre, St Petersburg), Jacques Lecoq, Monika Pagneux, Peter Schumann (of Bread and Puppet Theatre) and Anatoli Vasiliev.

From 1995 to its closure in 2001 McCaw recalibrated the IWF offer by giving each festival (now annual) a theme under an overarching banner title of 'The Body of Knowledge'. The themes were these:

1995 The Performer's Energy
1996 . . . and movement
1997 Voice/Dance/Movement & With the Whole Voice
1998 The Way of the Warrior
1998 A Common Pulse
1999 Between Character and Performer
2000 Passages and Dialogues
2001 The Sense of Space

McCaw explained his thinking behind this turn in the 10th anniversary booklet:

> In 1995 IWF began a projected series of seven festivals exploring fundamental aspects of the performing arts (e.g. rhythm, movement, space, character) . . . Since we are dealing with the essential building blocks in the performing arts, none can be completely isolated. The aim of each individual festival is to see how different performing traditions, disciplines, or artists conceive of the given theme. This demonstrates how many approaches there are to the phenomenon of performance. If one thinks of each theme as a problem, then each festival offers 20 different solutions, or, to put it musically, each festival has one theme and 20 variations.
>
> *(McCaw/IWF, 1998)*

As we have similarly remarked in relation to Mime Action Group (MAG), the work of IWF over 13 years merits a full-length research project, both to document in detail its activities and to reflect critically on the cultural forces which shaped

184 Training: from scarcity to abundance

its purpose and programmes and how, in turn, to investigate how IWF workshops helped to fashion the landscape of mime and physical theatre during this period. As a snapshot of a single year we studied a report sent to us by McCaw on the 1994 festival and here summarise its main points and reflections. Whilst each festival was different in content and became themed from 1995, we believe that the profile below offers a good enough feel for the IWF project as a whole to get a sense of its dynamics, and the challenges typically faced by McCaw and his fellow organisers.

The 1994 Festival had four centres: London, Glasgow, Nottingham and Londonderry (Derry) and a range of workshop and talks took place in these cities throughout September, October and November of that year. In London, the festival was badged 'The World Theatre Forum' and was based in the London Studio Centre. The programme began with 6 weekend workshops, followed by 6 five-day workshops, and concluded with a further 6 weekend events. The week-long workshops focused on voice (Liza Mayer and Zygmunt Molik), Butoh (Anzu Furakawa and Shiro Daimon), contemporary dance (Lucinda Childs) and the work of actor/writer, Nava Zukerman. The weekend workshops included Flora Lauten, Andrew Buckland with Lionel Newton, Nancy Meckler, Phelim McDermott, Guy Dartnell, Jos Houben, Sean Gandini, Gill Clarke, Peter Badejo, Bobby Baker and Mladen Materić.

Glasgow hosted a joint programme – 'A Romanian Affair' – after Manchester dropped out when hoped-for funding never materialised. Here, Romanian theatre directors, Gabor Tompa and Silviu Purcarete, taught at the Tramway, while Andrei Serban (once of Peter Brook's 1971 experimental company which performed *Orghast*) taught at the Cottier Theatre, a recently adapted church in Glasgow's West End. Serbian actor and director, Mladen Materic taught a 5-day workshop at the Royal Scottish Academy of Music and Drama (RSAMD) and the Centre for Contemporary Art (CCA), originally the Third Eye Centre, hosted talks and acted as an informal club for Festival participants.

In Nottingham, where the IWF had had a regular presence since 1992, under the theme of 'Stamping Ground', McCaw notes:

> Our work . . . has a much wider impact than in any other IWF venue because of the broader programme of work undertaken: in addition to the masterclasses, there is also a weekend conference, as well as five or six weeks' worth of activities in local schools. Thus, when looking for artists for the workshop programme one also has to find people who have the ability to communicate with professionals one week, and with school kids the next.
>
> *(McCaw/IWF, 1994)*

The IWF partnership with Nottingham dated back to 1991 and was deemed by McCaw and his team to be a model of collaboration. Here the relationship was with Nottingham Playhouse (Ruth Mackenzie), Dance 4 (Rachel Emmett),

Roundabout and the Education and Leisure Services Departments of Nottinghamshire County Council. In 1994 the visiting artists were: Salidummay and Nestor Horfila (Phillipines), David Freeman (Australia/UK), Lokendra Arambam (Manipur), Koffi Koko (Benin) and the London School of Capoeira (UK/Brazil). During the Nottingham programme, as well as running workshops, the artists gave talks to community and school groups and ran short taster workshops during the weekend conference.

Derry in this year marked the third visit of the IWF to the city and Festival events there were presented under the banner of 'Finding a Voice'. The 1994 programme in Derry had a strong street theatre dimension and saw the troupe Gog i Magog from Catalonia create a stilt-walking street procession, and the South African company FootPaul explore the 'voice of the street' in the city. Giovanna Marini, singer and collector of traditional music from Italy was to have completed the programme but had to cancel at the last moment due to illness. (See Chapter 4 for an account of Northern Ireland.)

McCaw's report on the 1994 Festival illustrates the scale and ambition of the event and provides a detailed archive, revealing the administrative complexities of organising the overall experience across four cities. The report, in addition to providing detailed facts and figures, also offers a host of perceptive reflections and thoughts on some of the wider cultural/political issues entailed in scheduling the kind of radical and ambitious programme which characterised IWF's aspirations and mission. Amongst the more thought-provoking observations from the report we have identified the following:

- Less appetite for workshops which were cross-art form in intention, practice and pedagogy.
- The difficulties of being 'a festival dedicated to providing new challenges and perspectives – to working on the cutting edge – means that IWF has to confront and try to overcome the habitual 'conservatism of the profession' (McCaw/IWF, 1994).
- Importance of each city having a space which acts as a social and convivial hub where participants and artists can gather after the daily work has finished. Glasgow's CCA worked perfectly in this respect.
- How to make cross-cultural exchanges meaningful, and not a response to 'post-colonial guilt or conformity to well-meaning but theoretical arts policy' (McCaw/IWF, 1994)?
- Inadequate staffing levels within IWF and the remorseless cycle of fundraising.
- Critical importance of researching each workshop – ability/experience of the artist as teacher, target participant group, level of difficulty, local support structures – before committing to the programme.

186 Training: from scarcity to abundance

Any reflection on the 13 years of IWF returns us not only to questions about the definition, nature and purpose of an activity called 'training', but also what sort of training for mime and physical theatre was needed in this period. Furthermore, to pose the question in terms of 'needs' obliges us to ponder on whose needs, who is defining those needs and who might satisfy them. And beyond this, even further, what were the economies of cultural production in these decades in relation to mime and physical theatre training? These questions – posed rhetorically at this juncture – generate complex, contingent and intertwined responses. We return to some of these questions in the rest of this chapter. However, as a postscript to this profile, and as an insight into debates about the cultural economy of the workshop phenomena, we note an exchange in the pages of *Total Theatre* in 1995 and 1996 between Rivca Rubin (founder/director of Physical State International [PSI]) and McCaw. In the Winter 1995 issue of *Total Theatre* Rubin wrote a strongly felt and impassioned critique of the current state of training – and training needs – under the title of 'The Relevance and Revelation (?) of the Workshop'. Rubin's targets were partly university theatre and performing arts programmes offering practice-based learning, and the plethora of short workshops she had observed over the time she had been running PSI. IWF was not named in her sights but in a response the following year McCaw felt obliged – unapologetically – to explain and defend the provision of short workshops. Rubin's main argument might be summed up like this:

> Many formal training courses today are covering too many subjects too superficially. In-depth training and profound understanding of one area as an initial base has almost become extinct. . . . We now have a conveyor belt production of 'master classes', taught mainly by flavour of the moment artists and some master makers, but rarely master teachers. . . . In an overcrowded market, why has it become so compelling to organise workshops? . . . Do we really care about the participant's development or are we satisfied with the notion that overall the artist will learn 'something'.
>
> *(Rubin, 1995: 11)*

So, essentially Rubin was commenting on what she perceived to be the low level of skill possessed by university students/graduates and early career professionals, and laying the blame at the feet of university courses and the 'overcrowded market' of workshop provision. McCaw, responding in the Summer 1996 issue of *Total Theatre*, did not engage with Rubin's claims about skill levels, but challenged her on what 'job of work' the short workshop aspired to undertake. For McCaw, IWF workshops were also a space for networking and sociability:

> A workshop is simply a space in which professionals can meet to exchange and explore ideas and skills, and to experiment freely without the pressure of the rehearsal schedule. The same workshop can answer a variety of professional needs: a means of reviving flagging morale and energy, a way through a creative block, or a new insight into the creative process.
>
> *(McCaw, 1996: 19)*

The debate would have benefitted from widening and deepening, and it is a shame, perhaps, that *Total Theatre* did not provide a forum for this to happen. Research into workshop participants' hopes and expectations and whether they felt these had been met by any particular workshop experience would have been very fruitful and salient. These short contributions from Rubin and McCaw set the parameters for a productive debate, but it seems now (in retrospect) that each author hoped for something different from workshops as generic forms of training. McCaw was defending a paradigm of workshop training which was unlike in form, content and purpose from that espoused by Rubin. Over 25 years on, in our interview, McCaw elaborated on what he valued in the workshop festivals he had curated. For him, whilst the actual experience of the workshop was, of course, critically important, it was the peripheral, the unintended and less formulaic qualities of the festival experience that he most valued. His comments serve as a 'final word' (for now) on IWF:

> More important than the actual workshops was working with people who were in the workshops, seeing how they learned, seeing their learning style. So I think it was oddly less about the content, and more about the encounters. The biggest thing for me was that it was a festival in which, in the evening, you heard people talking formally, but I also insisted upon the informality of it. You could meet other people, there were exchanges, it was about a community. It became much more a reflection upon this dynamic core of creativity, which is unrecognized, misunderstood and sometimes decried as an indulgence. . . . You could start thinking about a fundamental aspect or principle in performance from a new perspective.
>
> *(McCaw, 2020)*

Mime Action Group (MAG): workshop broker and enabler

In our profile of MAG in Chapter 3, and in scanning its multiple roles and initiatives, it was impossible not to remark on the considerable investment made in training through its own occasional workshop events, discursive forums which debated provision, needs and strategies, and as a ubiquitous pre-internet 'notice board' (see Figure 6.2) advertising a huge variety of training opportunities across the UK and beyond. Indeed, campaigning for training was hard-wired into MAG's objectives and ambitions from its formation in the mid-1980s. MAG's preoccupation with training was a double track exercise: supporting and broadcasting the multiple forms of preparation for those already committed to a professional working life in mime and physical theatre (or about to embark on one), *and* the provision of myriad workshop opportunities in schools and other community contexts. For many 'young' companies and artists it was in the latter territory that their teaching was played out, but for those with some longevity and the reputation that went with it, increasingly there would be an opportunity to share – to 'sell' – their skills with a more professional constituency of participants. Sometimes, these were to be billed as 'master classes'!

Training

Workshops &

Performance

International Workshop Festival
Bristol, Derry and Nottingham
Sept – Nov 1992
The 1992 Programme continues to consolidate the International Workshop Festival's reputation as the

Ecole Trapeze Grand Volant de Jean Pallacy

world's largest and most ambitious event committed to the exploration of theatrical creation.
At its core is a determination to help push theatre back to the very centre of our cultural life, to counter the vision of the performing arts as merely an adjunct to the entertainment and heritage industries.
In association with the Circus School , Fooltime, Bristol IWF will present Ariel Manoeuvres (9 – 20 Sept) bringing together some of the worlds leading circus artists. Participants include one of France's greatest Trapeze artist's Jean Pallacy and his famous Ecole Trapeze Grand Volant, who will bring their extraordinary flying trapeze to Bristol; juggling genius, KI Summers; Peking Oper's principal teacher, Liu Fu Sheng, as well as Ra Ra Zoo and Fooltime's own Frankie Anderson.
Moving to Derry in Northern Ireland, the Festival presents Voices of Liberation (11 Sept – 21 Oct) a season of workshops focusing on theatre created as a response to political conflict. Featured artists are Barney Simon from South Africa's Market Theatre, the leading Brazilian theatre Director, Augusto Boal; Wolfgang Stange and Amici; and Gardzience from Poland who will be working with performers from both Protestant and Catholic communities.
The Festival culminates in Nottingham with Stamping Ground (2 – 20 Nov) an ambitious programme bringing together groups of artists from across the world who use dance and theatre to challenge the threat to their endangered cultures. Companies in residence include Solaris/Lakota Sioux Project, Aboriginal and Islander Dance Theatre of Australia, Sardanists Freedom Fighter Allan Bolt and African Dance Legend Germaine Acogny, Director of Mudra Africa.
Information: The International Workshop Festival, 2 – 9 Mason's Avenue, London. EC2V 5BT. Tel 071 600 2242.

Cross Over
Movement, Mime, Masks, Object Theatre
Led by Ronald Wilson and John Mowat
(City and Guilds of London Art School, Kennington)
2 – 11 Sept 1992

Each day will open with a period devoted to Body Awareness, Rhythm and Release. This will be followed by a class on the fundamental techniques of Modern Physical Mime: fixed point, enlargement and reduction, rhythm and phrasing, counterweights and illusions.
Cost: £125/Concession £ 95
Details: Jennifer Ferguson, 56 Kestral Avenue, London. SE24 OEB. Tel 071 274 3821.

The Artist Within and the Archetypal Mask.
Led by Merle van den Bosch, John Wright, Scott Clark and Peter Badejo
Centre for the Expressive Arts, London
10 Sept – 10 December 1992
An ongoing course of 14 weeks held on Thursday evenings from 6pm – 9pm and two Saturdays from 10am -5pm.
The workshop will integrate Dance, Drama, Feldenkrais Movement Awareness, Spontaneous Theatre, Voice, Visual Art, Archetypal Mask and Black Dance and is open to professionals and non professionals.
Cost: £200/Concs £100
Details: Centre for the Expressive Arts, 22A Topsfield Parade, London. N8 8PP. Tel 081 340 4988.

Expressive Mime
Led by Adam Darius and Kazimir Kolesnik
Islington Arts Factory
21 Sept - 27 Nov 1992
Ten week course in Expressive Mime, Illusionary Mime, Make-Up, Voice Production, Acting, Ballet, Workshop & Production.
Details: The Mime Centre. Tel 081 455 2145.

Puppet Place and Headlights Community Arts, Bristol
MASK
Led by Sally Eaton and Nikki Griffiths
Sept 19 & 20 1992
This course will explore construction techniques.
Cost: £50/Concs £20
THE PUPPET WITHIN
Nov 20 & 22 1992
Participants will embark on a journey to discover the puppet within us all.
Cost: £95/Concs £30
For details on both courses contact: The Puppet Place, Hengrove School, Petherton Gardens, Hengrove, Bristol. BS14 9BU. Tel 0275 838800.

Self Portraits: Exploration of the Body Parts
Led by Didier Rouchon
Swathmore Centre, Leeds
Oct 1992 – Feb 1993
An intensive workshop held over 10 weekends focusing on integration of the body, mind and emotion through dance, movement, drawing and creative writing.
Details: Didier Rouchon on 0924 240587.

Chisenhale Dance Space, London
HANGING UP
Led by Jennifer Monson from New York
30 Sept - 3 Oct 1992
A four day Dance/Performance Workshop focussing on improvisation as a performance form.
Cost: C25/Concs £20
IMPRO-SENSATION WEEKEND
Led by Kathy Crick, Adele Levi, Lucia Walker, Kevin Finnan and Cindy Faulkner
17 & 18 Oct 1992.
A weekend of Contact Improvisation integrating sighted and non-sighted, emphasising the sense of touch as a form of communication.
Cost: Wkd £22/Concs £14
One Day £12/Concs £8
UNDER CONSTRUCTION
Led by Kate Brown, choreographer and Nicholas Ridout, writer.
Mondays, 2 Nov – 7 December 1992.
7pm-9pm
A performance project over six weeks combining movement and text.
Performance on 11th and 12th December.
Cost: £21 Full Course
THINKING OBJECTS
Led by Gary Stevens
Saturday 28th Nov 1992
Combining the visual artist and the performer, the workshop will focus on Steven's approach to the physical discipline.
Cost: £12/Concs £8
Chisenhale Dance Space also has other courses of interest. For further information contact Chisenhale Dance Space, 64 Chisenhale Road, Bow, London. E3 5QZ. Tel 081 981 6617.

Holborn Centre for the Performing Arts, London
PHYSICAL THEATRE
Led by Louder Than Words
Mondays, 28 Sept – 30 Nov 1992
7pm – 9.30pm
Physical techniques will be used to approach a range of texts, characterisation, ensemble work and devising.
For those with movement experience.
Cost: £7/£5.50 concs per class
MASKS AND MOVEMENT FOR PERFORMERS – AN INTRODUCTION
Led by Brige Bidell
Tuesdays, 15 Sept – 3 Nov 1992
7pm - 8.30pm
Cost: £60/£35 Concs
DANCING WITH MASKS
Led by Brige Bidell
Tuesdays, 10 Nov – 8 Dec 1992
7pm – 8.30pm
Using masks, creative dance and improvisation to create a piece of ritual theatre which will be performed at the final session for an invited audience. Advanced course.
Cost: £40/£25 Concs Full Course
JAPANESE PHYSICAL THEATRE
Led by Roy Leighton
Thursday 22 Oct 1992.
A one day workshop exploring Tadashi Suzuki's unique blend of Noh, Kabuki and Folk Theatre styles to develop control, strength and skill. Roy Leighton is only the second person from the UK to have studied with Suzuki. Cost: £25
COMMUNICATING YOUR VOICE
Led by Caryll Ziegler
Mondays, 21 Sept – 23 Nov 1992
7pm – 9pm
Study of breathing, relaxation, enunciation, and extension of the vocal range to enable the voice to be used more effectively.
Cost: £55/£45 Concs
The Holborn Centre also run courses and classes in Fencing, Tai Chi, Yoga and Contemporary Dance.
For further information contact: The Holborn Centre for the Performing Arts, 3 Princeton Street, London. WC1R 4AZ. Tel 071 405 5334.

Physical State International, Manchester
PSI, the Manchester based Performing and Visual Arts Training Project Agency.
MANY CULTURES – MANY DANCES
Led by Peter Badejo (Nigeria), Suraya Hilal (Egypt), Chandralekha (India) Pit Fong Loh and Ming Yam Low (China/Malaysia)
10 – 17 Oct 1992
An eight day course focussing on the dance of Nigeria, Egypt, India and China/Malaysia. Each of the tutors will lead a two day workshop.
The workshops can be taken separately or in combination.
Cost: From £25 to £160.
WEEKEND INTENSIVE COURSES
Anna Furse/ Paines Plough
6 – 8 Nov 1992
6pm Friday – 5pm Sunday
A mini laboratory for actors
Mark Murphy/V-Tol
7 & 8 Nov 1992
10am Saturday – 5pm Sunday
For those with previous dance experience
Lance Gries/Trisha Brown Company
13 – 15 Nov 1992
6pm Friday – 1pm Sunday
For those with previous dance experience
Volcano Theatre Company
21 – 23 Nov 1992
For performers, students, & those interested in physical theatre
Cost (per weekend)
Organisation/Funded Individuals £50
Waged Individuals £40
Unwaged/Students/Benefit Receivers £25
There are further concessions for block and group bookings.
Venue details upon reservation
For further information contact : Physical State International, 3 Crossland Road, Manchester. M21 1DT. Tel/Fax 061 860 6526.

Overseas

Voice and Movement
Cortijo Romero, Spain
15 – 22 Nov 1992
Frankie Armstrong and Darien Pritchard will lead a week of exploration in voice and movement in the mountains of Southern Spain.
Details: Studio E. Tel 081 459 5642.

Winter School in the Performing Arts of India
Cochin, Kerala
1 – 31 Jan 1993
Opportunity to study Kathakali, Kalarippayettu, Bharatanatyam and Living Dance (a contemporary Indian Form) including massage, yoga, martial arts training, and dance work.
Information: Ali Pretty, Gazelle Arts, 15 Evelyn House, Greatorex Street, London. E1 5NW. Tel 071 377 8980.

Theatre Biomechanics School
Russian Academy of Theatre Art, Moscow.
The RATA has announced that it is running a Theatre Biomechanics School in Jan 1993 for 8 weeks. The method of training has been developed by Gennady Bogdanov and Nikolay Karpov, the professors of RATA, on the basis of Vsevolod Meyerhold's actors training, stunt gesturality, classical biomechanic exercises, composition and the dramatic arts.
If you are interested in the School fax Irina Zhukova on (095) 290 05 97.

Education

Actions Speak Louder... Mime in the Community
Queen Margaret College, Edinburgh
7 – 11 Sept 1992
An introduction to basic mime technique and ways of adapting it to suit all kinds of community groups, including special needs.
Details: Pat Keysall. Tel 031 312 8329.

total theatre vol 4 no 2/3 summer / autumn 92

FIGURE 6.2 Workshop/training opportunities, Total Theatre, Volume 4, Number 2/3, Summer/Autumn 1992. By kind permission of Aurelius Productions & *Total Theatre* Magazine.

The drive to offer workshops with young people – in or out of school – was propelled by a blend of motives. Partly, this was an uncomplicated and generously benign sense of offering artistic experiences for participants (young and old) without any instrumental purpose. Here, such events were part of a culture which (still) validated exposure to the arts as an enriching and stimulating experience in its own right, and without additional economic justification. It is pertinent to note that the introduction of the Drama GCSE[4] (in England, Wales and Northern Ireland) in 1986 might have spurred schools to take up workshop offers. However, often in a rather uneasy relationship with such impulses, the obligation to offer workshops, usually contiguous with a performance, became an integral part of the funding deal either from the Arts Council[5] nationally and regional arts boards or from venues offering a theatre booking. As Annabel Arden drily remarked to us, 'basically, you didn't get the gig if you didn't offer a workshop' (2021)! In this context the obligation was unashamedly instrumental and commercial – you are more likely to sell tickets for a show if you have run workshops for groups near to the art centre concerned – but also born out of a broad and often ill-defined sense of accountability for public (taxpayers') money. Here, a modest form, of 'social engineering' can be seen to be at play.

MAG's role in supporting and enabling workshops in schools or communities was less concerned with advertising or promoting these since they were usually organised locally between venues, the company and the participant institution, but more with providing an infrastructure of advice and information for the artists concerned. To this end, in the mid-1990s MAG published a number of documents and guides and in 1994 commissioned mime animateur, Jac Wilkinson, to write and compile a *Guide to Mime in Education*. Aimed primarily at teachers, with a forward by the inspirational Ken Robinson[6], then Professor of Arts Education at Warwick University, the guide contained sections on how mime might figure and be taught within the National Curriculum (for England, Wales and Northern Ireland). It also featured case studies of practice by artists such as Pat Keysell, Jane Sutcliffe (based at the Midlands Art Centre [MAC]), Rowan Tolley, Trestle, Triangle and Volcano Theatre Companies, and an inventory of relevant contacts, terms, further reading and vocational training provided by schools and colleges. Triangle was based in Coventry and Mark Evans was working at the Coventry Centre for Performing Arts where Volcano ran workshops.

A year earlier in 1993, MAG had commissioned Neil Blunt of the Arts Training Programme at De Montfort University to research and write the first 'UK Mime and Physical Training Directory'. Running to 62 pages, its cover offered the strap line:

---

4 General Certificate in Secondary Education.

5 1992 Arts Council document 'Drama in Schools' promoted the idea that education in drama was about making, performing and responding to drama.

6 (Sir) Ken Robinson (1950–2020) was a writer, educationalist and academic. A passionate, funny and hugely articulate 'missionary' for the presence of art and creative practices within the school curriculum, he advised governments and extolled the belief that all children (indeed all people) were intrinsically creative if only they were given the right conditions to be so.

190 Training: from scarcity to abundance

> The first guide to provision of Mime, Physical Theatre and New Circus Training in the UK – contains over 200 listings and information on the training opportunities provided by Independent Schools, Colleges, Universities, Organisations, companies and Performers.
>
> *(Blunt and MAG, 1993)*

Priced at £5.99, the Directory (reprinted and updated in 1994) provided a mass of factual information and summarised the range of teaching provision offered by individual artists, companies, colleges, private drama schools and universities at that time. Beyond creative and performance workshops, the Directory also identified management and administrative courses. With a retrospective glance, it offers a very revealing profile of the UK mime, physical/visual theatre landscape in the mid-1990s – revealing not only the range and diversity of provision but also how artists and organisations described themselves and articulated the content and approach of their teaching. Almost 30 years on, we are prompted to consider how this publication (and others like it) were used and by whom. Such an unanswerable question does, however, invite a broader reflection on the multitude of guides, reports, directories and handbooks produced not only, of course, by MAG, but also by the national and regional Arts Councils and Boards. The apparent proliferation of such accounts – both then and now – invite searching questions about practical effects and consequences and a sense that, at their most routine and ineffectual, the immense production of printed words – in, we must remember, a pre-digital and pre-internet age – however wise and judicious, were a substitute or diversion from practical action on other fronts. A rhetorical question which must remain rhetorical in our publication.

These publications were also a way of sharing practice and a vehicle for the advocacy of mime and physical theatre. Many of these reports offered edited documentation of a range of signature educational events organised by MAG in the 1990s such as the Critical Practice and the London seminars. The titles of these slim documents reveal the zeitgeist of the times and the preoccupations not only of MAG's leadership, but also of venue directors, artists and companies. We list (verbatim) some examples of these here since they illustrate concerns of the moment:

- **Training for Tomorrow**: report on the NATIONAL CONFERENCE on mime and physical theatre training. 30/31 January 1993 at the Holborn Centre for the Performing Arts, London in association with the London International Mime Festival.
- **Critical Practice**: report on the SEMINAR focusing on the training and development needs of mime and physical theatre practitioners. 5 November 1993 at the Hawth, Crawley in association with the BEYOND WORDS FESTIVAL.
- **London Seminars**: report on the SEMINARS looking at opportunities for increasing access to training, artistic cultural exchange and the use of writing and directing in mime and physical theatre. 22 and 29

January 1994 at the South Bank Centre, London in association with the London International Mime Festival.

- *Education Day*: report on the day of discussions, workshops and performances at the Hawth, Crawley, in association with the BEYOND WORDS FESTIVAL. 12 October 1994.
- *Moving into Performance Report* (1995). A detailed record by John Keefe of the European Mime and Physical Theatre Workshop Symposium, held in Manchester, 1994.

Scanning these documents inevitably returns us to Khan's 1990 report and many of the issues she raised then are revisited in these events. The most salient of these seem to be: the debate around the need (or otherwise) for a British School of Mime and Physical Theatre; the imperative to develop intercultural training practices; access opportunities for Black and Asian artists and practitioners with disabilities; an increasing role for MAG; the need to initiate dialogue with drama schools and universities; and the importance of developing a language of *critical practice*.

In its history up until 2000, arguably MAG's most ambitious project was a 7-day long event held in Manchester between 12 and 18 September 1994. **Moving into Performance** (hereafter MIP) was billed as a 'European Mime and Physical Theatre Workshop Symposium', was jointly organised with the European Mime Federation based in Amsterdam, and was hosted by the School of Theatre at Manchester Metropolitan University. Beneath the designation, *Moving into Performance*, on the programme cover were four elliptical provocations, or points of reference, for the whole event and to inflect action and thought:

- EXCHANGE (Between forms, practitioners, vocabularies)
- TRANSLATION (From intention to final work, process to product)
- AUTHENTIC VOICE (The work's underlying truth, examining how process and staging contribute to the essence of the work)
- INNER STRUCTURE (Of the work, whether linear or non-linear, devised or authored)

The event combined five days (Monday to Friday) of four laboratory workshops run by Fritz Vogels[7] (Netherlands), Martin Gent[8] (UK), David Gaines[9] (USA) and Enrique Pardo[10] (France), each with a rapporteur who was to feed into the weekend

---

7 Vogels was founder and artistic director of Amsterdam's Griftheater.
8 Gent had been artistic director of dA dA dUMB Productions.
9 See Chapter 5 and Moving Picture Mime Show.
10 See Chapter 4 and Scottish Mime Forum.

192 Training: from scarcity to abundance

symposium which began on Friday afternoon and concluded late afternoon on Sunday. Almost 140 participants, including speakers, workshop leaders and organisers, attended for some or all of the seven days in what was a heady mix of sociability, heuristic learning (laboratory workshops), presentations, performances, lectures and – sometimes – heated exchange. The demographic of the event was almost a representative profile of those practices and artists which populated the landscape of physical and visual theatre in the UK at this time. The 'almost' here is an important qualification since while MIP also attracted figures from, for example, performance and live art, Enrique Pardo in a stimulating 'Burning Question' session asked 'Why is Odin not around? Is this a Decroux/Lecoq/Gaulier club? If so, what is the underlying performance philosophy bias?' (Pardo, 1995: 24). One might have added to Pardo's 'burning question' where are Lloyd Newson and other dance theatre practitioners? Pardo's provocation – if not entirely accurate – was justifiably posed and did indeed perceptively articulate something important about the landscape of UK mime and physical theatre during this period (something which is also addressed in Chapters 4 and 5). Early in the following year, MAG published a detailed report on MIP written by John Keefe. This is a very rich archive document since as well as identifying all the figures who felt it worthwhile to be present in Manchester for the workshops and/or the symposium, it reveals some of the main preoccupations, feelings and thoughts which were swirling around, particularly in the Symposium.

Eddying thoughts quoted by John Keefe in his report (1995) on Moving into Performance (1994)

- Visual theatre is not just a powerful technique for gingering up literary theatre (Joseph Seelig)
- Rejoice in the ending of silent mime and be happy to find a voice (Tom Leabhart)
- People don't know how to talk about their work, there's no common or shared language (Ris Widdicombe)
- We are training too many, too superficially with critical abilities, low or non-existent (Rivka Rubin)
- The dramaturg is one who brings in their biases as a positive intervention (Enrique Pardo)
- All networks and fora can only exist on a willingness to talk and share. Talking produces the seed that will become a flower, or turnip, or whatever. (Ruud Engelander)
- The mythic fox which we hunt, we have to find in ourselves instead of running from bush to bush to look for it. (Enrique Pardo)
- Find the mover in yourself who understands stillness (Fritz Vogels)
- This is the only opportunity I have had to sit down with people in the business and say 'what am I doing?' because you are always having to sell your stuff. (Jane Watson)

- Understanding process is complicated by the fact that there are two processes for an actor creating their own work: performer and director. (David Gaines)
- I do not want to be taught, but to share, discover, provoke, steal. (Chris Rowbury)
- We could have discovered these things more through the work we saw. They don't mean anything to me and no one uses these terms. (Walter Anichofer)
- Get rid of Decroux, Lecoq, Gaulier and Odin from this week – they are like armchairs. (Jonathan Kay)

There were no conclusions to MIP. They were probably not sought and would, in any case, have been impossible from such a large and (in some ways) diverse gathering. Murray was a rapporteur (for the Frits Vogels workshop) and remembers the event as a timely – and in many ways admirable – articulation of the disparate and sometimes conflicting interests and passions of the mime and physical theatre world. Of course, this was a largely Western European world, a largely white world, a world where men's voices seemed to be heard more loudly than women's and a world which, inevitably perhaps, often produced a frisson between the performance of intellectual or academic analysis and the lived material experience of making and performing stuff. The hugely generative ambition of MIP is best captured through Figures 6.3 and 6.4 which reveal the cast, contents and structure of the Workshop Symposium programme.

Learning mime in the community: a challenge to the conventions of drama teaching

It is debatable whether educational work with young people in schools or other contexts should be considered under the rubric of 'training'. Certainly, most of the artists running mime and physical theatre workshops in schools, for youth drama groups or with other community constituencies would regard 'training' as a rather grandiose term to describe what they were doing. And yet, if school children or teenagers in a youth drama club were learning physical and other theatrical skills which they could then take into productions, there was indeed an element of (non-professional) 'training' involved. We have established that for companies on tour offering workshops around their performances was a standard expectation and, indeed, often a contractual condition of funding support. Beyond this, however, in the 1990s certain companies also achieved funding purely for educational programmes in their own right and not simply as an event tagged on to a show[11]. These programmes were sometimes

---

11 In 1994 Trestle received three-year private sponsorship deal with Sainsbury's to teach mime and mask work in schools.

194 Training: from scarcity to abundance

8 APPENDICES

8.3 MOVING INTO PERFORMANCE PROGRAMME

Moving Into Performance Programme

Sunday 11 September 1994
Faculty meetings: Whole Faculty, Workshop Director & Facilitators;
Dramaturg & Rapporteurs; Workshop Director & Dramaturg; Facilitators & Rapporteurs; Administration

Monday 12 September 1994
WORKSHOP OPENING
Introduction by Workshop Director
Group meetings with respective Facilitators & Rapporteurs
Exchange Sessions
Burning Question: "Why is Odin not around? Is this a Decroux/Lecoq/Gaulier club? If so what is the underlying performance philosophy bias?"

Tuesday 13 September 1994
Exchange Sessions
1st Practical Session led by Enrique Pardo
Burning Question: "Can you tell us about a performance that moved you, moved your idea of performance?"

Wednesday 14 September 1994
Exchange Sessions
2nd Practical Session led by Enrique Pardo
Burning Question: "The cake; does 'physical theatre' refer to a collection of over-ambitious artists who want to have their cake and eat it, ie. be author, owner, director, dramaturg and performer?"

Thursday 15 September 1994
Exchange Sessions
3rd Practical Session led by Enrique Pardo
Burning Question: "Who is performance for? What is the intention?"

Friday 16 September 1994
Exchange Sessions
Workshop Plenary & Close
SYMPOSIUM OPENING
Welcome
Kenneth Rea, Symposium Chair
Welcome
Verena Cornwall, Co-Chair: Mime Action Group & Ide van Heiningen, Director: European Mime Federation
Opening Keynote Address
Joseph Seelig, London International Mime Festival
The M-Word
Workshop Report
North West Region Commissions Performance
Talking Pictures: CITY LIFE
Adele Myers Company: CORR-I-ADOR
Third Estate Music & Dance: RESORT OF EXTREMES
Rejects Revenge: SAD SEASIDE TOWNS WE HAVE TOURED TO
Post-Performance Discussion

44   mime action group *Moving Into Performance* REPORT

FIGURE 6.3   Moving into Performance programme (1), MAG, Manchester 1994. By kind permission of Aurelius Productions & *Total Theatre* Magazine.

geared towards teachers so that they could introduce basic mime and physical theatre 'techniques' and ideas into their daily teaching. At a fundamental and simple level the offer of a mime/physical theatre class or workshop was appealing to young people and their schools. The proposition often seemed new and unusual, it was about action and physicality and not – apparently – about learning and performing words

Training: from scarcity to abundance 195

||||||||||||||||||||||||||||||||||||||||||||||||||||||||||||||||||||| APPENDICES 8

Saturday 17 September 1994

Keynote Addresses
Tom Leabhart: *Post-Modern Performance*
Claire Heggen: *Theatre du Mouvement = the steps of a travel*

The Directors View
Pete Brooks, Insomniac Productions
Moniek Merkx, Suver Nuver Theatre

Network Exchange Session, Training The Physical, The Visual & The Spoken
Rivca Rubin, Physical State International
Mirna Zager, MAPA Zagreb
Ide van Heiningen, Ralf Rauker & Thilo Zantke, MAPA Berlin
Ineke Austen, Theatre Instituut Nederland
Chris Rowbury, Centre for Performance Research

Translations in Making and Performing
Barry Edwards and Terence Tiernan, OPTIK: *Watching What People Are*
Yurgen Schoora: *Translations*
Kenneth Davidson, Process Ten [28]: *Site specific performance; place as event*

The Clown
John Wright: *Tragic Clown*
Alex Chayka, Jart Theatre: *The specifics of humour in the ex-soviet union countries*

Questions of Dramaturgy
Enrique Pardo: *Dramaturgy and Magic: "...something is happening here, but you don't know what it is, do you Mister Jones?"*
John Keefe: *A Personal view of Dramaturgy*
Hans-Dieter Ilgner & Valerie Lucas: *Dramaturgy; Partner or Director's Slave?*

Ensemble Leporello, Performances
TWINS: With Afra Waldhor, Neil Cadger, Andrea Bardos, Bernard Eylenbosch. Music: Denis Pousseur.
Lighting: Isabelle Van Peteghem. Mise en Scene: Dirk Opstaele
MONSTREUX: With Afra Waldhor, Craig Weston, A. Charman, Gordon Wilson. Music and Tape: Craig Weston.
Lighting: Isabelle Van Peteghem and Marc Vandermeulen

Post-Performance Discussion

Sunday 18 September 1994

The Ensemble
David Glass, David Glass Ensemble: *The Problem of the Ensemble*
Frits Vogels, Griftheater: *Some facts about Griftheater*

Network Exchange Session, The Emergence of Networks & Fora in Europe
Brian Angus, The Mime Forum, Scotland
Simon Murray, Mime Action Group
Phil Gunderson, Bodily Functions
Elsbetia Pastecka, Poland
Ide van Heiningen, European Mime Federation

Text into Performance: A UK Perspective
Tim Etchells, Forced Entertainment
Hilary Westlake, Lumiere & Son

Symposium Plenary
CLOSE

mime action group *Moving Into Performance* REPORT   45

FIGURE 6.4   Moving into Performance programme (2), MAG, Manchester, 1994. By kind permission of Aurelius Productions & *Total Theatre* Magazine.

from a dramatic text. In the same way that physical theatre was constantly used as a marketing brand and descriptor – even if it remained opaque about what was being signalled – on publicity leaflets, so this appellation had a touch of the exotic to it and an implicit promise of fun and pleasure in store when applied to workshops.

It is likely that the larger or better-funded companies – such as the David Glass Ensemble, Trestle and Théâtre de Complicité – had time and capacity to think

196 Training: from scarcity to abundance

through and develop their educational work in a way that smaller or more poorly resourced companies could not manage. Over the last 20 years – and therefore outwith our time frame – Frantic Assembly, Théâtre de Complicité and the David Glass Ensemble (DGE) have established sophisticated and elaborate websites, significant parts of which are devoted to learning and teaching. These websites espouse the principles which underpin their teaching practice and – in the case of Théâtre de Complicité and Frantic Assembly – provide explicit links to teaching packs for secondary school teachers. Whilst this digitally sophisticated explication of their educational work is evidently a twenty-first-century phenomena, the seeds – or prefigurative forms – of this teaching and learning (and the passion which lay behind them) were being practiced and refined since the formation of these companies in the 1980s. We have already noted the commitment and imagination which the likes of Annabel Arden and David Glass espoused for the teaching dimensions of their practice. These articulations by Théâtre de Complicité and the DGE of their respective principles and objectives regarding educational practice are taken from twenty-first-century websites but speak of their enduring philosophy and aspirations.

Théâtre de Complicité

Education has been at the core of *Complicité's* practice for decades and we are proud to be a 'leading practitioner of devised theatre' on many GCSE, BTEC and A Level courses. Led by Complicité's Associates, highly experienced devising performers, our projects designed for schools, offer teachers and students a chance to experience and learn about the Company's collaborative processes which have play and risk-taking at the core. The roots of Complicité's practice can be traced back to the training of its members, many of whom studied at the Ecole Jacques Lecoq in Paris. This training is at the heart of the Company's Education programme, which reaches over 2,000 people in schools, colleges, clubs, museums and other institutions in the UK and abroad every year. Devising and collaboration form the foundation of our work; we encourage playfulness, risk taking and a willingness to fail. We believe that the Arts are not an add-on, they are not a luxury, they are not for the few. The techniques we use with students are the same building blocks that the Company employs every day in the rehearsal room. The aim of these workshops is to build group understanding of how to work together to create a shared visual language.

(Complicité Website, 2022)

David Glass Ensemble

In theatre we must engage, entertain and if we do this well we might, if we're lucky, educate.
The arts' job is to evoke, provoke and invoke through great storytelling.

We are not here to lecture but to reveal, seduce, delight, surprise and most of
all move the audience.
Let us fail at excellence, not succeed at mediocrity.
In theatre we play problems, not solve problems.
Life is inconvenient, messy and a struggle. Let theatre reflect this and you
might have an art form that has passion at its root and ordinary people
might want to see.

Workshops for Young People

It is a right and necessity for the young to learn the craft of performing
and theatre making to open and transform their bodies, minds, hearts and
worlds . . . We believe learning is a human right, not a commodity. Always
beginning in the body, our learning strand roots itself in the belief that young
people fundamentally want to have relationships with each other, the world
around them and themselves. . . . Workshops for young people will focus
on engaging them to think critically about the world around them, as well
as introducing them to foundational skills to build a life-long craft in the
theatre.

(David Glass Ensemble Website, 2022)

For companies whose work was sometimes or regularly designed for young
people there was a tacit element of learning and education in the reception of
their work. For example, much of the work of Northumbria (Hexham)-based
company, Théâtre Sans Frontières (TSF) – already profiled in Chapter 4 – was
created for young people, toured to schools and often, reflecting their international composition, performed in French or Spanish. This celebration of European languages certainly had a broad educational inflection to it and appealed
to school language departments as well as to drama teachers. TSF significantly
developed its educational work after 1999 and began to receive targeted funding in this respect. When touring in the 1990s, Artistic Director of TSF, Sarah
Kemp, writes:

As we were mostly doing two shows a day there wasn't usually time to do
workshops as well. Later, into the 2000s, we started developing a workshop
programme alongside the shows so schools could book a whole day and the
children could become creatively involved in the production. In autumn
1999 we began work on the *Tour de France* show and this involved workshop-
ping and discussion with children and teachers from North East primary
schools. We then made a pilot version which we took into the schools for
their feedback. Further development led to a full-scale show which then

198 Training: from scarcity to abundance

> toured theatres nationally. This was when Creative Partnership[12] money came on board and there was a lot more funding for projects with schools.
>
> *(Kemp, 2022)*

From the early 1980s this educational patchwork of mime and physical workshops and related projects was also populated by artists' residencies and the appointment of animateurs. The more we survey this heterogeneous provision the more it becomes clear that where activities arise and where imaginative initiatives are taken there is almost always a productive and resourceful matrix of mutually supportive relationships between energetic individuals and organisations. In conjunction with this individual skill and energy there were also, of course, enough material and financial resources to support and sustain the activities in question, whether these were to pay fees/salaries or to provide spaces for mime and physical work. An example of a building-based initiative which seems to exemplify this interwoven pattern of energies was Liverpool's Hope Street Community and Art Centre, and within this organisation, the Actor's Centre. In a *Total Theatre* article, Peter Ward, Assistant Director of Hope Street, writes:

> A unique organisation in the UK, Hope Street runs full and part-time train-ing courses in the performing arts within the environment of professional working theatres and arts organisations. Open to everyone over 18, it offers pre-vocational, vocational and professional courses.
>
> *(Ward, 1994: 8)*

The Hope Street project was partly funded from the European Social Fund (ESF) and had an agenda of economic regeneration across Merseyside, as well as cultural provision. Here, from the early 1990s, a spirit of collaboration with the Everyman and Unity Theatres, and with key figures from John Moores University, produced, by all accounts, a very fertile ecology for mime and physical theatre. We talked with Glenn Noble, currently teaching at Birmingham City University, but who had spent much of his early adult life in Liverpool as a physical theatre practitioner (Director of Spike Theatre), teaching at the City's Hope and John Moores uni-versities and was 'for six inspiring years' (Noble, 2021) Coordinator for the Physi-cal Theatre Programme at Hope Street. Noble became heavily involved in Hope Street activities during and after his time at university. He conveyed a sense of energy, flexibility and enthusiasm in relation to how the organisation was run – an openness to ideas and to many different user constituencies. He reflected:

> Everyman and Hope Street separated – Everyman went dark and into liquida-tion in 1994. So, the theatre closed but Hope Street became an independent

---

12 Established in 2002, Creative Partnerships was the UK government's creative learning programme with the objective of developing young people's creativity through artists' engagement with schools in nominated areas across England. Funding for these projects was cut in 2011. Creative Partnerships were widely used by theatre companies (and other artists) to fund work in schools.

organization. And at that point, Peter (Ward) had an idea of starting to create what would become the physical theatre program. To take the Actors Centre workshop seasons and do some joined-up sessions between guest artists over a period of time. I did the very first physical theatre course in '94. Hope Street had floors you could book and go and run your own sessions in, just test things out. So, there was this constant sense of well if I'm doing nothing next week what about two days in Hope Street. I'll just try some of this stuff again and devise and improvise and make stuff for the sake of it.

(Noble, 2021)

Whilst Hope Street was a particularly dynamic example of energetic individuals and different agencies coming together to create a 'critical mass' of action around physical theatre education and performance, it was not unique. As we have seen from the Northern Arts regional profile in Chapter 4, certain places became hubs for activity. Here, the Dovecot Art Centre in Stockton, the Brewery in Kendal and the Queen's Hall in Hexham all became such 'hubs' for a period of time. Outwith this region, Coventry, Bristol, Brighton, Dartington and (of course) London offer other case studies. In the West Midlands, for example, Mark Evans at the Coventry Centre for Performing Arts, Jac Wilkinson at Warwick Arts Centre, Jane Sutcliffe at the Midlands Art Centre (MAC) in Birmingham, Debbie Kingsley (Coventry City Council's Arts Development Officer) and performer/theatre maker Carran Waterfield (Triangle) worked productively together to create and sustain a proactive and lively environment for mime and physical theatre in this region. Evans ran regular weekend workshops with various practitioners (Trestle, Complicite, Volcano, Frantic, David Gaines, Julian Crouch, Bim Mason) during the 1990s, all funded by West Midlands Arts.

These configurations were born, on the one hand, out of the cultural force fields of the time, and therefore not peculiar to place and individual figures, but, on the other, were the product of singular sets of circumstances and relationships which combined to bring together certain people (arts officers and practitioners), agencies, colleges and universities, art centres and available funding pots. Within this matrix, as both cause and effect, we must also identify the animateur movement and heterogeneous projects described as residencies. Residencies were elastic and variously shaped 'occupations' which might last as little as a week, or spread – full or part-time – over several months. Usually, they consisted of one artist or company being based at an arts centre, or perhaps a whole city or region, with a remit to run courses/workshops, organise performances, undertake profile raising events for mime and physical theatre, to develop networks and to advance their own working practices. In March 1996 the Hope Street Actor's Centre organised a mime and physical theatre residency in conjunction with the Unity Theatre, Liverpool Institute of the Performing Arts (LIPA), Liverpool John Moores University and local arts officers and teachers. This 'residency' contained workshops, discussions and performances by Commotion, Rejects Revenge, John Wright, Andrew Dawson and Sally Cook. Between October 1988 and April 1989, clown and street theatre performer, John Lee, was awarded a mime residency in the South West Arts

200 Training: from scarcity to abundance

Region. In 1985/1986 the ubiquitous Pat Keysell was 'Mime Artist in Residence' at Dunfermline College of Physical Education in Scotland during which time she helped set up the Scottish Mime Forum and ran a Scottish Summer School of Mime in the summer of 1986. Finally, as we have already noted, David Glass, Peta Lily and the Gambolling Guisers had various teaching and rehearsal residencies in the Northern Region from the mid-1980s. Glass had residencies in Peterlee new town (County Durham) to teach and rehearse *The Dinosaur of Weltschmerz* and to work on and premiere *Solaris* at Newcastle's Gulbenkian Studio Theatre. Similarly, Lily developed and premiered her solo show *Piaf* at the Stanwix Theatre in Carlisle. On Teesside the Gambolling Guizers had two residencies with Frank Wilson at the Dovecot Art Centre. We should note also *de facto* residencies which were an integral part of festivals. Here, 'being resident' and having a 'residency' seem indistinguishable. The Brewery Arts Centre's International Mime Festival regularly incorporated short teaching residencies which included, for example, John Wright, Frankie Armstrong, Rick Zoltowski, Gerry Flanagan, Monika Pagneux, and Trickster as part of its annual programme.

A significant feature of almost all these residences was an attempt to blur the boundaries between teaching and development work in various community contexts *and* professional and creative development for the artist or company concerned. Whilst this impulse can be detected to a limited extent within more mainstream theatre work, it was most significantly within the fields of mime and physical theatre that these projects occurred in the three decades from 1970. Networks and networking were a key feature of these developments: practitioners and administrators drawn together by their passion for the work, and creating ways of connecting with each other and with audiences.

Clear distinctions between residencies and the work undertaken by animateurs remain hard to discern. Mime artists in residence were undertaking animateur work, and animateurs – on a salary – were 'in residence' usually for a finite period of time, although for longer than the typical residency. Whilst the National Association of Dance and Mime Animateurs (NADMA) was formally established in 1986, the term – and the role – began to gain currency across Europe in the 1970s. Dance academic, Jayne Stevens notes that:

> Between 1976 and 1979 the first dance animateur posts in the UK had been established and taken up by Veronica Lewis (in Cheshire), Molly Kenny (in Cardiff) and Marie McCluskey (in Swindon). The Arts Council of Great Britain's offer of seed funding for similar posts in 1981 led to growth of provision throughout the 1980s. By 1985 there were 31 dance animateurs in the UK and two years later the number had more than doubled to 75.
>
> *(Stevens, 2017)*

Since mime, as we have seen, was originally organised and supported under the Arts Council's Dance Department, mime animateurs had to be included in the categorisation. As funding for these posts began to grow from the mid-1980s the majority of animateurs were indeed from dance rather than mime. However, the pages of *MAGazine*, and then *Total Theatre*, contain references to and brief accounts of the work of mime animateurs dotted around the UK. These included:

- Pat Keysell followed by Deborah Barnard and Alicyn Marr at the Brewery Art Centre during the 1980s.
- Rick Kemp as Theatre and Mime Animateur in Luton, 1986/1987.
- Jac Wilkinson as Mime and Theatre Skills Animateur in Luton, 1988/1989.
- Lesley Moss in Coventry, 1989/1990.
- Sue Mitchell as Mime Development Officer for Greater London Arts (GLA) in the late 1980s, followed by Dance and Mime Animateur for Banff and Buchan in Scotland. By 1995 Mitchell had become Education Coordinator at Peterhead prison.
- Nigel Jamieson as Mime Development Worker for GLA in 1987/1988.
- Rowan Tolley as Yorkshire Mime Animateur in 1992/1993.

The animateur movement – whether dance or mime – was driven by the aspiration to encourage non-professional participation in these art forms. Its impulse emerged from the same paradigm as community arts practices more generally, and therefore, inevitably, contained different and not always mutually compatible strategies toward such active engagement and with varying ideological rationales and justifications for projects. In the 1980s these posts were typically co-funded by local authorities, regional arts boards and – sometimes – from the national Arts Council. By 1990, after mime had moved out of Dance into Drama in both the Arts Council and the regional arts boards the impulse to create mime animateurs seemed to wane. The job of the mime (or dance) animateur was hugely varied and often an isolated one with little infrastructural or artistic support. Usually without any training for the job, animateurs had to engage with many different organisations and constituencies in their areas, they often had only sporadic contact with the professional art forms which they were paid to develop and embed in the communities where they worked and lived. Stevens acutely encapsulated the challenges which faced animateurs, and although she is writing about dance, we can accurately substitute mime within this account:

> The demands placed on these dance animateurs were considerable. The role involved not only teaching dance and organising classes, workshops and performances but also developing the local dance provision by working with performing companies, venues, educational institutions, youth services and private dance schools. A national evaluation in 1986 noted that one person, usually working alone across an entire geographical region, was 'being asked to act as administrator, adviser, choreographer, dancer, diplomat, entrepreneur, fund-raiser, politician, promoter and teacher'.
>
> *(Ibid., 2016/17)*

FIGURE 6.5   Mark Saunders, mime workshop for children, Edinburgh 1983. By kind permission of Mark Saunders.

Whatever the difficulties faced by mime and – by implication – physical theatre animateurs, their presence in a region or a city spoke again of the enthusiasm and passion felt by a matrix of key figures and organisations at a particular time and in a particular place. Where they existed they were a crucial part of an unfolding but uneven ecology for mime and – later – physical/visual theatre.

Teaching mime and physical theatre in higher education: drama schools and universities in an ambivalent relationship

The final section of this chapter attends broadly to the presence of mime and physical theatre teaching in the higher education sector, both drama schools or conservatoires (private or public) and universities. In our research we found it difficult to draw up a comprehensive or accurate picture of this particular landscape of provision. As a general observation, it seemed that the explicitly named teaching of 'physical theatre' (or courses with similar nomenclature) did not really become noticeable until after 2000. This is not to say that higher education courses with a corporeal perspective or inflection did not exist prior to the turn of the century, rather that they were not unambiguously foregrounded as such on the curriculum.

As we have seen, the training of professional – or would-be professional – performers in corporeal skills and the making of physical theatre occurred in a relatively haphazard or heterogeneous way through short courses, workshops and master classes organised by experienced practitioners, often under the aegis of festivals (LIMF and IWF as the most prominent examples), art centres, theatres and residencies. Alternatively, or additionally, training took place in a more sustained manner across the English Channel at the Paris schools of Lecoq, Gaulier, Marceau and Decroux, and within organisations such as Odin Teatret (Holstebro), Gardzienice, the Grotowski Institute (Wroclaw) and the Grotowski Workcenter (Pontedera). In terms of longer programmes within the UK we have already noted in 1990s London the presence of 'schools' run by Philippe Gaulier, Steven Wasson and Corinne Soum, and Anja Dashwood. Alongside these, the longevity, ambition and endurance of the Desmond Jones School of Mime and Physical Theatre stands out as a rather extraordinary beacon and as possessing a notable list of professional alumni.

Desmond Jones School of Mime and Physical Theatre (1979–2004)

Jones, like a number of fervent proselytisers for the recognition of mime in the early to mid-1980s – including David Glass, Nola Rae, Pat Keysall, Nigel Jamieson, Mark Saunders, Helen Lannaghan and Joseph Seelig amongst others – was a passionately committed, dogged, charismatic, tireless – and often angrily indignant – advocate for the art form. In addition to running his school from a large, light and airy church hall in West London, Jones was active in MAG, regularly wrote entertainingly provocative short contributions in *Total Theatre* and served on Arts Council advisory committees. For Jones, mime was neither theatricalised dance nor theatre with a dash of movement, but an art form in its own right, and in this sense he echoed and embodied his mentor, Etienne Decroux, and his project of corporeal mime. In the early years, he had little sympathy for the term 'physical theatre', but he was also a pragmatist and his school was a small business to provide income for himself and his family. Jones had been an actor for stage, film and television and had undertaken some exploratory movement work on films such as *Quest for Fire, The Lover* and *Greystoke* before and during the early years of his school. He had trained with Decroux in Paris and attended a summer school with Jacques Lecoq, but he says:

> Although I based my work on Etienne Decroux, I began to forge my own path using everything I knew, all my varied experience, to teach a kind of movement-based theatre that could be used in everything from street theatre to straight theatre.
>
> *(Salm, 2004)*

Thus, by the late 1980s Jones' School of Mime had extended to 'and Physical Theatre' and thereby (reluctantly?) acknowledged that physical theatre had greater popular currency than widespread perceptions of mime and what it entailed. From the early 1990s for about ten years Jones was assisted by Ris Widdicombe. She had taken Jones' foundation and advanced courses as a student during 1990/1991 and

204 Training: from scarcity to abundance

then became his assistant on the former programme whilst keeping herself afloat financially on the Government-funded Youth Training Scheme (YTS). During the 1990s she was to become his regular teaching associate and became embroiled with Jones in thinking through how the School might develop. The School became structured around foundation and advanced courses and across four terms. In addition, in holiday periods he offered week-long morning and afternoon courses on specific themes, styles and techniques. Evans and Murray had both taken short courses with Jones (Evans had been a student on the Foundation programme in 1982), and Murray remembers taking a 5-day basic mime technique course with him in the late 1980s and then, a year or so later, a *Walking* and a *Body Popping* workshop, one in the morning, the other in the afternoon. The presence of these two short courses is an indication of Jones' imaginative eclecticism and his ability to harness and translate mime skills into other fields of popular performance. Murray has vivid, if incongruous, memories of the *Body Popping* 5-day workshop where Jones utilised Decroux's technical isolations for learning the punctuated 'popping' of specific body parts – arms, legs, chest and neck. The *Walking* workshop was a seriously detailed exercise in observing and identifying the mechanics of walking (our own and each other's) and then playing with these features so as to develop characterisation and dramatic scenarios.

The Foundation and Advanced course were the School's pedagogical spine but within these Jones taught an eclectic range and diversity of technical exercises, games and improvisations. A rich and sometimes eccentric syllabus indeed. The School was always international in its reach, typically with between one-third to a half coming from mainland Europe and beyond, and at the height of its success classes would contain between 20 and 30 students, comprise more women than men and with a range of ages. Over time Jones' classes began to cover less themes but he would invest longer periods to in-depth exploration of subjects and technical skills. The School never received any state funding or subsidy and in retrospect we feel that Jones never really received the recognition and respect that he deserved. Others too felt that in the absence of a formally accredited 'British School of Mime and Physical Theatre' – a subject of repeated discussion in various MAG forums – Jones' school was *de facto* that very institution. Over 25 years of running his school Jones remained a witty, insightful and highly committed maverick within a field of mavericks. Many of the practitioners we interviewed, and who feature in this volume, testified to the importance of Jones' courses and workshops in their own training and professional development[13]. Like Pat Keysell – with whom, ironically, he was often in furious disagreement – these two figures are amongst the 'unsung heroes' of this whole narrative. In describing his courses on School marketing publicity, Jones articulated his vision of mime like this:

---

13 Alumni of Jones' School are many, but include Ian Cameron, Gavin Robertson and Andrew Dawson (Mime Theatre Project), Peta Lily and Three Women Mime, Intriplicate Mime and Scottish Mime Theatre.

MIME is simply the drama of the body and of movement – movement that either supplants the need for words, or reinforces and deepens the thoughts and feelings lying behind the words. Many teachers sacrifice content for style. Too often the audience is aware of the style rather than the story. To me this is anti-theatre. Mime should be an integral part of the study of theatre. Certainly, the basis of all Physical Theatre is an informed and detailed knowledge of Mime.

(Jones, n.d.)

Universities and drama schools

We conclude this chapter with a cursory overview of the higher education sector: drama schools or conservatoires, art schools, colleges and universities. During our period, and to a lesser extent in the last two decades, the hegemonic pedagogy of actor training in drama schools remained rooted in Stanislavski and the teaching of Michel Saint-Denis who was very influential in the ethos of post-war drama schools. Although it is an over-simplification to pose these psychologically driven methods as incompatible with more physical and movement-based approaches to acting[14], it is the former, in the service of text-based naturalism, which was the dominant paradigm during the final three decades of the twentieth century. The conservatoires certainly gestured towards 'the body' through voice training and in a more limited way through movement classes which largely offered a more general corporeal preparation on the one hand, or very specific skills such as stage fighting and fencing on the other. Brechtian *Gestus* would, one imagines, invite considerations of embodiment and – more academically – figures such as Meyerhold, Artaud, Jarry, Craig, Beckett, Brook, (Michael) Chekhov and Marowitz might be referenced for their engagement with more physically material approaches to acting. Where drama schools and conservatoires employed staff, on a permanent or visiting basis, with a background of exposure to Lecoq, Gaulier, Pagneux, Grotowski or Barba, for example, there we might find alternatives to the dominance of Stanislavski or the Method. Whether the presence of tutors with such backgrounds fundamentally changed the centre of gravity of teaching programmes is questionable. Movement tutors – largely trained in Lecoq, Laban or Alexander – sought to find ways of blending what they taught so that it fitted with the overall Stanislavskian nature of the actor training in their institutions. When Mark Saunders (see Chapter 4) began to work full-time at the Royal Scottish Academy of Music and Drama (RSAMD) in 1992 there were already two Lecoq-trained teachers[15] at the institution (Joyce Deans and Pete Lincoln), but Saunders recalls:

---

14 Mark Evans' book 'Movement Training for the Modern Actor' (2009) is the first critical analysis of the key principles and practices informing the movement training of actors in the modern era.

15 Other Lecoq-trained movement tutors during the 1990s include Shona Morris and Lorna Marshall (Rose Bruford) and Jane Gibson who was Director of Movement at the (English) National Theatre between 1999 and 2009.

206 Training: from scarcity to abundance

> I introduced *Auto-cours* which didn't exist before I turned up . . . and put a condensed form of the 20 movements into place, and introduced various physical styles – masks, commedia dell'arte, bouffon, clown. I was also interested in the movement of the chorus and the balancing the space – the plateau type of exercises. I was directing quite a lot of Greek tragedies and I thought that would be really useful. I think it had an influence, but the overall pedagogy of the RSAMD certainly during the '90s was text-based naturalism. I was always left with a feeling that we were doing our funny Lecoq stuff and then they went into heavy Stanislavski mode for the next part of the day. I think the students could not connect these things at all. And I couldn't really blame them. But I was always thinking, how can I make the body alive and how can I keep the space alive and how can I keep the level of *jeu* between the actors alive throughout the whole piece.
>
> *(Saunders, 2020)*

The RSAMD was unusual in its affinity with the Lecoq School and its pedagogical lineage, but this is partly explained by the Lecoq family connection[16] to the Glasgow institution. At the other end of the country, Thomas Wilson who currently teaches at Rose Bruford College in Kent noted that the European Theatre Arts programme with a strong physical element was launched there in 1998. Wilson also recalls that in his undergraduate degree at St Mary's University in West London 'a physical theatre component was introduced in my second year (Autumn 1996) which then formed the basis for the creation of a full BA Physical Theatre after 2000' (Wilson 2022).

A more extensive investigation than space permits here into the relationship between non-university higher education provision and physical/visual forms of theatre might productively consider the role of Art Schools in the 1970s and 1980s (see Chapter 5). As the teaching of visual art became separated from craft and design after the Coldstream Report of 1960, and before it became formally incorporated into the university sector, performance or performance art (later described as live art) became a significant feature of student practice, often in the face of institutional disapproval. Here, strongly physical (though rarely technically virtuosic) practice based on action and material objects created performance work which often slid (unintentionally) into the field of physical theatre. Art colleges in Cardiff, Leeds, Bradford, Chelsea, Hornsea and Newcastle, for example, generated highly corporeal performance, often as political action or intervention. An illustrious example of such work was the Bradford Art College Theatre Group, established in 1968, with the active support of tutors, Albert Hunt and Geoffrey Reeves, which made spectacular, often large-scale, highly political theatrical performances. Hunt summarised his working methods in a manner not dissimilar from mime and physical theatre devising companies two decades later when he wrote: 'There will be games, improvisations and experiments, leading towards work on a script which we as a

---

16 Scottish born, Fay Lecoq (Jacques Lecoq's wife) was lead administrative director of the Paris school and trained at the RSAMD in the early 1950s. She met Jacques in 1957 whilst training with Decroux and they married in 1960.

FIGURE 6.6 Mark Saunders, mime workshop for students, Royal Scottish Academy of Music and Drama, Glasgow, 1991. By kind permission of Mark Saunders.

group will create' (Hunt, 1976). The role of art colleges during this period in fostering and encouraging the conditions of invention for performance work which has many connective tissues with the physical theatre practices we are examining in this volume warrants much deeper investigation than we can provide here.

The extent to which university theatre or drama departments over these three decades helped to generate the conditions of invention for mime and physical theatres is a complex one. At an explicit level, there is little tangible evidence that universities played any significant role in these developments, but beneath the surface there were undercurrents of dispersed, sporadic and fragmented teaching and learning activities which occupied, or fed into the fields of physical theatres. In the older and apparently more prestigious institutions the dominant pedagogical paradigm for theatre teaching was the analysis and production of dramatic texts. Many such departments either were part of literature departments or had broken off from them. Literary drama was the dominant mode of research and learning. However, university theatre/performance teachers with a training in various forms of movement practice would clearly shape their teaching through these influences during the final two decades of the twentieth century. Some selective examples provide an illustration: Mike Pearson and Richard Gough at Aberystwyth, Nigel Stewart at Lancaster, Paul Allain at Brunel University College and Goldsmiths, Sandra Reeve and Nick Sales at Exeter, Ruth Way, Roberta Mock, Terry Enright at Plymouth, Dymphna Callery at Wolverhampton, David Williams at Dartington, Mark Evans at Coventry, Franc Chamberlain and Jonathan Pitches at Northampton and Simon Murray at

208 Training: from scarcity to abundance

Ripon and York St John. Many of these figures would inflect their daily practice-based teaching in the university with perspectives, games and exercises from their own training experiences, or when working previously as professional practitioners. Although we have evidence of courses/modules, or indeed whole postgraduate master's programmes, entitled explicitly as physical theatre from around 2000, we could find little sign of these during our period. This is perhaps strange, as mime, mask work and physical theatre were popular with students, many of whom would have seen this kind of work on school trips or whilst at college or university.

The *UK Mime and Physical Theatre Training Directory* (MAG, 1993) has a section on universities and colleges with brief descriptions of their provision. Close examination of these entries offers little evidence of named physical theatre – much less, mime – provision. However, MAG's training directory in this respect at least indicates where university theatre or performing arts departments 'self-identified' as connecting or disposed to physical theatre practices. Seventeen institutions are listed and about one-third of these were drama schools or conservatoires. Of the universities listed it is significant that all of these were the (then) new, or relatively new, institutions such as Huddersfield, Wolverhampton, Manchester Metropolitan, Liverpool John Moores, Lancaster, Middlesex, Reading and Edinburgh's Queen Margaret College. It is significant that no Russell Group[17] university is included here. This possibly may be for sampling reasons but also because the Russell Group universities with longstanding drama/theatre departments (e.g. Glasgow, Manchester, Bristol, Birmingham and Exeter) were less disposed to embrace (or admit to) developments in late twentieth-century mime and physical theatre.

The Centre for Performance Research (CPR) at Aberystwyth University

In Chapter 4, we have identified in some depth the work of the Cardiff Laboratory Theatre (CLT) which spawned the CPR as an internal research unit in 1985. In 1988 the CPR became a formal separate entity and by May 1996 had moved to Aberystwyth University after Richard Gough had taken up a post as Senior Research Fellow in the Department of Theatre, Film and Television Studies a year earlier. It was at Aberystwyth where a CPR archive, library and resource centre were established and here Gough and Judy Christie, along with associate staff, delivered a remarkable series of educational, performance and research events of many different types and guises. In *A Performance Cosmology* published by Routledge and the CPR in 2006, Gough vividly chronicles the history of the CLT and the CPR between 1974 and 2005 in a chapter entitled 'Family album' (pp. 290–316). At Aberystwyth from 1995 until the end of our period we can only identify a few select examples which speak to the thematics of our book. However, from 1995 the

---

17 The Russell Group represents 24 leading research intensive UK universities. They tend to be the older or oldest UK universities but, for perplexing reasons, do not include Oxford, Cambridge or St Andrews.

CPR organised a series of symposia and workshops under the rubric of *Pastmasters* which – in chronological order up to 2000 – featured the practices and writings of Meyerhold, Artaud, Decroux, Brecht and Eisenstein, (Michael) Chekhov and Kantor and Cricot 2. The Decroux event included performances from Thomas Leabhart, Steve Wasson and Corinne Soum, and presentations from academics and artists from across the world. Murray participated in the Meyerhold, Artaud, Decroux and Kantor projects and remembers them as stimulating, provocative and highly convivial events which brought together practitioners and academics from far afield. Scrutiny of 'Family Album' reveals a whole jigsaw of additional educational and training events relating to the voice and its corporeal dynamics, Kalarippayattu, Beckett and other workshops led by Phillip Zarrilli[18] and a startling range of further workshops and performances led by such figures as Mike Pearson, John Rowley, Lorna Marshall, Enrique Pardo, David Zinder and Guillermo Gomez-Pina. There were many others. For this period, the relationship between the CPR and the Department at Aberystwyth seemed – from an outsider's perspective at any rate – as an unusual but highly generative and productive engagement between a higher education institution and an independent research unit.

FIGURE 6.7 CPR Past Masters Etienne Decroux workshops and symposium, Aberystwyth 1997.

Source: CLT/CPR Archives.

---

18 Phillip Zarrilli (1947–2020) was internationally renowned for training actors in psychophysical processes through Asian martial/meditation arts, and as a director/performer. He was Professor of Drama at the University of Exeter from 2000.

210 Training: from scarcity to abundance

Dartington College of Arts (DCA)

A higher education institution included in the directory which fits into neither category of university nor conservatoire was Dartington College of Arts (DCA). The College (1961–2010) situated on a beautiful rural estate at Totnes in Devon was an unusual and maverick institution that was neither purely a visual art college nor a conservatoire for dance, music and theatre although these four subject areas (plus Performance Writing from 1992) remained at the heart of the curriculum across its lifetime. Murray was Director of Theatre at DCA between 2004 and 2008 and recalls that the College used to position itself somewhat uneasily between the humanities of traditional universities and the practice-based teaching of the conservatoires with a strong element of the art school ethos. The history and work of the College is beginning to be written and to date, there is a patchwork of accounts (Cox, 2002; *Theatre, Dance and Performance Training Special Issue* 2018; Richards, 2015; Murray and Hall, 2011). DCA was a complex place with shifting curricula over the years. Always situated outside the mainstream of art practices and dedicated to critically reflective but heuristic pedagogies, DCA generated deeply embodied performance work which often strived to transgress the formal disciplinary boundaries between theatre, performance art, dance, writing and music.

We talked to David Williams who had worked at DCA between 1984 and 1986 (research assistant, teacher and assistant editor of Peter Hulton's *Theatre Papers*) and again between 1998 and 2009 where he was Professor of Theatre. For Williams, mime, as broadly understood, was never embraced (or named) within the Dartington project, but for him the most salient theatre teaching and performance making was a 'cross over between dance and theatre – models of practice which were plural, embodied – voice, text, movement, image. From the 1990s interdisciplinarity and, disciplinary leakage were encouraged' (Williams, 2021). During this period (the 1980s and 1990s) theatre at DCA embraced an eclectic mix of influences and visiting artists and companies, either teaching or in residence, included Steve Paxton, Laurie Booth, Richard Gough (CPR), Brith Gof, Goat Island, Reckless Sleepers, Forced Entertainment and Welfare State. In turn, the College 'produced' alumni companies such as Deer Park, Lone Twin, Desperate Optimists and graduates who joined or helped form existing companies, such as: Horse and Bamboo (Joe King, Sarah Frangleton), Wrights and Sites (Simon Persighetti), Goat Island (Mark Jeffrey) and Stan's Café (Sarah Archdeacon and Jake Oldershaw).

The story of DCA illustrates the difficulty of employing definitions and descriptors such as physical theatre to encapsulate work born out of cross-disciplinary learning and practice. Probably, 'physical theatre' was rarely claimed by these alumni in the companies (above) they formed or joined, but their practices were often deeply physical, usually collaboratively devised and almost always transgressed the rules and protocols of text-based mainstream drama. DCA in the 1980s and 1990s was also very much the progenitor and site of 'new dance' with figures such as Katie Duck, Mary Fulkerson, Laurie Booth and Steve Paxton present at the college either as permanent staff or as visitors. For Williams, in the Theatre field,

Training: from scarcity to abundance 211

FIGURE 6.8   *On the Braille in the Body.* Touchdown Dance integrated workshops with the visually impaired and the sighted at Dartington College of Arts, 1993. Featuring Gerry Overington and Dartington performer, Sharon Higginson. By kind permission of Kate Mount and Kevin Mount.

Source: Photographer: Kate Mount.

212 Training: from scarcity to abundance

FIGURE 6.9 Devised theatre class led by writer, Deborah Levy in Tilt Yard, Dartington College of Arts in the 1990s.

Source: Photographer: Graham Green.

these practices were 'equally important and constitutive of particular kinds of work made' (Ibid.). DCA in many ways speaks of and for the hybridity of this emerging performance work even if its explicit relationship with physical theatre was shadowy and unspoken. Notwithstanding Williams' claim that mime had little or no presence at the College during his time, we end with an anecdote by Joe Richards who was both student (1966–1968) and theatre tutor (1976–2010) for much of the life of the College. Richards submitted this little gem as a 'Postcard' for the special TDPT issue on DCA in 2018:

> *Early work at Dartington.*
> *In 1966 I was a nervous first year student at Dartington. There were eleven of us.*
> *One of my first sessions was with Mime Artist Julian Chagrín.*
> *The class consisted of building a wall with imaginary bricks.*
> *It required extraordinary concentration to sustain the sensation of the weight of a brick, a precise focus to remember where you had placed the previous one and an iron will not to catch the eye of my fellow students and burst out laughing.*
> *It was exhausting.*
> *After we had left the studio, I had to return to retrieve my precious kaftan.*
> *I witnessed Julian collecting in the bricks.*
>
> (Richards, 2018)

Concluding and continuing training

This chapter has attempted the impossible task of bringing together the multiple and disparate activities which engaged with mime and physical theatre training and education over three decades from 1970. We have particularly noted and reflected upon the extraordinary growth of the workshop 'industry', the uneven involvement in these practices from the higher education sector and the highly significant involvement of a small number of independent projects – MAG, CPR, IWF, DCA and Desmond Jones for example – which have all made productive interventions in training and education for and around mime and physical theatre during our period. To fit the tenor and the register of these performance practices the organisations and individuals we have identified and profiled might all be described as maverick, challenging and working imaginatively against the grain of established training practices of mainstream text-based theatre training.

7

ALL MIMES ARE EQUAL?

Artist/performer Anna-Maria Nabirye writes in an article reflecting on the online archive for *Total Theatre* magazine that, 'The archive is a key to knowledge, to seeing oneself reflected in the historical tapestry of culture and the arts. Representation is so important' (Nabirye, n.d.). For her it is necessary to recognise 'the history of where we stand and the journey that brought so many of us – me included – here' (ibid.). She champions the importance of 'owning the stories we tell ourselves, demanding more from the stories that are told to us, challenging who gets to tell the stories and who archives them for future generations' (ibid.). This chapter acknowledges and explores the importance of critiquing representation within mime and physical theatre on the basis of gender, race, ethnicity, class and disability. It sets out to ensure that important stories of difference and resistance within this field are heard, acknowledged and understood. The individual experiences of Black/Asian and/or female and/or disabled mime and physical theatre practitioners need to be seen within the context of a field that was often dominated by white, middle-class, non-disabled males. There are, of course, points of intersection between these identities, which we invite the reader to consider as they work through the chapter.

Addressing diversity and equality within the field of mime and physical theatre is not just about public attitudes and organisational structures, but also about recognising previously marginalised artistry, talent, skill and imagination. Postcolonialist, feminist and disability scholars have rightly critiqued the canon of twentieth-century theatre practice as largely male, white and non-disabled (Aston, 1995; Gilbert, 1996; and Kuppers, 2001), and even a brief survey of writing about mime and physical theatre during the late twentieth century would confirm a

DOI: 10.4324/9780429330209-7

similar analysis[1]. Quality and technique can too easily become ideologically constructed and judged in ways that support such cultural dominance. The rigours and risks of intensive physical training and performance might for instance be used to explain or excuse male non-disabled hegemony – ignoring the impact of performers such as Fern Smith (Volcano) and Nabil Shaban (Graeae). It is therefore important to centre the voices and achievements of those who have been marginalised. Indeed, the very term 'marginal' is in some senses problematic; this work was not on the margins of experience for those who created it or for whom it was devised.

The wider picture

The period of time that this book deals with was a period of significant change in relation to gender, race, ethnicity and disability. As noted in Chapter 3, several important Acts of Parliament variously addressed sex discrimination (1975) and race relations (1976). In 1981, approximately 9% of the population of England was Black, South Asian, Chinese or Mixed heritage, with a high percentage concentration in large urban areas. 1981 was declared by the United Nations as the International Year for Disabled People. In the UK, the Disabled Person Act (1986) and the Disability Discrimination Act (1995) both introduced significant changes to the rights of people with disabilities. In 1983, the disabled academic, Mike Oliver, introduced the concept of the social model of disability – a model which says that people are disabled by social barriers, not by their impairment or difference. Change within the theatre during this period was slow and localised, often dependent on the efforts of individuals and the support of organisations located where the pressure for change was most intense. Joff Chafer, who joined Trestle in the early 1980s, remembers that 'it felt there was a move to open things up, and in that diversity thing, actually bring everybody on board. It felt like things were possible and things were definitely changing' (Chafer, 2021). The Greater London Arts Association is an example of a regional arts association that made specific efforts to address inequalities, in part in recognition of the demographics of the Greater London conurbation and largely as a result of the radical and pioneering work of the then Labour-led Greater London Council. Naseem Khan's report, *The Arts Britain Ignores: The Arts of Ethnic Minorities in Britain* (1976), represented an important step in the growing recognition of cultural diversity and the importance of social equality. However, the National Arts and Media Strategy (ACE, 1992) makes no

---

1 Of the key texts on mime and physical theatre that focus on the last decades of the twentieth century, only that by Annette Lust (2003) contains sustained discussion of any marginalised groups (in this case, a chapter on 'Women in Mime', including a section on Nola Rae). None of the other texts (Chamberlain and Yarrow, 2002; Felner, 1985; Frost and Yarrow, 1990; Leabhart, 1989; Lust, 2003; Rolfe, 1979) addresses race, ethnicity or disability in any depth or detail.

216 All mimes are equal?

mention of Black, disabled or women practitioners until Chapter 7, and even less mention of gay and lesbian artists.

As has already been noted in Chapter 3, the dominant (but contested) arts agenda of the 1980s and 1990s was often about repositioning theatre as an entrepreneurial practice, as a means for creating cultural capital and making money. In this context, making work to give voice, empower, claim equality or speak out against oppression was increasingly marginalised in policy terms as either therapeutic activity ('it makes those people feel better about themselves') or activism ('it's politically motivated'). For artists and companies that rejected the dominant discourses, it was a struggle to establish their work as intrinsically valuable within an ideological frame for the arts that prioritised market value, virtuosic physical skill and flexibility. Capitalism at its bluntest reduces the cultural value of those who are perceived as less productive and efficient – physicality is not 'auditable'.

It has already been noted that many of the established 'master' teachers of mime were white, male and non-disabled. In the 1970s and early 1980s, as in the rest of the UK theatre industry, white male privilege meant that the opportunities to train, and to set up companies, create work and establish careers were not open to all. This cultural dominance, however, conceals the presence of the cultural diversity and resistance that already existed within UK theatre. The post-war period saw, over the 1960s to the 1980s, a significant growth in community theatre, alternative/experimental theatre and the exploration of class, feminism, race, disability and identity politics as significant drivers for new theatrical work. Mime and physical theatre offered a form of theatre that might seem particularly appropriate for such an expansion of access, participation and creation. It was cheap to produce and tour, the focus on physicality and comedy making it popular with young audiences and potentially able directly to address physical difference and/or inequality, through processes based on group devising. Yet the picture in reality is a lot less clear-cut. Mime and physical theatre, as part of the wider field of devised theatre, can be seen as an important space within which diverse performers were able to make their own work about the issues that mattered to them and to their communities. Its apparent simplicity of means potentially enabled anyone to 'have a go', and its aesthetic did away with the conventional signifying effects of sets, costumes and lighting. Physical theatre in the 1980s and 1990s increasingly refused to take for granted the image of the silent, white-faced (in multiple senses), illusion mime that was more popular in the late 1970s and responded creatively to the possibility that gesture, physicality and movement could be harnessed to say things that the hegemonic textual language of theatre cannot. Something of the 'punk' aesthetic of the late 1970s might be detected in the resistance to text and to the established hierarchies and conservative structures of theatre at this time. Mime and physical theatre in the UK found itself needing to be awkward and defiant in order to claim its space. The impact of the increased recognition of and access to non-European practices over the 1980s to the present, largely through festivals (International Workshop Festival, London International Festival of Theatre and London International Mime Festival) and international companies touring to the UK, also helped to open up the mime and physical theatre world to diverse approaches to training and making work. The growth, for example, in intercultural theatre practice during this period was supported by cheaper travel, growing recognition of the work of UK Asian, African and Caribbean theatre practitioners, funding from the British Council and easier access to non-Western performance traditions. Mime training itself – both in the Paris schools and in the schools set up in the UK – tended to eschew overtly political approaches to training and performance. However, their politics was embedded in the nature of the tasks and exercises, implicit in the internationalism of their student bodies, and evident in the humanism of the principles that informed their work. Those seeking to utilise mime and physical techniques to communicate explicitly political themes needed to look beyond these schools and the classical mime traditions. Important influences in the development of a more overtly politically aware approach to mime and physical theatre might include: awareness of the political work of the R. G. Davies' San Francisco Mime Troupe in California and Peter and Elka Schumann's Bread and Puppet Theater in Vermont; the work of the Italian actor/writer Dario Fo, who, together with his partner Franca Rame, ran a series of influential workshops in April/May 1983 at the Riverside Studios in London; the impact of Theatre-in-Education (e.g. M6 and Belgrade TIE), Community Theatre (e.g. Red Ladder) and Young People's Theatre (e.g. Greenwich Young People's Theatre and WAC Arts). All these were highly political and drew on popular forms and physical practices. At the same time the work of Augusto Boal was becoming known in the UK through a combination of his publications and workshops. The decline in Arts Council funding for explicitly political theatre in the UK during the 1980s meant that radical theatre practice tended to gravitate around the politics of identity as an alternative locus for resistance. The combined effect of accessibility, together with an increasing awareness of the particular political possibilities of physical performance, opened up new creative possibilities for challenging existing cultural hierarchies.

Working class mime

Socialist theatre in the UK during the twentieth century was drawn towards the use of movement and mime as forms of theatre that could communicate quickly and easily to their target audiences. Socialist theatre practitioners drew on the skills and traditions of working-class forms of entertainment, such as variety theatre and folk theatre, as they sought new structural systems (Warden, 2012: 46)[2]. Their work was inspired by the simple physicality and versatile platform stage of Copeau's work[3], and also by the constructivist influences of Vsevelod Meyerhold, Walter Gropius and László Moholy-Nagy. In general, there was a movement at this time to declutter the stage of illusion, a movement that provided a space for mime to prove its

---

2 See, for example, John McGrath's book *A Good Night Out* (1981) and the work of his 7:84 companies (England and Scotland).
3 Copeau presented *L'Illusion* at the Festival Theatre, Chichester, in 1928, using a simple platform stage to give back prominence to the human figure and its movement.

218 All mimes are equal?

value. Early Agit-Prop theatre in Britain encouraged actors to shift between characters, to use exaggerated characterisations and grotesque performance styles, and explicitly to play with narrative structure and form – all preparing the way for the mime and physical theatre of the 1970s and 1980s. Within UK avant-garde theatre between the World Wars, 'the body becomes an important aspect of performance, a political site of meaning construction as well as the fundamental element on an uncluttered, presentational stage' (Warden, 2012: 154). Blending the work of Dalcroze, Laban, Meyerhold[4] and Brecht, movement became an important and skilful process within the creation of socialist theatre. The over-arching idea was that, 'companies were developing specific working-class methods of movement based on particular working-class experience and inextricably connected to the industrial' (Leach, 2006: 82). The movement work of working-class theatre makers, such as Joan Littlewood, together with the history of physical performance within popular working-class entertainment (e.g. eccentric dancers such as Nat Ripley and Max Wall) illustrates the existence of working-class traditions in this field before the arrival of the French mime tradition in the UK. These working-class traditions, as Claire Warden (2012) argues, politicise the body through democratising the body, 'actively challenging the ownership of the physical by the hegemony . . . the body became a site of democratic intent, a method of challenging the political status quo and a source of individual (and indeed community) freedom' (2012: 159).

Despite this history, the arrival of the French mime tradition in the second half of the century was to eclipse such innovation. This is ironic given the strong socialist leanings of practitioners such as Decroux. The arts funding policy of the Thatcher government from 1979 also meant that working-class mime and physical theatre would struggle to get funding if it sought to promote a political agenda. Several of the practitioners interviewed for this book commented on the costs of training in the French mime tradition. As we have noted in Chapter 6, travel to France, staying in Paris and the cost of the school fees meant that in general only those with sufficient financial resources could afford to study with Decroux, Lecoq or Marceau[5]. The only other options were to try for one of the very few Arts Council bursaries or for one of the awards made by the French Government. For everyone else, it was a case of picking up training through workshops, short courses or modules offered within degree programmes. The cost of drama conservatoires and the dominance of the upper and middle classes within the student bodies at leading universities during the 1980s meant that power in the theatre industry tended to remain elusive for working-class artists. One notable exception to this was the provision at Hope Street in Liverpool (see Chapter 6). This had started as a training wing of the Everyman Theatre, providing workshops for unemployed actors in the city. Glenn

---

4 For Meyerhold, 'the basic law of Biomechanics is very simple: the whole body takes part in each of our movements' (Gladkov 1997, p. 96).

5 John Mowat considered studying with Lecoq in Paris, but couldn't raise the money: 'it would have been nice to have add a bit more of a full-time course, rather than three hours on a Tuesday evening and three hours on a Saturday afternoon at City Lit with Ronnie Wilson. It would have been nice. But no, I couldn't afford it' (Mowat, 2020).

Noble (2021) recalls how eventually Hope Street became a nexus for engagement with a range of companies, including small local companies with working-class performers. Alongside the training and workshop opportunities, Noble described the importance of accessible spaces: 'Hope Street had floors you could book and go and just run your own sessions in, and test things out' (Noble, 2021).

Although many companies focused on producing work that was popular, accessible and unpretentious, few if any identified as working-class in terms of personnel or target audience. In the 1994 UK Mime and Physical Theatre Directory, no company or artist listed does so. Working-class identity is almost impossible to trace within the recent history of mime and physical theatre. Few of the interviewees for this book spoke openly about their class background, and class is less immediately discernible than other forms of cultural diversity (e.g. gender, race or disability). In general terms, this has meant that class has often been invisible in mime and physical theatre, certainly in much of the work in the 1970s and early 1980s, which tended to be comic and structured around sketches. Nonetheless, both Théâtre de Complicité and Trestle have dealt with themes related to class identity (Théâtre de Complicité's *The Three Lives of Lucie Cabrol* (1994) was inspired by John Berger's book on peasant life, *Pig Earth*; Trestle's *Plastered* (1984) was inspired by characters from local pubs and hospital wards), and later companies have drawn inspiration from popular working-class culture such as Frantic Assembly's *Klub* (1995).

Women in mime and physical performance

Female, gay and lesbian mimes and physical theatre practitioners have faced similar obstacles and discrimination throughout their careers to those in the theatre sector as a whole. Women, as we have seen in Chapter 2, have always been present in the (her)story of mime during the last century; their relative absence in the established narratives however is an omission that deserves rectifying. These are artists not defined solely by their gender, but for the purposes of this chapter it is important to acknowledge how gender has played within their careers.

Chapter 2 recognised the importance of mid- to late-twentieth-century mime artists and teachers such as Irene Mawer, Pat Keysell and Claude Chagrin. In addition, it is important to recognise Nancy Meckler, who came from the USA to co-found Freehold theatre company (1969–1972), and who forged a career as a theatre director with a particular interest in non-naturalistic theatre and the physical expressivity of the actor. Nonetheless, for those women who looked to study mime and physical theatre during this period, female role models, although present, were relatively marginalised. In addition to those mentioned earlier, of particular note within the French mime tradition are: Monika Pagneux, who taught at the Lecoq School from 1965 to 1979 and then jointly ran another Paris school with Philippe Gaulier for several years in the 1980s; Sandra Mladenovich, who taught at the Lecoq School from 1978 to 1998; Pascale Lecoq, Lecoq's daughter, who has taught at the School since 1989 and is now the director of the School; Claire Heggen, co-founder of Théâtre du Mouvement (1975–), who has performed and taught across Europe; and Corinne Soum, co-founder of Théâtre de l'Ange Fou and of the Ecole de Mime Corporel Dramatique in Paris (1984–1995) and then London (1995–2014).

Monika Pagneux in particular offers a connection with many of the leading practitioners in twentieth-century theatre, dance and movement, including Mary Wigman, Peter Brook and Moshe Feldenkrais. Her pedagogy is distinctive and individual, drawing on these many experiences but never dominated by any of them, as well as being playful, joyous and liberating. Peta Lily talks about how Pagneux does not put herself out as the power centre in the class, but rather centres her work around her students (Lily, 2020). She has only recently allowed some of her work to be documented and distributed, believing passionately in the need for the work to be experienced rather than read, and perhaps as a consequence there is little published on her work (Evans, 2020: 324–326; Murray, 2010: 215–236; Pagneux, 2012). Her work has influenced a number of other women working within contemporary performance, most notably Annabel Arden, Linda Kerr Scott, Celia Gore Booth, Lilo Baur, Kathryn Hunter and Sarah Kemp, but it is not well known outside those who have studied with her. Annabel Arden is clear that,

> the whole sense of patterning and space and the composition of people and the way in which you can get people to work as a group, irrespective of their different physical capabilities. Everything I know about that came from her and everything I know about what the actor's body needs to play came from her. . . . She had worked with Feldenkrais himself, and she'd adapted all the key Feldenkrais exercises for the much less patient mind of an actor. And she'd adapted them for the function of play.
>
> *(Arden, 2021)*

What is important about Pagneux's work in the context of this chapter is her ability to empower the performer: 'She teaches me how to be myself, how to cope with the body I have, and makes me think about how I learn' (Arden in Luckhurst and Veltman, 2001: 2).

By the time that Mime Action Group published the *UK Mime and Physical Theatre training directory* in 1993, there were a substantial number of female mime artists, of mime and physical theatre companies founded, directed or run by women, and of companies employing significant numbers of women performers. Some names to note might include: Jane Sutcliffe (Metaphysique); Hayley Carmichael (Told by an Idiot); Mollie Guilfoyle (Intriplicate Mime); Hilary Ramsden (Dorothy Talk); Micheline Vanderpoel (The Right Size); Iris Walton (Still Life Mime Theatre and Cunning Stunts); Suzy Willson (Clod Ensemble), as well as Sarah Brignall, Lorna Marshall and Beatrice Pemberton. All of these women trained within the French tradition, mostly via Lecoq. Those women practitioners who trained outside the French tradition include: Linda Marlowe (who worked with Steven Berkoff for ten years); Franki Anderson (co-founder of Fooltime, trained in Laban's methods under Lisa Ullman); Kate Hale (Foursight Theatre Company, a Midlands physical theatre company founded and led by women); Debbie Isitt (Snarling Beasties and Cambridge Experimental Theatre); Wendy Houstoun (performed with DV8); Didi Hopkins (expert in Commedia Dell'Arte); and, Carran Waterfield (Triangle, trained with Odin Teatret). In addition, several important and influential women ran companies in the feminist theatre field, such as Beryl and the Perils, which made use of comic strip styles, acrobatics and clowning (Didi Hopkins was one of the founding members), and in the visual theatre field, such as Geraldine Pilgrim (Hesitate and Demonstrate) and Hilary Westlake (IOU) (see Chapter 5). This work was supported by a number of influential women administrators, including: Helen Lannaghan (London International Mime Festival and MAG), Sue Hoyle and Jane Nicholas (Arts Council England), Suzanne Burns (Northern Arts), Mhora Samuel (MAG), Deborah Barnard and Alicyn Marr (Kendal Brewery Art Centre) and Jac Wilkinson (Warwick Arts Centre and author of several important reports on mime). It is worth also noting the comment in the McCann Matthews Millman quantitative research report (1992), that '[as] is common with arts attenders, it appears that the majority (65%) of [attendees] for mime are female' (1992: 23). The role and experience of women as artists and audiences in this discipline area has been underestimated and undervalued historically.

Networking appears to have been mostly informal between women practitioners; there was, for instance, no specific provision within MAG for women to connect and support each other's work and development. However, one important international initiative was the Magdalena Project, founded in Wales in 1986 by a group of female theatre performers and practitioners. The project's website describes its vision in the following terms:

> the struggle of women in theatre is still couched very much in terms of winning a place within existing structures rather than in questioning the function of those structures. The Project has challenged this situation and encouraged women to examine their role in the future of theatre in more depth. Through looking at existing work by women, by sharing methodologies, by examining form as well as content or by making new material, the Project has been trying, practically, to reveal recurrent themes, vocabularies and images. . . . The Project aims to provoke the organisation of opportunities for women to explore new approaches to theatre-making that reflect, more profoundly, their own experiences and political priorities.
>
> *(Magdalena Project, 2018)*

The influence of Pina Bausch also merits attention – particularly in terms of her work, which explored how assumptions around gender could be challenged through dance, gesture and physical expression. Bausch provided a vision of the ways in which movement and gesture could be brought into play as a mode of resistance to patriarchal forms of behaviour – demonstrating the potential theatrical power of repetition and the eloquence of physical exhaustion as metaphors for male/female relationships. She had a profound impact on many dance and physical theatre practitioners in the UK throughout the latter half of the last century. Her work was impossible to watch without reaction, and it re-affirmed the idea that dance and physical theatre could be about something socially and politically serious and important which could be communicated through the body. She was also an important role model as a woman leading a major international dance/theatre company and choreographing her own work.

Working with the body as a central element of the performance and devising process had resonance for female performers during what was an important period for the historical development of feminism. Claire Heggen (Théâtre du Mouvement) draws an interesting parallel between the silence of mime and the silence that has historically been forced on women in society. She feels 'the function of mime is to be a memory, a witness of an occupied body, a "resistant body"' (King, 2004: 7), referring both to the experiences of Decroux in occupied France during the Second World War and to the ways that mime can speak to the embodied experience (the body memory) of women. Mime and physical theatre can therefore be seen as part of a drive, post-1968 and the Paris uprisings, to establish ways of working that were enabling for all those who were making theatre and performance within the feminist movement and seeking to challenge patriarchal attitudes to performance, the body, movement, performance making and difference. Of course, on a practical level, this also meant dealing with the everyday sexism of the time, which was no less prevalent in the theatre sector. As Geraldine Pilgrim recalls,

> I'll be brutally honest. It helped that Janet and I were seen as being very pretty young girls. There was absolutely no doubt about it. And I was very aware that that was helping us, and it really disturbed me. . . . I was very aware, and to be honest . . . I still am, that being a woman in the theatre, performance, live art, whatever it is, means that you are seen in a particular way.
> *(2020)*

Being in control of your own company, creating your own work and determining your own working conditions was one way of resisting such discrimination. Pilgrim (2020) probably speaks for a lot of women practitioners at that time when she states:

> Although I realise Hesitate and Demonstrate's work is respected, I sometimes feel that the company's work has never been acknowledged sufficiently . . . But we were no less important than any of those other companies that were run by men. Yet, you would think that we were. And being at art school at that time, and being a woman in the '70s and early '80s, was often really bloody difficult.

Sexist attitudes could additionally make getting bookings for shows more complicated. Angela de Castro suggests that women 'need to be "extra good", undergoing a struggle to prove yourself again and again to get the space to perform' (in King,

2004: 7). For Sian Williams (The Kosh), having her own company enabled her to ensure that women were protagonists in much of their work:

> it felt a good thing that we were often looking at things from a woman's perspective. But as far as working, I felt very equal. It never occurred to me in our work that I didn't have parity with what was going on.
>
> *(Williams, 2020)*

She also remarks how in some cases, working within co-founded companies that devised their own work could be a privileged position: 'I think I was sometimes not as aware of how unequal these things are; because I'd trained, and gone straight into working in a very wholesome environment, working in a cooperative' (ibid.). In any case, as in society at large at this time, women were aware of the ways in which sexist attitudes still informed most areas of creative theatre practice and training, and of the pressures to keep quiet and put up with it all: 'It was extraordinarily sexist when I think back about it, but we didn't really know any better, you know. We didn't really care and we accepted the whole mythology of, you know, the theatre is cruel' (Arden, 2021). Working in mime and physical theatre can forefront contact between bodies and clearly the potential for exploitative abuse of the physical trust, proximity and vulnerability that such work might necessitate is therefore an area of real concern. Abusive behaviours are seldom reported; however, quite recently, former members of the Polish company Gardzienice have made accusations about the historical behaviour of the director, Włodzimierz Staniewski. It is important to note that there are traditions of teaching, performing and directing that can be experienced as harassment, abuse and bullying when they step over the line from healthy provocation and/or clear haptic direction.

The body was, from the 1960s onwards, increasingly recognised as a contested space for feminist politics. In the UK, books such as Germaine Greer's *The Female Eunuch* (1970) and exhibitions such as Marianne Wex's *Let's Take Back our Space: 'Female' and 'Male' Body Language as a Result of Patriarchal Structures* at the ICA in 1982, raised awareness of the ways in which women's bodies were oppressed. By the 1990s, feminist theorists such as Judith Butler (1990 and 1993) and Iris Young (1990) had argued persuasively that gender was performative, created by the repetition of socially constructed modes of behaviour. Iris Young's article 'Throwing Like a Girl' suggested that women were capable of projecting their physical intentions purposefully through space, and that it was social conditioning that limited their ability to do so, not physical aptitude. In this context, mime and physical theatre became arenas in which women could actively challenge presumptions about what they could or should perform and how. Below are case studies on the careers of two female practitioners, Peta Lily (solo performer and teacher, founder member of Three Women Mime) and Fern Smith (Volcano Theatre). Lily offers an example of a woman who trained in conventional mime techniques and has gone on to adapt these in order to develop her own creative voice and her own approaches to teaching and making physical theatre. Smith came into physical performance through dance-based approaches (see Chapter 5) and a strong emphasis on risk, authenticity and physical energy – her performances have challenged some conventional notions of women's physicality. The case studies provide contrasting but complementary pictures of two women's physical theatre journeys.

Peta Lily

Lily grew up in Australia and her early influences included contemporary dance, the corporeal mime of Théâtre du Mouvement, and watching university productions that featured actors like Geoffrey Rush (who had recently returned from studying with Lecoq in Paris). She arrived in London at the end of the 1970s and started taking mime classes with Desmond Jones at the British Theatre Institute in Fitzroy Square. She began making mime shows with a fellow student, artist Tessa Schneideman, and later they joined with puppeteer Claudia Prietzel to form Three Women Mime (see Fig. 7.1):

> The first piece we made together at school was three women standing side by side, looking into a mirror, dressing and putting on make-up. Each gesture

FIGURE 7.1 Peta Lily preparing to perform in Three Women Mime's show *High Heels*, 1981. By kind permission of Peta Lily and Patrick Boillard.

Source: Photo © Patrick Boillaud.

further constrained their faces and bodies. For another piece, a cloth was hung so that only our legs were visible and our legs and shoe collection worked as a kind of puppetry, with diverse characters interacting, including a mother dragging a line of tiny shoes like a ball and chain. Tessa built a giant cream bun for one piece (in defiance of the fairly robust notion in those early days that mime should be a pure form consisting of a figure on a bare stage). In one piece three women in aprons and headscarves performed an entire circus using household objects. Over the course of three shows we addressed subjects including food issues, motherhood, the depiction of women in popular culture, and sexual violence.

(Lily n.d.)

She acknowledges the cross-fertilisation that was available at that time, with access to the 1981 UK summer school with Lecoq, classes with Gaulier and Pagneux in 1984, and seeing the work of so many other companies.

Performing at the Edinburgh Festival, Three Women had opportunity to both hone our work and to see other companies. The International Workshop Festival allowed us to study Butoh with Sankai Juku. The London International Mime Festival was a wonderful way to see work from practitioners outside UK. Three Women Mime were on the cover of *Time Out* as part of LIMF in 1982. Three Women were very successful. We were at a happy intersection, where conditions had supported women's theatre companies, plus the upward thrust of physical theatre. Three Women's shows toured constantly in the UK and in Europe: Germany, France, Holland and in Denmark we participated in a festival of feminist theatre. As a soloist, Peta Lily Company continued to appear at LIMF and tour UK and internationally.

(Lily, 2020)

Three Women Mime developed an innovative and particularly visual way of working. For one production, *Wounds* (1982), they worked with Hilary Westlake from Lumiere & Son, and in her interview, Lily referenced the impact of performers such as Rose English, whose interdisciplinary work challenged the nature of performance and imaginatively addressed gender politics. These experiences helped her develop a strong sense that mime and physical theatre could be about something important and that the work's visual impact needed to be thoroughly and carefully considered. Lily also benefitted from her Australian upbringing; coming from outside the codifications of British class and regionality gave her a position from which she could develop a different critical perspective. In 1983 she decided to go solo, in order to develop more sustained performance pieces. Working with director Rex Doyle, she created solo and two-handed shows throughout the 1980s and 1990s that blended her own experiences or obsessions with visual imagery and, more often than not, movement and gesture. Although she moved out of

226 All mimes are equal?

performance work from 1995 to the end of the decade for personal reasons, she has, since 2000 continued to work, teach and perform, developing her own strand of clown work which she calls Dark Clown[6].

For Lily, the importance of mime and physical theatre as an artist and as a woman lay in the opportunities to develop work that 'spoke directly to one's own actual experiences and to bring to light overlooked aspects that needed addressing. As a female practitioner, I could envisage new narratives, write and play the leading part, in fact, play all the parts' (Lily, 2020). At that time, there were very few solo female artists performing their own material. Lily's work as a mime and physical theatre artist was genre-crossing and recognised as innovative and she won several awards for her work, including an Edinburgh Fringe First for *Wendy Darling* in 1988 (see Fig. 7.2). She was also a significant and important member of the mime and physical theatre community at this time: a member of the Arts Council's Dance and Mime Panel for several years and an important contributor to the debates and discussions hosted by MAG around the future of mime and physical theatre in the UK. Since 1981, she has influenced and continues to influence performers, companies and practitioners in various fields through her teaching of mime, physical theatre, theatre making, Commedia dell'Arte and Dark Clown.

Fern Smith

Fern Smith met Paul Davies at Swansea University, and together they formed Volcano Theatre in reaction to the tameness of conventional drama in the late 1980s and fuelled by the excitement and energy of a politics of opposition developed over a decade of Thatcherism:

> there was almost an unspoken sense that culture and music actually mattered. And there was a place, perhaps, to talk about alternative visions, perhaps not even alternative visions, but to kick against the one that we were being offered. I suppose there was a sense of an oppositional energy . . . that really fuelled early Volcano.
>
> *(Smith, 2020)*

Alongside making theatre they initiated a festival programme called *The Revolution*, which brought performers such as mimes Peta Lily and Nola Rae, and artist/dancer Liz Aggiss, to Swansea to perform and run workshops. Volcano's work started with a desire to bring something of the energy and excitement available elsewhere in contemporary culture (sports, music, politics, film) into theatre performance. The movement elements of this work were influenced by the input of Nigel Charnock,

---

6 'Let's say that on one end you have emotions which you can expect to see and feel with the red nose clown: silliness, loveliness, enthusiasm, bossiness, grumpiness, possibly even anger – imagine that line extending towards pain, shame, guilt, existential horror, desperation and terror. That is the realm of expression for the Dark Clown' (Lily, n.d.).

All mimes are equal? **227**

FIGURE 7.2 Peta Lily in *Wendy Darling*, 1988. By kind permission of Peta Lily and Douglas Robertson.

Source: Photo by Douglas Robertson.

who directed several productions and introduced them to the kinds of dance and movement work and choreographic structures used by companies like DV8. This style of performance-making seems to have proved particularly eloquent in dealing with issues around sexuality and gender, which were coming to the fore in theatre and dance around this time. Volcano consciously set out to explore masculinity and femininity in some of their early work: 'There was something about a kind of a third gender, the mixture of the masculine and the feminine that was certainly something that I was always consciously exploring' (ibid.). Physical theatre offered a space where the representation of masculinity and femininity could be meaningfully explored: 'how else do you explore issues like this' (ibid.). Heddon and Milling whilst discussing Théâtre de Complicité's *The Street of Crocodiles*, point out the ways in which improvised devising can unwittingly replicate gendered physical interactions:

> Because the exercises or improvisations in the devising process are not concerned to explore sexual politics, or indeed politics in a broader sense, but emerge from a humanist individualism, the physical interaction that transfers from workshop into stage picture tends to reproduce predominantly heterosexual relationships, and traditional images of men carrying women – only very rarely do women performers carry male performers, and if they do so it is usually within an image suggesting oppression or struggle.
>
> *(Heddon and Milling, 2006: 180)*

Volcano's productions did however set out to explore sexual politics through movement. Smith's performance work was a clear declaration of female strength and a challenge to conventional perceptions of female physicality. As a performer, Smith had a powerful physical presence on stage and performed with an energy and commitment that challenged conventional notions of feminine physicality. Alongside other women physical theatre practitioners, such as Wendy Houstoun and Georgina Lamb, she offers a different vision of female physicality – active, energised and fearless. She now works as an independent artist, coach, celebrant and somatic practitioner (see https://fernsmith.uk).

Gender, sexuality and physical performance

The work of Lindsay Kemp (1938–2018) and his company offers probably the most distinctive example of mime performance that draws on gay experience, gay culture and a camp or queer aesthetic. Drawing on his training in mime and dance, his production *Flowers*, first performed in 1968 and based on the writings of Jean Genet, was an international success and openly dealt with homosexuality. Despite his success, there is little evidence that mime and physical theatre companies during the 1970s and early 1980s offered a space for the representation and/or celebration of gay or lesbian experience. Homophobia was still commonplace at this time and it is perhaps understandable that some performers may have chosen not to come out as gay or lesbian, and/or not to make work that fore fronted their gender identity. The British Social Attitudes survey suggests that by 1987 as few as 11% of the population believed that homosexual activity was not 'wrong' – by 2017 the figure had risen to nearly 70%. The introduction in 1988 of Section 28, a notorious piece of Conservative government legislation that prohibited the 'promotion' of homosexuality in schools, effectively silenced the political activity of many gay and lesbian organisations at this time, and resulted in self-censorship for many who might otherwise have wanted to explore their experiences through performance. Denise Wong recalls touring a Black Mime Theatre show, *Forgotten Heroes* (1995), which included a scene in which two men kissed, and reluctantly acquiescing to demands from the West Midlands schools to which they were touring to cut that scene. This the company only did when funding and the tour were being threatened. An opportunity to dialogue and create greater understanding was missed due to pressure from the regional funders and schools. Despite these socio-political conditions, and perhaps partially in reaction to them, a few artists explored the intersections between dance and theatre as a place within which gender and sexuality might be explored.

That this was a move away from mime and towards dance is significant. Gay and lesbian theatre over this period was usually text-based or company-devised political drama – Gay Sweatshop (1975–1981) and Split Britches (1980–) being perhaps the most well-known examples. UK Physical theatre didn't start to explore sexuality and gender explicitly until the work of DV8, a company whose experiences were rooted in dance. DV8 was founded in 1986 by Lloyd Newson in response to his frustration with an obsession with form over content in contemporary dance at that time. He also wanted to challenge the limitations of dance by including theatre, text and film in the work and by testing notions of trust, authenticity and risk. Productions such as *My Sex, Our Dance* (1986) and *Dead Dreams of Monochrome Men* (1988) involved a violent physicality that sought to communicate the emotional and physical nature of relationships in a more visceral and immediate way. The next case study focuses on Liam Steel, who, during the late 1980s and 1990s worked with a number of physical theatre companies, including DV8, Volcano and Frantic Assembly, on productions that challenged conventional notions of masculinity and sexuality.

Liam Steel

Steel began his career as a dance and visual theatre animateur in 1987. The job involved working alongside Ludus Dance company, whose work was centred around ensemble devising. Ludus had previously employed several other artists whose careers were to include physical theatre work, including Nigel Charnock, Wendy Houstoun and Sian Williams. Steel went on to work with The Kosh in 1991, before joining Volcano Theatre in Swansea for their 1992 production of *L.O.V.E.* This production was directed by Nigel Charnock, who introduced Steel to Lloyd Newson, which led to an invitation to join DV8 for their production of *MSM*. This was a show that explored the experiences of men who went 'cottaging' (having sex with other men in public toilets), and used interview material from 50 homosexual and bisexual men. Steel stayed with DV8 and was involved as a performer on a number of projects including *Enter Achilles* (1995), *Bound to Please* (1997) and *The Happiest Days of My Life* (1999). DV8's work offered a distinctive perspective on gay and straight male sexuality, presenting gay sexuality as a subject for physical theatre performance at a time when to do so was still politically risky in the UK. The work operated on two levels: firstly, revealing the sexual politics at the heart of the entire theatre and dance industry (what women or men are permitted to perform on stage); and secondly, connecting issues of sexual identity to wider themes of loneliness, the pressure to conform, and the compromises we make in order to be liked or loved. The aesthetics of risk, touch, embrace and exhaustion work to give these issues material presence on the stage and to challenge outmoded and conventional notions of authenticity.

> What I found myself was that the contact [improvisation] world and that whole world where women were suddenly lifting men, completely redrew the lines in terms of gender and what dance represented. . . . It was interesting that with DV8 and a lot of other companies at the time, such as Anna Teresa de Keersmaeker, there was the reductive accusation that the work was 'all just sexual politics'. As if the Royal Ballet having a row of all white women all exactly the same, that are stick thin, isn't making a statement about sexual politics.
>
> *(Steel, 2020)*

The experience of gendered identity is, in this manner, made explicit and integral to the work – Newson wanted 'to present reality as I see it in the world around me' (in Giannachi and Luckhurst, 1999: 113). Desire, in terms of multiple implications and effects, becomes the motor that drives the words, gestures, movements and actions. DV8 created a hybrid form of dance and theatre which facilitated this process. The combination of dance and theatre within this form of physical theatre drew on a professional context in which gay sexuality had a history. Whereas the world of French mime had been largely a world dominated by (apparently) heterosexual white males, the world of contemporary dance could draw on histories of gender diversity and plurality. DV8 took this as an opportunity to push back against traditional expectations of what dance and theatre could be about, and implicitly against how gender and sexuality might be explored on stage:

> physical theatre was sort of anti-establishment. It felt anti-establishment. It wasn't about being pretty, it wasn't about playing by the rules. And, in some ways, it was sort of the equivalent of what was happening with the rise of Punk.
>
> *(Steel, 2020)*

There is not a hint of mime in DV8's work. Their work is consciously positioned in opposition not only to conventional notions of dance, but also to the traditional conceptions of mime. Newson openly rejected anything arcane or elitist. DV8's work reveals a suspicion of pretence – evident in the use of real objects and real physical contact (objects such as beer glasses and blow-up dolls become animated and expressive in *Enter Achilles*, for instance). In reality, there was probably little divide between dance-based physical theatre and mime-based physical theatre, or Grotowski's work – the move away from conventional and traditional forms was indeed a common feature. Nonetheless, few artists seem to have crossed over between the dance/theatre and mime traditions of training and making work. Liam Steel is one example of those who did, but his career is the exception rather than the rule. It is interesting how, despite several shared points in common, the difference between forms (training traditions, cultures and processes of making) seemed pronounced enough to prevent more sustained collaboration and cooperation.

It's worth concluding with the words of Pete Brooks of Impact Theatre Cooperative, who suggests that:

> There is an erotics of performance based in the body. I came to understand this when I saw a lot of contemporary dance in the early '70s. . . . I realised there was an erotics that you can't get in film. It's also to do with presence, with the erotics of presence and the proximity of the body in performance. I think the success of a company like DV8 is to do with its eroticism. I think theatre has to say to itself 'what can we do that no-one else can do?'. . . What it can do is create that kind of erotic tension . . . because it's dealing with real people doing real things in front of a real audience. Hovering around that is this whole idea of sexuality, and sexual charge. . . . Women, gay men and lesbians have found a voice to discuss their sexuality, but because it's still a patriarchal culture you need to have a very sly view, a very crafty view to deal with issues of being a heterosexual man.
>
> *(Brooks in Dawson, 1993: 8)*

Dance-based physical theatre has done much to address anxieties around touch in teaching and performance, in particular male-to-male touching. It has created both spaces in which closeness can be physicalised in dynamic and exciting yet safe ways, and also eloquent models for intimacy in performance.

Race and mime

During the 1980s and 1990s, a number of theatre and dance companies emerged that drew on or spoke to the life experiences and cultural heritages of the Black and Asian communities in the UK. At the same time, important interventions such as *The Art Britain Ignores* by Naseem Khan (1976) highlighted and made the case for the value of Asian and Black arts within British culture. Some of these companies (for example Black Theatre Cooperative, Tara Arts, Tamasha, Talawa and Temba) brought to their work a desire to celebrate the physicalities inherent in their own cultural backgrounds. In 2003, Jatinder Verma, former director of Tara Arts, lamented that, 'When it comes to Asian or Black Arts, there is no History, only "moments of significance". So we lurch from moment to moment of visibility, separated by a void of invisibility' (2003). This is no less true within mime and

232 All mimes are equal?

physical theatre. Even if the histories are intermittent and partial, they do exist and it is important, wherever possible, to remember them. Steve Ward, for instance, records the ethnic diversity in the Victorian circus, including: Pablo Fanque (born William Darby), the first Black circus owner in Britain; Carlos Pablo Paddington, an artiste on the *corde volante*[7], the slack rope and as an equestrian, who also cross-dressed and was actually a 'she'; and Tom Handford, a Black clown, who eventually owned his own concert hall (Ward, 2021). The children's television presenter Derek Griffiths, whose mime skills were almost entirely self-taught, is perhaps one of the few Black mimes to find popular success in this period for his work on BBC's *Play School* (1971–1981).

A full history of Black and Asian physical performance in the UK is still to be written – the next sections aim to recognise some significant achievements, people and events over the period in question. One place to start from is with a Black theatre production that toured to the UK from South Africa during the early 1980s – *Woza Albert!* This show is an interesting example of a Black physical theatre production from early in this period. Its reception and impact are of relevance to the issues raised in this chapter.

Market Theatre: Woza Albert!

The arrival in the UK of *Woza Albert!*, a Market Theatre (Johannesburg) production of a play (Mtwa, Ngema and Simon, 1982) created, devised and written by Percy Mtwa, Mbongeni Ngema and Barney Simon, and performed by Mtwa and Ngema, offered Black British theatre makers a vision of ways in which mime and physicality could be an integral part of communicating Black experience (in this case, of apartheid in South Africa). The production was performed at the Edinburgh Festival and then in London in August and September 1982. The play was inspired by the idea of Christ's second coming happening in South Africa. It deliberately used 'poor theatre' techniques – physicality, mime, vocal effects, rapid changes in characterisation, clowning – inspired by Grotowski's *Towards a Poor Theatre* and Brook's *The Empty Space* (see Fig. 7.3). It was quickly recognised as a powerful and politically purposeful piece of Black physical theatre. It is intriguing that it did not directly lead to more visible examples of Black physical theatre in the UK. Was the success of *Woza Albert!* in South Africa due in part to the lack of a theatre infrastructure in the townships, meaning that such a dynamic and entertaining show, presented simply, connected directly with its intended audience. In the UK, theatre was more established as a form of commercial entertainment, and presenting this kind of politically engaged theatre in the West End of London inevitably weakened its socio-political impact. In fact, the only Black British company that set out two years later explicitly to create work within the field of mime and physical theatre was Black Mime Theatre.

---

7 The *corde volante* is also known as the Mexican Cloud Swing. The rope hangs between two points and the performer sits in the middle, using the rope as something like a trapeze.

FIGURE 7.3 Mbongeni Ngema and Percy Mtwa in *Woza Albert!*, 1981. By kind permission of Ruphin Coudyzer.

Source: Photo © Ruphin Coudyzer FPPSA.

Black Mime Theatre and Denise Wong

Founded in 1984 by David Boxer and Sarah Cahn, Black Mime Theatre provides evidence that mime and physical theatre could also belong and speak to the Black community in the UK. Denise Wong trained in Community Theatre at Rose Bruford College, where mime was part of the course following a long tradition built on Rose Bruford's own friendship with Irene Mawer. Wong then worked with several theatre companies before joining Black Mime as a founding member. David Boxer had trained at the Lecoq School and brought that initial influence into the early work of the company. Wong had wanted to go to the Lecoq School but the financial demands of studying in France meant that it wasn't possible; Black Mime Theatre filled the gap for her. When Boxer left in 1986, Wong became artistic director and directed all of the company's productions until its closure in 1997. Deeply committed to the development of a contemporary Black physical theatre aesthetic, she instigated annual two-week training programmes for Black women, bringing in leading teachers and developing young performers' confidence and enthusiasm for the genre: 'We are trying something new: looking for a way to change British culture by enriching it with real Black experience, Black talent' (Wong in Goodman, 1993: 166).

Black Mime expanded in 1990 to create a Women's Troop (see Fig. 7.4) and then in 1992 Wong created the Ensemble which merged the men's and women's

FIGURE 7.4 Black Mime Theatre (Tracey Anderson, Cassi Pool and Arosemaya Diedrick) in *Drowning*, 1991. By kind permission of Denise Wong and Simon Richardson.

Source: Photo by Simon Richardson.

companies. The company exploited the potential connections between the street culture of 1980s Black urban communities (music, graffiti art, dance, film, video, comic strips and hip hop) and the techniques offered within physical theatre in order to create a playful and energetic style of their own. Black urban street culture grew out of contemporary urban experience and drew on skills from other traditions as it needed them. Black Mime Theatre's eclectic playing style meant that while the work clearly spoke to young Black communities it also appealed to a wider audience who enjoyed its vibrancy and willingness to engage with contemporary issues. Black Mime Theatre's work displayed a strong emphasis on immediacy and relevance; work that was rough but rooted: 'The emphasis on visual, rather than verbal, imagery meant that barriers based on age, race, class and so on could to an extent, be overcome' (Goddard, 2002: 46).

This was, of course, work that grew out of opposition to nearly two decades of Conservative government. As we have seen earlier, government arts policy had led to a commercial and subsidised theatre sector that had mostly capitulated and become enmeshed with sponsorship, income generation and business approaches to the arts. Outside pop music, street culture and dance, there was little contemporary arts activity that spoke directly to the life experience of Black people in Britain. The increase in Black theatre during the 1980s was in no small part due to very specific initiatives, such as the supportive climate provided by the Greater London Council (GLC). The GLC's support for women and for Black artists encouraged companies to explore the experience of these communities of people. Theatre of Black Women was founded in 1982, Talawa was founded by Yvonne Brewster in 1985, and Tamasha was founded by Kristine Landon-Smith and Sudhar Bhuchar in 1989.

Shank (1996: 3) describes an 'official culture' in Britain whose people were white and middle class, but is clear that 'This "official" view of British culture does not reflect its true complexity'. Goodman (1993) points out how Black Mime Theatre Women's Troop was influenced by a range of other cultures and traditions, but suggests, 'This is not to say that the Women's Troop has not been successful in expressing a "Britishness" in its work, but it is rather to question the notion of "Britishness" when there is so much cultural diversity amongst British people' (Goodman, 1993: 167). It is of note that Black Mime Theatre put considerable effort into their relationship with their audiences: they would contact local communities in advance of their arrival at a venue, offer workshops to local schools, colleges and community centres, and also were one of the few companies at the time to survey audiences and take account of their demographics (Goodman, 1993: 167). In fact, the McCann Matthews Millman report into UK mime audiences noted that: 'Of all the pieces of printed material shown to respondents, the BLACK MIME THEATRE leaflet appeared to do most to alter the respondents' perceptions' (1989: 65). The founding of the Women's Troop positions Wong as an important intersectional figure in UK mime. Goodman reports that when asked why she decided to form the Women's Troop, Wong referred to the conditions of professional life for Black female performers: 'As Black women performers in Britain, they haven't exactly been nurtured and trained to the point where they are full of self-confidence' (Wong in Goodman, 1993: 171). Goodman suggests that:

> When working in mime – a marginalized form of performance, without the safety net of a text – the identity between performers and characters, events on stage and in 'real life', is enhanced. When the performers are also black women, doubly marginalized by definition from the 'white male norm', that level of marginalization and vulnerability is further enhanced.
>
> *(1993: 171)*

Furthermore, as Wong suggests,

> when we add to that mime is still such a 'white' art form (there is still an appalling lack of black people, or women, working in mime), then what we're doing is very political, very challenging, very provocative . . . . It's amazing that in 1991 in a multi-cultural society, an art form [mime] still

remains almost exclusively white, and largely male. So Black Mime Theatre Women's Troop has to be political and also feminist, in some sense.

(Wong in Goodman, 1993: 172–173).

Nicola Abram highlights the importance of Black Mime's work in reconnecting mime with everyday life over technique: 'Black Mime Theatre . . . repurpose an art form commonly perceived to be eccentric and elitist in order to represent everyday practices. The minimalistic staging and simple mime have a defamiliarizing effect, promoting a critical perspective on these activities' (Abram, 2020: 137). The company's experience also reflects the power dynamics and systematic racism within the British Theatre industry at this time. Reflecting on the career prospects for the women she worked with in the Black Mime Women's Troop, Wong states that:

So many of these women haven't worked much, and it's not for lack of talent or energy. Black women are assessed in certain ways, by white people with a white vision of what black people are, or what 'black roles' should be. Some groups now try for integrated casting, but then black performers will tend to be rewarded for not disturbing the balance, not standing out too much. Multi-racial productions need black performers who can conform, blend in and just be noticeable, but not agitate. This kind of approach will make British theatre stagnate. Black culture can add a whole new dimension: maybe it's too great a threat.

(Wong in Goodman, 1993: 174)

Her own experience as an artistic director is also telling. She admits that she had a steep learning curve as a young Black woman placed in charge of a Black theatre company in the late 1980s. She acknowledges the support that she had from others in putting together funding applications, and in budgeting and running the company. It is easy to underestimate how vitally important this knowledge is and how difficult it can be to access it.

You were either in the know or you weren't. And if you weren't, you would struggle and struggle to get support. I'm sad to say that this lack of handing down knowledge created a closed shop that wasn't colour bound. And if it wasn't for people like officers within GLAA, Philip Bernays, and other officers who gave us support, we would never have got off the ground. It seemed ludicrous that those with the knowledge felt their positions were secure if they didn't support up and coming new groups. Everyone knows greater diversity creates inspiration and challenges the establishment norms.

(Wong, 2020)

The approach of the company was bold, brave and anti-establishment. Their work instinctively spoke to those who might be socially marginalised through a mix of class, gender and race – a 'warts and all' approach that apparently didn't always go down well within some parts of the Black community. Wong acknowledges the influence of Steven Berkoff on their work:

> He was very influential. It was his way of having that sort of direct impact on an audience and being very 'in your face' and unapologetic in his style of work. Also the work of Black director Rufus Collins was instrumental in creating a Black aesthetic that was instantly recognised by the audience. He paved the way for me to want to create a theatre that was very much about now rather than having aspirations to imitate the establishment aesthetic.
>
> *(ibid.)*

It is worth reflecting on the relative invisibility of Black Mime Theatre and the artists who came out of/after it. The written histories and records of this time contain scant reference to their work, with Goodman (1993) and Goddard (2003) being notable exceptions. The company was doubly marginalised as a small-scale and a Black touring company working within an art-form dominated by white people. Black Mime Theatre received generous funding from the Arts Council – £100,000 for the first year of the franchise period and continuing funding for the next five to six years. In funding terms, this puts them alongside other established mime and physical theatre companies such as Trestle and Théâtre de Complicité, a position not uniformly reflected in their critical recognition. The removal of funding in 1997–1998 forced a sudden and unexpected end to the company – a jolt that disrupted Wong's own career and meant that legacy and influence were harder to create and more difficult to map. There is little record of the reasons for the removal of funding – Wong speculates that it related to her taking some limited time off from the company for her own professional development, which may have been misconstrued as a lack of long-term commitment.

For Wong the reason for the company's success is fairly straightforward:

> it was the fact that we were able to start tapping in to our own experiences, and also the experiences of the Black community, and put those up on stage, and hold a mirror up to ourselves. We always spent time researching our subjects and set aside time for 6 weeks of training before embarking on each production.
>
> *(ibid.)*

At the same time, the company's work also proposed that mime wasn't just a white middle class art form:

> we're all part of this art form, and this art form speaks to all of us . . . it wasn't just Black audiences who were attending it was the whole spectrum of society who you would see attending our performances. I felt that it did speak to everyone. I would often get frustrated when watching establishment mime individuals/groups and wonder why black faces were missing on stage

238 All mimes are equal?

and in the audience? It felt like an art form with an 'old boys club' mentality and no one seemed to care until David Boxer (who worked and trained with Moving Picture Mime) saw young black kids body popping and thought if they can do that, they can do mime. He in fact created Black Mime for this purpose. I was lucky to be in the first tour alongside Carlton Dixon as a performer with David directing us in *Tall Stories*. That show created a buzz in the schools we toured and laid the foundations for an urban retelling of mime that spoke to today of today. Ours was a mime that energised and modernised mime, using dance, music, song and text with movement.

(ibid.).

Benji Reid and Hip-Hop Theatre

Benji Reid began as a body-popper and street dancer and then went on to train in dance at the Northern School of Contemporary Dance. He worked on several productions with Black Mime Theatre, as well as performing with the David Glass Ensemble and Trestle. Benji traces the explosion in robotics (a form of mime-based performance focusing on mechanical movements of the body and the isolation of specific limbs and body parts) to the 1970s, and the start of street dance and body-popping back to the early 1980s. He identifies both as specifically American influences, out of New York street culture: 'mime, popping and street dance had a really close relationship, especially in the '80s' (Reid, 2020). For Reid,

> robotics was actually a kind of separate entity, in terms of street dance. And then popping came along, that was almost like the 3D version, the new updated version. But it was using robotics as a basics, in terms of how you could animate the body, in terms of isolation, but then adding fluidity in terms of 1) different types of character, but 2) also in terms of how the body could wave.

(ibid.)

These forms represented key styles of movement performance that grew out of Black culture and spoke directly to young Black people. There are associations with traditional mime, and some mime teachers capitalised on these connections to offer classes that aimed to identify how mime technique might 'enhance' robotic and body-popping performance[8] (see the section on Desmond Jones in Chapter 6). For Benji, training in contemporary dance represented a way in to movement-based performance that seemed accessible and potentially offered a freedom to develop

---

8 Pat Keysell writes rather dismissively of performers, 'who have made a fetish out of "clics" and "snaps" and all kinds of extreme contortions of the body' (1990: 4). The emphasis on neutrality, purity and efficiency of movement in the French tradition needs to be understood as partly a culturally constructed position, which some might seek to use to justify such a critique of Black movement practices.

his own style. His dance training no doubt also represented a point of connection with David Glass, who had also trained as a dancer, but it was Black Mime Theatre that opened his eyes to the ways in which physical performance could be relevant to him and his own life experience. He recalls,

> I absolutely loved working with David Glass, but I was still a black young man working in a multi-cultural company. I wasn't necessarily speaking to things that were culturally relevant to me at that time. Working with Black Mime was where the cultural relevance came in – with the mime, and the story-telling and the singing. For me, I felt like that three years, between David Glass and the two years with Black Mime, was my holistic training into physical theatre.
>
> *(ibid.)*

After Black Mime Theatre and David Glass, Reid went on to work with Jonzi D in the mid-1990s, creating a series of performances including *The Aeroplane Man*, *Silence Da Bitchin'*, and *Cracked*. This was the start of what Reid identifies as hip-hop theatre: 'basically, I was one of the pioneers of hip-hop theatre. There was me and Jonzi as the pioneers of hip-hop theatre' (ibid.). This is an important moment in the development of physical theatre – what is significant is the way in which a cultural development of physical performance such as hip-hop theatre, which clearly has some association with physical theatre, evolves not within the conventional physical theatre field but on its margins, claiming its own space. Identifying it as hip-hop theatre both asserts its cultural difference and celebrates its own cultural roots, whilst also enabling mainstream (white) physical theatre to ignore its significance and its implications.

> Because the great thing about working in hip-hop theatre was that I could really flex my muscles as a director. I could start to work with what my vision was, or our vision was. Using the elements of hip-hop in terms of b-boying, popping, DJing, MCing – using them four elements, how do we introduce that into theatre that wasn't just about slapping a rap on top of a traditional theatre piece? How could we use rap as the basis of story-telling? So, we were using rhyme as a way of carrying the story, but we were also using popping and breaking as a way of animating it. For us it was a brand-new departure at that point in time; it was a great departure point in terms of what Black theatre could be. We were right at the very cutting edge of this new language called hip-hop theatre.
>
> *(ibid.)*

Since the end of the 1990s, Reid has continued to create innovative work, sometimes crossing over several disciplines, including photography (see www.benjireid. com). He formed his own hip-hop theatre company, Breaking Cycles, which was funded by the Arts Council until, in an echo of the fate of Black Mime Theatre,

240 All mimes are equal?

it was disinvested when the Council changed its funding strategy from Regularly Funded Organisations to National Portfolio Organisations in 2011.

Another black performer, Kwesi Johnson, also worked with Black Mime between 1995 and 1997. He also moved into Hip Hop theatre and his work reflects a similar attempt to combine contemporary Black culture, contemporary dance and physical theatre. Johnson trained at the Northern School of Contemporary Dance and also worked with Can*do*Co, Phoenix Dance and Lloyd Newson. He referred to himself as a 'griographer' – a term that combines Western notions of choreography with the African tradition of the griot[9] or storyteller, someone whose role would be both to entertain and to curate the oral histories and cultural traditions of the community.

Work opportunities for black performers

Having examined the work of Black practitioners such as Wong and Reid, and the successes of Black Mime Theatre, it is worth reflecting on the position of black performers in relation to work opportunities within the mime and physical theatre sector in the UK. Black Mime was one of a number of Black and Asian theatre companies funded at this time. However, opportunities for Black performers outside these companies during this period were still limited. This is not to say that companies did not employ Black performers or did not want to: Tyrone Huggins was one of the founder members of Impact Theatre and worked with Hesitate and Demonstrate; Josette Bushell-Mingo worked for Kaboodle; Leo Wringer and DeObia Oparei both appeared in Théâtre de Complicité's 1992 production of *The Winter's Tale*; and Benji Reid worked for Trestle in *Beyond the Blue Horizon* (1997). But, nonetheless the opportunities were limited and the work seldom tackled Black British life experience. Companies were not unaware of these omissions. In interview, Annabel Arden talked to us about the important role theatre director Annie Castledine played in pushing Théâtre de Complicité to become less 'white':

> Annie, of course, was way ahead of her time, particularly when it came to matters of diversity. She championed several really important black actors: Josette Bushell-Mingo, Patrice Naiambana, David Harewood, Jenny Jules amongst many others. She was always alert to the politics of identity. We worked with her on *The Winter's Tale*, which I directed. That was the first time that Complicité worked with black actors, we worked with DeObia Oparei and with Leo Wringer . . . it was Annie who was the influence on us. She would castigate us, 'You're so white, so suburban!' And we said, 'No.

---

9 The griot was a term that became more widely understood following the success of Youssou Ndour in the UK popular music scene. Ndour came from a griot family in Senegal, and became widely known in the UK following a number of collaborations with Peter Gabriel, Neneh Cherry and others in the 1990s.

We're not. We're from all over Europe', 'Yes, but you're all white and you're all middle class. You haven't got a political bone in your body.' I mean she was really tough with us.

(Arden, 2021)

Arden remembers 'wanting really to reach out . . . to make a multi-racial company of Complicité' (ibid.). The company's 1992 artistic policy statement referred to its equal opportunities policy and to holding 'exploratory workshops' in order to meet and work with more diverse performers. In her view, the difficulty in doing so was not any lack of talented and interested Black performers,

> but what we realized, of course, was that we made work that came from us, from a shared if varied culture, from who we were. Now, in order to have made the work we wanted to make, we didn't really know how to address those questions that would come up of difference, real difference, within the rehearsal room, to address all those questions of power, to really take it on, you know. We were instinctively self-protective, because we knew how we could make our work, and it was delicate, so we wanted to protect the creative process which we were just beginning to find out about. . . . You know, we were very privileged actually. To be able to spend that many hours a day, doing the stuff that we did, and not having to worry too much about money, wasn't just because there was some supplementary benefit. It was because we had large parental homes to live in.

(ibid.)

This honest, candid reflection on what it felt like trying to negotiate how to progress the development of a company from a particular social position speaks to several different perspectives on equality and diversity. The cohesion that comes from having shared experiences of devising and performing work is powerful and useful, but can get in the way of engaging other people in the process unless openness, equality and communication are worked on from the start. It also points to the economic challenges discussed elsewhere – who can afford to make work as an emerging theatre company. Arden also points out that the physical nature of the work inevitably brings the focus towards the body, which can then become a site for racial tensions, awkwardnesses and challenges:

> I think one of the difficulties at the time was our lack of political vocabulary concerning the body. You know, you do have to go through something when you work intimately, physically, with other people. I think you have to really encounter each other at a level beyond language. And the neutral mask (one of the core aspects of our training) was asking that: What happens when you put the mask on? And nobody was really able to interrogate what it might feel like for a black person to put that mask on.

(ibid.)

242 All mimes are equal?

Joff Chafer, who was a long-term member of Trestle during the 1980s and the 1990s, confirms that that company did have some diversity training: 'I think it must have been an Arts Council thing or an ITC thing' (Chafer, 2021). For him, one clear benefit was that,

> it did make you question, 'Okay so you're not allowed to positively discriminate, but you've got to get it out to places . . . if you're advertising . . . you've got to get it to the places where everybody has an equal chance of seeing it. And recognizing that just putting something in *The Stage* or in the back of *Total Theatre* or whatever isn't enough.
>
> *(ibid.)*

Given the obstacles facing them, it is perhaps not surprising that few Black performers chose mime and physical theatre as a form of performance to explore. As has been noted in Chapter 6, although Naseem Khan's 1990 report on training in mime made a number of important recommendations, there was a subsequent failure to consider how training opportunities could best cater for Black and Asian physical theatre performers. During this period the growth in street dance, hip-hop culture, Black contemporary dance, devised theatre and popular music provided more accessible outlets for young Black people's creativity.

Mime, physical theatre and interculturalism

UK Asian dance and physical theatre performance traditions have been largely overlooked in relation to the history of mime and physical theatre during this period, with the exception of the work of academics such as Royona Mitra (2015) and Phillip Zarrilli (1998), despite there being long and well-established histories to such practice. This period saw the steady development of traditional and contemporary Asian dance at professional and community level in the UK[10], as well as tours by some influential Asian companies, such as Habib Tanvir's Naya Theatre. These influences did not directly impact on much of the mime and physical theatre performance work created within the European lineage; but, if there were no Asian mime companies in the European sense of the word, that should not diminish the importance of Asian practices of dance and story-telling and the cultural value of these practices to the British-Asian communities and to later live art and performance practices[11]. Mark Evans recalls there being a vibrant and well-established Asian performing arts ecology in the West Midlands during the

---

10 At a professional level, the work of Akram Khan and Shobana Jeyasingh represents important examples.

11 Such as the work of Motiroti (founded in 1991), which combines visual art, live art performance and new technology whilst drawing on intercultural themes and Asian performance modes and traditions.

1990s, including the dance work of Sonia Sabri, Piali Ray, Nahid Siddiqui and Kusumika Chatterjee.

In some respects, one of the unintended effects of the International Workshop Festival, despite its intentions, may have been to 'other' or 'exoticise' Asian practices as ways for white middle-class performers to develop their skills and careers. Without the opportunity to examine in detail who attended these workshops it is difficult to draw definite conclusions. However, it is tempting to suggest that these events, rather than diversifying the field of performers, instead functioned to widen the cultural experience of white participants. Such widening is not without merit, but inevitably raises issues of parity of opportunity and access.

The impact of African, Asian and other non-Western dance/theatre over this period can also be seen in the rise of intercultural performance practice in the UK. This was evident through productions, projects and festivals such as: Pan Project, the early work of Trickster Theatre Company and the UK performances of the *Mahabharata* directed by Peter Brook (The Tramway, Glasgow, 1988). It can also be seen in the teaching of Eastern techniques by White practitioners such as Kenneth Rea and Philip Zarrilli, or through the teaching of expert practitioners of non-Western performance traditions at events such as the IWF (see Chapter 6). This intercultural physical practice has some of its cultural roots in the primitivism of Artaud, the artists of the early twentieth-century avant-garde and the contemporaneous fascination with Asian dance and somatic practices (such as yoga and Balinese dance drama). Intercultural performance, mime and physical theatre all shared a disappointment with what they saw as the morbidity of British theatre at this time. They also shared a conviction that new forms of theatre were needed that would challenge British cultural conventions, especially around the dominance of text and voice.

As early as 1973, the British Theatre of the Deaf produced *Under the Sun*, a show based on folktales from around the world and underpinned by a sense of the body as a universal reference point and by an anthropological interest in the diversity of theatre forms. This is indicative of the Eurocentric humanism[12] that informed much of the intercultural performance practice at this time. Triangle Theatre's 1994 production of *Tributaries*, featuring Carran Waterfield, Vayu Naidu and Joji Hirota, revealed the difficulties of making intercultural work where the performers' approaches are unable to integrate in a coherent manner (Trowsdale, 1997: 246). Heddon and Milling (2006) critique Théâtre de Complicité's focus on white European experience and what they perceive as the desire of the company to present this as representing a universal experience. They cite *Mnemonic* (2000) as an example of this – in particular the scene where the place of the anonymous ice-man, preserved in a display, is taken by members of the company in turn, implying that the ice-man

---

12 Humanism has been critiqued for espousing a universalist approach to human nature, ignoring significant cultural differences. Edward Said made the case for reclaiming humanism in a more democratic and socially inclusive form, whilst maintaining an ambivalence towards its tendencies ignore oppression and suffering in its pursuit of common ground.

244 All mimes are equal?

can stand for all of us and we for him. The thematic core of the show is suggested as the notion of the 'body as collective mnemonic, the lowest common denominator' (Freshwater, 2001: 218). Heddon and Milling ask to what extent such work performs 'a very significant political act of forgetting all the different bodies whose encultured forms were not represented by the company' (2006: 182). None of this is to suggest that such work was not well-intentioned, but that changes in political and cultural awareness of the power structures at operation in such exchanges have shifted our understanding of their potential implications.

Underpinning this interest in performance practices from around the world was a rise in the profile of performance studies and intercultural performance as academic fields. These were fields of study, research and practice that emerged from the work of theatre scholars such as Richard Schechner, and which opened up academic interest in intercultural and interdisciplinary performance (Schechner, 1985). Two UK companies are interesting to examine in relation to intercultural performance in this period.

Jamieson is very open about the ways in which Trickster's early work in the mid-1980s was inspired by the traditions of the Kwakiutl people, the indigenous First Nations people who inhabit(ed) what is now the western coast of British Colombia, Canada:

> the first two shows we did were based on Kwakiutl culture. And I think we did the first one and thought, 'My God, we could do that so much better, and much more profoundly'. And that was finding all those plundered incredible masks, which were all held . . . you know, because as we stretched our sticky hands around the Empire we confiscated their sacred goods, particularly their masks. So, we found these incredible masks and then started looking at these Edward Curtis photographs of these incredible rituals and this period, *Time of Lies*, when the whole community came together for this sort of communal storytelling. And it used lots of illusion and magic tricks and tunnels under the ground to make people appear and disappear. So, I think that that was the start of that journey.
>
> *(Jamieson, 2020)*

Jamieson is honest and open about the colonial associations implicit in this early work – what would in twenty-first-century terms be understood as cultural appropriation. The company was obviously inspired by the Kwakiutl traditions and the ways that masks, tricks and acrobatics were integrated into performance. In many senses their work represents an example of the ways in which many European theatre practitioners looked to the traditions of other cultures for ways of re-invigorating practices that had become tired, text-bound, lacking in physicality, dynamism or spirituality. This is certainly a trend that can be seen to have impacted on the work of Ariane Mnouchkine/Théâtre du Soleil and of Peter Brook's International Centre for Theatre Research in Paris. Trickster's work is by no means defined solely by their intercultural performances; nonetheless, it had a formative influence on their style and physicality.

FIGURE 7.5   Trickster Theatre Company (Robert Thirtle and Roger Ennals) in *Time of Lies*, 1982. By kind permission of Tessa Musgrave and Trickster Theatre.

Source: Photo © Tessa Musgrave.

Pan Intercultural Arts (initially known as Pan Project)

Pan Project was founded in 1986 by a group of performers interested in drawing together different cultural traditions to create performance for a multi-racial society. In contrast to Trickster, Pan Project was made up of performers and practitioners from a wide range of cultures and disciplines. Early members included the performers John Martin (who had trained with Lecoq), Gordon Case and Jacqui Chan and the dancers Ranjabati Sircar and Mala Sikka, as well as musicians and singers. Key figures within the company included the Nigerian dancer, choreographer and performer Peter Badejo and the Indian actress and dancer Mallika Sarabhai. Sarabhai toured her 1989 production of *Shakti – The Power of Woman* nationally and internationally, and also played the part of Draupadi in Peter Brook's *Mahabharata* for 5 years. Badejo arrived in the UK in 1989 from Nigeria, already a leading figure in African dance. He created an extensive number of African dance performances, and received an OBE for his contribution to this field.

The work of Pan Project was important and significant in the ways in which it promoted non-European traditions of physical performance and spoke to issues pertinent to diverse audiences[13]; it also had relevance for audiences seeking better

---

13 Franc Chamberlain (2020) recalls workshops with Pan Project in the 1980s that included Lecoq-based practice alongside Japanese Noh and Balinese Topeng theatre techniques.

246 All mimes are equal?

to understand the complex nature of multi-cultural Britain during the late 1980s and the 1990s. Its multi-cultural membership was a model for equality and inclusion which was trail-blazing at that time. Nonetheless, John Martin's vision of the Pan Project's intercultural performance as a 'process of meeting, cross-pollinating and producing new and relevant work' (2004: 4) now feels somewhat romantic in relation to the colonial power structures potentially at play within intercultural performance production.

Pan Project's inclusion of East Asian performers was also significant, as even fewer opportunities existed for people from these communities. Despite interest in the skills and techniques involved in Peking Opera and Japanese Noh and Kabuki theatre, and in the Chinese martial art system of Tai Chi, it was not until the founding of Yellow Earth (now New Earth) in 1995 that there was a movement-based company that sought to explore East Asian life experience and employ East Asian physical performers[14]. Yellow Earth also, in 1999, commissioned David Glass to direct an adaptation of Dennis Potter's *Blue Remembered Hills*. Performed by a multi-racial ensemble, the company explored a highly physical style based on Glass' own European performance heritage. Glass had previously worked on projects in East Asia with his own Ensemble (and continues to do so) and developed his own form of intercultural process[15]. The challenge, then as now, was to ensure that collaboration and exchange were genuine and did not privilege those already in possession of power.

Disability, mime and physical theatre

As a final section within this chapter, we will consider disability as a 'master sign' of difference, and one that has too often been socially employed to exclude performance by disabled people from the field of mime and physical theatre. We will reflect upon the impact of the physical work of companies such as the British Theatre of the Deaf, as well as the ways in which changes in policy and developments in disabled performance (e.g. Graeae and CandoCo) can be seen as paving the way for integrated productions such as DV8's *The Cost of Living* (2003), the Graeae/Paines Plough/Frantic Assembly production of *On Blindness* (2004) and the work of companies such as The Lawnmowers (formed as a community group on Tyneside in 1986, and as a theatre company in 2000).

Paddy Masefield, a disabled theatre director and administrator, wrote in a speech for an Arts Council event in 1992 how he was aware of three doors that would-be

---

14 Kumiko Mendl, one of the founder members of Yellow Earth, was inspired to explore mime after watching a Moving Picture Mime Show performance. She trained with Lorna Marshall at City Lit Institute in London and then at the Lecoq School.

15 In addition, both Complicité (*The Elephant Vanishes*, 2003) and Steven Berkoff (*Metamorphosis*, 1992) have produced work in Japan, with Japanese performers, each offering different approaches to collaboration and exchange.

arts workers had to negotiate. He describes the 'men only' door and the 'whites only door', and finishes by describing how

> the third door had no need of a sign. It merely had huge steps in front of it, high handles, impossibly heavy hinges, no raised lettering, narrow lifts inside, more stairs, sudden drops, cluttered corridors that led to inaccessible inner sanctums of power.
>
> *(Masefield in Pointon and Davies, 1997: 107)*

A powerful literal and metaphorical description of the problems facing many disabled performers who wanted to make and perform physical theatre (or any theatre) at this time. Even accessing the spaces in which workshops, classes and rehearsals happened could be a major obstacle. However, this is also a trajectory that points towards the later success of events such as the London Games 2012 Paralympic Opening ceremony and the Birmingham Rep/Ramps on the Moon production of Gogol's *The Government Inspector* (2016), all of which reveal ways in which the aesthetics of physical performance can be adapted and respond to the capabilities and needs of disabled performers over the following decades.

The Winter 1996/1967 issue of *Total Theatre* includes a multi-authored article entitled 'Physical Ability'. Adam Benjamin (at that time, artistic director of Can-*do*Co) starts his section of this article by stating how physical-based performance 'provides a particular set of challenges for performers with physical disabilities' (1997: 12). He suggests that the lack of confidence on the part of those leading disability performance groups to engage disabled people in physical performance meant that many disabled people resorted to sports for the opportunity to express themselves physically and to engage with risk and challenge. He writes, 'In Can-*do*Co we have made a conscious choice to pursue the highest levels of physical achievement with our students, and to create an environment in which risks can be taken' (ibid.: 13). This implies that during this period, misunderstandings around the needs and capabilities of disabled performers may have meant that there was a tendency on the part of non-disabled theatre makers either to over-protect disabled people, and/or to work to lower expectations of what they could do or achieve. Benjamin wryly suggested that, 'In many cases when someone falls out of a wheelchair there is a greater risk of heart failure in those watching than of any serious damage to the person who has just ditched' (ibid.: 12). He points out that the problem with caution over risk is that 'everyone can take part, but no-one can excel' (ibid.: 13). In the wider sector, the introduction of the 1995 Disability Discrimination Act meant that non-disabled physical theatre companies, venues and promoters needed to pay more attention to the needs of disabled audiences and artists. The introduction of Lottery funding, also in 1995, was welcome at a time when additional resources were needed. The fact that the funding forms included questions about access for disabled people was also an encouragement for companies to engage positively and actively with this agenda (Lucas, 1996: 13). However, the emphasis was often on the needs of audiences rather than creatives, and, until

248 All mimes are equal?

the 2010 Equality Act, there were still plenty of loop holes that arts organisations could use in order to avoid providing equitable and fair levels of access.

Graeae Theatre Company

Graeae Theatre Company was founded in Coventry in 1980 by Nabil Shaban and Richard Tomlinson. The company wanted to challenge popular misconceptions of disability that associated it with powerlessness and helplessness. Graeae's training was generally workshop based during this period – partly because that enabled control over content and ethos, but also perhaps because so few of the existing training institutions actively recruited disabled students. During the 1990s, Graeae had workshop sessions with Lloyd Newson (DV8), and a week-long training programme with Amanda Wilsher from Trestle Theatre (Lucas, 1997: 13). As a disabled-led theatre company, Graeae was alert to the particular lived experience of disabled performers. The reality of disabled people's experience in the late 1970s and early 1980s was generally that they would only be accepted into theatre on non-disabled terms (Tomlinson, 1982: 9). This means that at this time, the decision to make disabled theatre was in and of itself an act of resistance. Making theatre placed disabled people as 'initiators of activity, they are in charge, they can take control' (Tomlinson, 1982: 10). In the midst of a society that expected disabled people to be submissive and acquiescent, Tomlinson pointed out that 'performance gives power' (Tomlinson, 1982: 12). Although the company did not set out to be a physical theatre company, its work often fore-fronted the physicality of its performers and explored ways in which their particular movement potentialities could be integrated in to the shows and the thematic content. Disability can often be about physical differences; thus, physical presence is central to the visibility of disabled people on their own terms. At the point at which Tomlinson was writing, Graeae had only just begun to explore the use of mime and non-verbal communication. He explains that this was in part because there was little interest in 'developing movement for people with unusual gaits. Present practices try to make them seem more "normal"' (Tomlinson, 1982: 72). Over the following two decades, encouraged perhaps by CandoCo, the use of movement and physicality within the work of disabled theatre companies developed and expanded. Nonetheless, although some Graeae shows have been devised, the majority have been scripted with an emphasis on text and message, perhaps not unlike the work of other special interest companies such as Talawa and Gay Sweatshop. The use of scripts emphasised the companies' status as serious organisations making culturally significant work.

British Theatre of the Deaf

The British Theatre of the Deaf [BTD] makes an interesting case study for a number of reasons. Firstly, the common nature of the disability shared by the company members facilitated the exploration and development of a consistent physical style. Secondly, the nature of the shared disability also meant that the focus on mime was a natural fit for performers whose form of communication uses movement and gesture. Although relatively short-lived – the company had disbanded by 1977 – the history of the BTD draws together several themes and a number of important people in the history of UK mime. Unfortunately, it is a part of the history of UK mime and physical theatre that has been largely ignored; the language of Deaf people and the culture that springs from it has not been appropriately respected or understood[16].

The company began as the Royal National Institute for the Deaf (RNID) Mime Group, which was set up in 1961 by Pat Keysell (see Chapter 2). This Mime Group continued over the next few years, producing a number of successful amateur shows during the 1960s. However, the turning point came in 1968, when Keysell was funded by the Winston Churchill Memorial Trust to visit the USA. During her time there, she was heavily influenced by the National Theatre of the Deaf's use of 'sign-mime' – a form of heightened sign language:

> Sign-mime seems to me an ideal way through the limitations. It is capable of great pace, and strong enough to reach the back of a theatre without loss of impact. It is beautiful and exciting to a hearing audience, it makes them realise that deaf people are artistic, perceptive, intelligent because it conveys so much more than the average human voice – it is like music, it goes beyond speech.
>
> *(Keysell in Stewart, 2015: xix)*

On her return, she pushed for the group to be renamed the British Theatre of the Deaf, and for the instigation of an annual summer school to help develop skill levels and recruit new members. By 1974 the company had toured to the Edinburgh Festival Fringe and begun to undertake professional tours of their productions. The company was initially semi-professional, subsidised by the Royal National Institute for the Deaf and largely composed of older members who were retired and younger members who could fit classes and performances around their work commitments.

Claude Chagrin was one of the tutors on the first BTD summer school in 1969, and she persuaded Laurence Olivier to become patron of the company. As well as what she referred to as 'modern mime', Keysell also taught the group 'classical mime', which was probably more in line with Commedia, the mime of Marcel Marceau and with ballet mime – stock characters and situations, and a more expansive style. What places her work most convincingly within the Lecoq tradition is that for her mime provided opportunities for the sharing of experiences in learning how to mime actions – observation was recognised as an essential part of learning mime. Company member Ian Stewart recalls the work being watched in 1965 by Henrietta Fairhead, 'a well-known Mime and Dance Movement specialist

16 For a detailed history of Deaf sign language and its reception by the hearing world, see Rée (1999).

teacher' (Stewart, 2015: 27), someone rather more in the Ginner-Mawer tradition (see Chapter 2), who was impressed and wrote an appreciative article on the group's work. Keysell herself was drawn to the work of Lecoq and was impressed by the way that he trained his students 'to shed all imitation, all artificiality, all the tricks and manners, to strip mime down to the bare essentials of unadorned communication' (Keysell in Stewart, 2015: 39). In particular she perceived that Lecoq was 'more interested in what he calls "collective mime" and this was of immense value for the work I do with groups of deaf people who have a great gift for mime' (Keysell in Stewart, 2015: 39). Lecoq's vision of mime as a profound form built on observation and a deep understanding of the communicative power of movement resonated deeply with her sense that mime was not just a convenient tool for Deaf performers, but that it had the ability to convey meanings that went deeper than words.

The relationship between the work of the company and the world of mime in the 1960s and early 1970s is interesting and revealing. Apart from Chagrin's input, the summer schools also involved classes in Laban-based movement, mime classes with Ben Benison (who Keysell would have known from her work on *Vision On*), mask classes with Peter Bridgmont (who had worked with Joan Littlewood's Theatre Workshop) as well as lectures from special guests, such as the theatre director Clifford Williams[17]. It is worth noting that, according to Stewart, Deaf audiences were both supportive and critical of the work. Keysell was aware of the tensions inherent in being the non-disabled director of a disabled theatre company. She gave a talk on 'Mime for Deaf Children and Adults' at an Arts for the Benefit and Care of Disability event at Dartington in July 1978, in which she admitted that: 'I always speak or write about working with deaf people with very much mixed feelings nowadays because I am so aware of how much they prefer to speak for themselves' (Keysell in Stewart, 2015: iii). Holding the group together became an increasing challenge for Keysell. Despite her passion and ambition for the work, the challenges faced by the company come over very clearly in Keysell's letters – 'it is not so much that I am tired of the Theatre of the Deaf but tired of the impossible conditions under which we have to work' (Keysell in Stewart, 2015: 99). It proved increasingly difficult to sustain what was for too long an amateur company trying to work on a professional basis. It was not until January 1974 that the company received its first Arts Council grant of £3,000. The American National Theatre of the Deaf received $350,000, whilst BTD received, at most, no more than £12,000 from the Arts Council. Keysell left the company in March 1977, it was disbanded shortly after her departure. Disappointingly few obituaries of Pat Keysell reference her work with the RNID Mime Group and the BTD.

---

17 See Chapter 2 for more on Benison and Clifford Williams, and Chapters 2 and 4 for more on Keysell.

Moving towards a repertoire that consisted of sign-mime, pure mime, dance movement and poetry-signing, and towards the development of extended pieces, was important in defining a form of theatre that was not a limited version of conventional theatre, but that communicated in a distinctive way and developed performances in which the actors could excel. The turning point was achieved as audiences begun to accept the work in its own right and not make concessions for the performers being Deaf. In this respect, the achievements of the group are an important example of a wider movement within disability theatre to create work that celebrated the culture and life-experience of those making it.

Despite its problems, the work of the BTD had a legacy and it is possible to see evidence of its impact in the work of Deaf performers in the 1990s. Aaron Williamson, a Deaf dance performer who also taught for a period at Dartington College of Arts, wrote in *Total Theatre* of combining 'silence, utterance and movement into a bodily evocation of my own deafness' (Williamson, 1996: 14). The way Williamson describes his movement work is very reminiscent of the sign-mime developed by Keysell and BTD. The work of Graeae, BTD and Keysell has been important in terms of moving away from what Petra Kuppers describes as a 'theatre of socially acceptable comportment' (2017: 4), in which disabled people have their disability and their disabled identity trained out of them, repressing the expression of their disabled identity. Kuppers dismisses perceptions of disability as simply a reservoir of meanings, and argues for disability to be recognised as a way of being in the world. Mime and physical theatre have, for significant periods, been viewed as inaccessible for many disabled people, the result of 'a social imagination that did not conceive of disabled people (and others) as "citizens"' (Kuppers, 2017: 49) Kuppers argues that because of this, much disability performance happened on the edges and margins. The naming of BTD is in this respect complex as whilst it celebrates the identity of its members, it gives the impression that the work is not for a hearing spectatorship.

The histories of Graeae and BTD, and of other companies such as Mind the Gap (formed in 1988) and Heart n Soul (formed in 1987) point us towards the marginalisation of generations of disabled physical performers. During the last decades of the twentieth century we can note significant changes which challenged public and professional understandings of mime and physical theatre as activities only available to those who were non-disabled. The success of performers such as Kathryn Hunter (*Anything for a Quiet Life* (1987) and *The Visit* (1989), for Théâtre de Complicité), Tim Barlow (*My Army* (1989), for Théâtre de Complicité) and David Toole (*Can We Afford This?* (2000), for DV8) illustrated that change was possible. Hunter's career should indicate how disability need be no impediment to success as a performer within physical theatre and beyond, and Barlow showed how disabled life experience could be central to the making of theatre. Dominant concepts of virtuosity, agility, strength and beauty have been contested, as has the notion that disabled people are not best placed to represent their own physicality and their own life experience on stage.

252 All mimes are equal?

Conclusion

In writing this chapter, we acknowledge the need to discuss the histories and practices of difference and resistance. However, we also see these histories and practices as ongoing and continually present. This means being aware that within the writing of history we need to ensure that however difficult the histories of difference, exclusion and discrimination are they should always be included and recognised. Much European mime and physical theatre training draws on Western European notions of the neutral body – a concept derived from Jacques Copeau and Suzanne Bing's work in the 1920s and passed on through the teachings of Lecoq, Gaulier and others. The social models of gender, race and disability challenge the physical cultural hegemony implicit in some conceptions of neutrality. Both Mark Evans (2009) and Carrie Sandahl (2005) critique the concept of the neutral body as a notion that derives from concepts of industrial productivity and efficiency. As Ann Cooper Allbright puts it: 'Many of our ideas about autonomy, health, and self-determination in this late twentieth century culture are based on a model of the body as an efficient machine over which we should have total control' (Allbright, 1998: 65). This is a conceptual framework which immediately disadvantages disabled actors who wish to engage with the fields of mime and physical theatre. As Evans states:

> In so far as the disabled actor is culturally perceived as clumsy, awkward, inefficient, weak, or in any other sense incomplete, then that actor is a cause of anxiety for an industry which assumes bodies which are beautiful, graceful, responsive and efficient.
>
> *(2009: 105)*

The assumption is that being disabled is somehow inescapable, and that it cannot be written over.

> Implicit in the various manifestations of the neutral metaphor is the assumption that a character cannot be built from a position of physical difference. The appropriate actor's body for any character, even a character that is literally disabled or symbolically struggling, is not only the able body, but also the extraordinarily able body.
>
> *(Sandahl, 2005: 262)*

What has not been adequately recognised outside the field of disability arts and performance, is that physical theatre, of all the forms of theatre, has the most potential for playing with the distance between performer and character, revelling in the ways that different bodies represent on stage, and challenging assumptions about who can perform what and how.

This chapter has sought to reflect on the impact of the various obstacles to equality within mime and physical theatre during this period. These can be identified as:

- Low income for emerging artists (difficult for those from disadvantaged backgrounds – social class, disability, ethnicity/race);
- Lack of physical access (spaces for workshops and performances that were not accessible for disabled performers);
- Expectations around physical ability;
- The background of those in positions of power, such as artistic directors (often male, non-disabled, white and privileged);
- Accessibility of training (largely located in London and other large cities, little available free/low cost);
- Opportunities tending to be London-centric, involving high living costs;
- And the general public perception of mime as white, non-disabled, European and niche.

This lack of opportunity also created a shortage of role models. It took commitment and effort to bridge the divides represented by class, race/ethnicity, gender and disability, and only certain companies markedly succeeded in doing so.

This returns us to the importance of the stories of individuals as well as of the critique of organisational infrastructures. We must not lose sight of the individual artists and their struggles and successes, their lived experience as artists. Female, Black and disabled artists fought during this period to be allowed to define their own practice for their own audiences and to challenge theatre conventions and the social assumptions underpinning them. Mime and physical theatre might, in hindsight, have offered female, Black and disabled practitioners more creative opportunities to explore and express the lived experiences of their own embodiment, physicality and culture. That this did not happen as fully as it could have reflects not only on these art forms but also on the wider social, cultural and theatrical landscapes at this time and some of the long-standing structural and systematic inequalities that shaped them. Despite the marginalisation, the inequality and the under-representation, all these artists and companies formed a crucial part of the landscape we are writing about and their work appealed not only to their own communities but also to a wide and varied range of audiences beyond those communities. They were, of course, of this field and not apart from it, and should be recognised as such notwithstanding the marginalisation that they experienced.

8

CONCLUSION – THE RISE AND FALL OF MIME AS A CULTURAL PHENOMENON

For a period in the 1980s mime percolated into the popular consciousness and into popular culture. The general interest around mime at this time can, for instance, be evidenced in the ways in which it captured the imagination of pop artists and music video makers. The impact on popular music had started in the 1970s. Lindsay Kemp's relationship with David Bowie has been covered in Chapter 2; however, the singer Kate Bush also attended Kemp's classes in mime at the Dance Centre in Covent Garden in 1976, and Kemp helped her develop the movement work for her early performances. Arlene Phillips worked with Kemp and appeared in *Flowers* in 1974 before forming Hot Gossip, the dance troupe that made her famous. The mime group Shock[1] formed in 1979 and performed as a support act for Depeche Mode, Gary Numan, Ultravox, and Adam and the Ants. In 1982, Tik and Tok (formed by former members of Shock) started performing robotic mime[2] and working with Duran Duran, Depeche Mode and Vangelis. Peta Lily appeared in a number of iconic pop videos including: 'Video Killed The Radio Star' (1979); 'Vienna' (1981); 'While You See a Chance Take It' (1981); and, 'Planet Earth' (1981). Howard Jones employed a mime artist, Jed Hoile, to perform alongside him for his hit single 'New Song' (1983). In 1981 Simon McBurney, Neil Bartlett and Rick Kemp performed a clown show to 3,000 people in Hammersmith Palais as a warm-up act to the punk band Bauhaus – 'one of the most remarkable evenings of

---

1 Mime artists involved in Shock included Tim Dry (who trained with Desmond Jones and with Lindsay Kemp), Barbie Wilde (who trained with Desmond Jones) and Sean Crawford.
2 Robotic mime is the mimicking of mechanical movement. It eventually became more strongly associated with Hip-Hop dance culture, but in the late 1970s and early 1980s Mark Evans remembers it as an element of Decroux-based mime training at the Desmond Jones School. Some mime artists, such as Andy Sinclair, have made it a significant part of their performance offer (www.andyjsinclair.co.uk/index.html).

DOI: 10.4324/9780429330209-8

Conclusion – the rise and fall of mime **255**

my life' (McBurney in Giannachi and Luckhurst, 1999: 70). Mimes were able to work physically in response to the visual imagery that informed the music videos or gigs, and offered a heightened physical performance style that suited the tastes of the post-punk New Romantic period. By the late 1980s and the early 1990s, the success of popular black music and Hip-Hop culture meant that techniques such as robotics and body-popping had become very popular – Simon Murray remembers attending a short course in such techniques at Desmond Jones' school in London. Michael Jackson popularised the Moonwalk, the mime walk that was known in French as the '*marche sur place*', in 1983. In fact, Jackson had learnt the move from the British dancer Jeffrey Daniel (a member of the soul group Shalamar), who performed it on *Top of the Pops* in 1982[3]. The move has a long history in dance, going back at least until the 1920s[4].

By the 1990s, music tastes and popular interest in mime had changed quite profoundly. The role of mime in relation to popular music seemed to have been ceded to dance at some point during the late 1980s. The dancer/choreographer Michael Clark's collaborations with Mark E Smith and The Fall are one notable example of this shift. Dance-based physical theatre companies such as Frantic Assembly, founded in 1994, were more interested in contemporary club culture and the dance music that was part of it. DJ Andy Cleeton collaborated with Frantic Assembly, creating soundscapes for some of their work. He recalled how the first time he saw a Frantic Assembly show, he 'thought it was like being at the most exciting nightclub in the world' (Gardner, 1998: 15). Frantic, Volcano and DV8 all drew on contemporary popular music as part of the cultural references they wanted to embed in their work. The Wedding Present's music video for the song 'Brass-neck' (1989) indicates the growing influence of the sort of dance/physical theatre performance work that was emerging by the end of the 1980s[5].

Mime companies also drew on other forms of popular culture as sources for their work. In 1984 Mime Theatre Project (Andy Dawson and Gavin Robertson) created a mime version of the 1960s children's television series *Thunderbirds*, which toured extensively, and was revived in London's West End as late as 2000. Children's television provided several mimes with opportunities for work. In 1988

---

3 Jeffrey Daniel, in his ToTP routine, uses not only the 'moonwalk', but also mimes pulling on a rope and uses robotics, body-popping and ticking (breaking a movement into shorter sections punctuated by frozen moments).

4 It appears to have been variously used by performers, dancers and variety acts, and has links to the eccentric dance routines of Wilson, Keppel and Betty, to Chaplin's dance in *Modern Times* (1936), and to Max Wall's funny walks. The 'moonwalk' is thus representative of the fragmented, dispersed and culturally complex history of mime.

5 Interestingly, Théâtre de Complicité seemed more interested in classical music; for example, *Come In!*, the evocative music of contemporary Russian composer Vladimir Martynov, was used for *The Street of Crocodiles* (1992). This was undoubtedly influenced by the work of the composer and arranger Gerard McBurney (older brother of Simon and an expert in Russian music) as Music Director for many of their productions.

256 Conclusion – the rise and fall of mime

Wayne Pritchett[6] presented a television programme *Body Talk* for the BBC, using mime to assist young children to think about how their bodies worked; and Mick Wall, who trained with Lecoq in the 1970s, was involved in *Dizzy Heights* on Children's BBC from 1990 to 1993. Popular television comedians such as Benny Hill, Harry Worth and Tommy Cooper drew on a long history of visual gags and physical routines within UK variety performance, a tradition carried over into the final decade of this period by Rowan Atkinson's Mr Bean, a largely silent comic character first presented on UK television in 1990.

Finally, it is important to recognise the extent to which the mask also developed a place in popular culture during this period. Increasing interest in anthropology and psychology during the 1960s and 1970s, fuelled for example by Erving Goffman's work on the presentation of the self (1956) or Desmond Morris' popularisation of human anthropology (1969), meant that the notion of the mask as a cultural, social and psychological artefact gained significant traction in intellectual circles and within the popular imagination. Keith Johnstone's work on mask and trance (1981: 143–205) taps into this interest, although it is not an aspect of mask performance that interested Lecoq, whose work on masks tends to focus on the dynamics of the actor's performance rather than psychological or anthropological concerns. More broadly, the intellectual and political impetus for a cultural shift towards mime and physical theatre echoed a distrust of words and text and an enthusiasm for action, transformation and physical liberation that informed so much of the experimental theatre in the 1960s and pointed towards the postmodernism of the 1980s.

By the late 1990s, the corporeal mime of Decroux and the illusion mime of Marceau seemed to have declined in visibility and the field was dominated by the influence of Lecoq and Gaulier. By 1998, Annette Lust was reflecting in *Total Theatre* that Decroux's teachings were 'not fashionable in contemporary British theatre' (1998: 16). Theatre de L'Ange Fou, which was founded in France by Steven Wasson and Corinne Soum, who had trained with Decroux and worked as his teaching assistants, was based in the UK from 1995 until 2014. Their work was important and transformational for those that studied with them, but it is hard to trace an impact as persistent and wide-ranging as that of Théâtre de Complicité, for instance. The particular magic of illusion mime and the abstraction of corporeal mime had made sense in the austerity of the 1970s and the early 1980s – when funding was less generous and the public taste for 'fringe' theatre was focused on simple and direct staging. This kind of mime struggled however to connect with an audience and funders looking for innovation, spectacle and playfulness as the cultural economy started to thrive in the late 1980s and the 1990s. The taste for the various practices that were branded as physical theatre in the 1990s led to a ubiquity

---

6 Pritchett had started performing mime in 1963. In 1975 he studied mime with Desmond Jones and shortly after he went on to direct the Canadian Mime Theatre at Niagara-on-the-Lake, Ontario, until its closure in 1979. He was joint winner of the TV talent show *New Faces* on 25 March 1975.

and a multiplicity which eventually diluted physical theatre's identity as a separate form. By the second decade of the twenty-first century, it was integrated into a wide range of theatre practices – from young people's theatre to mainstream commercial theatre (e.g. *Warhorse* and *The Curious Incident of the Dog in the Night-time*).

At the same time that mime and physical theatre were gaining some audience recognition and being embraced by popular music and culture they were struggling to obtain traction in academic circles. Other European practitioners such as Grotowski, Barba, Meyerhold and Kantor were a little more attractive to academic researchers – their work was perceived as serious, complex, rigorous and dealing with challenging themes. Perhaps more importantly it did not eschew text. By comparison, the French mime lineage seemed to be regarded as niche in its rigid emphasis on silence (Decroux and Marceau), old-fashioned in its modernist aesthetic (Decroux) or populist in its focus on playfulness, improvisation and comedy (Lecoq and Gaulier). Physical theatre in Eastern Europe represented an intellectual robustness that UK professional practice (with the exception of a few companies) tended not to aspire to (as the context did not, for the most part, demand it). Knowledge of the work of Grotowski and those companies inspired by him (Odin Teatret, Gardzienice and Song of the Goat) has for instance been sustained through research and teaching in UK universities[7], despite its limited impact on professional performance practice, in ways that the work of Lecoq and Decroux generally has not.

Making content – mime and physical theatre about something

There was, in some quarters, an assumption that much of the UK mime and physical theatre work in the 1980s lacked political significance or depth and focused instead on the virtuosic physicality of the performers. Michael Billington, theatre critic for *The Guardian*, notoriously opined during a BBC programme on Théâtre de Complicité's production of *The Street of Crocodiles* (1992) that, 'the moral content of theatre is being subordinated to a display of technique' (Billington in 2002: 36). Billington was talking largely about the company's early work, but he was also wrong on two counts – firstly he had failed to acknowledge that mime and physical theatre shows were about something (e.g. loneliness, futility, failure, connection, vanity for example), and secondly, he ignored the ways in which the medium was part of the message (physicality is an ideal medium through which to explore such emotional states) thus perpetuating a dichotomy between form and content. Certainly, Lecoq himself was aware of the danger of pure technique – he recalled, in his book *Théâtre du Geste* (1987), demonstrating the technique of walking on the

---

7 For example, Nick Sales and Sandra Reeve (Exeter), Paul Allain (Goldsmiths and Kent), Adam Ledger (Birmingham), Jane Turner (MMU), Alison Hodge (Royal Holloway) and Nigel Stewart (Lancaster).

258 Conclusion – the rise and fall of mime

spot to a group in Padua, only to get the response from an old Italian actor, '*Che bello! Che bello! Ma dove va?*' ('It's good! It's good! But where are you going?'). Practitioner Peta Lily is clear that making mime and physical theatre was always about having something to say: 'From the beginning of my solo career, I wanted to make work that was about subjects, work that would invite emotional engagement and thought' (2020). She recalls how,

> Over the years, I realised how much personal compulsions or themes were informing each show. . . . A fear, a quibble or a worry often gave an unusual premise which would then incite a process of exploration and unfolding of story – with the underlying motive to connect and communicate to the audience.
>
> *(ibid.)*

For David Glass, the meaning of the work emerges within the process, not just as content but as the nature and quality of the experience given to the audience: 'for a little while, your training, your focus, makes them feel they have more focus . . . we're actually turning the audience into artists for a little while' (Glass, 2020). For Glass, the relationship with the audience is in essence therefore fairly simple:

> I realize that all theatre, all art, is really an evocation or a provocation. Provocation is like tickling someone. . . . You provoke laughter, you don't ask them to laugh, you provoke them to laughter. And you evoke worlds in their mind, you know, once upon a time . . . whatever, you evoke.
>
> *(ibid.)*

Even with work that aimed to be popular and accessible, such as the work of Black Mime Theatre, great care was taken to ensure that themes were researched and personal experience was appropriately mined: 'We would do huge amounts of research, lots of role-playing and personal excavation in terms of what our personal stories were and how they then related to the story or the nature of the work that we were making' (Reid, 2020). Denise Wong remembers that the process 'always started with an idea of the subject matter, what the play was going to be about' (2020). The idea might come from the news or a discussion:

> when we had the women's troupe, there was a discussion in the office where myself, the administrator and some volunteers were talking and we ended up discussing our mothers. And then we thought, that's going to be the next show – we're going to do a show on mothers.
>
> *(ibid.)*

Similarly, their show on alcoholism, *Drowning*, came about from an article that Denise had read in a newspaper. Then the process would develop outwards from the director's initial idea:

Conclusion – the rise and fall of mime   **259**

I would do research. Once the actors came on board they also would do some research. We'd go and meet with various organisations. We'd talk to them. We'd hear their experiences. Look at various texts that could support us. Then I would come up with a few scenarios and the actors would act them out. I would just pick the parts that I felt worked reasonably well and then would develop them.

(ibid.)

From the 1980s changes in the political climate in the UK made it difficult to get funding for the creation of overtly political theatre. However, there is a less obvious but none the less deep political message implicit in mime and physical theatre's rejection of set structures, the emphasis on playful relationships between all involved, and the choice of simple design aesthetics. As the focus for theatre makers shifted from party politics and the effects of wider socio-economic forces towards the politics of identity and the interpersonal (following Carol Hanisch's provocation that 'the personal is political' (1970)), it is perhaps no surprise that devising and making practices reflected some of that focus – turning towards '[g] roup dynamics, relationships, and interactions between people' (Oddey, 1996: 9). As companies brought more people into the devising process and acknowledged their creative contribution, they enabled the construction of a more richly textured vision, pulling in multiple perspectives and offering the audience a more complex and stimulating experience as a result. Toby Sedgwick probably speaks for many mime and physical theatre practitioners during this period, when he recalls that, 'subliminally we must have reflected aspects of that political agenda in our work, but we didn't consciously want to write about things that were happening in that time – although it was a huge period of change' (2020).

Devising allowed composition and dramaturgy to move away from strict linear narrative structures and to employ approaches drawn from dance (task-based building blocks and contact improvisation), fine art (aleatoric structures, visual composition, surrealism, abstraction, sculptural concepts, imagery), music (canon, rhythm, jazz forms), cinema (close ups, pans, montage) and games (loose set structures, audience engagement). By the end of this period, companies increasingly sought to integrate different art forms. This was in part a development shaped by the influence of postmodern theory and the flattening of hierarchies between forms of cultural expression but also supported by the influence of international companies from Europe and the USA as experienced through the London Mime Festival, the London International Festival of Theatre and the International Workshop Festival.

Companies such as Théâtre de Complicité clearly undertook a deliberate journey away from work that might be seen as trivial and comic towards grander themes with international significance (e.g. *The Three Lives of Lucie Cabrol*, *Street of Crocodiles*, and *Mnemonic*). As with many other companies, their work was very often the result of group improvisation, chance, play and a kind of fluidity around conventional notions of objects, characters and place – so that multiple physical imaginations cohered to create work that embodies a message of our physical interconnectedness. The idea of *complicité* is at the heart of the meaning of the company's work – it is more than just an approach to making theatre, it is a cultural and political statement about the importance of collaboration, connectedness and internationalism. Often in the company's work there is an implicit recognition and awareness of being European, and of the importance of this international identity as something worthy of interrogation and celebration. Although explicit in Théâtre de Complicité's work, much of the same ethos informs the work of other companies over this period – such as Trickster, DV8 and Trestle. For such companies, the physicality was the message – unruly, playful, transgressive and transformative, it provided audiences with a vision of the world that pushed against compliance, complacency and self-aggrandisement.

> By the mid '90s we had had over 15 years of Tory government and I am sure physical theatre developed out of a reaction to those times. In many ways, the form was anti-establishment. It *felt* anti-establishment. It wasn't about being pretty. It wasn't about playing by the rules. I guess it was sort of the equivalent of what was happening with the rise of Punk. It felt like the form was kicking back against something, that we had something that needed to be said.
>
> *(Steel, 2020)*

Through all this work, meaning emerges through the process. The challenge with improvisational and task-based work is always how to develop beyond a series of short sections that appear only thematically linked. The use of tasks or building blocks can however enable meaning to be layered as happy accidents arise and different sequences overlap. Meanings are seldom handed to audiences on a plate or fixed early on but rather allowed to percolate as the movement sequences are worked on. The dramaturgical coherence of productions is a collaborative effort, shaped by a director but from multiple sources.

Critical reception

The critical reception for mime and physical theatre has always been mixed: 'Audiences liked it, critics generally didn't' (Rae, 2020). Mime's position somewhere between dance and theatre in the funding structures was also reflected in the recognition given by the press and media – in the 1960s and 1970s, it tended to fall to dance critics to review mime. One of the most supportive of these was Fernau Hall (1915–1988), the dance critic of The Daily Telegraph. His reviewing helped to put mime on the cultural map. He was interested in all kinds of visual theatre, from a range of cultural heritages. For Nola Rae, Hall was, '[q]uite instrumental in getting mime better known' (Rae, 2020). She recalls that a lot of other papers simply were not interested – they likened mime to circus, and they didn't review circus.

The challenge came as mime started to break out of its traditional formats, so that the alignment with dance started to look less and less appropriate or convincing: 'When we came on the scene it was quite interesting, because the only critics were dance critics, it wasn't under the auspices of theatre at all, they didn't know how to categorise what we did' (Sedgwick, 2020). This complicated things, because the importance of good reviews and media attention was clear, yet mime was arising in a new space somewhere between dance, theatre, comedy and variety. John Ashford pointed out in the early 1980s that the 'division between "straight", respectable theatre and popular entertainment has left the British critic without a basic approach to work which is not necessarily about what is done but about the way it is done' (John Ashford in Craig, 1980: 98). The arrival of the London listing magazines *Time Out* (in 1968) and *City Limits* (in 1981) began a change that certainly benefitted London-based mime artists. Having work listed under distinct headings made it easier to find, and these new publications were quite happy to list almost everything that was submitted. The reviewers for these magazines came with a more open mind towards work that didn't fall easily into the old compartments. The combined effect of this was to create profile and recognition for the artists and to develop a knowledgeable and devoted audience base. Reviewers such as Lyn Gardner[8], who was a founding member of *City Limits* magazine, and Judith Mackrell, a dance critic who reviewed much of DV8's early work for *The Guardian* in the 1990s, were both supportive of the new work that emerged at this time. *Time Out* and *City Limits* spoke to a particular London demographic – young, urban and looking for the latest thing to see. Thus, the opportunities for reviews and coverage were another reason why mime activity tended to gravitate towards London and the kinds of festivals that might attract critical attention (Edinburgh Fringe, London Mime Festival and some of the regional events). *Total Theatre* magazine offered reviews of a range of work within the field, and although its readership was essentially other mime and physical theatre practitioners, it did offer reviews from a more informed perspective. In this respect, *Time Out*, *City Limits* and *Total Theatre* represent additional symptoms of the economic, cultural, administrative, funding and artistic shifts that have been identified throughout this book. These publications recognised the needs of a new generation of performers/makers, administrators and audiences – a generation with increased access to higher education, less restricted travel, better funding, numerous small-scale venues and with a desire for new kinds of artistic experience.

Mime and physical theatre into the new millennium

After 2000, mime and physical theatre skills and techniques increasingly became integrated into the wider theatre ecology. Julian Chagrin reflected on the way that mime's influence seemed to dissolve over time when we interviewed him for this book: 'Mime didn't become anything actually. There were just a few good people doing it. But as a thing, it didn't really become anything' (Chagrin, 2020). As

---

8 Gardner went on to be a critic for The Independent, and in 1995 joined *The Guardian*, where she took the lead on reviewing alternative and fringe theatre work. Since 2017 she has written for *The Stage*.

262 Conclusion – the rise and fall of mime

text and words became much more prominent in mime and physical theatre, their 'purity' as forms became less obvious and less compelling. As a result the terms became increasingly vague and imprecise and companies gradually became less comfortable with the nomenclature. Although physical theatre remained popular within schools and colleges after 2000 (largely due to the willingness of companies to undertake extensive education work), the long-term cultural dominance of text, the interests of funders and venue programmers, and the decline of the small-scale touring circuit all made mime and physical theatre hard as career choices. In addition, the arrival of digital technology started to move interest away from the body and towards the virtual. Although some practitioners, such as Simon McBurney, have found ways of integrating the digital and the physical, in general digital technology has complicated the notions of the authentic physical body as the primary site for experience. Annabel Arden believes that Simon McBurney's work with digital technologies,

> is so good because it's deeply embedded, deeply physically integrated into the show. Simon has been experimenting with video imagery and the use of live cameras on stage even as early as *The Street of Crocodiles*. The recent shows have a complex narrative which makes it clear to the audience where the images originate – and tie them to the action through the agency of the actor. So the medium becomes PLAYFUL.
>
> *(Arden, 2021)*

Total Theatre magazine continued publishing into the new millennium, finally ceasing to produce printed issues in 2012; however, by this time the magazine had become a forum for virtually all practices outside the mainstream theatre and offers an illustration of the ways in which mime and physical theatre had become subsections of something much bigger, more amorphous and harder to define. We can imagine Desmond Jones decrying this tendency as dissipation, a diminution of a form with sharp and well-defined skills and aesthetics.

A trawl through the pages of *Total Theatre* reveals long lists of the many companies that have come and gone over this period and into the first decade or so of the new century. It would be foolish and naive to claim that all UK theatre has been influenced by mime and physical theatre, and yet equally wrong to ignore the shift that has happened. Some of the successful movement directors of the twenty-first century cut their teeth in the physical theatre field (e.g. Toby Sedgwick and Steven Hoggett), and movement direction has become a central and integrated feature of many productions over the last decade or so. Recognising the body in performance, means recognising *all* bodies and what they signify – the integration of physical theatre practice has run concurrent to the ways in which multiple and diverse types of bodies and physicalities are increasingly recognised and celebrated in UK theatre. At the point at which we write a number of huge global shifts, variously informed by the COVID-19 pandemic, the #MeToo movement and the Black Lives Matter movement, have led to calls for radical change within theatre training and production. Theatre and performer training are in a period of unsettlement and acute self-examination unlike anything they have experienced for a long time. Though highlighted by current events, it is possible to see this predicament as only the end of a slow process that has been unfolding for some time. David Glass stated 25 years ago that

> [t]heatre is our attempt to literalise that which is an internal world for us. . . . But I do think theatre is dying in conventional terms. . . . I don't think theatre has any great value in our society any more. . . . You are more likely to see theatre at a rock concert, or on a street corner or in a refugee camp. People don't want to be spectators, they want to be 'spect-actors', to be involved. In workshops when I teach it's like a piece of theatre where everyone is the actor and the audience at the same time. And I like that.
>
> *(Glass in Olsen, 1997: 11)*

The companies that survived into the 2000s, such as Théâtre de Complicité and Frantic Assembly, continued to evolve, with key members leaving and the work changing in response to new challenges and opportunities. For Complicité, Annabel Arden states:

> I don't think it could ever have stayed together as a company – in its original form – and I think that was the secret of its success. Because everybody had such individual creative drive and talent, it was bound to spin off into a million directions. The interesting thing is how we have continued to regroup and reform creative partnerships over a forty year period. I co-directed with Simon in Berlin at the Schaubühne in 2020 having not worked so closely with him for 20 years almost. In his current project he will re-unite with many longstanding colleagues. The movements of the tribe are unpredictable but, in a way, cyclical.
>
> *(Arden, 2021)*

Finally, as we enter a period of profound and radical challenge within the theatre arts (equality/diversity, climate change/energy crisis, war/forced migration, gender violence/culture wars, political/economic uncertainty), we might want to reflect on the ways in which physical performance could help find cultural articulation for such traumatic experiences, the interrogation and celebration of diverse identities, and new ways of making/creating. Mime and physical theatre can be seen as theatre forms that mirrored the traumatic experience and memory of early twentieth-century crises such as the Spanish Flu pandemic and First World War. Aspects of mime can be interpreted as allegorising such past experience – for example, the way that Lecoq's training integrates themes of exodus and explores the contemporary relevance of the tragic chorus. In such contexts, physical performance can act as a place of repair, solace and expression, and also as a space that suggests what is not present, what has been lost, silenced or removed. It will be interesting to see whether these new challenges rejuvenate an interest in what physical theatre has to offer.

BIBLIOGRAPHY

Abram, Nicola (2020) *Black British Women's Theatre: Intersectionality, Archives, Aesthetics*, Basingstoke: Palgrave Macmillan.

Alfreds, Mike (1979) *A Shared Experience: The Actor as Storyteller* (Theatre Papers – The Third Series (1979–80), no. 6), Dartington: Dartington College of Arts.

Allain, Paul (1997) *Gardzienice: Polish Theatre in Transition*, London: Routledge.

Allbright, Ann Cooper (1998) 'Strategic Abilities: Negotiating the Disabled Body in Dance', in Dils, and Allbright (eds.), *Moving History/Dancing Cultures: A Dance History Reader*, Middletown, Co: Wesleyan University Press, pp. 56–66.

Ansorge, Peter (1975) *Disrupting the Spectacle*, London: Pitman.

Arts Council England (ACE) (1992) *Towards a National Arts and Media Strategy*, London: Arts Council England.

Aston, Elaine (1995) *An Introduction to Feminism and Theatre*, London: Routledge.

Baldwin, Jane (2003) *Michel Saint-Denis and the Shaping of the Modern Actor*, London and Westport: Praeger.

Barba, Eugenio (1986) *Beyond the Floating Islands*, New York: PAJ Publications.

Barker, Clive (1977) *Theatre Games: A New Approach to Drama Training*, London: Methuen.

Bausch, Pina (2007) 'What Moves Me', *Acceptance Speech at the Kyoto Award Ceremony*. Available at: www.pinabausch.org/post/what-moves-me. Accessed: 9 August 2022.

Benjamin, Adam (1997) 'Physical Ability: CandoCo Dance Company', *Total Theatre*, 8(4), 12–13.

Berkoff, Steven (1995) *Meditations on Metamorphosis,* London: Faber and Faber.

Berkoff, Steven (1996) *Free Association: An Autobiography*, London: Faber and Faber.

Blunt, Neil, and MAG (1993) *UK Mime and Physical Training Directory*, London: MAG.

Boal, Augusto (1992) *Games for Actors and Non-Actors*, London and New York: Routledge.

Braun, Edward (1969) *Meyerhold on Theatre* (translated and edited by Edward Braun), London: Eyre Methuen.

Brook, Peter (1968) *The Empty Space*, Harmondsworth: Penguin Books.

Brown, Bryan (2018) *A History of the Theatre Laboratory,* New York: Routledge.

Bruford, Rose (1958) *Teaching Mime*, London: Methuen.

Butler, Judith (1990) *Gender Trouble: Feminism and the Subversion of Identity*, New York: Routledge.

Butler, Judith (1993) *Bodies That Matter: On the Discursive Limits of 'Sex'*, London: Routledge.

Callery, Dymphna (2001) *Through the Body: A Practical Guide to Physical Theatre*, London: Nick Hern Books.

Carter, Huntly (1925) *The New Spirit in the European Theatre 1914–1924: A Comparative Study of the Changes Effected by War and Revolution*, London: Ernest Benn.

Chafer, Joff, and Wilsher, Amanda (1994) *Trestle Theatre Company: Teachers' Pack*, Barnet: Trestle Theatre Company.

Chamberlain, Franc, and Yarrow, Ralph (2002) *Jacques Lecoq and the British Theatre*, London: Routledge.

Chisman, Isabel, and Wiles, Gladys (1934) *Mimes and Miming*, London: Thomas Nelson and Sons.

Clements, Paul (1983) *The Improvised Play: The Work of Mike Leigh*, London: Methuen.

Climenhaga, Royd (2013) *The Pina Bausch Sourcebook: The Making of Tanztheater*, New York: Routledge.

Climenhaga, Royd (2018) *Pina Bausch*, Abingdon and New York: Routledge.

Cohn, Ruby (1975) 'The Triple Action Theatre Group', *Educational Theatre Journal*, 27(1), 56–62.

Communicado Theatre Company (2021) *Communicado Theatre Company: About.* Available at: https://communicadotheatre.co.uk/about/. Accessed: 29 October 2021.

Complicite (2003) *Complicite Plays 1: Street of Crocodiles, Mnemonic, The Three Lives of Lucie Cabrol*, London: Bloomsbury.

Complicité (2022) *Complicité: Education.* Available at: www.complicite.org/education.php. Accessed: 29 March 2022.

Cook, Jonathan Paul (n.d.) *Jonathan Paul Cook on Footsbarn, Communal Living, and Rural Theatre.* Available at: www.artcornwall.org/interviews/Jonathan_Paul_Cook.htm. Accessed: 5 April 2022.

Cox, Peter (2002) *Origins Dartington College of Arts*, Dartington: Dartington College of Arts.

Craig, Sandy (ed.) (1980) *Dreams and Deconstructions: Alternative Theatre in Britain*, Ambergate: Amber Lane Press.

Crawley, Marie-Louise (2020) 'Dance as Radical Archaeology', *Dance Research Journal*, 52, 88–100.

David Glass Ensemble (2020) *David Glass Ensemble: Education and Partnerships.* Available at: http://davidglassensemble.co.uk/wp-content/uploads/2020/07/Learning-PDF-Updated-29-July-2020.pdf. Accessed: 25 March 2022.

David Glass Ensemble (2022) *Lost Child.* Available at: https://davidglassensemble.co.uk/projects/lost-child/. Accessed: 28 February 2022.

Dawson, Sarah (1993) 'In Conversation With Pete Brooks', *Total Theatre*, 5(2), 8.

Dawson, Sarah (1994) 'IOU Outdoors', *Total Theatre*, 6(2), 6.

Donahue, Thomas (2007) *Jacques Copeau's Friends and Disciples: The Théâtre Du Vieux-Colombier in New York City, 1917–1919*, New York: Peter Lang.

Dorcy, Jean (1961) *The Mime*, New York: Robert Speller and Sons.

Dorney, Kate, and Merkin, Ros (eds.) (2010) *The Glory of the Garden: English Regional Theatre and the Arts Council 1984–2009*, Cambridge: Cambridge Scholars Publishing.

Drijver, Rieks (1998) 'Theatre of the Imagination', *Total Theatre*, 10(2), 14–15.

Drljaca, Mileva (1993) 'Challenged and Acting', *Total Theatre*, 5(1), 13.

Etchells, Tim (1999) *Certain Fragments: Contemporary Performance and Forced Entertainment*, Abingdon and New York: Routledge.

266 Bibliography

Evans, Mark (2009) *Movement Training for the Modern Actor*, Abingdon: Routledge.

Evans, Mark (2015) 'The Myth of Pierrot', in Crick, Olly, and Chaffee, Judith (eds.), *The Routledge Companion to Commedia dell'Arte*, New York: Routledge.

Evans, Mark (2017) *Jacques Copeau*, New York: Routledge.

Evans, Mark, and Fleming, Cass (2019) 'Jacques Copeau', in Pitches, Jonathan (ed.), *The Great European Stage Directors: Copeau, Komisarjevsky, Guthrie* (Vol. 3), London: Methuen.

Evans, Mark, and Kemp, Rick (2016) *The Routledge Companion to Jacques Lecoq*, Abingdon: Routledge.

Felner, Mira (1985) *Apostles of Silence: The Modern French Mimes*, London: Associated University Presses.

Forced Entertainment (n.d.) *About Us*. Available at: www.forcedentertainment.com/about/. Accessed: 20 January 2022.

Forgan, Liz (2016) *The Arts Council at 70: A History in the Spotlight 31 May 2016* (London: Cultural Trends & King's College London). Available at: www.kcl.ac.uk/cultural/resources/reports/the-arts-council-at-70-report.pdf. Accessed: 5 May 2022.

Frazer, James George (1890) *The Golden Bough*, London: Macmillan and Co.

Freshwater, Helen (2001) 'The Ethics of Indeterminacy: Theatre de Complicité's Mnemonic', *New Theatre Quarterly*, XVII(3), 212–218.

Frost, Anthony, and Yarrow, Ralph (1990) *Improvisation in Drama*, Basingstoke: Macmillan.

Fry, Michael (2015) 'Théâtre de Complicité', in Saunders, Graham (ed.), *British Theatre Companies 1980–1994*, London: Bloomsbury, pp. 165–188.

Gardner, Lyn (1998) 'They're No Angels', *The Guardian*, 14–15.

Gaskill, William (1988) *A Sense of Direction: Life at the Royal Court*, London: Faber and Faber.

Gaulier, Philippe (2006) *Le Gégèneur: Jeux, lumière, théâtre/The Tormentor: Le jeu, Light, Theatre*, Paris: Éditions Filmiko.

Giannachi, Gabriella, and Luckhurst, Mary (eds.) (1999) *On Directing*, London: Faber and Faber.

Gilbert, Helen (1996) *Post-colonial Drama: Theory, Practice, Politics*, London: Routledge.

Ginner, Ruby (1963) *The Technique of the Revived Greek Dance*, London: The Imperial Society of Teachers of Dancing.

Goffman, Erving (1956) *The Presentation of Self in Everyday Life*, Edinburgh: University of Edinburgh Press.

Gordon, Mel (1974) 'Meyerhold's Biomechanics', *The Drama Review: TDR*, 18(3), 73–88.

Graham, Scott, and Hoggett, Steven (2014) *The Frantic Assembly Book of Devising Theatre* (2nd edition), Abingdon and New York: Routledge.

Grantham, Barry (2000) *Playing Commedia: A Training Guide to Commedia Techniques*, London: Nick Hern Books.

Greer, Germaine (1970) *The Female Eunuch*, London: Palladin.

Grotowski, Jerzy (1969) *Towards a Poor Theatre*, London: Eyre Methuen.

Hall, John, and Murray, Simon (2011) 'Arts for What, for Where, for Whom: Fragmentary Reflections on Dartington College of Arts, 1961–2010', *Theatre, Dance and Performance Training*, 2(1), 54–71.

Hanisch, Carol (1970) 'The Personal Is Political', in Firestone, Shulamith, and Koedt, Anne (eds.), *Notes from the Second Year: Women's Liberation*, New York: Radical Feminism, pp. 76–78.

Heddon, Dee and Milling, Jane (2006) *Devised Theatre: A Critical History*, Basingstoke: Palgrave Macmillan.

Hodge, Alison (2010) *Actor Training* (2nd edition), Abingdon and New York: Routledge.

Hunt, Albert (1976) *Hopes for Great Happenings: Alternatives in Education and Theatre*, London: Eyre Methuen.

Bibliography 267

Jamieson, Nigel (1984) *Draft letter to Jane Nicholas at Arts Council in MAGazine* (Autumn)

Jenkins, David, Legge, Meg, and Palmer, Scott (1988) *The Kosh at Trinity,* Coventry: University of Warwick (unpublished draft).

Johnstone, Keith (1981) *Impro: Improvisation and the Theatre*, London: Eyre Methuen.

Jones, Desmond (1985) 'Alive and Kicking', *Magazine*, p. 4.

Jones, Desmond (1991) 'The London International Mime Festival – A Retrospective', *Total Theatre*, 3(1), 9.

Jones, Desmond (n.d.) 'Course Information Document' (unpublished).

Kabosh (2021) *Kabosh: About Us.* Available at: https://kabosh.net/about-us/. Accessed: 22 November 2021

Keefe, John (1991) 'A Way Through the Mimefield: The Mime Training Report', *Total Theatre*, 3(3), 4.

Keefe, John (1995) *Moving Into Performance Report*, London: Mime Action Group.

Kemp, Sarah (2022) 'Unpublished Correspondence with Authors', 25 March 2022.

Keysell, Pat (1990) *Mime Over Matter: A Mime Workshop Book*, London: John Clare Books.

Khan, Naseem (1990) *A Way Through the Mimefield: The Mime Training Report*, London: Arts Council England.

King, Miriam (2004) 'Cos I'm a Woman, W-O-M-A-N', *Total Theatre*, 16(1), 6–8.

Kipnis, Claude (1974) *The Mime Book*, London: Harper Colophon Books.

Kitowska-Łysiak, Małgorzata (2022) 'Tadeusz Kantor', *Culture.pl: Artists.* Available at: https://culture.pl/en/artist/tadeusz-kantor. Accessed: 29 November 2022.

Kuppers, Petra (2001) *Disability and Performance*, London: Harwood Academic Press.

Kuppers, Petra (2017) *Theatre & Disability*, Basingstoke: Palgrave.

Lang, John (1994) 'The Next Wave in Prague', *Total Theatre*, 6(3), 20–21.

Lawson, Joan (1957) *Mime: The Theory and Practice of Expressive Gesture*, London: Pitman.

Leabhart, Thomas (1989) *Modern and Postmodern Mime*, Basingstoke: Macmillan.

Leabhart, Thomas (2019) *Etienne Decroux* (2nd edition), Abingdon and New York: Routledge.

Leach, Robert (2006) *Theatre Workshop: Joan Littlewood and the Making of Modern British Theatre*, Exeter: Exeter University Press.

Lecoq, Patrick (2016) *Jacques Lecoq: un point fixe en Movement*, Paris: Actes Sud-Papiers.

Lewis, Tim (2016) 'Interview – Lindsay Kemp: 'I Was Destined for Stardom . . . I'm Still Waiting for It'', *The Observer*, 24 April. Available at: www.theguardian.com/stage/2016/apr/24/lindsay-kemp-destined-for-stardom-david-bowie-kate-bush. Accessed: 3 February 2022.

Lily, Peta (n.d.) 'Peta Lily: Invention and Re-invention', *Total Theatre*. Available at: http://totaltheatre.org.uk/archive/recollections/peta-lily-invention-and-re-invention. Accessed: 16 December 2021.

Lucas, C (1997) 'Physical Ability: Graeae Theatre Company', *Total Theatre*, 8(4), 13.

Luckhurst, Mary, and Veltman, Chloe (eds.) (2001) *On Acting: Interviews with Actors*, London: Faber and Faber.

Lust, Annette (1998) 'Decroux and the Art of Articulation', *Total Theatre*, 10(2), 16–17.

Lust, Annette (2000) *From the Greek Mimes to Marcel Marceau and Beyond: Mimes, Actors, Pierrots, And Clowns: A Chronicle of the Many Visages of Mime in the Theatre*, Lanham: Scarecrow Press.

Macintosh, Fiona (2011) 'The Ancient Greeks and the 'Natural'', in Carter, Alexandra, and Fensham, Rachel (eds.) *Dancing Naturally: Nature, Neo-Classicism and Modernity in Early Twentieth Century Dance*, Basingstoke: Palgrave Macmillan.

Magdalena Project (2018) *Background*. Available at: www.themagdalenaproject.org/en/content/background. Accessed: 21 January 2022.

Marchant, Graham (2001) 'The Funding of Drama Student Training in Britain', *New Theatre Quarterly*, 17(65), 31–44.

Matthews, John (2012) 'What is a Workshop?', *Theatre, Dance and Performance Training*, 3(3), 349–361.

Mawer, Irene (1925) *The Dance of Words*, London: Dent & Sons.

Mawer, Irene (1936) *The Art of Mime: Its History and Technique in Education and The Theatre*, London: Methuen & Co.

McBurney, Simon (1994) *Live 1*, London: Methuen, pp. 13–24.

McBurney, Simon (2008) *A Disappearing Number*, London: Bloomsbury.

McCann Matthews Millman (1989) *The UK Mime Audience: Qualitative Research Findings and Report*, Cardiff: McCann Matthews Millman.

McCann Matthews Millman (1991) *Marketing Mime: Promoters and Practitioners – Working in Partnership*, Cardiff: McCann Matthews Millman.

McCann Matthews Millman (1992) *Mime Audience Survey: Quantitative Research Report 1991/92*, Cardiff: McCann Matthews Millman.

McCaw, Dick (1994) *Report on 1994 Festival. Personal document for International Workshop Festival* (Unpublished).

McCaw, Dick (1996) 'Dear *Total Theatre*: A Fraternal Reply to Rivca Rubin', *Total Theatre*, 8(2), 19.

McCaw, Dick (1998) *10th Anniversary Celebrations/Report. Personal Document for International Workshop Festival* (Unpublished).

McGrath, John (1981) *A Good Night Out: Popular Theatre: Audience, Class and Form*, London: Methuen.

Mime Action Group (MAG) (1995) *The Mime, Physical Theatres and Visual Performance Project. Report from MAG to Northern Arts Board*, London: MAG.

Mime Forum Scotland (1995) *Mime Forum News*, Edinburgh: Mime Forum Scotland.

Mitra, Royona (2015) *Akram Khan: Dancing New Interculturalism*, Basingstoke: Palgrave Macmillan.

Morris, Desmond (1969) *The Naked Ape: A Zoologist's Study of the Human Animal*, London: Corgi Books.

Moussinac, Leon (1931) *New Movement in the Theatre: A Survey of Recent Developments in Europe and America*, London: Batsford.

Mtwa, Percy, Ngema, Mbongeni, and Simon, Barney (1982) *Woza Albert!*, London: Methuen.

Murray, Simon (2002) '"Tout Bouge": Jacques Lecoq, Modern Mime and the Zero Body', in Chamberlain, Franc, and Yarrow, Ralph (eds.), *Jacques Lecoq and the British Theatre*, New York: Routledge.

Murray, Simon (2018) *Jacques Lecoq* (2nd edition), New York: Routledge.

Murray, Simon, and Hall, John (2011) 'Arts for What, for Where, for Whom? Fragmentary Reflections on Dartington College of Arts, 1961–2010', *Theatre, Dance and Performance Training*, 2(1), 54–71.

Murray, Simon, and Keefe, John (2007) *Physical Theatres: A Critical Reader*, New York: Routledge.

Murray, Simon, and Keefe, John (2016) *Physical Theatres: A Critical Introduction* (2nd edition), New York: Routledge.

Myerscough, John (1988) *The Economic Importance of the Arts in Britain*, London: Policy Studies Institute.

Nabirye, Anna-Maria (n.d.) 'Passing The Baton', *Total Theatre*. Available at: http://totaltheatre.org.uk/archive/artist-writers/passing-baton.

Newson, Lloyd (1994) *Live 1*, London: Methuen, pp. 43–54.

Newson, Lloyd (1999) 'Lloyd Newson', in Giannachi, Gabriella, and Luckhurst, Mary (eds.), *On Directing*, London: Faber and Faber, pp. 108–114.

Nietzsche, Friedrich (1872) *The Birth of Tragedy from the Spirit of Music* (Die Geburt der Tragödie aus dem Geiste der Musik), Leipzig: E. W. Fritzsch.

Oddey, Alison (1996) *Devising Theatre: A Practical and Theoretical Handbook*, London and New York: Routledge.

Olsen, Jo (1997) 'The Inner World of David Glass', *Total Theatre*, 9(3), 10–11.

Pagneux, Monika (2012) *Inside Out: Theatre/Movement/Being, Robert Golden Pictures*. Available at: https://vimeo.com/253941723. Accessed: 29 May 2022.

Pakula, Pablo (2011) *Jerzy Grotowski's Influence on British Theatre, 1966 – 1980 (Histories, Perspectives, Recollections)*, unpublished PhD thesis, University of Kent.

Pardo, Enrique (2001) 'My Theatre', *Total Theatre*, 13(1), 9.

Peake, Mervyn (2006) *Gormenghast, Adapted for the Stage by John Constable*, London: Oberon Books.

Pearson, Mike (1998) 'My Balls, Your Chin', *Performance Research: On Place*, 3(2), 35–41.

Perugini, Mark (1925) *The Mime*, London: The Dancing Times.

Perugini, Mark (1928) 'On decadence in art', *The Link*, 3(3), 27–29.

Phillips, Graeme (1992) 'A Thriving Picture', *Total Theatre*, 4(4), 10.

Pickersgill, M. Gertrude (1947) *Practical Miming*, London: Pitman & Sons.

Pointon, Ann, and Davies, Chris (1997) Framed: Interrogating Disability in the Media, London: British Film Institute.

Rea, Kenneth (1989) *A Better Direction: A National Enquiry Into the Training of Directors for Theatre, Film and Television*, London: Calouste Gulbenkian Foundation.

Rea, Kenneth (1994) '10 Years of Mime Action Group', *Total Theatre*, 6(3). Available at: http://totaltheatre.org.uk/archive/features/10-years-mime-action-group. Accessed: 7 January 2022.

Rees, Phil, and Butt, Faisal (2004) 'Ethnic Change and Diversity in England, 1981–2001', *Census and Society*, 36(2), 174–186.

Richards, Joe (2018) 'Early Work at Dartington', *Theatre, Dance and Performance Training*, 9(3), 339.

Richards, Sam (2015) *Dartington College of Arts – Learning by Doing: A Biography of a College*, Totnes: Longmarsh Press.

Ritchie, Rob (1987) *The Joint Stock Book: The Making of a Theatre Collective*, London: Methuen.

Rolfe, Bari (1979) *Mimes on Miming: Writings on the Art of Mime*, London: Millington Books.

Rothenberg, Ellis (1992) 'Larger than Life: A Festival of Delight and Provocation', *Total Theatre*, 4(2–3), 5.

Rubin, Rivca (1995) 'Training Today – The Relevance and Revelation (?) of the Workshop', *Total Theatre*, 7(4), 11.

Saint-Denis, Michel (1960) *Theatre: The Rediscovery of Style*, London: Heinemann.

Saint-Denis, Michel (1982) *Training for the Theatre*, London: Heinemann Educational Books.

Samuel, Raphael, MacColl, Ewan, and Cosgrove, Stuart (1985) *Theatres of the Left: 1880–1935 Workers' Theatre Movements in Britain and America*, London: Routledge and Kegan Paul.

Sanchez-Colberg, Ana (1996) 'Altered States and Subliminal Spaces: Charting the Road towards a Physical Theatre', *Performance Research: On Risk*, 1(2), 40–56.

Saunders, Graham (2015) *British Theatre Companies 1980–1994*, London: Bloomsbury.

270 Bibliography

Savran, David (1988) *Breaking the Rules: The Wooster Group*, New York: Theatre Communications Group.

Schechner, Richard (1985) *Between Theater and Anthropology*, Pennsylvania: University of Pennsylvania Press.

Shank, Theodore (ed.) (1996) *Contemporary British Theatre*, Basingstoke: Macmillan.

Slowiak, James, and Cuesta, Jairo (2007) *Jerzy Grotowski*, New York: Routledge.

Spalding, Alistair (1992) 'Beyond Words – A Mime Festival in Crawley', *Total Theatre*, 4(2–3), 5.

Station House Opera (n.d.) 'Station House Opera – About – History'. Available at: www.stationhouseopera.com/about.php?section=4. Accessed: 16 December 2021.

Stebbings, Paul, and Smith, Phil (2020) *TNT: The New Theatre*, Axminster: Triarchy Press.

Stevens, Jayne (2017) 'The Bubble That Didn't Burst: Dance Animateurs in the 1980s', *Animated*, Autumn/Winter 2016/2017, 8–9.

Stewart, Ian (2015) *My Years with the British Theatre of the Deaf: 1963–1977*, London: Quay Media Solutions.

Tashkiran, Ayse (2020) *Movement Directors in Contemporary Theatre: Conversations on Craft*, London: Methuen.

The Times (2017) 'Adam Darius: Obituary', *The Times*, 27 December. Available at: www.thetimes.co.uk//article/adam-darius-7v507zvmr. Accessed: 28 January 2022

Théâtre de Complicité (1993) *Current Artistic Policy*, London: Théâtre de Complicité (unpublished document).

Thompson, Edward (2013) *The Making of the English Working Class*, London: Penguin.

Tolley, Rowan (1993) 'The Yorkshire Connection', *Total Theatre*, 5(1), 12.

Tomlinson, Richard (1982) *Disability, Theatre and Education*, London: Souvenir Press.

Total Theatre (1997) '*Total Theatre* Awards at the Edinburgh Festival Fringe', *Total Theatre*, 9(1), 20.

Total Theatre Network (2021) *Total Theatre Awards*, Available at: www.totaltheatrenetwork.org/totaltheatreawards. Accessed: 3 December 2021.

Triple Action Theatre (1972) 'Triple Action Theatre: The Classical Theatre of the 1970s', Held in the Arts Council of Great Britain Archives, V&A Theatre and Performance department.

Trowsdale, Jo (1997) '"Identity – Even if It Is a Fantasy': The Work of Carran Waterfield', *New Theatre Quarterly*, XIII, 231–247.

Tufnell, Miranda, and Crickmay, Chris (1990) *Body Space Image: Notes Towards Improvisation and Performance*, London: Virago.

Turner, Jane (2004) *Eugenio Barba*, New York: Routledge.

van Gyseghem, André (1943) *Theatre in Soviet Russia*, London: Faber and Faber.

Verma, Jatinder (2003) 'Asian Arts in the 21st Century', *Keynote Address, DNAsia Conference, Watermans Arts Centre*, 24 March.

Volcano Theatre (2021) *Volcano: A Timeline of Volcano*. Available at: https://volcanotheatre.wales/timeline/. Accessed: 17 November 2021.

Ward, Peter (1994) 'A Rough Guide to HOPE STREET', *Total Theatre*, 6(1), 8.

Ward, Steve (2021) *Artistes of Colour: Ethnic Diversity and Representation in the Victorian Circus*, Philadelphia: Modern Vaudeville Press.

Warden, Claire (2012) *British Avant-Garde Theatre*, Basingstoke: Palgrave Macmillan.

Wardle, Irving (1978) *The Theatres of George Devine*, London: Jonathan Cape.

Waterman, Stanley (1998) 'Carnivals for Elites? The Cultural Politics of Arts Festivals', *Progress in Human Geography*, 22(1), 54–74.

Watson, Ian (1995) *Towards a Third Theatre: Eugenio Barba and the Odin Teatret*, London: Routledge.

Welsford, Enid (1935) *The Fool: His Social and Literary History*, London: Faber and Faber.

Williams, Raymond (1997) *Marxism and Literature*, Oxford: Oxford University Press.

Williamson, Aaron (1996) 'Physical Ability: Aaron Williamson', *Total Theatre*, 8(4).

Wisniewski, Tomasz (2016) *Complicite, Theatre and Aesthetics: From Scraps of Leather*, Abingdon: Palgrave Macmillan.

Young, Iris (1990) *Throwing Like a Girl*, Bloomington: Indiana University Press.

Zarrilli, Phillip (1998) *When the Body Becomes All Eyes: Paradigms and Practices of Power in Kalarippayattu, a South Indian Martial Art*, Oxford: Oxford University Press.

Interviews

Allain, Paul (2020) Unpublished interview with the authors, 4 December.

Arden, Annabel (2021) Unpublished interview with the authors, 12 February.

Barnard, Deborah (2020) Unpublished interview with the authors, 14 October.

Berkoff, Steven (2020) Unpublished interview with the authors, 3 July.

Buckley, Geoff (2018) Unpublished interview with the authors, 23 November.

Burns, Susanne (2020) Unpublished interview with the authors, 7 July.

Caig Wilson, Alan (2021) Unpublished interview with the authors, 5 January.

Cameron, Ian (2021) Unpublished interview with the authors, 5 January.

Case, Justin (2020) Unpublished interview with the authors, 20 November.

Chafer, Joff (2021) Unpublished interview with the authors, 7 January.

Chagrin, Julian (2020) Unpublished interview with the authors, 17 July.

Chamberlain, Franc (2020) Unpublished interview with the authors, 25 September.

Ennis, Stewart (2020) Unpublished interview with the authors, 29 October.

Foley, Sean (2021) Unpublished interview with the authors, 13 January.

Glass, David (2020) Unpublished interview with the authors, 3 July.

Gough, Richard (2020) Unpublished interview with the authors, 1 October.

Hoyle, Sue (2021) Unpublished interview with the authors, 10 March.

Jamieson, Nigel (2020) Unpublished interview with the authors, 29 October.

Lanaghan, Helen, and Seelig, Joseph (2020) Unpublished interview with the authors, 25 June.

Lily, Peta (2020) Unpublished interview with the authors, 10 June.

Mason, Bim (2020) Unpublished interview with the authors, 19 November.

McCaw, Dick (2020) Unpublished interview with the authors, 3 December.

Mowat, John (2020) Unpublished interview with the authors, 20 November.

Noble, Glenn (2021) Unpublished interview with the authors, 8 January.

Pilgrim, Geraldine (2020) Unpublished interview with the authors, 16 October.

Rae, Nola (2020) Unpublished interview with the authors, 22 May.

Reid, Benji (2020) Unpublished interview with the authors, 22 October.

Samuel, Mhora (2020) Unpublished interview with the authors, 15 July.

Saunders, Mark (2020) Unpublished interview with the authors, 3 December.

Sedgwick, Toby (2020) Unpublished interview with the authors, 26 June.

Seelig, Joseph, and Lannaghan, Helen (2020) Unpublished interview with the authors, 25 June.

Smith, Fern (2020) Unpublished interview with the authors, 11 December.

Steel, Liam (2020) Unpublished interview with the authors, 19 November.

Williams, David (2021) Unpublished interview with the authors, 19 February.

Williams, Sian (2020) Unpublished interview with the authors, 12 November.

Wilson, Frank (2021) Unpublished interview with the authors, 26 February.

Wong, Denise (2020) Unpublished interview with the authors, 17 July.
Wright, John (2020) Unpublished interview with the authors, 17 September.

Correspondence

Allain, Paul (2022) Correspondence with authors, 27 May.
Grant, David (2021) Correspondence with authors, 5 November.
Kemp, Sarah (2022) Unpublished correspondence with authors, 25 March.
Lannaghan, Helen (2021) Unpublished correspondence with the authors, 27 November.
Lister, Robert (2021) Unpublished correspondence with the authors, 20 January.
Maguire, Tom (2021) Unpublished correspondence with authors, 31 October.
Stewart, Eileen (2022) Unpublished correspondence with the authors, 25 June.
Wilson, Thomas (2022) Unpublished correspondence with the authors, 4 April.

INDEX

7.84 Theatre Company 101, 107–108, 113

Aberystwyth 34, 38, 80, 108, 115–116, 122, 137, 139, 207–209
Abortion Act (1967) 43
acrobatics 10, 11, 33, 34, 160, 221, 244
Adventures in Motion Pictures 78
Alaverdy, Melissa 59
Alfreds, Mike 164, 173, 177, 182n
Allain, Paul 139, 207, 257n
Anderson, Franki 220
Anti-Apartheid Movement 43
Antonioni, Michaelangelo 21
Arden, Annabel 103, 104, 127, 128, 133, 137, 161, 167, 168, 178, 189, 196, 220, 223, 240–241, 262, 263
Arndt, Annabel 58
Artaud, Antonin 38, 113, 205, 209, 243
The Arts Council at 70: A History in the Spotlight Symposium (2016) 44, 49
Arts Council of Great Britain/England 58, 61, 63, 64, 69, 76, 83, 85, 88, 91, 94, 97, 103n, 127, 159, 169n, 170, 173, 178, 189
Arts Council of Northern Ireland 45
Arts Council of Wales 44
Arts for Everyone (A4E) Lottery scheme 49
Arts Lab, The 16
Arts Theatre, London 9
Association for Business Sponsorship of the Arts (ABSA) 50
Atkinson, Rowan 9, 256
auto-cours 16, 129–131, 135, 136, 162, 206

Badejo, Peter 184, 245
ballet 11, 15–16, 19, 25, 27, 52, 54, 249
Barba, Eugenio 38, 104, 107–109, 110, 111, 113, 116, 117, 120, 121, 139, 141, 169, 171, 175, 177, 178, 205, 257
Barbican Arts Centre 71
Barclays New Stages Award 50–51
Barlow, Tim 251
Barnard, Deborah 58, 65, 76–79, 201, 221
Barrault, Jean-Louis 8–9, 15, 16, 20, 61, 97
Barr, Margaret 35–36
Bartlett, Neil 19, 127, 254; *see also* Gloria
Battersea Arts Centre 31, 58
Bausch, Pina 35, 37, 121, 147, 178, 221
Beck's Beer 50, 51
Beckett, Samuel 11, 205, 209
Benchtours 105–108
Benison, Ben 25, 29, 250
Benjamin, Adam 247
Berkoff, Steven 22, 24, 35, 43, 119, 123, 126, 127, 129–130, 149, 176, 220, 237; *Decadence* 24, 35; *East* 23; *Greek* 24; *Metamorphosis* 23–24, 29n, 35, 246n; *Salome* 24; *Sink the Belgrano* 24, 43, 126n; *The Trial* 24
Beyond Words mime festivals 74, 86, 190–191
Billington, Michael 257
Bing, Suzanne 8, 15, 142, 252
Black Mime Theatre 3n, 5, 58, 70, 83, 85, 87, 127, 129, 146, 176, 177, 229, 232, 233–238, 239–240, 258; Ensemble 233; Women's Troop 233, 235–236

274 Index

Blueprint for Regional Mime Development 63
Booth, Laurie 210
Bouge-de-la 85, 146
Bourne, Val 53
Bowie, David 17, 18n, 19, 69, 254
Boxer, David 233, 238
Brewery Arts Centre, Kendal 20, 58, 65, 68, 70, 73, 76–79, 88, 89, 90, 91, 93, 94, 96, 199, 200, 201, 221
Brith Gof 108, 109, 111, 128, 138, 210
British Council 31, 122
British Summer School of Mime 10, 156, 173
British Theatre of the Deaf [BTD] 5, 19, 20, 243, 246, 248–251
Brook, Peter 3, 16, 38, 64, 93, 140, 178, 205, 220, 243; *The Empty Space* 3, 232; *Mahabharata* 16n, 107, 121, 243, 245; Theatre of Cruelty season 38, 138; *US* 138
Brooks, Pete 104, 106, 231
Bruford, Rose 11, 12
Bruvvers Theatre Company 93–94
Buckley, Geoff 24–25, 87, 130, 131, 176
Burns, Jo 49
Burns, Susanne 53, 56, 88–90, 91, 94, 96, 179, 221
Bushell-Mingo, Josette 240
butoh 19, 184, 225
Bush, Kate 16n, 254
Byland, Pierre 31

Cahn, Sarah 233
Caig Wilson, Alan 96–98, 100, 103–105, 107
Cameron, Ian 96–98, 100, 104–105, 107, 204n
Campaign for Nuclear Disarmament (CND) 43
Campbell, Ken 64, 136, 183
CandoCo 91
Cardiff Laboratory Theatre [CLT] 108–112, 113, 115, 138, 139, 177, 208, 208
Carmichael, Hayley 134, 164, 165, 220
cartoons 21, 31, 135, 160, 167n
Case, Justin 29–30, 31, 33, 127, 128, 131, 176
Castledine, Annie 240
Centre for Performance Research (CPR) 34, 38, 80, 84, 108, 115–116, 122, 177, 208–209, 213
Chafer, Joff 2, 142–145, 146, 215, 242
Chagrin, Claude 20–22, 24–25, 103, 130, 219, 249

Chagrin, Julian 9, 20–22, 23, 25, 29, 31, 71, 97, 127, 131, 212, 261
Chamberlain, Franc 173, 176–177, 207, 215n, 245n
Chaplin, Charlie 10, 255n
Charabanc Theatre Company 118
Charnock, Nigel 64, 117, 149, 226, 229
Chase, Michael 142
Chatterjee, Kusumika 243
Cheshire, Harold 11–12
Chisenhale Dance Space 58
Christie, Judie 80, 115, 208
City Limits 261
City Lit 22, 69, 172, 218n, 246n
Civil Rights Movement 43
class 7, 126, 128, 214, 216, 217–219, 225, 234, 235, 236, 237, 241, 243, 253
Cobb, John 94
Cockpit Festival of Mime and Visual Theatre 68
comedy 3, 10, 20, 21, 29, 30, 37, 39, 126, 137, 146, 151, 160, 179, 216, 257, 261
Commedia dell'Arte 10, 11–12, 15, 34, 141, 142, 146, 158, 177, 181, 206, 221, 226, 249
Committee for Encouragement of Music and the Arts (CEMA) (1940) 44
Communicado 99, 101–103, 107–108
Complicité, *see* Théâtre de Complicité
contact improvisation 147, 230, 259
Copeau, Jacques 8, 15, 124, 142, 217n, 252; Ecole du Vieux-Colombier 8
Cork Report (1986) 45, 50, 52
Council of Regional Arts Associations (CORAA) 56
County Durham 48, 88, 89, 90, 179, 200
Coventry 12, 70, 84, 87–88, 121, 138–139, 183, 189, 199, 201, 207, 248
Craig, Edward Gordon 37, 205
Crick, Olly 142
Crocker, Helen 103, 172, 173
Cultural industries 51–52
Cumbria 20, 48, 76, 79, 88, 89, 94

Dance and Mime Department (Arts Council) 52, 53, 54, 58
Dance Umbrella 53
Daniel, Jeffrey 255
Daniel, John 59
Darius, Adam 16, 172, 177
Dartington College of Arts 35, 84, 85, 147, 171, 199, 207, 210–213, 250, 251
Dashwood, Anja 172, 203
Davies, Paul 148, 226

Dawson, Andrew 12n, 57, 71, 84, 100, 199, 204n, 255
de Castro, Angela 222
Decroux, Etienne 8–9, 15, 33, 55, 61, 71, 97n, 98, 116, 120, 131, 134, 162, 169, 171, 173, 180, 192, 193, 203, 206n, 209, 218, 222, 254n, 256, 257
De Keersmaeker, Anne Teresa 147, 230
Delsarte, François 11
Demarco, Richard 36, 104, 107, 121
devised theatre 1, 65, 124, 125, 128, 137, 196, 216, 242
devising 6, 32, 78, 94, 118, 119, 124–132, 135, 137, 138, 139, 140, 142–143, 145–146, 148, 149, 151, 153, 157, 160, 161, 162, 176, 179, 196, 216, 222, 228, 229, 241, 259
Disability Discrimination Act (1995) 215, 247
Divorce Reform Act (1969) 43
Dorney, Kate 41, 42
Dovecot Arts Centre, Stockton 63, 68, 75, 89, 90–93, 199, 200
Drama Department (Arts Council) 52–53, 54, 64, 83, 166
DV8 19, 50, 53, 87, 93, 116, 117, 122, 148–150, 151, 168, 221, 227, 229–231, 246, 248, 251, 255, 260, 261; *Bound to Please* 229; *Dead Dreams of Monochrome Men* 229l; *Enter Achilles* 149, 168, 229, 231; *Happiest Days of My Life* 229; *MSM* 229; *My Sex, Our Dance* 229
Dyos, Linda 57

Edinburgh Festival 16, 36, 68, 69, 70, 76, 79, 91, 97, 99, 103, 115, 121, 225, 226, 232, 249, 261
Edwards, Jango 27
Ellu, Tina 58
English, Rose 177, 225
Ennis Stewart 96, 106
Enterprise Allowance Scheme 42
Equal Pay Act (1970) 43
Etchells, Tim 64, 124, 157
ethnicity 214, 215, 253
European Economic Community (EEC) 43
European Mime Federation 62, 84, 103, 191
European Union (EU) 43, 122
Evans, Mark 8n, 10, 18n, 87, 108n, 147n, 149, 154n, 173, 177, 189, 199, 204, 205n, 207, 220, 242, 252, 254n
Everett, Kenny 9
Extemporary Dance 148

Faulty Optic 70, 78
Feldenkrais, Moshe 105, 220
Felner, Mira 2, 10, 215n
feminism 4, 39, 153, 216, 222
Fo, Dario 10, 119, 217
Foley, Sean 132, 133
Footsbarn 32–33, 85, 128
Forced Entertainment 124, 148, 149, 157, 161, 177, 210
Forgan, Liz 43–45, 48
Frantic Assembly 87, 108, 122, 127, 148, 149–150, 151, 177, 196, 199, 219, 229, 246, 255, 263
Freehold 16, 38, 138, 139–140, 161, 219

Gaines, David 31, 87, 135, 177, 191, 193, 199
Gambolling Guizers 63, 89–91, 200
Gardner, Lyn 255, 261
Gardzienice 138, 139, 176, 176, 203, 223, 257
Gaulier, Philippe 31, 94, 105–107, 108, 116, 117, 120–121, 128n, 133, 134, 137, 138n, 142, 146, 158, 169, 171, 172, 173, 175, 176, 177, 178, 192, 193, 203, 205, 219, 225, 252, 256, 257
gender 7, 118, 126, 148, 214, 215, 219, 221, 223, 225, 227–229, 230, 236, 252, 253, 263
Genet, Jean 18, 228
Ginner, Ruby 12–15, 250
Glass, David 3, 26, 31, 53, 54, 55, 57, 59, 64, 69, 71, 78, 89, 90, 91, 103, 104, 133, 159, 160, 161, 162–166, 177, 178–180, 200, 203, 238–239, 246, 258, 263; David Glass Ensemble 83, 86, 164n, 166, 167n, 195–197, 238; *Gormenghast* 164–166
Gloria 131
Glory of the Garden report 41, 45, 56, 64
Goat Island 91, 210
Gob Squad 75, 91
Goddard, Janet 154
Gordon, Fiona 137
Gough, Richard 38, 80, 108–117, 139, 177, 207, 207–208, 210
Graeae 91, 215, 246, 248, 251
Grant, David 117–120
Grantham, Barry 15–16
Greater London Arts (GLA) 56, 57, 58, 180, 201, 215
Greater London Council (GLC) 215, 235
Griffiths, Derek 232
Grimaldi, Joseph 10

276 Index

Grotowski, Jerzy 26n, 37–38, 61, 99, 108,
109, 111, 113, 116, 117, 120, 121, 124,
138–139, 140, 142, 169, 171, 203, 205,
257; *Towards a Poor Theatre* 140, 232
Guide to Mime in Education 63, 87, 189
Guildhall School of Music and Drama 43,
55, 176
Guilfoyle, Molly 57, 220
Gulbenkian Studio Theatre 89–90, 93, 200

Hall, Fernau 260
Hall, John 171, 210
Hanlon-Lees Troupe 10
Harman, Paul 93
Harris, Chris 28–29, 85, 131
Hawth Art Centre, Crawley 59n, 63, 74,
86, 190–191
Haynes, Jim 26
Heddon, Deirdre 65, 125, 128n, 137, 147,
161, 228, 243, 244
Heggen, Claire 104, 219, 222
Hesitate and Demonstrate 153, 154–155,
177, 221, 222, 240
Hip-Hop 160, 234, 238–240, 242,
254n, 255
Hoile, Jed 254
Hope Street Centre, Liverpool 84,
198–199, 218–219
Hopkins, Didi 221
Houben, Jos 12n, 71, 104, 184
Houstoun, Wendy 149, 221, 228, 229
Hoyle, Sue 53–54, 55–56, 58, 221
Hunter, Kathryn 220, 251
Hunter, Paul 134, 164

Impact Theatre Co-operative 91, 231, 240
Improbable 70, 128, 157
improvisation 8, 24, 25, 29, 30, 39, 118,
119, 124, 125, 128–130, 133–135, 137,
138, 139, 142, 146, 160, 161, 176, 179,
230, 257, 259
Institute for Contemporary Arts (ICA) 33,
71, 223
International Workshop Festival (IWF) 55,
62, 68, 90, 121, 174, 180–187, 216, 225,
243, 277
Intriplicate Mime 57, 71, 204n, 220
IOU 83, 124, 153, 156–157, 221

Jackson, Michael 255
Jamieson, Nigel 2, 54, 55, 57, 64, 121,
158, 159–160, 161, 180–181, 201,
203, 244
Jennings, Mel 58

Johnstone, Keith 24n, 64, 124, 128, 142n
Jones, Desmond 2, 7, 20, 30n, 54–55,
59, 71, 98, 103, 159, 172, 173, 177,
203–205, 213, 224, 238, 254n, 255,
256n, 262
Jooss, Kurt 35, 36

Kaboodle 33, 83, 84, 240
Kabosh Theatre Company 118–119
Kabuki 17, 19, 23, 164, 246
Kantor, Tadeusz 36–37, 121, 209, 257
Keaton, Ben 57, 69, 71
Keefe, John 3n, 4, 60, 63, 85, 125, 147n,
170–171, 173, 191, 192
Kemp, Lindsay 16, 17–19, 23, 24, 71, 99,
100, 103, 127, 129, 228, 254; *Flowers* 18,
23, 99, 228, 254
Kemp, Sarah 63, 94, 197–198, 220
Kendal 58, 65, 68, 70, 74, 76–78, 84, 88,
89, 96, 199, 221
Keynes, John Maynard 44
Keysell, Pat 2, 19–20, 54, 58, 59, 76, 88,
98, 100, 103, 104, 105, 107, 108, 189,
200, 201, 204, 219, 238n, 249–251
Khan, Naseem 45, 170, 215, 231, 242
Kinear-Wilson, Ninean 142
Kneehigh 33, 71, 85, 91, 128, 167n
Koch, Aurelian 146
Kosh, The 148, 151–152, 161, 223, 229
Kuppers, Petra 214, 251

Laban, Rudolf 35–36, 121, 205, 218, 250
LAMDA -38 138, 176
Lannaghan, Helen 54, 56, 57, 58, 65, 68,
70–72, 74, 76, 78, 203, 221
Larger than Life Festival 73, 86
Laurel, Stanley 10
Leabhart, Tom 9, 10, 86, 124, 158, 192,
209, 215n
Lecoq, Jacques 5, 8, 10, 15, 20–22, 24,
25, 31, 32, 33, 61, 85, 97, 98, 99, 103,
105, 107, 108, 116, 117, 120, 121, 131,
133, 135, 136, 138n, 142, 146, 162, 169,
171, 172, 173, 175, 178, 179, 181, 183,
192, 193, 203, 205–206, 218, 220, 224,
225, 245, 249, 250, 252, 256, 257; Ecole
Jacques Lecoq (Lecoq School) 16, 21,
23, 28, 29, 31, 32, 54, 98, 105, 130, 133,
135, 136, 137, 146, 158, 164n, 173, 177,
196, 203, 206, 219, 233, 246n; LEM
(Laboratoire d'Etudes du Mouvement)
10, 147; *The Moving Body* 8, 133n, 173
Lecoq, Pascale 219
Lee, Jennie 45

Lily, Peta 54, 57, 70, 78, 90, 91, 153, 156, 160, 177, 200, 204n, 220, 223, 224–226, 227, 254, 258
Littlewood, Joan 34, 35, 94, 218
Living Theatre, The 17, 38
Local Arts Development Agencies (LADAs) 63
London Contemporary Dance School 54, 162
London International Mime Festival (LIMF) 4, 27, 53, 68–73, 74, 76, 87, 91, 100, 121, 153, 190, 191, 216, 221, 225, 259, 261
Lumiere & Son 124, 153, 156, 225
Lust, Annette 5, 10, 158, 214n, 215n, 256
Lyddiard, Alan 63, 93, 122

MAGazine 56–59, 64, 66, 68, 79, 201
Magdalena Project 156, 221
Magni, Marcello 137
Maguire, Tom 117–119
Manchester Metropolitan University School of Theatre 62, 84, 139, 191, 208
Marceau, Marcel 3, 8, 9, 10, 15, 16n, 17, 18, 22, 23, 24, 27, 31, 33, 68, 71, 72, 99, 120, 131, 134, 137, 173, 203, 218, 249, 256, 257
Maree, Lynn 56
Marowitz, Charles 38, 205
Marr, Alicyn 58, 65, 76, 78, 201, 221
Martin, John 29, 176, 245
masks 8–9, 20, 25, 29, 30, 31, 87, 94n, 98, 106, 124, 126, 134, 135, 142–146, 159, 176, 177, 181, 193n, 208, 241, 250, 256
Mason, Bim 33, 71, 85, 133, 158–159, 172, 173, 199
Materic, Mladen 177, 184
Maude-Roxby, Roddy 25
Mawer, Irene 10, 11, 12–15, 219, 233, 250; The Institute of Mime 13; L'Enfant Prodigue 13–14
Max Prior, Dorothy 60
Mayes, Penny 57
McBurney, Simon 37, 132, 137, 161–162, 168n, 177, 254–255, 262
McCaw, Dick 121, 174, 178, 180–187
McDermott, Phelim 128n, 147, 184
Meckler, Nancy 38, 139, 140, 184, 219
Melkveg, The (Amsterdam) 33
Merkin, Ros 41, 42
Meyerhold, Vsevelod 34–35, 109, 121, 124, 141–142, 205, 209, 217, 218, 257
Milling, Jane 65, 125, 128n, 137, 147, 161, 228, 243, 244

Mime Action Group (MAG) 4, 54, 56–66, 153, 183, 187–193, 220; *see also* Total Theatre
Mime Centrum Berlin 62
The Mime, Physical Theatres and Visual Performance Project: A Report from Mime Action Group to Northern Arts Board 63
Mime in Schools 63
Mime Theatre Project (MTP) 3, 57, 78, 204n, 255
Mitchell, Sue 100, 201
Mitra, Royona 242
Mnouchkine, Ariane 177, 244
moonwalk 255
Moore, Geoff 156
Moving Being 108, 109, 113, 115, 156, 177
Moving into Performance (MIP) 62, 84, 191–193, 194–195
Moving into Performance Report (MIP) 63, 191, 192
Moving Picture Mime Show (MPMS) 31–32, 53, 54, 70, 78, 87, 103, 122, 127, 135–136, 137, 142, 146, 160, 177, 238, 246n
Mowat, John 69, 71, 90, 131, 218n
Mowlam, Marjorie (Mo) 64
Mtwa, Percy 232–233
Mulgrew, Gerry 103–104
Mulqueen, Mark 63, 90, 91, 94, 96
Mummer&Dada 32–33, 85, 146n, 158–159, 161
Murray, Simon 2, 3n, 4, 10, 59, 60, 63, 77, 85, 88, 93–94, 95, 108, 125, 133n, 137, 147n, 167, 171, 173, 177, 179, 193, 204, 207–208, 209, 220, 255

National Lottery 4, 44–45, 47–50, 75, 92, 247
National Theatre (London) 12, 22, 25, 100, 146, 164n, 205
National Theatre of Scotland 100
neo-liberalism 41
Newson, Lloyd 116, 148, 149, 150, 192, 229, 230, 240, 248
Ngema, Mbongeni 232–233
Nicholas, Jane 52–53, 54, 64, 221
Noble, Glenn 128n, 198–199, 218–219
Northern Arts 46n, 48, 50, 53, 56, 63, 75, 76, 84, 88–96, 179, 199, 221
Northern Festival of Mime, Dance and Visual Theatre 68
Northern Ireland 5, 45, 80, 81, 82, 83, 103, 117–120, 185, 189

278 Index

Northern Region 5, 47–48, 50, 53, 63, 81, 83, 88, 92–96, 200
Northern Stage 63, 93, 122
Northumberland 48, 88, 89, 94
North West Arts 46n, 49, 84, 88

Oddey, Alison 125, 145, 153, 162, 259
Odin Teatret 87, 104, 107, 109, 111, 112, 113, 121, 138, 139, 141, 175, 192, 193, 203, 221, 257
Ogilvie, George 20, 29
Oliver, Peter 26
Olympic Games, London 2012 247
Oparei, DeObia 240
Open Space, The 38
O'Rorke, Lucy 146
Oval House 26, 29, 172

Pagneux, Monika 31, 78, 90, 94, 120, 121, 133, 134, 169, 173, 175, 177, 178, 183, 200, 205, 219, 220, 225
Paines Plough 54, 246
Pan Project 243, 245–246
Pardo, Enrique 104, 123, 177, 191–192, 209
Paupers' Carnival 108, 139
Paxton, Steve 210
Pearson, Mike 38, 99, 108–113, 115, 116, 117, 139, 207, 209
Peepolykus 33, 131
Peking Opera 114, 126
People Show, The 16, 70, 109, 153, 161
Perugini, Mark 11, 13n
phenomenology 4
Phillips, Arlene 254
Phoenix Dance Company 89, 240
Physical State International (PSI) 62, 84, 178, 186
Pierrot 10, 11, 12, 13, 14, 18, 20n, 24
Pilgrim, Geraldine 26, 104, 154–155, 177, 221, 222
Pip Simmons Theatre Company 16, 91, 108, 161
Platel, Alain 116, 147
A Policy for the Arts: First Steps (White Paper, 1964) 45
Prietzel, Claudia 153, 224
Pritchett, Wayne 256
Project funding 47, 49
Purcell Room 71

Queen Elizabeth Hall 71
Queen's Hall Art Centre, Hexham 50, 89, 90, 93, 94, 199

race 214, 215, 216, 219, 231–242, 252, 253
Race Relations Act (1965) 43
RADA 25, 176
Rae, Nola 2, 9, 10n, 19, 27–28, 29, 53, 54, 57, 59, 68–69, 70, 78, 90, 103, 122, 127, 131–132, 203, 215n, 226, 260; London Mime Theatre 27
Ralf Ralf 70, 78
RAT Theatre 99, 108, 109, 138, 139
Ray, Piali 243
Rea, Kenneth 55, 159, 243
Redcliffe-Maud, Lord 47, 48
Regional Arts Associations (RAA) 41, 46, 56, 58, 61, 83, 88, 97, 215
Regional Arts Boards (RAB) 4, 5, 41, 44, 46, 58, 61, 83, 97, 178, 189, 190, 201
Reid, Benji 238–240, 258
Rejects Revenge Theatre Company 84, 88, 199
residencies 5, 26, 35, 47, 67, 86, 87, 90, 107, 111, 113, 138, 139, 180, 198, 199, 200, 203
Revenue/Regularly Funded Organisations 47, 50, 94, 240
Richards, Joe 212
Ridout, Matthew 57
Right Size, The 3n, 70, 83, 85, 86, 131, 132, 157, 220
Riverside Festival 68, 70, 73–75, 90, 91, 92, 121
Robertson, Gavin 57, 71, 100, 204n, 255
Robinson, Ken 189
Rose Bruford College 12, 20, 28, 30n, 176, 205n, 206, 233
Royal Ballet School 16, 27, 54
Royal Festival Hall 71
Royal Shakespeare Company (RSC) 12, 25, 38, 138, 139, 140, 146n
Roy Hart Theatre 104n, 177
Rubin, Rivka 84, 178, 186, 187
Rumbelow, Steve 140
Rush, Geoffrey 224
Ryan, David 58, 59

Sabri, Sonia 243
Sadler's Wells 58, 59n, 71, 74, 115, 121
Saint-Denis, Michel 8, 9, 15, 124, 142n, 205; and La Compagnie des Quinze 8; London Theatre Studio 8; Old Vic School 8, 24n
Samuel, Mhora 57–59, 63, 86, 221
Sarabhai, Mallika 245
Saunders, Graham 54

Saunders, Mark 90, 96, 98–103, 105, 107, 176, 202–203, 205–207
Schneideman, Tessa 153, 224
Scotland 5, 20, 43, 46, 76, 80, 81, 82, 83, 96–107, 108, 113, 117, 118, 120, 200, 201
Scottish Arts Council 44, 97, 98, 100, 103, 106
Scottish Mime Forum (SMF) 97–98, 103–105, 107–108, 191n, 200
Scottish Mime Theatre (SMT) 103, 108, 204n
Second World War 8, 9, 11, 12, 13, 15, 37n, 43, 44n, 97n, 222
Sedgwick, Toby 2, 31–32, 53, 71, 135–136, 259, 261, 262
Seelig, Joseph 27, 54, 55, 68–69, 71–72, 74, 76, 78, 192, 203
sexuality 227, 228–229, 230, 231
Sexual Offences Act (1967) 43
Shaban, Nabil 215, 248
Shock 254
Siddiqui, Nahid 243
Simmons, Pip 16, 91, 108, 161
Simon, Barney 232
Smith, Fern 35, 148, 166, 167, 215, 223, 226–228
Smith, Phil 139, 141–142
Smith, Rae 157, 164
Soum, Corinne 131, 172, 202, 209, 220, 256
South Bank Centre 71, 74, 191
South East Arts 46n, 63, 83, 86
Southern Arts - 46n 73, 83, 85
South West Arts 46n, 83, 85, 199
Spalding, Alistair 58–59, 63, 74, 75
Splinter Group Mime 91, 93–94
sponsorship 4, 41n, 50–51, 92, 193n, 234
Staniewski, Włodzimierz 38, 223
Stan's Café 70, 87, 157, 210
Stan Won't Dance 19
Station House Opera 157
Stebbings, Paul 139, 141–142
Steel, Liam 148, 149–150, 177, 229–231, 260
Stockton-upon-Tees 68, 70, 74–75, 89–91, 121, 199
street theatre 32–33, 75, 87, 127, 160, 181, 185, 199, 203
Structure of feeling 51, 92, 117
Support For The Arts In England And Wales: A Report To The Calouste Gulbenkian Foundation 47

Talawa Theatre Company 58, 231, 235, 248
Tamasha 231, 235
Tara Arts 231
Taylorism 34
Teatr Laboratorium 37, 109, 114, 177
Teesside 48, 75, 88, 89, 90, 200
Temba Theatre Company 231
Thatcherism 41, 48, 126, 226
Thatcher, Margaret 41, 43, 44n, 48, 218
Theater Institute Nederland 62
Théâtre de Complicité, 3, 31 35, 37, 50, 51, 53, 54, 70, 78, 83, 87, 90, 93, 103, 119, 122, 123, 125n, 126, 127, 128, 130n, 131, 133, 137, 146, 148, 159, 160, 161, 164, 166, 167, 168n, 176, 177, 178, 195–196, 199, 219, 228, 237, 240–241, 243, 246n, 251, 255n, 256, 257, 259, 260, 263; *Anything for a Quiet Life* 35, 137, 251; *A Minute Too Late* 137; *Mnemonic* 37, 146, 243–244, 259; *Street of Crocodiles* 125n, 146, 164, 166, 167, 228, 255n, 257, 259, 262; *Three Lives of Lucie Cabrol* 37, 167, 219, 259; *The Visit* 35, 137, 164n, 251; *The Winter's Tale* 240
Theatre de L'Ange Fou 131, 172, 220, 256
Théâtre du Mouvement 104, 173, 219, 222, 224
Theatres Act (1968) 43, 128
Théâtre sans Frontières (TSF) 49–50, 63, 90, 91, 93–95, 197
Thirtle, Robert 143, 160, 245
Three Women Mime 5, 153, 156, 204, 223, 224, 225
Tik and Tok 254
Time Out 26, 225, 261
TNT 35, 138, 139, 141–142
Tolley, Rowan 83, 87, 189, 201
Tomlinson, Richard 248
Toole, David 251
Total Theatre 34n, 55, 58–59, 60, 64–66, 68, 70, 71, 72, 73–74, 79, 82, 83, 90, 121, 122, 170, 174, 178, 180, 186, 187, 188, 194, 195, 198, 201, 203, 214, 242, 247, 251, 256, 261, 262
Total Theatre Awards 24, 27, 64–65
Total Theatre Network 58, 64–65
Trading Faces 142
Tramway, Glasgow 104, 107, 121, 202, 243
Trestle 3n, 50, 53, 54, 57, 63, 70, 83, 86, 87, 89, 91, 122, 124, 127, 134, 135, 142–146, 159, 177, 189, 193n, 195, 199, 215, 219, 237, 238, 240, 242, 248, 260

280 Index

Trickster 53, 54, 55, 71, 78, 90, 122, 127, 142, 143, 146, 157, 159–160, 177, 180, 200, 243, 245, 260
Triple Action Theatre 138, 139–141, 177
Tyneside 48, 88, 89, 246

UK Mime and Physical Theatre Training Directory 63, 208, 220

Vandekeybus, Wim 64, 147
Vanderpoel, Micheline 220
Vision On 19, 25, 250
visual theatre 3, 4, 26, 29, 43, 52, 62, 64, 68, 72, 74, 76, 78, 79, 91, 117, 124, 131, 153, 155, 181, 190, 192, 202, 221, 229, 260
Volcano Theatre Company 35, 87, 117, 189, 223, 226, 229; *L.O.V.E.* 117

Wales 5, 38, 44, 46, 80, 81, 82, 83, 108–117, 118, 120, 128, 138, 139, 189, 221
Wall, Max 21, 218
Wall, Mick 71, 87, 146n, 256
Wall Street Productions 91, 93–94, 167n
Walton, Iris 220
Wasson, Steve 131, 172, 203, 209, 256
Waterfield, Carran 87, 139, 199, 221, 243
Wearside 48, 88, 89
Welfare State International 153, 156, 177, 210
Westlake, Hilary 156, 173, 177, 221, 225
West Midlands Arts 46n, 83, 87, 199
Whose Line Is It Anyway 30, 128
Widdicombe, Ris 192, 202

Wigman, Mary 121, 220
Wildcat Theatre Company 101, 107–108
Wilding Report (1989) 45, 46, 83
Wilkinson, Jac 63, 87, 189, 199, 201, 221
Williams, Clifford 11, 12, 146n, 250
Williams, David 177, 207, 210, 212
Williamson, Aaron 251
Williams, Raymond 51
Williams, Sian 151–152, 223, 229
Willson, Suzy 220
Wilsher, Amanda 248
Wilsher, Toby 63, 144
Wilson, Dorothy 87
Wilson, Frank 63, 74–75, 90–92, 200
Wilson, Harold 41
Wilson, Ronnie 69, 172, 218n
Wilson, Thomas 206
Wissel Theatre 78
Wong, Denise 129, 146, 176, 177, 229, 233–238, 240, 258
Wooster Group, The 161
Workers' Theatre Movement 34
Woza Albert! 232–233
Wright, John 64, 84, 90, 128n, 133–135, 139, 142, 145, 161, 164, 199, 200
Wringer, Leo 240

Yellow Earth (now New Earth) 246
York Arts Centre 16, 26, 87
Yorkshire and Humberside Arts 46n, 83, 86
Young, Iris 223

Zarrilli, Phillip 209, 242, 243
Zoltowski (Kemp), Rick 71, 90, 200–201, 254

Saunders, Mark 90, 96, 98–103, 105, 107, 176, 202–203, 205–207
Schneideman, Tessa 153, 224
Scotland 5, 20, 43, 46, 76, 80, 81, 82, 83, 96–107, 108, 113, 117, 118, 120, 200, 201
Scottish Arts Council 44, 97, 98, 100, 103, 106
Scottish Mime Forum (SMF) 97–98, 103–105, 107–108, 191n, 200
Scottish Mime Theatre (SMT) 103, 108, 204n
Second World War 8, 9, 11, 12, 13, 15, 37n, 43, 44n, 97n, 222
Sedgwick, Toby 2, 31–32, 53, 71, 135–136, 259, 261, 262
Seelig, Joseph 27, 54, 55, 68–69, 71–72, 74, 76, 78, 192, 203
sexuality 227, 228–229, 230, 231
Sexual Offences Act (1967) 43
Shaban, Nabil 215, 248
Shock 254
Siddiqui, Nahid 243
Simmons, Pip 16, 91, 108, 161
Simon, Barney 232
Smith, Fern 35, 148, 166, 167, 215, 223, 226–228
Smith, Phil 139, 141–142
Smith, Rae 157, 164
Soum, Corinne 131, 172, 202, 209, 220, 256
South Bank Centre 71, 74, 191
South East Arts 46n, 63, 83, 86
Southern Arts - 46n 73, 83, 85
South West Arts 46n, 83, 85, 199
Spalding, Alistair 58–59, 63, 74, 75
Splinter Group Mime 91, 93–94
sponsorship 4, 41n, 50–51, 92, 193n, 234
Staniewski, Włodzimierz 38, 223
Stan's Café 70, 87, 157, 210
Stan Won't Dance 19
Station House Opera 157
Stebbings, Paul 139, 141–142
Steel, Liam 148, 149–150, 177, 229–231, 260
Stockton-upon-Tees 68, 70, 74–75, 89–91, 121, 199
street theatre 32–33, 75, 87, 127, 160, 181, 185, 199, 203
Structure of feeling 51, 92, 117
Support For The Arts In England And Wales: A Report To The Calouste Gulbenkian Foundation 47

Talawa Theatre Company 58, 231, 235, 248
Tamasha 231, 235
Tara Arts 231
Taylorism 34
Teatr Laboratorium 37, 109, 114, 177
Teesside 48, 75, 88, 89, 90, 200
Temba Theatre Company 231
Thatcherism 41, 48, 126, 226
Thatcher, Margaret 41, 43, 44n, 48, 218
Theater Institute Nederland 62
Théâtre de Complicité, 3, 31 35, 37, 50, 51, 53, 54, 70, 78, 83, 87, 90, 93, 103, 119, 122, 123, 125n, 126, 127, 128, 130n, 131, 133, 137, 146, 148, 159, 160, 161, 164, 166, 167, 168n, 176, 177, 178, 195–196, 199, 219, 228, 237, 240–241, 243, 246n, 251, 255n, 256, 257, 259, 260, 263; *Anything for a Quiet Life* 35, 137, 251; *A Minute Too Late* 137; *Mnemonic* 37, 146, 243–244, 259; *Street of Crocodiles* 125n, 146, 164, 166, 167, 228, 255n, 257, 259, 262; *Three Lives of Lucie Cabrol* 37, 167, 219, 259; *The Visit* 35, 137, 164n, 251; *The Winter's Tale* 240
Theatre de L'Ange Fou 131, 172, 220, 256
Théâtre du Mouvement 104, 173, 219, 222, 224
Theatres Act (1968) 43, 128
Théâtre sans Frontières (TSF) 49–50, 63, 90, 91, 93–95, 197
Thirtle, Robert 143, 160, 245
Three Women Mime 5, 153, 156, 204, 223, 224, 225
Tik and Tok 254
Time Out 26, 225, 261
TNT 35, 138, 139, 141–142
Tolley, Rowan 83, 87, 189, 201
Tomlinson, Richard 248
Toole, David 251
Total Theatre 34n, 55, 58–59, 60, 64–66, 68, 70, 71, 72, 73–74, 79, 82, 83, 90, 121, 122, 170, 174, 178, 180, 186, 187, 188, 194, 195, 198, 201, 203, 214, 242, 247, 251, 256, 261, 262
Total Theatre Awards 24, 27, 64–65
Total Theatre Network 58, 64–65
Trading Faces 142
Tramway, Glasgow 104, 107, 121, 202, 243
Trestle 3n, 50, 53, 54, 57, 63, 70, 83, 86, 87, 89, 91, 122, 124, 127, 134, 135, 142–146, 159, 177, 189, 193n, 195, 199, 215, 219, 237, 238, 240, 242, 248, 260

280 Index

Trickster 53, 54, 55, 71, 78, 90, 122, 127, 142, 143, 146, 157, 159–160, 177, 180, 200, 243, 245, 260
Triple Action Theatre 138, 139–141, 177
Tyneside 48, 88, 89, 246

UK Mime and Physical Theatre Training Directory 63, 208, 220

Vandekeybus, Wim 64, 147
Vanderpoel, Micheline 220
Vision On 19, 25, 250
visual theatre 3, 4, 26, 29, 43, 52, 62, 64, 68, 72, 74, 76, 78, 79, 91, 117, 124, 131, 153, 155, 181, 190, 192, 202, 221, 229, 260
Volcano Theatre Company 35, 87, 117, 189, 223, 226, 229; *L.O.V.E.* 117

Wales 5, 38, 44, 46, 80, 81, 82, 83, 108–117, 118, 120, 128, 138, 139, 189, 221
Wall, Max 21, 218
Wall, Mick 71, 87, 146n, 256
Wall Street Productions 91, 93–94, 167n
Walton, Iris 220
Wasson, Steve 131, 172, 203, 209, 256
Waterfield, Carran 87, 139, 199, 221, 243
Wearside 48, 88, 89
Welfare State International 153, 156, 177, 210
Westlake, Hilary 156, 173, 177, 221, 225
West Midlands Arts 46n, 83, 87, 199
Whose Line Is It Anyway 30, 128
Widdicombe, Ris 192, 202

Wigman, Mary 121, 220
Wildcat Theatre Company 101, 107–108
Wilding Report (1989) 45, 46, 83
Wilkinson, Jac 63, 87, 189, 199, 201, 221
Williams, Clifford 11, 12, 146n, 250
Williams, David 177, 207, 210, 212
Williamson, Aaron 251
Williams, Raymond 51
Williams, Sian 151–152, 223, 229
Willson, Suzy 220
Wilsher, Amanda 248
Wilsher, Toby 63, 144
Wilson, Dorothy 87
Wilson, Frank 63, 74–75, 90–92, 200
Wilson, Harold 41
Wilson, Ronnie 69, 172, 218n
Wilson, Thomas 206
Wissel Theatre 78
Wong, Denise 129, 146, 176, 177, 229, 233–238, 240, 258
Wooster Group, The 161
Workers' Theatre Movement 34
Woza Albert! 232–233
Wright, John 64, 84, 90, 128n, 133–135, 139, 142, 145, 161, 164, 199, 200
Wringer, Leo 240

Yellow Earth (now New Earth) 246
York Arts Centre 16, 26, 87
Yorkshire and Humberside Arts 46n, 83, 86
Young, Iris 223

Zarrilli, Phillip 209, 242, 243
Zoltowski (Kemp), Rick 71, 90, 200–201, 254